T0385723

American
Catholics

American Catholics

A History

LESLIE WOODCOCK TENTLER

Yale UNIVERSITY PRESS/NEW HAVEN & LONDON

Yale University Press books may be purchased in quantity for
educational, business, or promotional use. For information,
please e-mail sales.press@yale.edu (U.S. office) or sales@yaleup.
co.uk (U.K. office).

Set in Minion type by IDS Infotech Ltd.
Printed in the United States of America.

Library of Congress Control Number: 2019950194
ISBN 978-0-300-21964-7 (hardcover : alk. paper)

A catalogue record for this book is available from the British
Library.

This paper meets the requirements of ANSI/NISO Z39.48-1992
(Permanence of Paper).

10 9 8 7 6 5 4 3 2 1

As always, for Tom

Contents

Preface

I cannot remember a time when I was not fascinated by Catholics, not because I was raised in the faith—I was not—or even necessarily because I lived in a heavily Catholic neighborhood. That was true only after my tenth birthday, when my family moved to suburban Detroit. I did have a Catholic grandmother, who was far and away my favorite relative, but her influence was presumably muted by my parents' anti-Catholicism. My father, who in adolescence had briefly hoped to become a priest, left the church as a young adult and embraced the Socialist Party. My mother, an even more passionate leftist, lost her first husband in the Spanish Civil War, when he fought with the Abraham Lincoln Brigade. Widowed while still in her teens, she never forgave the church its support of General Franco. Hostility to Catholicism was part of the air I breathed as a child. I knew that Senator Joseph McCarthy was a Catholic and that this explained just about everything long before I knew what his offenses were. Some years later, I was bemused to learn that Wisconsin's junior senator had been the cause of my first remembered minor miracle—my parents' purchase of a television. Longtime holdouts, they were brought around by the prospect of watching the Army-McCarthy hearings.

My parents' anti-Catholicism was of the genteel variety, more quiet assumptions than overt bigotry, and sat oddly with their otherwise tolerant view of the world. What I mainly imbibed from it, I think, was a sense that Catholicism mattered. Whatever one's view of the church, it was not an institution that could be ignored. That truth became especially evident when we moved to Detroit, where local politics in those distant days was dominated by the Catholic tribe. Most were Democrats, I could not help noting, which made them quite different animals from Wisconsin's by-now-late junior senator. Indeed, my parents seemed to admire many of these Catholic politicians, although they continued to deplore certain instances of Catholic political muscle-flexing. Chief among these were Catholic opposition to the public funding of birth-control programs and Catholic pressure on local businesses to close for three hours on Good Friday afternoon—a practice still quite widely observed in the later 1950s. My mother was also dismayed—the word is not too strong—by the very large size of most Catholic families on our suburban block.

Unlike my mother, however, I rejoiced in the exuberant fertility so evident in our neighborhood. Where she saw overburdened parents and a looming population crisis, I saw a swarm of playmates and an abundance of houses where mess-making children were tolerated. As I grew older and began to course about the city, I came to admire additional aspects of Catholic otherness. Detroit was then honeycombed with enormous Catholic churches, most of them with schools attached, along with a plethora of Catholic institutions that serviced the entire city—colleges, hospitals, recreation centers, and social service agencies of a quite astonishing variety. The old Polish neighborhoods were especially intriguing, given the lavish décor of their churches and the numerous small businesses—I have fond memories of the bakeries—that anchored those neighborhoods and gave them a kind of vital density. Catholics increasingly came to seem like a people who had literally built a civilization of their own—one that possessed an enviable warmth and rootedness. That I was certainly romanticizing matters did not detract in later years from my continued interest in this not-inconsiderable achievement.

Whatever romance might have been brewing between me and the Catholic Church went underground during my college and graduate school years. I was quite passionately involved in the antiwar movement and other forms of student activism, proving that I was, after all, very much my parents' daughter. But for me, at least, politics could not provide answers to certain ultimate questions, which I think in retrospect were lurking beneath my earlier fascination with Catholicism. Having married an exemplary Catholic and begun a family, I found it almost natural to join the tribe myself. This step was possible, I hasten to add, only because of the Second Vatican Council and the reforms that came in its wake. Still my parents' daughter, I doubt that I could have converted to the church in what I quite reasonably regarded as its triumphal mode. I needed a church that, while claiming to possess ultimate truth, was also willing to concede that it did not have all the answers. I thought I had found it in postconciliar Catholicism.

A practicing social historian by the time I converted, I did not turn immediately to Catholics as a focus of my research. My first book, which barely mentioned religion, had to do with women's employment in the early decades of the twentieth century. That many of my subjects were Catholic did not at first impress me. But as I tried subsequently to figure out ways to understand what I vaguely termed "working-class culture," religion came into focus. At least in the U.S. context, after all, religion has been a powerful force in many working-class communities. An initial foray into the archives to study a long-term and episodically violent dispute in a local Polish parish stimulated something like a second conversion. Catholics were to be my principal subject from now on. I had much to learn to come up to speed in what was essentially a new field of study, such being the balkanized nature of American history in the academy. Thirty-odd years later, I am still learning. But I did discover in the course of my first "Catholic" project that I quite enjoyed being situated both within and outside that religious tradition, which is where my personal history has placed me. It seemed to make it easier to balance both appreciation of the tradition and a critical perspective on it. Whether I have succeeded in the pages that follow in achieving an equitable balance is up to the reader to judge.

A happy consequence of becoming a historian of American Catholicism was acquiring a new set of colleagues, most of whom had been laboring in this particular vineyard for the whole of their scholarly careers. Thanks to their superior training and venturesome minds, the field was even then undergoing a genuine renaissance. Freed from immigrant defensiveness, the "new" Catholic history provided a fresh take on the past, attentive to lay religious experience and the essential variables of gender, ethnicity, race, and class. The field has only grown stronger in the intervening years, more sophisticated theoretically and more imaginatively shaped by a heightened sensitivity to the insights of anthropology, psychology, and literary studies. Without the work of my accomplished colleagues, this book would not have been possible. I do not hold any of them responsible for my interpretations or emphases, with which some may disagree. But I am indebted to them all. Thanks are due as well to the many archivists who have labored, often in straitened financial circumstances, to make Catholic sources available to researchers.

The pages that follow survey almost five hundred years of Catholic experience in what became the United States. Surveying so long a period entails hard choices. What to include and what to ignore? My first priority, despite the paucity of relevant sources, has been to emphasize lay religion in all its variety. What did it mean to be a "good Catholic" at particular times and in particular places? How many Catholics, and which ones, were best able to approximate the ideal? What about the religious imaginations of the seemingly lukewarm? One cannot understand the religious experience of the laity without knowing something about the priests and vowed religious who served them and did so much to establish the emotional climate of the local church—and who, lest we forget, were once lay Catholics too. So I have given generous attention to these groups, as well, although here too the sources are far fewer than I would have liked. I have also tried throughout to focus on the larger American context and its impact on the Catholic Church as it evolved in the territory that eventually became the United States. A somewhat more difficult but equally important endeavor has been to explore how that same church shaped the American world around it. The United States would have been a different kind of country without its Catholic minority—of that I am convinced. I have tried to illuminate, in the course of the narrative, the principal reasons why I think so.

The Catholic Church in North America from its very beginnings encompassed far more human variety than any other—something that is still true today. In that sense, this most un-American of churches, for so it has long been regarded, constitutes a metaphor of sorts for our shared experience as a nation. What is more central to our national history than the creation of one out of many—the building of a nation almost entirely peopled by immigrants and their descendants? In learning about Catholics, then, even non-Catholic Americans will come to a richer understanding of their national past. Diversity led to conflict in both church and nation. It also flowered into cultural richness. Catholicism itself made for diversity in a nation that had long regarded its essence as Protestant. Conflict resulted, but a new civic richness too, as Americans began to think in more generous ways about religious liberty. Although Catholics long imagined themselves as a people set apart, they have helped to shape the

American drama from the very beginning—even prior to the emergence on
these shores of an independent nation. Participation in that drama has also
helped to shape the people that American Catholics became. Thus it is an
intertwined story that we now embark on, with meaning for Catholics and
non-Catholics alike.

Part I
On the Fringes of Empire

Eusebio Kino, S.J.

(1645–1711)

The year is 1663. A gifted student of mathematics lies gravely ill in a village in the Austrian Tyrol, not far from his birthplace near Trent. Fearing imminent death, young Eusebio Kino appeals to the recently canonized St. Francis Xavier, one of the original members of the Society of Jesus and famed for his missionary labors in India and Japan. Should he survive, young Kino vows, he too will join the Jesuits and become a missionary. Kino did in fact recover. He entered the Society two years later, at the age of twenty, hoping to serve in its China missions. His superiors sent him instead to New Spain, or present-day Mexico, where he arrived in 1681. Assigned initially to the new mission territory of Baja California, Kino gained fame for his subsequent exploration and mission founding in what is now the Mexican province of Sonora and the southernmost tier of today's Arizona—a district known then as the Pimería Alta. This remote and geographically forbidding region constituted the northernmost frontier of Spain's New World empire, which at its height encompassed the Caribbean islands, half of South America, most of Central America, present-day Mexico, Florida, the southwestern United States, and its Pacific Coast.

Kino's remarkable career was propelled by the same forces that shaped the early centuries of Catholic Christianity in the Americas. His was the first global age—a time when developments in navigation made possible not only European discovery of the Americas in 1492 but also greatly expanded trade with Asia and the Pacific islands. The rise of vast maritime empires followed. First Portugal and Spain, then France, the Netherlands, and Great Britain established overseas colonies in Africa, Asia, and the Indian subcontinent as well as the New World. The fortunes of Catholicism in the Americas until the end of the eighteenth century were profoundly shaped by the resulting imperial rivalries. Kino was sent to establish missions in Baja California as a kind of advance guard of Spanish colonization less because of the region's natural resources—it had few beyond a reputed pearl fishery—than Spain's need to protect its Pacific sea route to the Philippines from the depredations of privateers who flew the flag of rival powers. Doing so meant strengthening its claim to California's coast—a claim established in 1542 when Juan Rodriguez Cabrillo commanded the first European expedition to sail the length of what is now the most populous U.S. state.

Kino's was also an age of religious revitalization. The Protestant Reformations of the sixteenth century greatly strengthened existing reform impulses within Catholicism, which led in the post-Reformation century to heightened standards of training and discipline for the parish clergy and a new emphasis on the religious education of the laity. The ministry of preaching assumed greater significance, promoting not just doctrinal literacy but a more personal religion of the heart. The God of fear did not disappear—hell was regularly and graphically preached, while strict standards were upheld when it came to attendance at Mass and reception of the sacraments. But the emphasis in preaching was increasingly on the abundance of God's grace, the accessibility of salvation, and the will of a tenderly loving Father that all should be saved. Among the Catholic peasantry, these various reforms had resulted by the mid-seventeenth century in a more disciplined religious practice than had prevailed on the eve of the Reformation and a higher level of religious literacy. Among educated elites, the results were even more remarkable. It was here that "heart religion" flourished most mightily, especially among women, giving rise to a new intensity in lay devotion and a newfound zeal for acts of charity.

The earliest and most striking characteristic of the Catholic (or Counter-) Reformation, as this time of renewal is generally called, was the founding of religious orders. The Jesuits, established in 1540, were the most significant of these, although mention should also be made, given later developments in American Catholic history, of the Capuchins (1526) and the Vincentians (1633), along with the following communities of women: the

Ursulines (1535), Visitation sisters (1610), and Daughters of Charity (1633). Many of the new religious orders, along with a number of older communities that had undergone internal reform, produced notable missionary vocations. The Jesuits, to pick the most prominent example, by the time of Kino's birth had missions in Africa, India, Japan, China, and the Philippines; throughout South and Central America; and in the recently founded French colonies in present-day Canada. Many more Jesuits then, as now, were teachers rather than missionaries. But in the sixteenth and seventeenth centuries, it was missionaries and especially missionary-martyrs who dominated the Society's pantheon of Christian heroes. Eusebio Kino's education and intellectual gifts had prepared him for success in any number of secular pursuits—among other things, he was an accomplished cartographer—but his times were such that the missionary's calling might easily have seemed the most admirable and morally essential.[1]

Whatever his piety and idealism, however, the missionary priest was also—indeed, some would say primarily—an agent of empire. The earliest missionaries arrived in the New World in the context of military conquest; those who arrived later depended on the conqueror's military forces for protection and were expected to serve an imperial agenda. The missionary was an ambassador of sorts, valued for his ability to establish alliances with indigenous clan and tribal leaders and provide intelligence to the secular power. He was also a "civilizer," especially in the Spanish colonies, imposing—or attempting to impose—an alien discipline of life and work on the newly baptized. The missionary was expected to mold not simply new Christians but newly minted Spaniards, loyal subjects of the king—a project that even a non-Spaniard like Kino regarded as unproblematic. Most missionaries, it is true, came to see themselves as protectors of the indigenous population and sometimes protested their exploitation by the military or European settlers. But as a corollary of conquest, New World missions—regardless of the imperial power that sponsored them—were compromised at the outset. They served both God and Mammon.

Fortunately for Kino the missionary, his was an unusually itinerant career. During his twenty-four years in the Pimería Alta, he embarked on at least fifty journeys through that vast region, routinely traveling thirty or more miles a day for weeks or months at a time. Although he founded, and subsequently visited, a number of missions in the course of his travels and baptized numerous Indians—some four thousand, he estimated toward the end of his life—he also functioned as an explorer, describing and mapping a territory he thought destined for eventual Spanish settlement. Seldom present for long periods even in the Sonora missions that he directly administered, Kino was spared the moral ambiguities attendant on the painful business of replacing one culture with another. Unlike a resident mission pastor, he did not have to discipline Indian neophytes who engaged in traditional bouts of drinking and dancing or harbored ritual objects from the pagan past. Nor was he obliged to do personal battle against polygamy—ordering a high-status man to abandon all but his original wife was frequently a dangerous business—or the tolerant view of divorce so widely found in Indian cultures. Kino's arrival in his far-flung missions was, at least in his telling, typically celebrated with all-night festivities on the part of the Indian faithful. Jesuits resident in the missions he founded encountered a different response—sullen, resentful neophytes and occasional mass desertions of the mission compound. Several were murdered in the course of Indian rebellions.[2]

Kino died in 1711 at one of his Sonora missions, regarded by his closest Jesuit companions as nothing less than a saint. "He prayed much, and was considered as without vice," in the words of Father Luís Velarde. "He never had more than two coarse shirts, because he gave everything as alms to the Indians."[3] Ever the optimist, he could hardly have imagined the 1767 expulsion of the Jesuits from all their New World missions or the ultimate collapse of the mission project in what is now Arizona. But two of the missions he founded there have extant churches, protected today as national monuments, and Kino himself is memorialized in the U.S. Capitol's Statuary Hall as an Arizona founder. Let us bear in mind the complexities of his life and legacy—morally troubling in some respects, profoundly admirable in others—as we embark on our exploration of Catholicism's American advent—first via Spain, then France, and finally a small minority of early English settlers. Some of those who birthed the Catholic Church on American soil were doubtless saints, although even saints' lives can have unintended consequences. Saints or sinners, however, those colonial Catholics were just as much founders of today's American nation as the Calvinist Protestants who settled early New England—and not only because they got here first.

Spain's North American Frontier

Initial Spanish probes into the territory that is now the United States date from 1513, when Juan Ponce de León reached the Florida coast on a voyage from Puerto Rico. The indigenous population of North America at the time was at least seven million, with five million of these inhabiting the present-day United States. Some population estimates, it should be noted, range much higher. These earliest Spanish ventures were notable for their brutality. Many expeditions, not all of them legal, were mounted for the purpose of enslaving Indians, indigenous death rates in the Spanish-occupied Caribbean having caused acute labor shortages. The most celebrated—Francisco Vázquez de Coronado's expedition from Mexico north to present-day Nebraska and west to the Grand Canyon, and Hernando de Soto's epic trek through present-day Florida, Georgia, Alabama, Mississippi, Tennessee, and probably Arkansas—inflicted horrific violence on the indigenous people. Although priests accompanied both Coronado and de Soto, no real evangelizing took place. Indeed, missionaries who came subsequently to areas once traversed by these expeditions found their ministries hampered by Indian memories of Spanish mayhem.[1]

Ironically, the Spanish vision of empire placed a high value on Indian conversion. The Spanish arrival in the New World coincided with the expulsion from Spain of all practicing Jews and Catholic Spain's final triumph over Iberia's Muslim principalities. The conjunction seemed providential, especially to Spain's devout. Surely conquest and conversion of the New

World was the next stage in God's unfolding plan for the nation. More pro-saically, Spain's exploitation of the New World's riches depended on Indian labor, and a Christianized population would presumably be a more tracta-ble one. But the Spanish vision of empire had a certain generosity at its core. Indians were expected to become Spaniards—low-status Spaniards, to be sure, but members nonetheless of a New World Hispanic polity. Mar-riages between Spanish men and Indian women were encouraged from the outset, and it was not long before a mixed-race Hispanicized people came into being, some of whom eventually achieved high rank.

In such a vision of empire—simultaneously generous and profoundly coercive—the missionary played a central role. Generally responsible for making initial peaceful contact with the local indigenous population, the missionary was then expected to transform them into Christianized sub-jects of the Spanish Crown. The mission ideal, most fully realized by the Jesuits in eighteenth-century Paraguay, was a mission community whose members, in various stages of conversion and Hispanicization, could pro-duce enough to feed themselves and nearby military installations. Mission-aries nearly always preferred that a mission's residents be kept from contact with outsiders who might interrupt the process of cultural transformation, and that meant Hispanic soldiers and settlers as well as nonmission Indians. But Spanish hunger for indigenous labor doomed missionary hopes in this regard and led to frequent conflict between missionaries and secular au-thorities. Indian resistance was a factor too. Even baptized Indians retained attachments to non-Christian kin and tribal ways, while the more assimi-lated resented the restricted contours of mission life.

Despite such obstacles, the Spanish missions in what is now the United States typically passed through a time of prosperity, with numerous converts living peaceably in thriving mission settlements. This was espe-cially true in the present-day states of Florida, southernmost Georgia, New Mexico, and California. Indian religious devotion in mature commu-nities like these, observers sometimes noted, exceeded that of most local Spaniards. But even religiously vibrant missions eventually collapsed, sometimes because of Indian rebellions or intra-Indian warfare but most often because of disease. Indian contact with Europeans meant exposure to infectious diseases hitherto unknown in the Americas, including smallpox, diphtheria, influenza, and measles, to which many Spaniards had complete or partial immunity. The indigenous population of central Mexico had declined by as much as one-third within a decade of the Spanish arrival. Similarly horrific losses occurred subsequently in parts of the present-day United States.[2]

Spain's missionary era in what is now the United States encompassed well over two hundred years. The earliest missions, in Florida and New Mexico, were founded on the eve of the seventeenth century. The last, in California, were begun in 1769, shortly before the American Revolution. By that time the missions in Florida had been largely abandoned for better than fifty years, while those in Texas and Arizona—founded in the 1690s— were nearing a state of collapse. The various missions occupied strikingly disparate natural environments and tried to reach Indian peoples at vary- ing stages of social development. Their histories differ accordingly. Only with regard to Florida, however, can it be plausibly argued that the mission enterprise, though destined to failure, had no significant impact on subse- quent developments in the history of American Catholicism.

La Florida

Although St. Augustine was founded as a Spanish military outpost in 1565 and a Catholic parish was established there, successful Indian missions in Florida date only from the 1590s. Previous evangelizing efforts by the Do- minicans (1558), Jesuits (1566–70), and Franciscans (1573–75) had ended in dashed hopes and, in some cases, martyrdom at the hands of hostile Indians. The Jesuits' departure was prompted by the murder of eight of their number who had tried to establish a mission without military protection on the shores of Chesapeake Bay in present-day Virginia, then regarded by the Spanish as the northern portion of a vaguely defined entity known as La Florida. It was only with the return of a few Franciscans to the vicinity of St. Augustine in 1584 and especially the arrival of twelve more in 1595 that initial mission success began. Martyrdom was still available: rebellion among the Guale Indians in 1598 led to the deaths of seven Franciscans and temporary abandonment of the entire mission project. But the Guale and neighboring Timucua people were essential to the survival of the garrison at St. Augus- tine, which depended on these native agriculturalists for food and labor, and the garrison itself was essential to Spain in view of recent French attempts to establish a presence on La Florida's Atlantic coast. For reasons of empire, then, the Franciscan missions were resumed as early as 1612.

Despite difficult conditions, those missions enjoyed surprising success. By 1655 some forty Franciscan friars were ministering to as many as twenty-six thousand Christianized Indians in a mission territory that stretched across the Florida panhandle and into the southernmost tier of present-day Georgia. Working first among the Guale and Timucua and later among the Apalachee, Florida missionaries initially directed their conversion efforts at local chiefs, who upon consenting to baptism received Spanish names, Spanish clothing, and other exotic gifts and were honored thereafter as Spanish allies. "Once a few chiefs took the step of accepting Christianity," according to historian John H. Hann, "it behooved their neighbors to do the same, especially those who were head chiefs, lest one of their subordinates do so and thereby possibly supplant them by becoming the chiefdom's broker with the new power source." Spanish goods carried with them an aura of power and were highly prized by local Indians, especially iron tools, seeds of plants like peaches and melons, and such domesticated sources of meat as pigs and cattle, indigenous Americans at the time of contact having domesticated no quadrupeds other than the dog. (Firearms were coveted too, but the Spanish took care to keep them from Indian hands.) High-status Indians were especially intrigued by Spanish literacy and printed books. In the circumstances, Spanish religion very likely assumed an aura of potency as well and may help to explain—along with the promptings of local chiefs—why so many Florida natives sought to be baptized.[3]

Florida's missionaries, their numbers stretched thin, apparently made few attempts to gather the newly baptized into segregated mission communities. They lived instead, nearly always alone, in villages where a baptized chief was resident, from which they visited nearby hamlets for purposes of worship and catechesis. Despite their immersion in Indian life, few Florida Franciscans appear to have mastered any of the local languages, instead relying on Indian interpreters who had managed to pick up Spanish. What translation of this informal sort meant for the Christian message is impossible to know; certainly those missionaries who did gain facility in an Indian language, whether in Florida or elsewhere, often claimed that it simply lacked words to convey certain Christian concepts. Many years later, in 1790, a Rumsen-language catechism, devised for the California missions by indigenous translators, used a word for "soul" that is best rendered in English as "viscera"—the physical insides of the body.[4]

But liturgy teaches too, and probably better than the catechism. Images of Jesus, Mary, and the saints decorated Florida's churches—built by Indian labor, always of wood—and perhaps substituted emotionally for the idols that were sometimes burned at the local missionary's command. Indian neophytes reportedly loved to sing—even the catechism was often set to music—and Mass sometimes proceeded in those primitive churches with Indian choirs chanting the responses in Latin. Devotional confraternities were introduced to each mission shortly after its founding as a means of encouraging disciplined prayer among the newly baptized. As early as 1602, at the Timucua missions of San Pedro and San Juan de Puerto, Confraternities of the True Cross were staging Holy Week processions reminiscent of the Old World. "They performed their flagellation and procession on Holy Thursday in accord with Spanish custom," witnesses testified, "and assisted the priest in making the monument in which the Eucharist was enclosed. Warriors with their arms stood guard before it was opened on Good Friday."[5]

Once a generation of Indian children had grown up as Christians, speaking and even literate in Spanish thanks to mission education, what had been a Spanish religion became Indian property too. "Do they confess as Christians? I answer yes," in the words of one Franciscan. "Many persons are found, men and women, who confess and who receive [the Eucharist] with tears, and who show up advantageously with many Spaniards." But even in mature missions, Indian Christianity possessed a distinctive flavor, and the lives of Christian Indians were marked by a curious blend of old and new. It was customary, for example, to bury mission Indians—nearly always sans coffins—in the nave of the local church, where overcrowding might result in remains stacked six feet deep. It was also customary, on All Souls' Day, for Christian Indians to offer pumpkins, beans, and maize to their dead—a ritual that echoed an Indian tradition of offering food to deceased kin whose bones were stored in charnel houses or buried in mounds. Franciscan missionaries may well have worried that the ritual smacked of ancestor worship. But they generally tolerated such behaviors, saving their authority for weightier transgressions like polygamy or the worship of idols.[6]

Given the evident vitality of mission religion for much of the seventeenth century, what explains the ultimate collapse of the Florida mission enterprise? Disease was a constant adversary. Smallpox, measles, and other epidemic scourges had by midcentury reduced the Apalachee population to about ten thousand—some 20 percent of the total in 1513. The Timucua and

Guale were even more severely devastated. Depopulation left the missions increasingly vulnerable to attack; the Guale missions on the Atlantic coast were partly destroyed by pirate raids as early as 1680. By century's end, with the French ensconced along the lower Mississippi and English settlers resident at Charleston, South Carolina (founded 1760), Spain's Florida holdings were under severe military pressure. A motley settlers' militia from Charleston, supplemented by non-Christian Indian recruits, laid siege to St. Augustine in 1702, largely destroying the town. Subsequent raids by the same forces obliterated many of the Florida missions, with Indian captives reduced to slavery. Those Franciscans who remained in La Florida increasingly retreated to the relative safety of St. Augustine, now rebuilt, where they served a growing population of Spaniards and a handful of Indian refugees. The town had a thriving parish life until 1763, when Spain ceded Florida to the British.[7]

The missions were also weakened by the secular government's exploitation of the local Indian population. Indian labor was needed on farm sites close to St. Augustine, for construction projects, road maintenance, and militia service. Indian bearers carried goods between St. Augustine and the various missions, sometimes traveling the width of the Florida panhandle—work that was grueling, sometimes fatal, and bitterly resented. Missionaries stood outside the system, at least formally, since local chiefs drafted workers to fill a mission's quota. Missionaries, in fact, spoke out on occasion against the forced-labor regime. But missionaries also drafted workers for mission farms and construction projects. More problematically, from the Indian perspective, they enforced a strict discipline with regard to conduct and religious observance. Indians who missed Mass or catechism could be publicly whipped, either by the priests or their Indian assistants. Not surprisingly, Indian revolts in the early stages of mission history—the Guale revolt in 1597 and that among the newly missionized Apalachee in 1647—resulted in Franciscan deaths and destruction of mission churches. But the Timucua revolt of 1656, by which time a generation and more had grown up as Christians, targeted neither priests nor churches. The enemy this time around was the Spanish military.[8]

Nothing remains of the Florida missions, the locations of which are still sometimes unknown. And nothing remains of the Indian peoples who were once so numerous in the region. The Spanish missions in California and the American Southwest fostered a mixed people—part Spanish, part

Indian, and sometimes part African—whose mostly Catholic descendants survive to this day, augmented over the centuries by migration of a similar stock from Mexico and Central America. Although Florida saw a limited number of marriages between Indians and Spaniards plus numerous casual sexual contacts, no mixed population survived there long term. Apart from allowing Catholics to claim a symbolic "first"—St. Augustine is the oldest European settlement in what is now the United States—the Florida missions cannot be said to have shaped American Catholic history in any significant way. But the human drama they embody is surely worth remembering.

New Mexico

Franciscan priests entered present-day New Mexico in 1598, shortly after their advent in La Florida. As in La Florida, initial contact was marked by horrific violence. The first Franciscans accompanied a military expedition led by Juan de Oñate, which, having encountered resistance in the Ácoma pueblo, inflicted vicious retaliation on that hapless Indian fortress in 1599. Over eight hundred Indians died, and dozens more were deliberately maimed. Oñate governed the "Kingdom of New Mexico" for another seven years before he was forced to resign, not because of his brutality but for failing to deliver a profit to the Crown from this newest Spanish colony, which Philip III of Spain was reportedly ready to abandon. At this juncture, however, the Franciscans announced the baptisms of some seven thousand New Mexico Indians, including numerous women and children taken captive at Ácoma and brought to live as quasi-slaves among the Spanish colonists. Influential at the Spanish Court, the friars saved the nascent colony. Santa Fe was established as its capital in 1610, with a Spanish governor in residence and a surprisingly modest military presence. No clergy other than Franciscans were permitted in the colony, which gave them unusual independence from secular authority. Outside the immediate Santa Fe area and at least in the colony's earlier years, the Franciscans were in charge.[9]

The Franciscans who served in seventeenth-century New Mexico are often described as close to zealots—fervently millenarian in their outlook and ascetic in their personal lives. New Mexico, they believed, had been given to them by God to establish a church like that of Apostolic times, uncorrupted by the greed and license that marked even putatively Catholic nations in the world they saw around them. Their millenarian hopes were strengthened in 1631 upon learning that a Spanish nun—María de Ágreda—had been having visions of herself being bodily transported to New Mexico and preaching to the Indians. With vast excitement they recalled the report of a fellow Franciscan in 1623: Indians he had recently encountered had told him of being instructed in Christian doctrine by a woman in Franciscan robes. Surely it was María de Ágreda, come all the way from Spain! Miracles and mystical visions were integral to Franciscan spirituality, not just in the seventeenth century but for many generations thereafter. Junípero Serra, famed founder of the California missions in the later eighteenth century, believed firmly in the Ágreda legend and found in it a source of both purpose and consolation.

Evangelization in New Mexico met with great success initially. By 1631, sixty-six Franciscans were ministering to about sixty thousand baptized Indians, most of them agriculturalists living in compact towns—*pueblos,* in Spanish, which is why Spaniards called the various Indian peoples of the area by that name. As in Florida, conversion efforts were directed first at local chiefs, whose attraction to Spanish goods and respect for Spanish power often prompted a quick consent to baptism. Mass baptism of their subjects usually followed. In the early years of mission activity, none of the missionaries knew any of the local languages, and only a handful learned one thereafter. Thus, as in Florida, evangelization was carried out via Indian interpreters, sacred images, music, and liturgical ceremony. New Mexico's mission churches were generally larger and more elaborately decorated than those in Florida and musical life there more ambitious. New Mexico's missions, according to one authority, may have boasted as many as seventeen organs by the 1640s. Trumpets and shawms, an oboe-like instrument, also accompanied Indian choirs that apparently sang polyphony. New Mexico Franciscans also used drama to convey not just religious precepts—a shepherd's play featured at Christmas—but the intimate link between Spanish power and the new religion. "The Christians and the Moors," depicting the final defeat of Iberia's Muslims in 1492, was frequently staged.[10]

What did conversion mean in such circumstances, particularly for adults? In many cases, very likely, conversion meant simply accepting that the Spaniards' power was greater than their own. Southwest Indians were plagued by frequent warfare and accustomed to Indian conquerors who imposed their gods on the vanquished. Other outcomes were certainly possible. Hearts might well be moved by Christian ritual and the message of a loving God, who was also a suffering human. Still, the Franciscans were taking no chances. Once resident in an Indian town, the missionary established classes for the local children, who came every morning to the church to learn Spanish—to read and write as well as speak it, although only a minority became fully literate—as well as Christian prayers and doctrine. Every child was taught to sing and those sufficiently gifted to play a musical instrument. Within a generation, then, most missions probably housed a number of committed Christians, some of them zealous. Christian boys were reportedly used by some Franciscans to ferret out idols in pueblo households so that they might be publicly burned.[11]

Christianity was often a source of division in the densely populated pueblos. Much of it was generational—witness the idol-hunting boys exposing their nominally converted elders to likely punishment. But mission discipline also caused trouble, especially with high-status men. All baptized Indians were required to attend Mass, catechism, and evening Vespers daily; those absent without excuse were punished, sometimes by whipping. Sexual sins were punished even more severely, by such public humiliations as imprisonment in the stocks or the shearing of one's hair. Pueblo Indian customs with regard to sex were lax by Christian standards—polygamy was permitted among those of high rank, casual divorce was common, and tolerance was afforded men who chose to dress and function as women. Not surprisingly, sexual discipline was a serious point of contention throughout the mission era. The Franciscans themselves did not generally administer punishment but left it to their Indian assistants—church wardens and catechists whose exalted status rested largely on their knowledge of Spanish. Indian males once accustomed to authority could hardly have looked with equanimity on the rise of this missionary-made elite.

Epidemic disease in New Mexico was never as lethal as in Florida, with a dry climate and sparser settlement hindering its spread. Nonetheless, the Pueblo Indian population was probably halved in the course of the seventeenth century. A smallpox epidemic in 1636 killed an estimated twenty thousand and apparently ushered in a time of growing Indian disaffection. Disease and periodic drought suggested, at least to nominal converts, that Spanish religion lacked the power they had once imputed to it, and some resumed the secret practice of indigenous religious rituals. A declining population of Indians led in some cases to smaller missions being forcibly consolidated, which caused further alienation. Nor did it help that some

Franciscans—their numbers were small but potent as example—were ne-glecting their vows of celibacy and fathering half-Indian children. The slen-der evidence in this regard dates mainly from the 1660s and after, suggesting that Indian disaffection and missionary isolation had eroded the zeal so evident among earlier Franciscans. "All the pueblos are full of friars' chil-dren," Father Nicholas Freitas reported almost casually in 1671, and while his account is clearly exaggerated, it suggests a sea change in Franciscan morale.[12]

Diminishing Indian numbers also led to intensified Spanish exploita-tion. Christianized Indians were obliged, as elsewhere, to labor on mission farms and ranches. (Spaniards introduced New Mexico to cattle, sheep, pigs, and horses.) Although work of this sort was more regimented than precon-tact Indians had known, other demands on Indian labor were far more bit-terly resented. Certain Spanish inhabitants of New Mexico were permitted by Spanish law to exact tribute from the local Indians in exchange for putative military protection. That same law prohibited local Spaniards from exacting tribute in the form of labor. But in isolated New Mexico, the law was readily flouted, and Indians were regularly required to work for Spanish soldiers and settlers as well as make tribute payments of cloth, skins, and corn. Settlers sometimes laid claim in addition to land still defined as Indian property. As the Indian population declined and settler numbers increased, the burden of tribute—known in Spanish as *encomienda*—grew ever more onerous. New Mexico's missionaries did object to the system, often vigorously, generating serious conflict with the colony's governors. But Franciscan authority waned as settlement expanded, and such protests had little ultimate effect.[13]

Accumulated grievances led in 1680 to the deadliest Indian rebellion in the history of Spanish North America. The great Pueblo Revolt was pre-ceded by years of drought in the 1670s and a consequent revival of indige-nous religious practice in many stricken Indian settlements—surreptitious practice, to be sure, but sufficiently widespread that New Mexico's governor in 1675 launched a military campaign intended to suppress idolatry and punish Indian shamans. The campaign did little beyond stoking Indian re-sentment. It was shamans who orchestrated the multipueblo revolt of 1680, with a man named Popé—a Tewa Indian—generally said to have been their charismatic leader. More than four hundred settlers were murdered out of a population of some twenty-eight hundred, along with twenty-one Fran-ciscans, many of whom were put to death following ritualized torture.

Churches were desecrated and destroyed and Christian paraphernalia burned, and many onetime Christians immersed themselves in streams to wash away the effects of baptism. In the course of what can only be called a religiously inflected cultural revolution, the Spanish were forced to retreat to present-day El Paso, ceding New Mexico to the Indians. They did not return until 1692, when the Spanish military finally secured the submission of most of New Mexico's pueblos.[14]

The Franciscans returned to New Mexico too, albeit in a chastened mood. Continued Indian submission could not be assumed; indeed, five more friars died in the course of a 1696 uprising. Authority both secular and clerical was in consequence imposed with a lighter hand. The encomienda was ended, while missionaries now tolerated the practice of indigenous rituals not overtly in conflict with Catholic doctrine. The result of the latter was open engagement in a frankly synchronistic religion. Christian saints assumed attributes of the Katsina—spirits of the dead who brought life-giving rain—and local gods; images of the Virgin linked her symbolically to the Corn Mothers, central to Pueblo creation myths. Did this altered symbol system represent an acculturated Christianity? Or was Indian Christianity simply a veneer—surface conformity to an alien faith that masked continued adherence to ancient religious beliefs? Durango's Bishop Pedro Tamarón y Romeral thought it was the latter. On a pastoral tour of New Mexico in 1760, he encountered many Indians who never went to confession, although deathbed confession via an interpreter was still standard practice in the missions. Not truly understanding Spanish and tended by priests who knew no Indian languages, these nominal Christians, in the bishop's telling, were ignorant of Christian doctrine. "This point saddened and upset me, . . . and I felt scruples about confirming adults."[15]

By the time of Bishop Tamarón's visit, New Mexico's Indian missions had lost their vigor and were more and more marginal to its Catholic life. Religiously speaking, the future belonged to the putatively Spanish settlers, whose numbers were growing steadily. Those settlers or *gente de razon* (people of reason), as the bishop called them, were almost all of mixed ancestry, descended in varying combinations from Spaniards, Indians, and sometimes Africans. Settlers arriving from Mexico were already a mixed people, having lived for generations under Spanish colonial rule. Once in New Mexico, where settler women were in short supply, surplus males either married Indian women (as their priests advised), lived with them in nonmarital unions of uncertain tenure, or exploited them sexually. The widespread practice of Indian slavery in New Mexico—another formally illegal practice that the colony's isolation permitted—made sexual exploitation easy, as did the drafting of Indian women for domestic labor by means of the encomienda. Indian women sometimes abandoned the offspring of such unions at the local mission, where a priest would baptize the child and place it with a Christian family. Known as "children of the church," such youngsters were estimated to constitute roughly 10 percent of the population of New Mexico's Spanish towns in the eighteenth century.[16]

The permeability of racial boundaries in Spanish colonial society expanded the reach and meaning of the Indian missions, whose effects were not confined to exclusively Indian communities. The missionaries' great, if unintended, triumph was precisely the mixed society into which so many Indians were eventually incorporated. That society was held together by the Spanish language and Catholicism—not necessarily, in the case of the latter, as a deeply internalized faith but certainly as ritual practice. Indian women who married settlers, Indian men who left the missions in pursuit of work in town or on a ranch—pioneers like these bought social membership by means of language and religious conformity. What might have begun for the first generation as superficial adherence to the Spaniards' religion, moreover, could easily become in the next a valued religious inheritance, as the vivid traditions of New Mexico Catholicism rather strongly suggest. Especially after the annexation of New Mexico by the United States in 1848, Catholicism served more and more as a principal source of identity and cultural integrity for a newly conquered people.

Unlike the case of Florida, New Mexico's mission churches have largely survived, although all were eventually abandoned by the Spanish Franciscans. Some survive as carefully tended ruins; others continue to function as parishes. Among the most evocative is San Estevan del Rey in Ácoma pueblo, site of the 1598 massacre. The fortress-like church, begun in 1629 and today a national historic site, is the only New Mexico mission church to have come through the Pueblo Revolt unscathed, although its resident priest was murdered. The site bears witness simultaneously to Spanish cruelty, Indian resistance, and Franciscan heroism. (The priest in question kept to his post despite plentiful rumors of an imminent Indian uprising.) In an isolated pueblo like Ácoma, indigenous religion clearly did retain some elements of precontact vitality. Well into the twentieth century, according to

Mission and church at Ácoma, 1905; photograph by Edward Curtis (Library
of Congress, LC-USZ62-195585; courtesy of the Library of Congress,
Washington, DC)

historian David J. Weber, the Pueblo Indians "simultaneously practiced Catholicism through the intermediary of a Catholic priest, and indigenous
religious traditions through native priests—'compartmentalizing' the two
religions rather than synthesizing them."[17] Here is another contrast to Florida: the survival in New Mexico of Indian peoples and cultures, if inevitably
in attenuated fashion.

Texas and Arizona

The first missions in Texas and Arizona were founded roughly a century
after their counterparts in Florida and New Mexico. That intervening century saw a gradual ascent of liberal values among the Spanish elite—a new
interest in reform, a new enthusiasm for science and critical history, even a
growing respect for non-Western cultures. The fundamental nature of the
Spanish colonial project did not change; its purpose remained the exploitation of indigenous peoples and their resources. Nor could administrators

necessarily control the behavior of military and civilian personnel on distant imperial frontiers. But an increasingly enlightened corps of colonial
administrators did seek to minimize harm among their subject populations, in the name of efficiency as well as humanity. A parallel liberalization
was evident in ecclesiastical circles, with efforts to improve education for
missionaries and encourage the learning of local languages. Here too there
were limits to how fully reform aspirations could be realized. But the change
in mentality was significant.

Although Spanish explorers had crossed portions of present-day Texas on numerous occasions in the sixteenth and seventeenth centuries, the
first missions were not established there until 1690. Prior to this time, the
Spanish Crown had evinced little interest in what is now Texas—a region so
remote from the heart of Spain's American empire as to seem compara-
tively worthless. But by the 1680s, with France laying claim to the entire
length of the Mississippi, Texas assumed strategic importance as a buffer
zone against the French. Despite its strategic potential, however, Texas was
envisioned as a civilian colony rather than a string of military outposts.
Carnage like that at Ácoma in 1598 did not mar the mission era in Texas,
itself a testimony to Spain's gradual liberalization. Juan de Oñate had
marched to Ácoma behind an image of the Virgin as La Conquistadora, as
Coronado had earlier done. A much smaller expedition of Franciscans and
their military escort into the mission fields of Texas in 1716 carried an image
of the Virgin of Guadalupe—the Mother of God in the guise of a young
Indian woman.[18]

Texas was a Franciscan preserve, with mission founding occurring
initially among the Hasinai people of eastern Texas. (The Spanish called
them "Tejas"—a rough approximation of the term employed by the Hasinai as a greeting—from which the name "Texas" derives.) The earliest
missions were short lived: restiveness among the Indians caused their abandonment in 1693. A second initiative, which began in 1716, gave rise to
missions on the Rio Grande, along the San Antonio River, and on the Texas
Gulf Coast. There were twenty-one missions in Texas by 1722, not all of
which endured long term. A third wave of mission founding took place
between 1745 and 1762, with the very last mission dating from 1793. Success
in some missions, if realized at all, was fleeting. Those in isolated regions
were vulnerable to attack by hostile Apaches. In others, the seminomadic
habits common to most Texas Indians proved too great a barrier to conver-

sion. Indeed, except in a handful of missions, conversion rates were disappointing.[19]

The Franciscans enjoyed their greatest success in a cluster of missions in and around present-day San Antonio (founded 1718). Here they came closest to realizing the ideal of a "congregated" mission, where life was centered on work and devotion, and Indian contact with the outside world was kept to a minimum. Each of the numerous missions in the vicinity of San Antonio housed more than two hundred people, whose labor over the generations gave rise to magnificent churches, sturdy houses and outbuildings, irrigated fields, and thriving herds of livestock. But despite their evident vitality, insulated missions of this sort could not be sustained. A permanent sedentary existence proved unpalatable to a great many baptized Indians, who often left the mission temporarily to hunt, fish, or trade. Others rebelled against missionary efforts to suppress indigenous games and rituals or discipline sexual offenders. The danger of attack by hostile Indians, from which few Texas locales were truly immune, did constitute something of a Franciscan trump card: residence in the fortified missions of San Antonio provided much-valued protection. Even so, many Indians with enduring mission connections eventually became sufficiently Hispanicized to join the local Hispanic community, either by means of marriage or the autonomous sale of their labor. As in New Mexico, language and religious conformity paved the way to social membership, though not—at least initially—at any but the lowest status.[20]

By the later 1770s, missions were falling out of favor with many Spanish officials, who regarded them as far too costly and, given their paternalism, incompatible with liberal values. There was increasing pressure too from Hispanic farmers and ranchers, hungry as their numbers grew for access to mission lands. Many Texas missions by this time had declining populations, the result in part of what was called "fugitivism"—Indians leaving without permission despite its being against the law—and in part of disease and consequent low fertility. Such pressures led in the 1790s to initial steps toward secularization, a sometimes lengthy process by which missions were converted into parishes served by diocesan clergy. (Texas was then in the Diocese of Guadalajara.) Once a mission was fully secularized, its Indian inhabitants were free to leave and live as independent workers; its lands were also disposed of—in theory to the mission Indians but in practice nearly always to local settlers. All the missions in Texas were fully secularized after Mexico achieved independence from Spain in 1821. The last Franciscan living in Texas died in 1833—murdered under mysterious circumstances shortly after baptizing an Anglo newcomer by the name of Sam Houston.[21]

The missions in present-day Arizona began in 1691, when the re-doubtable Eusebio Kino arrived at Guevavi, a Pima Indian village just north of the present international boundary. Kino, who had already worked for several years in the missions of Sonora, preached to the locals at Guevavi to evident good effect, for they offered some of their children for baptism. Kino established a mission there and at neighboring Tumacácori and a third mission (San Xavier del Bac) just south of present-day Tucson in 1692. The local Indians were mostly hunter-gatherers, though some who lived near water also tended crops. In a land of drought and climatic extremes, the getting of food was a principal focus of Indian life and something that played an outsized role in local mission history. That missionaries brought hitherto-unknown seeds and domesticated animals—the peripatetic Kino was a father of sorts to the vast herds of cattle and sheep that soon flour-ished in the region—greatly enhanced their authority. It also corrupted mission life, at least as the missionaries saw it. "Indians do not come to Christian service when they do not see the maize pot boiling," in the words of Guevavi's pastor in the 1730s.[22]

The Arizona missions belonged to the Jesuits until their expulsion from Spain's American dominions in 1767. Frank rivals to the Franciscans when it came to missionary labor, the Jesuits did enjoy certain advantages. Their missionaries typically received a more rigorous training than their Franciscan counterparts, particularly when it came to local cultures and languages. Not every Jesuit in the Americas mastered an Indian language, nor was every Franciscan ignorant in this regard. But on the whole, the Je-suits were the more accomplished linguists. Eusebio Kino began his study of the Pima language—common to many Indians in the Pimería Alta, al-though spoken in various dialects—shortly after his arrival in the Americas. The extent of his mastery is not wholly clear, but several of his successors at Guevavi were said to have been fluent speakers. (Since the Jesuits who came to the region were mostly German, Austrian, or Swiss, they had already mastered Spanish.) But despite this notable advantage, the Jesuits in Ari-zona produced few enduring conversions. No more than five Jesuits served the vast region at any given time, with one or two being more typical. And the Indians who greeted the itinerant Kino with such enthusiasm were far less responsive once a resident pastor arrived.

The methods employed in the Jesuits' missions were in most respects similar to those of the Franciscans. Preaching was central, preferably without an interpreter. On his first visit to San Xavier del Bac, Kino situated the locals in the context of salvation history, before concluding with the usual peroration on heaven and hell. Saint James had brought the Gospel to Spain many centuries earlier, he told them. "And I showed them on a world map how the Spaniards and the Faith had come by sea to Vera Cruz and entered Puebla and Mexico City and Guadalajara and Sinaloa and Sonora and now the lands of the Pimas at Nuestra Señora de los Dolores del Cosari, where already there were many baptized, a house and church, bells and images of saints, many provisions, wheat and maize, many cattle and many horses." Along with its aura of equality—Indians, after all, were invited to membership in a global Christian community—the masterful sermon also suggested that conversion meant access to food and a rich ceremonial life. His listeners were pleased, Kino tells us, and brought him some children for baptism. Kino administered the sacrament immediately, since children below the age of reason—seven or possibly eight, by most reckonings—could be baptized without being catechized. Older candidates had first to master the Christian basics, unless they were at the point of death.[23]

Eager to have a resident priest, the as-yet-unbaptized Indians at Guevavi set about building a proper house. Kino taught them to build in adobe, unknown in the region, and supervised the planting of the mission's first crops. Those at Tumacácori and Bac followed suit. Building a church came next—spartan at first but destined to be imposing. "The churches in this valley are remarkable," a surprised U.S. soldier reported well over a century later. The Jesuits endowed even modest churches with costly altar furnishings and a plentitude of colorful images—the latter useful for teaching doctrine. They cultivated musical life as well and mounted processions on popular feast days. Mission life at its most fully realized featured a compulsory round of morning prayer, followed by daily Mass and catechism, "prayed or sung," after which priest as well as people adjourned to labor in field, stock barn, or kitchen. "It is necessary that the father go, shovel in hand, to the garden and work there until the Ave Maria chime so that things do not go to ruins," as one disgruntled Jesuit explained.[24]

The remote Pimería Alta was unappealing to all but the most zealous, and the Jesuit order was stretched thin by its global missionary commitments. After Kino paid a final visit to Guevavi and its neighbors in 1702, there were no resident pastors in what is now Arizona until 1731. Jesuits who arrived subsequently often suffered from physical ailments—Guevavi especially was an unhealthy site—and apparent low morale. The ebullient Kino had described the Pima as something close to nascent Christians, eager for baptism and instruction. The resident pastors who succeeded him told a different story—one of Indian indifference to religious teaching, resentment at having to labor, and resistance to discipline. Nor had the Pima abandoned the rituals of their supposedly abjured paganism, some of them fueled by a potent cactus liquor. Whenever his parishioners "were contemplating a nocturnal dance and revelry," according to Jesuit Joseph Och, they contrived to get rid of him, sometimes by inventing a dying Christian living far from the mission who wanted the father to hear his confession.[25]

Indian discontents ran deep, at least at Guevavi and Bac, where a 1751 revolt cost the lives of two Jesuits and at least one hundred settlers and peaceful Indians. But disease, desertion, and attacks by hostile Apache were ultimately more damaging. By 1766, Guevavi's population was down to a reported fifty souls, despite repeated Jesuit efforts to replenish the mission by importing Indians who lived at a distance. By the 1760s, if not before, Jesuits in the Pimería Alta were ministering to almost as many Hispanic soldiers, miners, and ranchers as Indians—although here too the Hispanic population, into which some local Indians married, was partially of Indian descent. The region's German Jesuits apparently regarded local Hispanics as both indolent and cruel, largely due to their ruthless exploitation of the region's Indians. They were drinkers, too, in the Jesuits' telling, as well as sexually profligate and unwilling to go to confession.

The Jesuits' ordeal in Arizona, if such it was, ended abruptly in 1767, when every member of the order was expelled from the Spanish Americas. In an era of centralizing monarchies, the Jesuits' vow of loyalty to the pope—himself a secular power in Europe—and the order's cosmopolitan ethos rankled Europe's imperial rulers. The order was suppressed in the Portuguese empire in 1759 and France in 1764; it would be suppressed entirely in 1773 by order of Pope Clement XIV, under pressure from Europe's Catholic kings. The Jesuits expelled from New Spain suffered real abuse at the hands of the soldiers who rounded them up and those who imprisoned them at local ports to await extradition to Spain. At least twenty of those working in present-day Mexico died as a result, including one who had previously served at Guevavi.

The Jesuit missions in the Pimería Alta were given to the Franciscans, who served in the region until 1842, by which time the region's missions were moribund. The mission frontier in Arizona remained where it had been under the Jesuits, Apache hostility ensuring that no mission north of Bac could survive. The 1830s saw the first American settlers arrive in present-day Arizona, which was annexed to the United States in 1848, although its southernmost tier remained a nominal Mexican possession until 1854. A U.S. soldier in 1848 passed by Tumacácori, which in the Franciscan years had been the area's principal mission, and remarked on the size and beauty of its church. There had not been a priest in residence for many years, he noted, but the handful of Indians still at the mission had cared lovingly for the church's furnishings: "all its images, pictures, figures &c remain unmolested, and in good keeping." Shortly thereafter, the Indians abandoned Tumacácori for fear of the Apache. But they took with them all the church goods they could carry—images, vestments, and sacred vessels.[26]

California

Twenty-one missions were established in California by Spanish Franciscans between 1769 and 1823, stretching from present-day San Diego to just north of San Francisco Bay. California's numerous coastal Indians—an estimated sixty-five thousand lived in what became mission territory—were hunter-gatherers, organized in relatively small bands and speaking as many as one hundred distinct languages. Such social realities posed daunting obstacles to evangelization, at least as the Franciscans saw it. How to catechize, much less Hispanicize, a seminomadic population? Experience said it could not be done. "Congregated missions" were the obvious solution—Franciscan-run villages where interested Indians might be prepared for baptism. Once baptized, the new Christian would be legally required to live at the mission and participate in its tightly organized round of worship, work, and instruction. (Flight brought pursuit, sometimes by the military.) The language problem, awkward at first, would eventually be solved by teaching selected boys Spanish. Once these youngsters acquired fluency, they could function as interpreters and even evangelize on their own.[27]

Conversions were initially slow to come, given the linguistic circumstances. But the Indians were generally friendly—a brief uprising at Mission San Diego shortly after its founding in 1769 was a signal exception—and enormously curious about the Spanish newcomers, whose goods excited admiration and perhaps a sense of awe. The first baptisms, which usually occurred within six months of a mission's founding, were invariably those of infants or children who often enough were seriously ill. Baptism, alas, seldom effected the hoped-for cure. Presenting a child for baptism may also have been a ritual means of establishing ties with the new power source—a mode of alliance that did not require the parents to live at the mission. And as was everywhere the case, the missions attracted Indians by their stores of food. Even in the lush environment of coastal California, hunter-gatherers knew periodic hunger. Their ability to sustain themselves, moreover, was quickly compromised by the Spanish presence: herds of livestock attached to the missions destroyed many native plants, as did mission agriculture, while new diseases reduced the population of many small Indian bands.

Life in a congregated mission was frankly designed to remake its Indian inhabitants. The day was carefully parceled out, its various activities announced by a bell: recitation of the catechism, daily Mass, morning chores, noon prayers, midday dinner, and afternoon work, with a second catechetical lesson in the evening. The talented also got musical instruction, for all the missions had choirs and most had small orchestras. Indian men were set to work as farmers and stock tenders, despite their pasts as free-ranging hunters, while women's tasks kept them close to the mission and under the watch of the friars, who apparently regarded nearly all Indians as inherently licentious. In most California missions, unmarried women and girls nearing puberty were sequestered at night in their own dormitory—an arrangement that proved disastrously unhealthy as mission populations grew and sanitation remained primitive. Sexual discipline was policed in other ways as well: polygamous males who wanted baptism had to abandon their "surplus" wives, divorce was prohibited, and so were homosexual liaisons. California's Indians, like a great many others, recognized a kind of third sex—men who dressed and otherwise identified as women, even to the point of marrying as such. Fray Francisco Palóu indignantly recalled a mission Indian who tried to justify the homosexual act in which he had been caught on the grounds that his partner was his wife.[28]

As Fray Palóu was learning, it was no easy matter to refashion adults. With only two Franciscans typically resident in a mission and mission populations that ranged as high as twenty-eight hundred souls, compromise was inevitably the order of the day. In the early years moreover, the missions could not house all who entered; most Indian converts and catechumens lived in adjacent villages, where private life could proceed with at least a degree of autonomy. Even baptized Indians insisted on regular visits to nonbaptized kin and the right to engage in certain traditional practices, particularly those surrounding the hunt. Initially committed to a regime of strict segregation, the Franciscans were soon forced to institute a policy of annual leave—a period of several weeks when Indians might legally absent themselves from the mission and its discipline. Even the standards for baptism were ultimately subjected to compromise. When large groups entered a mission together—whole villages migrated into the missions of the San Francisco Bay region during a drought in the mid-1790s—catechesis prior to the baptism of adults was often truncated. Catechumens in the earliest days of the missions typically waited months or even years for baptism. By 1801, the wait was down to just a few weeks.[29]

Compromise had its limits: sexual sin was always punished, as were absences from Mass or catechetical instruction. Unexcused absence from the mission itself was a particularly serious offense, but as a violation of Spanish law, it was punished by the military, as were theft, rape, and murder. The usual punishment was public whipping, assuming that the offender was male. (For modesty's sake, women were whipped in private.) More grievous or chronic offenses might be punished by confinement in the stocks or a term at hard labor. Capital punishment, however, was rare— even for rebels and murderers. As in Franciscan missions elsewhere, the California Franciscans themselves did not usually administer punishment, leaving that task to their Indian assistants or the soldiers at a nearby presidio. But some apparently did wield the lash, at least on occasion, and at times intemperately. Reforming currents by the late eighteenth century made physical punishment of this sort increasingly hard to justify, and Franciscans writing on the subject betrayed a certain defensiveness. Charged with the immensely difficult task of civilizing a primitive people, they argued, missionaries were forced to employ a regime of exemplary punishments, which they inflicted only upon provocation and with the greatest reluctance.[30]

Physical punishment in the California missions emerged as a subject of national debate in 2015, thanks to the Washington, DC, canonization of Junípero Serra by Pope Francis I. Born in Mallorca in 1713, Serra spent his early years as a Franciscan teaching philosophy in the seminary at Palma.

Fervently ascetic and inclined to mysticism, he abandoned his academic career for a missionary vocation at the age of thirty-five, traveling to New Spain in 1749. Serra served initially in the missions of the Sierra Gorda, an isolated region north of Mexico City, and subsequently as Master of Novices at the Franciscan College of San Fernando in Mexico City itself. In this latter assignment, he gained local renown as an impassioned preacher—he traveled a preaching circuit at regular intervals—and a reputation among his confreres as an exemplar of prayer and self-discipline. He regularly inflicted physical pain on himself as a mode of penance, both in the context of private prayer and while preaching. As historian Steven Hackel explains, "At the conclusion of his sermons, when he recited an act of contrition, Serra would raise his crucifix in his left hand and then, in emulation of Saint Jerome, grasp a large rock with his right hand and pound his chest with such force that many expected him to fall dead."[31]

Assigned to the former Jesuit missions in Baja California in 1767, Serra served there only briefly before being sent to establish new missions in the unexplored territory to the north, where the advent of Russian traders signaled the need for a Spanish presence. Traveling overland to present-day San Diego, a journey of some seven hundred miles, Serra founded a mission there in 1769, the first of the nine he established in Alta (or Upper) California prior to his death in 1784. He lived primarily at Mission San Carlos in Carmel, among the Rumsen Indians, but made regular visits to the others in his capacity as Father-President. Never much of a linguist— despite near-daily immersion, he could not master Rumsen—Serra shone as an administrator and, often enough, as a politician. In this latter capacity he emerged as an ardent defender of the local Indians, who were frequently abused by Hispanic soldiers. Keeping mission Indians segregated, in Serra's view, was a means of protecting them from rape and murder as well as temptations to sin. Ever practical, he also advocated marriage between local soldiers, themselves of mixed-race origin, and Indian women who had been baptized.

Serra did indeed defend corporal punishment in the missions and on occasion prescribed it himself. At the same time, he opposed capital punishment, even in the case of Indian rebellion. "As to the killer, let him live that he can be saved," he wrote in the wake of a second uprising at Mission San Diego, in which a Franciscan had been killed, "for that is the purpose of our coming here and its sole justification." What to make of this seeming contradiction? Let us remember Serra's own ascetic practice: even a lifelong Christian, in his evident view, had to subdue the promptings of the flesh with harsh physical discipline. Withholding punishment for sin, especially in the case of a Christian neophyte, meant risking the eternal destiny of a vulnerable soul. "This should be a good lesson for them," he wrote with regard to the three rounds of whipping prescribed for a group of Indians who had absconded from Mission San Carlos on several occasions, "and it will be of spiritual benefit for everyone." Uneasily aware of external criticism and even of disciplinary excesses by certain confreres—"there probably have been some irregularities on the part of some Padres"—Serra continued to defend the system. It was not until the 1830s that a new generation of Franciscans spoke out against physical punishment and took steps to reduce its incidence.[32]

At Serra's death in 1784, eighteen Franciscans were serving some 5,125 neophytes in the nine California missions he founded. Dramatic growth was to follow. At the death of Serra's successor, Fermín Francisco de Lasuén, in 1803, more than forty Franciscans were at work in eighteen missions with a combined population of 15,562. But if Serra missed his missions' flowering, he was spared their greatest tragedy. Disease was always a mission problem. But mission death rates in Serra's day were relatively low, at least in part because mission populations were not yet large and crowded together. Growth brought greater density, with its attendant problems of sanitation, along with the scourge of epidemics. It was not long before most California missions had death rates, especially among women and children, at least as high as the worst in seventeenth-century Europe. Fertility among mission Indians was also unnaturally low, very likely due to endemic syphilis—an affliction brought by the Spanish, whose forebears in their turn had probably acquired it from the indigenous peoples of the Caribbean. In the demographic circumstances, mission populations could be sustained only by the continual importation of Indians from the hinterland, where an ongoing crisis of subsistence made the mission seem, for all its disease, like something of a refuge.[33]

Death stalked the California missions into their final chapter, which began with their gradual secularization in the 1820s and 1830s. Indians who left the missions, as they were now free to do, were typically the most Hispanicized—able because of their skills and mastery of Spanish to make a living among California's small but growing population of Spanish-speaking settlers. Few remained long on the land, drifting instead toward such nodes of settlement as San Jose (founded 1777) and Los Angeles (founded 1781), where the fortunate made lives for themselves, their children often becoming part of the mixed-race world around them. Others were desperately poor, sometimes homeless, and increasingly prey to alcoholism. Their fate was especially grim once American settlers flooded the region after gold was discovered near San Francisco in 1848. State-sponsored killers among those settlers, along with poverty and disease, decimated California's remaining Indian population in the middle decades of the nineteenth century.[34] The missions themselves, abandoned in the 1830s by all but the old and the sick, were eventually reduced to ruins.

Those ruined missions, however, had an afterlife of sorts. Helen Hunt Jackson's *Ramona* (1884), a wildly successful novel, fueled a national romance with "Spanish California" and a view of mission history that had little to do with its tragic realities. (Hunt was a critic of U.S. Indian policy, which she compared unfavorably to that of Spain.) Promoted as tourist sites after the turn of the twentieth century, the crumbling mission churches were stabilized, and most were gradually restored. Junípero Serra too gained new visibility as a result of Hunt's fiction and scholarly writings. Long revered by the state's Hispanic minority, Serra gained admirers among California's Anglo elite, who chose him as one of two Californians to be honored in 1931 in the U.S. Capitol's Statuary Hall. A campaign for Serra's canonization was under way soon after. While sainthood would surely have boosted tourism, the Anglo elite could not make it happen. When victory came in 2015, it honored the now-enormous presence of Hispanics in the American Catholic Church—descendants of the mixed people that Spanish conquest, for all its brutality, had ultimately brought into being.

In 1879, Robert Louis Stevenson paid a visit to Serra's Mission San Carlos, then in derelict condition. It was the feast of its patron saint, and a good many Indians had come for the Mass. Their devotion impressed the visiting author. "An Indian, stone-blind and about eighty years of age, conducts the singing; other Indians compose the choir; yet they have the Gregorian music at their finger-ends, and pronounce the Latin so correctly that I could follow the meaning as they sang." Had their mission forebears been as genuinely Catholic? At first glance, it seems unlikely, given the linguistic and cultural barriers that distanced mission Indians from their Franciscan overlords. But there are signs that some, perhaps many, mission Indians were able to appropriate Catholicism on their own terms. Church images painted by Indian artisans sometimes incorporated Indian attributes in depictions of saints and martyrs. Christ appears to be an Indian in a crucifixion scene housed at Mission San Gabriel, while the Roman soldiers look like Spaniards. Communal singing, reportedly popular, was a way of asserting liturgical ownership. Devotion to Mary had emotive appeal, especially among Indian women. Even the rebellious could betray an attachment to the norms of Catholic practice. Two Indian men, apparently ill, announced their intention of abandoning Mission San Francisco to die among their people. But before they left, both went to confession.[35]

Prominent among the Marian images so ubiquitous in the mission churches was the Virgin of Guadalupe. Based on an alleged apparition near Mexico City in 1531, the image is that of an Indian maiden. Not surprisingly, Guadalupan devotion first took root among the mixed population of New Spain, which was partly of Indian descent. By the mid-eighteenth century, the devotion was sufficiently widespread that the Virgin of Guadalupe was proclaimed patroness of New Spain by Pope Benedict XIV. She remains the most popular symbol of Hispanic Catholicism, both in Mexico and the United States. We can read in her an acknowledgment of Indian suffering during the long colonial ordeal, as well as a tribute to Indian endurance. Even Spaniards, after all, came to honor her unmistakably Indian image. She can also be read as a source of forgiveness for New Spain's mixed people, who sometimes abused the Indians from whom they were so recently descended. Honoring the Virgin of Guadalupe, they honored their Indian past and were freed to embrace their own mixed status with a new sense of pride. She continues to play this healing role for recent waves of Hispanic immigrants to a not-always-welcoming United States.[36]

T · W · O

France in America

Although Jacques Cartier claimed what is now eastern Canada for France in 1534, a permanent French presence in the region dates effectively from 1608 and the founding of Quebec. Unlike Spain, France did not envision a New World empire of conquest but one based on trade, primarily in furs, with the indigenous people. Large numbers of soldiers were not required for such an endeavor—their presence, indeed, might alienate the Indians who were the source of furs and other natural wealth. If the region's Indians suffered immensely as a long-term result of the French presence, they were never subdued militarily. Nor did the French initially envision extensive civilian settlement, another potential cause of Indian alienation. Even in 1627, two decades after Quebec's founding, New France had only eighty-five colonists, all of them male. Missionaries, however, had a place in the system. Living among the indigenous people, they anchored a commercial empire—interpreting the French presence, mediating relations between Indians and peripatetic French traders, and, it was hoped, transforming Indians by means of conversion into dependable French allies.[1]

Given an expanding British presence to the south, Indian alliances grew increasingly important as French territorial ambitions grew. Especially in contested border areas such as present-day Maine, missionaries were frontline sources of intelligence and deeply involved on occasion in Indian warfare against the English, Indians being crucial allies of the badly out-

numbered French. France and England went to war on five separate occasions between 1689 and 1763, bringing periodic mayhem to the colonial
backwoods, with both sides slaughtering civilians and seizing hostages. Although Catholic priests could not bear arms—canon law prohibits this—
French priests blessed Indian raiding parties and the taking of Protestant
hostages, some of whom became Catholics after long detention in New
France. New England's Protestant divines beat the war drums too and also
condoned the taking of hostages. But as far as the English were concerned,
French priests bore singular responsibility for frontier violence. The Jesuit
Sebastian Râle, reviled in New England as the "great Incendiary" among the
mostly Catholic Wabanaki, was murdered by an English militia at his Ken-
nebec River mission in 1723. His scalp was borne in triumph to Boston.[2]

Despite the rigors of the Canadian winter and potentially hostile Indians, French missionaries pushed steadily into present-day Canada and the
northern half of present-day Maine as the seventeenth century unfolded.
An extensive mission to the Wendat (Huron), agriculturalists living north
of Lake Ontario, was under way by the 1640s, with probes extending from
its heartland into the Iroquois nations in the Finger Lakes region of the
present-day state of New York. French missions appeared around the perim-
eter of the Great Lakes in the 1660s and then along the Mississippi. Detroit
was founded as a French military outpost in 1701 and New Orleans in 1718,
with St. Louis established as a trading station in 1764. Although France lost
Quebec to the British in 1759 and ceded the rest of its North American possessions in the Treaty of Paris in 1763, French settlers remained—hence the
indisputably French founding of St. Louis after the end of French rule. The
bishop of Quebec, sole Catholic prelate then resident in North America,
retained ecclesiastical jurisdiction over the region's Catholics until 1791 and
ministered on occasion to Catholics on the U.S. side of the border for many
years thereafter. French was widely spoken in the region even after American
independence, and communal life had a Catholic flavor.

The missions of New France in the seventeenth century—the century
of their greatest expansion and vigor—were dominated by the Jesuits,
whose missionary ethos fit neatly with French imperial purposes. Committed to learning indigenous languages and flexible when it came to evangelizing strategies, Jesuits were better suited than most to solitary living
among the Indians, even those who were hunter-gatherers. Theirs was what
might today be called a "ministry of accompaniment." Securing residence

in an Indian village, sometimes only because it was a stipulated condition of trade, the missionary participated as best he could in the round of tribal life, thereby improving his grasp of the language and knowledge of local culture. If invited, he joined the winter hunt, where he along with the rest of the men endured bitter cold, intermittent hunger, and vermin-infested clothing. He generally adopted an Indian name at some point in his sojourn, by which he was thereafter addressed, and took care to acquire survival skills akin to those of his hosts. Conscious that the people he lived among had little to spare and conscious too of his own isolation, the successful missionary did all he could to avoid being a burden. "If you can travel naked and carry a horse's load on your back—as they do—then you will be considered worthwhile in their eyes and you will be recognized as a great man—otherwise not!" the Jesuit Jean de Brébeuf warned young colleagues in France who hungered for the missions.[3]

Brébeuf and his fellow Jesuits took a lively interest in indigenous culture, if mainly as a means to evangelical ends. How to convey the Christian message in culturally resonant terms? The challenge led most Jesuits to serious inquiry into native religion and an effort to discern therein vestiges of belief in a recognizably Christian God. It was troubling, they conceded, that even the settled tribes of New France had "neither Temples nor Priests"—something the French were not to encounter, at least in recognizable form, until the turn of the eighteenth century and a short-lived effort to establish missions among the Tunica in present-day Mississippi. But closer study brought comfort. The Wendat Feast of the Dead, according to Brébeuf, proved that they "believe in the immortality of the soul," while their natural virtues—he admired especially the Indians' hospitality, ritual gift-giving, and stoicism in the face of death—suggested an innate, if corrupted, notion of the true God. So did Indians' capacity to reason, about which the Jesuits betrayed few doubts, comparing them favorably in this regard to French peasants. "It is so evident that there is a Divinity who has made Heaven and earth that our Hurons cannot entirely ignore it." The Gospel could flourish in authentically Indian soil, as the Jesuits saw it; no wholesale remaking of culture was necessary. Baptized Indians were not expected to learn French or adopt French dress; the Jesuits, indeed, quickly came to oppose assimilative policies for any but a handful of gifted youngsters.[4]

This surprising openness to Indian culture shaped Jesuit mission practice in distinctive ways. Hymns and chants in the Indian vernacular featured in worship—the Jesuits produced the requisite texts—and sermons were regularly interrupted by questions and even minidiscourses from high-status men in the congregation. The preacher himself might well be a layman, even when the missionary was fluent in the local language, due to Jesuit respect for Indian standards of oral performance. Dancing, integral to tribal cultures, was part of the liturgy at the great feasts of Christmas and Easter, while mission churches were bedecked with the glass-bead offerings and wampum collars brought to Mass by the Indian faithful. Relatively few tribal ceremonies were off-limits to mission Christians, who continued to live on a daily basis according to most tribal norms. Nor did the Jesuits attempt to institute congregated missions on the Spanish model, even in settings where most locals had been baptized. The baptized were free to come and go, and even avowedly Christian villages had nonbelievers in residence.[5]

For all their openness to Indian culture, however, the Jesuits remained inflexible when it came to sex, doing implacable battle—hell figured prominently—against polygamy, divorce, and nonmarital couplings of every variety. (The Jesuit Jacques Marquette was stunned to find among the Illinois Indians the same "third sex"—males living as women—so widely encountered by the Spanish.) Sexual lapses by the baptized brought punishment, including public flogging. That some young women at the mission village of Kahnawake were by the 1670s renouncing marriage in response to Jesuit preaching and the example of women religious in nearby Montreal suggests how disruptive of culture an abrupt shift in sexual ethics could be. Prisoners of their own culture, the Jesuits simply ignored this reality, just as they ignored the cultural consequences of asserting their own authority at the expense of local shamans. Disease disrupted cultures too, and Europeans brought disease. Smallpox was especially lethal in the first half of the century: at least half the Mohawk population of present-day New York State may have died in an epidemic brought by Dutch traders in 1634. The appearance of disease in a mission was generally blamed on the missionary, whom even non-Christian Indians regarded as spiritually potent. Brébeuf, honored as a village chieftain when times were prosperous, was several times assaulted by Indian adversaries when epidemics threatened.[6]

Jesuit missions among the Wendat, the single most ambitious such undertaking in the history of New France, enjoyed a brief flourishing in the mid-1640s. Some twenty-seven hundred baptisms were reported in 1647, when the pace of conversion was accelerating. But if the Christian minority was growing, the Wendat remained a divided people and, as such, arguably demoralized. When the Iroquois mounted a series of ferocious raids on their villages in 1648 and 1649, armed with firearms secured from Dutch traders, they offered little resistance. Numerous Wendat were taken captive, some of them destined to supplement an Iroquois population depleted by warfare and disease. Many others were slaughtered, along with four Jesuit priests, Jean de Brébeuf among them. Brébeuf and his confrere Gabriel Lalemant died together after prolonged ritual torture, having baptized as many as they could upon learning of an imminent attack. Wendat survivors bore witness to the grace and courage with which the two met their agonizing deaths.[7]

A graphic account of the two priests' martyrdoms—for so their deaths were instantly labeled—appeared subsequently in the *Jesuit Relations,* an annual account of the New France missions with immense appeal in devout French circles. Martyrdom lay at the heart of Counter-Reformation spirituality, at least in a symbolic sense: fervent Christians of both sexes spoke the language of self-abnegation and sometimes embraced extreme modes of penance. Brébeuf's earliest surviving writing is in just such a mode: "I sense within myself a consuming desire to suffer something for Christ's sake. . . . Only when opportunities for suffering are given me will I be hopeful of my salvation." Iroquois aggression in the 1640s produced no fewer than eight Jesuit martyrs whose deaths were celebrated in the *Relations:* along with Brébeuf and Lalemant, they include *donné* René Goupil, a lay assistant vowed to lifelong service with the Jesuits, killed by the Iroquois in the Finger Lakes region in 1642; priest Isaac Jogues and *donné* Jean de La Lande, murdered nearby in 1646; and Fathers Antoine Daniel and Nöel Chabanel, both of whom died among the Wendat. Eventually known to Catholics as the North American Martyrs, the eight were canonized in 1930—an honor withheld from the hundreds of Wendat Christians who also perished at the hands of the Iroquois.[8]

The Wendat were decimated as a people by the Iroquois invasions. The largest remnant fled west, to the Great Lakes and beyond, where they gradually amalgamated with the Petun, themselves refugees from Iroquois aggression, and assumed a new tribal identity. The Jesuits eventually followed, founding a series of Indian missions around the Great Lakes and among the Illinois people, first visited by Jacques Marquette in 1673. These missions were marked by the same evangelical sophistication as earlier Jesuit efforts: missionaries mastered native languages, in which they produced catechisms and prayer books; liturgies were infused with Indian themes and images; native rituals were, where possible, endowed with Christian meaning. Impressive successes were occasionally reported: the Kiskakon Ottawa announced their intention to convert as a tribe in 1668, while the Jesuit Claude Allouez (1622–1689), a twenty-year veteran of missions in the upper Great Lakes, was said—no doubt hyperbolically—to have baptized ten thousand indigenous people from more than twenty tribes. When a delegation of Illinois Indians visited New Orleans in 1730, some forty years after mass conversions among their people, their piety was the talk of the town. "Every evening they recited the rosary," reported a local Jesuit priest, "and every morning they heard me say Mass." The Indians chanted in their native language during the liturgy, alternating verses with Ursuline nuns from the local convent, who sang in Latin.[9]

France's surrender of its North American possessions in 1763, followed shortly thereafter by papal suppression of the Jesuit order, doomed the Great Lakes Indian missions, which were soon abandoned. The small but growing French settlements along the Mississippi and its tributaries suffered quasi-abandonment too. When Father Pierre Gibault, a priest of the Diocese of Quebec, visited the village of Vincennes in 1770, its mostly French inhabitants had not seen a priest for seven years. "When I arrived," he tells us, "everyone crowded down to the banks of the river to receive me. Some of them fell to their knees, too overwhelmed to speak; others could speak only through their sobs." A local layman had been administering baptisms and conducting funerals in the interim, but only a priest could hear confessions. And it was confession for which Catholics hungered at every stop on Gibault's travels. He had been besieged at Mackinac by Indians and French *voyageurs* alike "who desired to make their confessions covering a period of three to ten years." Gibault had neither the linguistic capacity—he spoke no Indian languages—nor the time to hear them all.[10]

The internal radicalization of the French Revolution in the early 1790s sent a wave of French priests to North American shores. Twenty-three arrived in the young United States over the course of the decade—a minuscule fraction of the estimated thirty thousand leaving France at the time but enough to almost double the number of Catholic priests in the new nation. Most were members of the Paris-based Society of St. Sulpice, a community of diocesan priests who specialized in seminary education. Sulpicians provided the faculty for the first Catholic seminary in the United States, founded in 1791; they also served as missionary-priests in frontier communities where French was spoken. Among them was Gabriel Richard, sent first to the Illinois country in 1792 and then to Detroit in 1798, where for thirty-four years he was not only pastor but school founder and teacher, farmer and fisheries manager, newspaper publisher, entrepreneur and inventor, preacher to local Protestants, and delegate to Congress from the Michigan Territory (1823–25). "He has the talent of doing, almost simultaneously, ten different things," an admiring Bishop Joseph-Octave Plessis marveled in the course of a visit from Quebec. Educated to a high standard and infused with an austere spirituality, French Sulpicians exerted an outsized influence on American Catholicism in the first half of the nineteenth century, especially via their seminary teaching and the eight who served as U.S. bishops.[11]

French colonization in what is now the United States did not produce a significant mixed people, as happened in the Spanish dominions, although French policy actively favored the marriage of Indian women and French men. Numerous such marriages did occur, but the French population was simply too small to have long-term demographic effect. With quickening immigration from Ireland and Germany in the 1830s and after, the French-speaking presence in the American church dwindled into relative insignificance. Not until the late nineteenth century, with Catholic immigration from Quebec flooding the mill towns of New England, could Franco-Americans once again wield ethnic clout in U.S. Catholic circles. But numbers do not tell the whole of the story. Just as the American church was profoundly affected by a relative handful of French priests during its formative years, so the relatively small French presence in colonial North America helped to shape the consciousness of millions of American Catholics.

The Great Lakes region and the Mississippi Valley were destined to become the nation's industrial heartland and the site of its principal transportation nodes. It mattered that a region so central to the nation's economy and identity should have been built from the first by Catholics as well as Protestants. The region's schoolchildren learned a founding myth in which French missionaries and explorers—the latter transformed into Catholic gentlemen—played a leading role, cementing a Catholic claim to full membership in the American experiment. Growing up in Michigan in the 1950s, when state history was still a staple of public education, I learned more

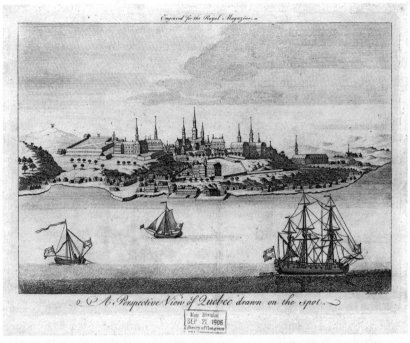

"A Perspective View of Quebec, drawn on the spot," by James Hullett,
ca. 1750–70 (Library of Congress, LC-USZ62-110425; courtesy of the Library
of Congress, Washington, DC)

about the Great Lakes Jesuits than the Puritans' John Winthrop, even
though I absorbed these lessons in the state's Dutch Calvinist heartland. My
youthful perceptions of American history were shaped accordingly. Heavy
Protestant migration into the region after the early nineteenth century
brought anti-Catholicism in its wake, which shaped local politics for generations. But religious enmities were more muted there than in eastern cities like New York and Boston, and the region's Catholic life developed in a
notably less defensive mode. Largely for this reason, the region has long
been fertile soil for a wide variety of progressive Catholic movements.

The cult of the North American martyrs provides particularly fruitful
insight into Catholic uses of the French past. Shortly after the deaths of
Brébeuf and Gabriel Lalemant in 1649, their bones were carried to Quebec,
where Brébeuf's remains were credited with a series of miraculous healings.
His reputation for sanctity, along with that of his martyred companions,

spread to Jesuit missions worldwide and also to France, where the archbishop of Rouen gathered testimony in premature anticipation of proceedings leading to canonization. Brébeuf and those who died on what became
Canadian soil were eventually embraced as saints by nationalist Catholics
in Quebec—a cult that had vigorous life well into the twentieth century.
That cult had little resonance in the United States, given its connections to
Francophone politics in Canada. But by the later nineteenth century, Jesuits
in the United States were promoting an Americanized version of the cult,
establishing Our Lady of the Martyrs Shrine in 1885 near Auriesville, New
York, the presumed but never proven site of the murder of Jogues and his
two companions. The U.S. bishops had already petitioned Rome for the
canonization of Jogues and René Goupil, adding the name of *donné* Jean de
La Lande in 1906. The Canadian bishops filed their own petition in 1886 but
only for those who had died in Canada.[12]

Success was relatively slow to come—the eight were canonized only in
1930—and the cult in the United States was hampered by an absence of rel-
ics. But its nationalist dimensions are evident. By dying on what became
American soil, Isaac Jogues and his martyred companions acquired honorary standing as Americans and even as founders of the nation. One additional "founder"—irony is the keynote here—emerged from this Catholic
reimagining of the nation's past. She was Catherine Tekakwitha, a young
Mohawk convert, born in the village where Jogues and his companions had
earlier died. Orphaned as a small child and badly disfigured by smallpox,
Catherine converted to Catholicism in her late teens, emigrating a few years
later to the majority-Christian community of Kahnawake near Montreal.
Here she emerged as a leader in a circle of devout young women, who regarded themselves as indigenous counterparts to local French religious sisters. Catherine and certain of her companions pledged themselves to
celibacy, while the group as a whole embraced penitential practices of the
most extreme sort, undergoing rigorous fasts and inflicting harsh punishments on their bodies. When Catherine died in 1680, at the probable age of
twenty-four, this alarming asceticism—local Jesuits had tried in vain to
tame it—was at least a partial cause.

Catherine gained a reputation for sanctity in the final months of her
young life, in part because of the serenity with which she endured her final
suffering. Her body was scarcely cold before miracle stories began to circu-
late, although mainly among French settlers rather than indigenous con-

verts, who initially held a bit aloof. Catherine's intercession was credited with numerous healings, perhaps most notably of an English boy brought as a hostage to Kahnawake in 1703 from his home in Massachusetts; he was allegedly cured of smallpox by the application of wood from Catherine's coffin. Catherine's bones were eventually transferred to the Kahnawake mission church, which became a site of pilgrimage, certainly for Indians but also for the French, whose "wilderness" such shrines helped to sacralize. A saint by popular acclamation, she was proposed for formal canonization only in 1884, when the U.S. bishops included her name in their petition advancing the cause of Jogues and René Goupil, presumably because of her putatively American birth. Finally canonized in 2012, she is now an emblem in the United States of yet another founding story—one centered on Indian endurance. This is nowhere more true than in the Catholic pueblos of New Mexico, where images of Catherine are nearly as ubiquitous as those of the Virgin of Guadalupe.[13]

The women religious so admired by Tekakwitha and her circle should also be seen as a French legacy to the American church, given the roles they played in New France and the subsequent importance of French women's communities in American Catholicism. The six French sisters who arrived in Quebec in 1639—three were Ursulines, and three were members of an Augustinian order devoted to hospital nursing—were the first to serve in North America. (None served on the northern fringes of the Spanish empire, while the first convent in the former English colonies dates from 1790.) The Ursuline order, founded in Brescia in 1596, grew rapidly in France, where its commitment to the education of girls had especially strong appeal. The convent established at Quebec was soon the site of a school, attended by both French and Indian girls and particularly devoted to the conversion of the latter. The Ursulines who served in Quebec and later at Trois-Rivières and Montreal regarded themselves as missionaries as well as teachers, having come to New France with a passion for the Indian missions. "There are so many of these who write to us," according to the Jesuit superior in Quebec in 1635, "and from so many Convents, and from various Orders of the strictest discipline, that you would say that each one is first to laugh at the hardships of the Sea and the barbarism of these countries."[14]

Although the Ursuline order was semicloistered, its Quebec convent was a vibrant center of social and religious life. Indians of both sexes came and went freely, sometimes for the available meals but also to hear religious instruction or simply to satisfy their curiosity. Very much in the spirit of their Jesuit contemporaries, the sisters worked hard at learning at least one Amerindian language. The Ursuline superior at Quebec, Mother Marie de l'Incarnation (born Marie Guyart), eventually mastered several, in which she could also write. During her long Canadian residence—she died in 1672—she produced catechisms, prayer books and a dictionary in Algonquin, a Wendat catechism, and a catechism and dictionary in Iroquois. Revered for her holiness of life, Mother Marie was also honored as an expert on Indian language and culture, sought out by newcomers to New France for purposes of orientation. Inspired to go to Canada by the *Jesuit Relations,* which circulated in her convent at Tours, Mother Marie found there an outlet for her vast spiritual energies. "Although she was largely ignorant of the world beyond Tours," in the words of historian Natalie Davis, "she had a vivid sense of the urgency of global evangelization."[15]

The fluidity of colonial society and its enormous social needs meant a wider world for women religious and encouraged them to regard their vocations in newly flexible and activist terms. Ursulines in New France nursed the sick during epidemics, although their ministry in Europe had centered on education; those in the convent at Trois-Rivières, responding to urgent local needs, embraced nursing as an ongoing apostolate. When twelve Ursulines arrived at New Orleans in 1727, the first women religious to serve in what is now the United States, their initial contract with the city specified nursing as their primary commitment. The sisters still managed to open a school but found themselves also caring for orphans and serving as catechists to a broad interracial public. Women religious were invariably respected as women of prayer and self-sacrifice; several in New France, Marie de l'Incarnation among them, were popularly regarded as saints. (Mother Marie was canonized in 2014, with Pope Benedict XVI invoking the durability of her local cult as a principal justification.) But in New France, as later in the United States, the piety most admired in sisters was a piety of action.[16]

Adaptable and surprisingly independent, women religious in New France created a template of sorts for the nascent church in the United States. When bishops in the United States recruited sisters for their dioceses or encouraged the formation of local women's communities, they wanted women who could teach, nurse, and care for the destitute. Contemplatives—cloistered religious whose sole ministry was prayer—were in their view a luxury that no young church could afford. Nor did the bishops have much patience with orders that defined their apostolate narrowly—flexibility was essential, especially in the pre–Civil War decades. France also continued to be important as a source of women religious. Poor Clares took up residence in Washington, DC, as early as 1798, precursors of what became the first community of Visitation Sisters in the United States. In 1818, five Religious of the Sacred Heart arrived in frontier St. Louis, led by Mother Rose Philippine Duchesne; they were soon running a free day school, a boarding school where tuition was charged, and an orphanage. (A devotee of Marie de l'Incarnation, Mother Duchesne was herself canonized in 1988.) Sisters of St. Joseph came from France to that same city in 1836, while Sisters of Providence, led by Mother Théodore Guérin (canonized 2006), arrived in the Diocese of Vincennes in 1840, followed in 1843 by Sisters of the Holy Cross. Others could be mentioned. Many communities of women founded in the United States, moreover, based their rule on French models, especially those associated with Saints Vincent de Paul and Francis de Sales.

The Ursulines who came to New Orleans in 1737 struggled financially, as did many later communities in the United States. Unable to demand cash dowries from young women who wanted to join them, given the poverty of the local population, the Ursulines became entrepreneurs, deploying the modest income from their elite boarding school into investments in land and slaves. They owned over eighty slaves as of 1796, which placed the community among the larger slaveholding entities in the city. The strategy ultimately made for a highly public mode of economic independence, which served the community well as New Orleans passed from French to Spanish to American hands. It also constitutes a moral problem for present-day Catholics, especially since the Ursulines were far from the only religious order to own slaves in North America. A number of communities did so, including French Jesuits in the vast Louisiana Territory and English Jesuits in Maryland.

Although generally reputed to be compassionate in their treatment of slaves, keeping families intact and providing religious instruction, religious communities could not ultimately shield them from the system's cruel logic. When the French Jesuits were expelled from the Louisiana Territory, for example, many of their slaves were sold at auction. Still, extant records do not suggest that slave-owning religious had moral qualms about the practice. The Ursulines courted controversy in colonial New Orleans by educating free women of color, even welcoming them into their elite boarding school along with whites until the turn of the nineteenth century. But they had no apparent difficulty with the buying of slaves or the selling of those whose conduct they regarded as reprobate. Slavery, it is fair to note, was sufficiently widespread in colonial America among Indians as well as Europeans to possess an aura of legitimacy. Marie Rouensa, an Illinois Indian married to a Frenchmen and a catechist in the Jesuit mission at Kaskaskia, died in 1727 as an exemplary Christian. Her estate included five slaves—four Africans and an Indian boy. This justification—if such it was—is far harder to invoke for those communities that still held slaves on the eve of the Civil War.[17]

In 1673, the Jesuit Jacques Marquette embarked with Canadian-born trader Louis Jolliet on an epic voyage down the Mississippi, whose course was still a mystery to Europeans. Paddling as far as the river's juncture with the Arkansas, Jolliet's expedition ascertained that the Mississippi emptied into the Gulf of Mexico rather than, as some had assumed, the Chesapeake Bay or the Pacific. A veteran of the Great Lakes missions who spoke six Indian languages, Marquette went ashore wherever he could to evangelize the Indians, although the expedition soon traveled beyond the range of the languages he knew. "This is a seed cast into the ground, which will bear fruit in its time," was his hopeful comment on a sermon preached to the Arkansas Indians by means of signs and the halting translation of a local man with limited command of the Illinois tongue. Warmly welcomed toward the start of the journey by the Kaskaskia, an Illinois tribe, Marquette vowed to return and establish a mission among them. His knowledge of their language partly accounts for the warmth of his welcome. But so does Marquette's magnetic presence and his ability, in the words of a Jesuit confrere, to be "all things to all men—a Frenchman with the French, a Huron with the Hurons, an Algonquin with the Algonquins."[18]

Although the arduous voyage had compromised his health, Marquette returned to Kaskaskia, a tribal village on the Illinois River, in the spring of 1675. He preached his inaugural sermon to some five hundred Illinois chiefs and elders, with more than a thousand young men standing in ranks behind them. His stay was short—he was, in fact, dying—but it gave birth to an eventually thriving mission, although one that was subsequently moved to a new location on the Mississippi as the Indian population migrated westward. Due in part to the conversion of a locally prominent family, the Kaskaskia were soon a mostly Christianized people, who seem to have used the new faith to make sense of their rapidly changing world and navigate relations with a growing population of French settlers. The Jesuit Gabriel Marest, in residence at Kaskaskia in 1712, described a village where life was centered on Catholic practice—daily catechesis for the not-yet-baptized, followed by community-wide attendance at Mass and evening devotions. "They generally end the day with private meetings, which they hold in their own houses, the men apart from the women," where hymns were sung and the Rosary recited.[19]

Given that his words were intended for the edification of pious French readers, we can safely assume that Father Marest was painting an overly rosy picture. But Indians could be genuine converts, and the durability of Catholicism among the Kaskaskia suggests that such was the case for many of them. They could also make Catholic Christianity their own, fusing its rituals almost seamlessly with their own traditions. Consider the aftermath of Marquette's death, which occurred on his return journey from Kaskaskia to Mission St. Ignace on the Straits of Mackinac in 1675. Two years after the priest's burial on a remote Lake Michigan beach, a party of Kiskakon Ottawa, converts of some ten years' standing who had been evangelized by Marquette, exhumed his body and extricated his bones, which they boiled, "as is their custom." With the bones arranged in a birch-bark box, as a Jesuit witness told it, "they set out to bring them to our mission of St. Ignace. There were nearly 30 canoes which formed, in excellent order, that funeral procession," which was joined in due course by "a goodly number" of Iroquois and Algonquin. After a funeral Mass, Marquette's bones were buried in the church at St. Ignace. "The savages often come to pray over his tomb," where miracles were occasionally reported.[20]

A century later, New France was no more, and the Jesuit order had been suppressed. But the seeming evanescence of the French presence in what is now the United States should not detract from its importance, both for the reasons earlier discussed and for the Jesuits' remarkable openness to the Indian other. As the eminent historian John Demos wrote after immersing himself in French Jesuit sources, "The early Jesuit missionaries, I came to think, had seen—truly *seen*—Indians more fully than other 'white' colonists." Those Jesuits had plenty of cultural blind spots and were anything but relativists. In their certainty that truth was single and knowable and their passion for martyrdom in its pursuit, they are almost as remote from the twenty-first century as the Indians they came to evangelize. But in their ability to live among the Indians, speaking their language and adhering to many tribal ways, French Jesuits came closer than other colonials to a genuine transcultural encounter, which gave rise not just to respect for the other but to a richer sense of Christian universalism. Something of this spirit is evident in a Christmas hymn written by Jean de Brébeuf in the Wendat language, probably in 1642, an English version of which has long been popular in Canada. The holy child, in the English translation, is housed "within a lodge of broken bark." Wrapped in a ragged rabbit skin, he is surrounded by an aura even more beautiful than the "earliest moon of wintertime." Drawn by this glorious light, the "hunter braves" and chiefs draw near to present their gifts of pelts—the indigenous equivalent, in this generous vision, of gold, frankincense, and myrrh.[21]

Catholics in the British Colonies

Catholics were a minuscule presence in Britain's North American colonies before 1763, when the Treaty of Paris gave Britain control of both Florida and Quebec, where substantial Catholic populations had of necessity to be accorded tolerance. Matters were otherwise in the thirteen colonies that became the United States. Constituting about 1 percent of the colonies' population on the eve of the American Revolution, Catholics lived almost exclusively in Maryland and Pennsylvania, where they suffered serious legal disabilities. Even in Maryland, despite its initial charter having been granted in 1632 to a Catholic proprietor, Catholics were for much of the colony's history excluded from political and civic life. This was also the case in Pennsylvania, at least according to the law; William Penn, the colony's famously tolerant proprietor, did not regard Roman Catholics as authentic Christians. Penn was pragmatic, however, and the colony's small population of Catholics—less numerous by far than Maryland's—experienced greater toleration in practice than anywhere else in the colonies.

Colonial Protestants, like their coreligionists in England, saw Catholics as opposed to personal liberty and loyal to a hostile foreign power, by which they meant the pope. Catholics were thus a threat to English nationhood both culturally and politically. Heightened religious tension in the mother country, which occurred episodically, nearly always led to greater repression in the American colonies. Catholics were legally banned from many jurisdictions in the seventeenth century and even beyond, especially in Calvinist New England, where anti-Catholicism functioned with particular power as a source of identity and social cohesion. A Massachusetts law of 1647 forbade Catholic priests from entering the colony on pain of banishment; a second offense was punishable by execution. (Priests shipwrecked off the colony's coast were exempt from punishment, but only on condition that they leave the colony forthwith.) As in the mother country, where Catholics suffered often crippling legal disabilities and on occasion risked martyrdom, anti-Catholicism permeated colonial culture and to a large extent defined it.

Maryland's first Catholic settlers arrived in the Chesapeake Bay in the winter of 1634, borne thither in two ships, the *Ark* and the *Dove.* Although the expedition had sailed under Catholic auspices—Cecil Calvert, the second Lord Baltimore and a Catholic, held the colony's charter—the majority of those on board were Protestants, servants for the most part to the twenty Catholic "gentleman adventurers" who had made the trip. Centered on St. Mary's, a palisaded village perched on bluffs above the Potomac River, the new colony grew slowly. Disease was a constant scourge, and a surplus of men hindered family formation—a problem the English seldom solved, whether Catholic or no, by intermarriage with local Indians. Still, with profits to be made by cultivating tobacco in Maryland's fertile soil, new settlers trickled in. By the early 1640s, the colony's English population stood at roughly four hundred, of whom about one-quarter were Catholic—a higher percentage, as it happens, than Catholics in colonial Maryland would enjoy again.[1]

Those first Catholic settlers were accompanied by Jesuits, who initially hoped to convert the local Indian population. Only a handful of converts resulted, largely due to the priests' small numbers, their vulnerability to locally endemic diseases like malaria, and bouts of intra-Indian warfare. Hostility from neighboring Protestants was a factor too: an armed invasion in 1645 resulted in the temporary expulsion of all five Jesuits from the Maryland colony and an end to the Indian missions. Despite their longing for missionary heroism, which they shared with their French and Spanish counterparts, Maryland's Jesuits served mainly as chaplains to its European settlers. In this capacity, they owned and managed large plantations, their principal means of support in a colony where English law prohibited the establishment of the Catholic Church. For much of the seventeenth century, the Jesuits' plantations were worked by indentured labor, then plentiful in Maryland. But by the early eighteenth century, as indentured labor grew scarce, the Jesuits relied increasingly on slaves. By 1765, the order owned 192 enslaved persons of African descent who labored on its expanded network of plantations in Maryland and eastern Pennsylvania.[2]

In the opening years of the Maryland colony, the Catholic minority enjoyed something approaching full religious liberty. Mass was celebrated publicly—the first was said by Andrew White, S.J., on St. Clement's Island in the Potomac in March 1634—and Jesuits proselytized among local Protestants, especially the sick and dying. So vigorous a manifestation of Catholic life would not have been possible in England, even under the relatively benign regime—from a Catholic perspective—of Charles I. Nor did it last long in Maryland. With the outbreak of the English Civil War in 1642, dissident Protestants in Maryland and neighboring Virginia began to mobilize against Maryland's Catholic elite, staging no fewer than three armed revolts between 1645 and 1660. The Calverts did manage to retain their colonial charter but only by ceding a large share of governing power to Protestants, who made up an increasingly large majority of Maryland's population. The colony's 1649 Act of Religious Toleration, justly celebrated as the first law in the English-speaking world to protect religious liberty, was passed by a Maryland assembly about to lose its Catholic majority.

Despite rising Protestant numbers and the altered political circumstances, Maryland's Catholic elite continued to participate in the colony's governance until 1689, when a popular revolt—very much prompted by England's Glorious Revolution, which brought the Calvinist William I to the throne—stripped Catholics of their rights, both political and religious. Presumably because of the wealth of the colony's Catholics and its need for population, the extent of actual repression varied—conditions for Maryland's Catholics were never as dire as those in England. But by the early eighteenth century, Catholic practice in Maryland was confined to the home and private chapels, while even high-status Catholic men were excluded from public life. Proscription in this relatively mild form seems to have worked for the good of religion, with itinerant priests reporting an upsurge in lay piety and a heightened sense of Catholic identity. When religious tensions eased in the wake of the Treaty of Paris, Maryland's Catholics began once again to build public chapels, although they were still forbidden by law to do so. The first Catholic church in Baltimore dates from the mid-

1760s. Catholics then constituted about 8 percent of the colony's population, a portion of them slaves.

Colonial Catholicism was always priest-poor, although less so in Maryland than Pennsylvania, many of whose Catholic settlers were Germans and thus not readily served by English-speaking Jesuits. (German Jesuits were sent to Pennsylvania in the 1740s, but their numbers were small.) Catholics who settled elsewhere might never see a priest, especially in the backcountry. Given the rural residence of Maryland's Catholics, the Jesuits who served them had to itinerate, saying Mass as infrequently as once a month at various stations around a circuit. By 1760 there were fifty Catholic chapels in Maryland, many in manor houses, and these were regularly visited. Itinerant priests did their best to serve Pennsylvania's rural Catholics too. But happily for all concerned, given the burdens of itinerant ministry, some Catholics in that colony took up residence in a booming Philadelphia, where a Catholic parish was organized in 1733. The first urban parish in the English colonies, St. Joseph's represented the future, not simply because of its location but also because of its increasingly multiethnic congregation.

An itinerant priest's life was physically demanding, requiring that he travel by horseback for as many as twenty miles to visit his congregations. A few traveled farther, most notably Joseph Mosely, S.J., assigned to the Eastern Shore of Maryland in the late 1750s and serving there for the next thirty years. Because of the extent of his pastoral territory, Mosely wrote to his sister in England, "I often ride about 300 miles a week, and never a week but I ride 150 or 200. . . . We ride almost as much by night as by day, in all weathers, in heats, cold, rain, frost or snow." Unlike most of his Jesuit confreres who had at least periodic recourse to communal life at one of the Maryland plantations, Mosely almost never saw a fellow priest. When not on the road, he lived alone on a small plantation near the Wye River that was worked by a handful of slaves—"a true eremite at home," as he put it, although "thronged sufficiently" when he visited his missions. Steeled by his Jesuit spiritual formation, Moseley professed to be contented: "If I've suffered, I've equally sinned, and have my faults. I've often seen poor, miserable, abandoned families in poverty, want and misery, suffering far more than all I've ever suffered: we are all God's creatures: what right have I to be better off than they?"[3]

Priests who "rode circuit" spent long hours in the hearing of confessions—"from very early in the morning until 11 o'clock," according to

Joseph Mattingly, S.J., whose mid-eighteenth-century childhood had been spent in a Maryland mission station. Then the community assembled for Mass, which frequently opened with communal recitation of the Litany of Loreto, a Marian devotion of immense period popularity. The Mass was in Latin, as were the readings from Scripture, with the Gospel repeated in the vernacular. There might be vernacular hymns as well, since the Maryland Jesuits generally favored devotional use of the local language. Unless the occasion was a great Christian feast, few or no members of the congregation would typically receive communion—only the notably devout communicated more than two or three times a year, as was indeed the case throughout the contemporary Catholic world. The Mass concluded with a sermon, which might be lengthy and was typically doctrinal in content. After a midday meal, at which the priest broke his fast, the afternoon was devoted to the instruction of children and perhaps a prospective convert or a couple preparing for marriage. Vespers and benediction generally followed.[4]

An itinerant priest depended on the laity in many aspects of his ministry—for board and lodging, for cleaning the chapel and preparing it for services, for alerting those who lived at a distance to the priest's imminent visit. Perhaps most important, he expected the laity to assemble for worship in his absence. A priestless Sunday properly observed meant prayer and spiritual reading in a family or communal setting with a male member of the laity presiding, although women were frequently the organizers and motive force behind this mode of observance and often responsible for catechizing the young. Women far outnumbered men in the sodalities organized by the Jesuits to stimulate piety among the laity, typically either the Confraternity of the Blessed Sacrament for those with access to a chapel that housed the consecrated Host or the Confraternity of the Sacred Heart. Members of the latter pledged to make a "morning offering" of the upcoming day's activities to Jesus, which historian Emmet Curran has called "a modest but profoundly Jesuit way of finding God in all things." Limited evidence suggests that this devotion had appeal across class lines, especially among women, and its advocates clearly promoted its accessibility to the unlettered. "The great ones and the rich of the world have here no superior advantage over the poor and those of the common sort, because it rests wholly on the dispositions of the heart."[5]

For all their emphasis on "heart religion," Maryland's Jesuits were steeped in an austere spirituality of a distinctively English variety. Theirs was the interior piety of a persecuted people long confined to an underground church, and such was the faith they preached to their congregations. The pious ideal was largely private—prayer at prescribed intervals throughout the day, set times devoted to meditation, nightly examinations of conscience—and, in view of later developments, surprisingly Christocentric. By means of a disciplined spiritual practice, the individual was encouraged to cultivate an interior communion with Christ. The cult of the saints, so prominent in French and Spanish Catholicism, had only a muted presence in the English colonies, although devotion to the Virgin Mary was broadly popular. The prevailing ethos was consoling, reflecting a strong tradition of Jesuit humanism: while human sinfulness was generously acknowledged, the underlying view of human nature was fundamentally optimistic. Aided by the sacraments, believers could find salvation in lives of quiet virtue. But as was everywhere the case in Counter-Reformation Catholicism, there was emphasis too on what Catholics call the Four Last Things: death, judgment, heaven, and hell. The most popular Catholic prayer book in the English colonies, Bishop Richard Challoner's *The Garden of the Soul,* featured "a short exercise, as a preparation for death, that may be used every day."[6]

Despite the order's devotion to the ministry of education, Maryland's Jesuits did not found a school until 1677. It did not long flourish. By the early eighteenth century, prosperous Maryland Catholics were sending at least some of their sons to one of two English Jesuit colleges in exile on the Continent. Of the eighty-two sons of Maryland Catholics educated in Europe between 1759 and 1773, fully fifty-four embraced a priestly vocation, with forty-nine becoming Jesuits. Even daughters were sent abroad for schooling, albeit in much smaller numbers and nearly always in service of an incipient religious vocation. At least twenty-five Maryland women traveled to Europe to join a contemplative order, a step that almost guaranteed a permanent exile from family. This remarkable crop of vocations—Americans constituted 13 percent of the Jesuits' English province by 1773—testifies to the vitality of Maryland's Catholic subculture. In an institutional sense, however, Maryland Catholicism remained severely underdeveloped.[7]

Among the young men sent to Europe for schooling was John Carroll, born in 1735 to a Maryland family linked via his mother to the colony's founders. After study at St. Omer's College in French Flanders, Carroll joined the Society of Jesus and subsequently taught at the order's colleges in Liège and Bruges. He would probably have remained there for the rest of his life were it not for two stunning developments, the first of which was papal suppression of the Jesuit order in 1773. Carroll was in Rome as events reached their climax. Shocked by what he saw of politics at the papal court, he was soured thereafter on the close-to-incestuous ties that bound church and state in countries like Portugal and Spain. Catholic Europe, he wrote in an unguarded moment, had exposed him to "scenes of iniquity, duplicity, and depredation." He retained an especially deep suspicion of the Sacred Congregation for the Propagation of the Faith (usually called the Propaganda), which he, like many other Jesuits, believed had played a role in their order's demise. Apparently planning to request a transfer to blessedly distant Maryland as rumors of suppression swirled, he was nonetheless stung by the formal announcement. "I am not, and perhaps never shall be, recovered from the shock of this dreadful intelligence," he wrote to his brother. "The greatest blessing which in my estimation I could receive from God would be immediate death."[8]

Carroll sailed for home in the spring of 1774, when he encountered the second great upheaval to his hitherto quiet life—the accelerating movement toward American independence. That the movement in its final stages was fueled by anti-Catholic rhetoric—Thomas Paine called monarchy "the Popery of government"—presumably gave Carroll at least momentary pause. But Maryland's Catholic elite by the time of his return were mostly aligned with the patriots' cause, evidently having persuaded themselves that the anti-Catholic excesses of their countrymen were largely symbolic—a resonant if unfortunate shorthand for English abuses of colonial liberties. Of none was this truer than Carroll's distant cousin Charles, a member of the Maryland delegation to the First Continental Congress in 1774. (Charles Carroll served in an "unofficial" capacity at the first Congress, since he was barred as a Maryland Catholic from holding public office.) Matters, moreover, were moving quickly. Permitted once again to vote and hold office by the end of 1775, Maryland's Catholics entered the political lists with astonishing rapidity, nearly all of them on the patriot side. More than 40 percent of the colony's younger elite males—members of the gentry who came of age between 1750 and 1775—were serving in government by 1777. As for Charles Carroll, by now a voting member of the Second Continental Congress, he gained enduring fame as the only Catholic to sign the Declaration of Independence.[9]

John Carroll himself was eventually caught up in something like political action. At the invitation of the Second Continental Congress, he accompanied a three-man delegation to Quebec late in the winter of 1776 in an ultimately futile attempt to persuade the locals to join the fight against Britain. As a Catholic priest and a fluent French speaker, Carroll's value to the effort was obvious. He also impressed Benjamin Franklin, a fellow delegation member and confirmed anti-Catholic, with his gentility and learning—the beginning of an unlikely friendship. But apart from this venture, Carroll stood apart from politics for the duration of the war, as was true of his ex-Jesuit confreres in the infant United States. (All twenty-three priests then serving in the country had been members of the order.) Surviving sermons from the period contain no discernible political content. But nearly every Catholic priest took an oath of loyalty to the new American government, which was generally read as support for the Revolution itself. Even Joseph Moseley, remote from political news on Maryland's Eastern Shore and feeling himself "between hawk and buzzard" at the outbreak of war in 1775, eventually took the oath and urged his congregations to do so.[10]

If Catholics were more disposed than colonial Protestants to support independence, which is a reasonable assumption, not every Catholic was a patriot. Many German Catholics opposed the break with England, as did a portion of the Highland Scots who had immigrated to New York's Mohawk Valley. German Catholics even contributed a regiment to the Loyalist cause. Irish Catholics, by contrast, seem mostly to have favored independence, along with their Anglo-American counterparts, and were well represented in the officers' ranks of the American army and navy. Irish hostility to England is easily explained. But given the anti-Catholicism endemic to colonial culture and the legal disabilities under which they had suffered, the position of Maryland's Catholics is less so. If there were any Catholic Loyalists in Maryland, they did not act publicly in support of the Crown. Nor were Maryland's Catholics inclined to neutrality; they expressed support for independence, donated money to the cause, and volunteered for military service in disproportionate numbers.[11]

The wealth of the colony's Catholic leaders was doubtless an explanatory factor—some of Maryland's richest planters were Catholics who enjoyed high social standing. Whatever disabilities they incurred because of their religion, Maryland's Catholic elite had flourished with regard to the things of this world. Matters were otherwise in England, where concerted repression had led by the late eighteenth century to mass defections from the faith among the Catholic nobility and gentry. Separated by an ocean from the mother country, the colony's Catholics and especially its leaders were indisputably better off, as those Catholics certainly knew. Buoyed by this awareness, the prospect of a break with England might well have been easier for Catholics to countenance than it was for colonial Protestants. Perhaps anti-Catholicism, so ubiquitous a factor in colonial life, was at root an English import, with tolerance the natural mode for an increasingly diverse New World order. The prospect was worth entertaining. A tradition of lay activism among Maryland Catholics may have played a role as well. Accustomed to taking initiative in their spiritual lives, the colony's Catholics— despite their longtime exclusion from politics—may have gravitated naturally to secular activism as the old political order waned.

Developments on the colonial side as early as 1775 served to validate Catholic hopes. Efforts to enlist the Quebecois in the fight for independence resulted in an immediate muting of anti-Catholicism, at least in elite circles. In November of that year, George Washington banned celebrations of Pope's Day—a popular English holiday on which the pope was burned in effigy—in the Continental Army. The custom, he said, was "ridiculous and childish." When Catholic France agreed early in 1778 to fight alongside the American rebels, most pro-independence Protestants greeted the development as providential. French intervention proved militarily decisive, which further diminished the public expression of anti-Catholicism. Shortly after the battle of Yorktown, where the French forced surrender of the principal British Army, a Mass of Thanksgiving was held at St. Mary's Church in Philadelphia, attended by members of the Continental Congress and the Pennsylvania Assembly. A French priest preached—one of the more than one hundred chaplains to arrive with the French troops.[12]

The revolution also wrought a profound change in the legal status of Catholics. Virginia, Maryland, and Pennsylvania enfranchised Catholics, or the property-owning males among them, in the war's early stages. Every state constitution in the immediate postwar years embraced at least a limited form of religious freedom, although several restricted officeholding to Protestants. But the right to hold office was everywhere extended, often in less than a decade, to Catholics and then to Jews—a development foreshadowed and partially caused by the federal Constitution's ban on religious tests for public office. Most states also ended their religious establishments or weakened them significantly. John Carroll, for one, was delighted. "I am glad . . . to inform you that the fullest & largest system of toleration is adopted in almost all the American states," he informed an English comrade in 1779, attributing purported signs of greater toleration in England to the American example. His confrere Joseph Moseley, still riding circuit on the Eastern Shore, put matters more bluntly in 1784. "The toleration here granted by the Bill of Rights"—he was referring to a Maryland statute—"has put all on the same footing, and has been of great service to us."[13]

American Catholics at the close of the war remained under the authority of the Vicar Apostolic of London—an untenable situation, from the Catholic perspective, given latent anti-Catholicism and the widespread distrust of England that haunted the newly independent states. Acutely aware of the problem, John Carroll organized his fellow priests into what he called a "General Chapter," which drew up a "Constitution for the Clergy" of the United States and provided for a representative form of clerical church governance. The representative body so created petitioned Rome for a resident superior in 1783—not a bishop, they hastened to add, given current American sensibilities, but one who could lead the church with universally recognized authority. Carroll was the obvious choice, since the body had already voted to make him their procurator, or leader. His appointment as Superior of the Mission came late in 1784, granting him certain episcopal faculties including the ability to administer confirmation. That the appointment came from the Propaganda, of which Carroll remained deeply distrustful, was troubling to him, but his status as something less than a bishop seems to have mollified those many Americans who were fearful of Roman authority.

Carroll soon saw a need for greater authority than his initial status seemed to confer, especially when dealing with recalcitrant clergy, all of them recent arrivals. Hence a second appeal to Rome in 1788, signed by Carroll and two of his priests, requesting the appointment of an American bishop. "Especially deputed by our brother priests who exercise the ministry with us in the United States," the three also asked that "the choice of the bishop, at least in this first instance, be left to the priests here who have the care of souls." A papal appointment would have ruffled Protestant sensibilities, as the priests surely knew. But more was involved than deference to a dominant republican ethos. Bishops in Europe had traditionally been elected by priest-members of cathedral chapters, save where Rome had transferred that right to monarchs. The American situation was obviously anomalous, there being neither king nor cathedral. (Congress had refused a consultative role with regard to episcopal appointments when the Propaganda floated the option in 1783.) Presumably for this reason, the request was granted. Carroll was elected bishop by his priests in 1789, with Baltimore as his See city. The United States nonetheless remained a mission territory—a status Rome would not alter until 1908—and thus under the ultimate jurisdiction of the Propaganda.[14]

Carroll, like his confreres, very much hoped that future American bishops would be elected by the clergy or, as Carroll strongly preferred, by a seasoned elite among them. Such a mode of selection would not only conform to republican expectations but also—and this was far more important—strengthen the hand of American bishops in their dealings with Rome. The papacy, as Carroll saw it, ought to function primarily as "a center of Ecclesiastical unity," its authority "purely spiritual." The pope's temporal power—the monarchical Papal States still occupied much of the Italian peninsula—constituted, in Carroll's view, a major obstacle to Catholic prospects in the United States. So did the near-exclusive use of Latin in the liturgy. "The greatest part of our Congregations must be utterly ignorant of the meaning and Sense of the publick Offices of the church," he wrote to a clerical colleague in 1784, asserting on another occasion that most of his clergy also favored a vernacular liturgy. He endorsed reform in the secular sphere, as well. When the Maryland Assembly proposed in 1784 to tax the state's residents for the general support of all churches, Carroll joined a number of Protestants in opposition, suggesting a principled embrace on his part of the religiously neutral state.[15]

Carroll also endorsed the exercise of limited lay authority at the parish level, permitting congregations to elect lay trustees who held title to and managed parish property. Many congregations made use of the privilege, although others allowed their priest—visiting or otherwise—to appoint them. However selected, trustees were essential in those many locales that lacked a resident priest. In every sort of parish, moreover, trustees were useful for raising money. Even in the 1780s, the Catholic Church in the United States was too populous to subsist on revenue from the former Jesuit plantations, already diminishing in profitability. More and more churches depended solely on lay contributions for survival—and trustees, mostly chosen from a community's most affluent members, were often significant sources of funds. The honor of office, it was widely assumed, would prompt them to be especially generous. The laity, moreover, were apt to give more when some of their own were keeping the books—or so experience seemed to indicate.

Although functioning well in a great many places, the trustee system also caused instances of high-profile conflict, particularly during the first half-century of American nationhood—a subject explored at greater length in chapter 5. Encouraged in part by Protestant example, some boards of trustees claimed the right to hire and dismiss their priests—something no Catholic bishop could countenance. To do so, in Carroll's words, would make every priest a potential "victim of the most capricious despotism." New York's St. Peter's Church was the scene in 1787–88 of the first of numerous bitter battles over precisely this question. Carroll's efforts at mediation—he traveled to New York for this purpose—met with public humiliation. He was twice pulled from the altar by angry parishioners when he attempted to say Mass at St. Peter's.[16]

The Catholic population over which Carroll assumed jurisdiction was in the 1780s still concentrated in Maryland. Roughly 15,800 Catholics lived in that state, he told the Propaganda in 1785, some 20 percent of them slaves. Half as many lived in Pennsylvania, "but very few Africans." Some fifteen hundred were now resident in the state of New York, he had recently been told, and New York City had just witnessed the organization of its first Catholic congregation—the soon-to-be-turbulent St. Peter's. No more than two hundred could be found in nearby Virginia, where an itinerant priest said Mass just four or five times a year. As for those Catholics "said to live scattered here and there in that state and in the others," as well as those living "in the territory near the so-called Mississippi," they were "destitute of all religious services." Carroll simply had no priests to send them. Maryland had just nineteen priests in 1785 and Pennsylvania only five, which meant that many established congregations still lacked a resident priest.[17]

Even on remote frontiers, Catholic settlers were apparently eager to have a priest among them. "I receive applications from every part of the U. States . . . for Clergymen," Carroll told an English confrere, "and considerable property is offered for their maintenance." But despite the religious commitment implicit in such requests, Carroll had no high opinion of lay piety, evidently convinced that devotion invariably withered where priests were few in number. Even among those native-born Catholics with at least monthly access to Mass and the sacraments, fervor was too often lacking, at least in

Carroll's view. Many confessed and received communion only once a year—the canonical minimum for Catholics since a papal bull to that effect in 1215. Among immigrant Catholics, moreover, most of whom derived from Ireland or Germany, "hardly anyone is found . . . who observes the duty of religion," by which the bishop presumably meant the obligation to confess and receive communion annually. Carroll attributed these failings in part to the bad example of American Protestants, among whom regular churchgoing was in fact much less frequent than would later be the case. They were also to blame, according to Carroll, for the "rather free conduct" of young Catholics with regard to the opposite sex, particularly their fondness for dancing, and a near mania for novel reading, "especially among girls." With the rising generation so readily corrupted and their parents unwilling or unable to provide religious instruction, Carroll feared for the future.[18]

The bishop's views in this regard should be taken with the proverbial grain of salt. He had relatively little contact with immigrants, especially those suffering the worst effects of poverty and social dislocation. As a celibate priest, moreover, he had limited existential grasp of life as most laity knew it. Carroll himself acknowledged that he and his priests spent long hours hearing confessions—"at times confessions cannot be heard in less than three hours" preceding Mass, he noted in 1787. He also knew firsthand of priestless congregations where devotional life flourished under lay leadership. As a pastor, he could even admit that dancing, while certainly dangerous, was not necessarily mortally sinful or a sign of cultural collapse. "To prohibit dancing entirely would, I fear, be a rash exercise of authority, & the cause of innumerable sins & drive some out of the Church," he wrote in 1796 to a priest in Vincennes. Given the radical shortage of priests, a good many Catholics in Carroll's day certainly drifted from the church. But the principal cause, very likely, was less Protestant example than marriage across confessional lines in those many places where Catholics were a minuscule minority.[19]

Carroll dealt with his clergy shortage by recruitment in Europe, which resulted in increased, if still insufficient, manpower and a series of episcopal headaches. Priests arriving in the 1780s, primarily from Ireland and Germany, enabled Carroll to send pastors to places hitherto bereft—not just New York and Boston but southern locales where Catholic numbers were small but growing rapidly, including Charleston, South Carolina, and the Kentucky frontier. Not every man could endure the rigors of ministry in such difficult circumstances, and some new recruits did not stay long. Others arrived without adequate testimonials from their bishops in Europe or with testimonials to which their conduct soon gave the lie. "You cannot conceive the trouble, I suffer already, & still greater, which I foresee, from the medley of clerical characters coming from different quarters, & various educations, & seeking employment here," Carroll confided to an English confrere in 1789, rightly suspecting that at least a few bishops were ridding themselves of problem priests by exporting them to America. More than a few were alcoholics, a handful were charged with sexual offenses, and most resisted Carroll's authority whenever he tried to discipline them.[20]

The "bad priest" problem would not be solved in Carroll's lifetime. Given a dearth of native vocations and rapid growth in the Catholic population, most bishops depended on imperfectly vetted clerical imports throughout the antebellum years and sometimes even beyond. But Carroll got a welcome respite in the early 1790s, when the first of an eventual twenty-three priests from Revolutionary France sought refuge in the United States. Mostly members of the Society of St. Sulpice, these priests almost to a man were disciplined, devout, and highly educated. Carroll sent several with uncertain English to regions of his vast diocese where French was still the common language, including posts in the Great Lakes region and along the Mississippi. Others were sent to Kentucky, to which many of Maryland's Catholics had immigrated, as well as points farther south. Frontier Kentucky was served by four priests at the close of the 1790s, when priests were ministering for the first time in Georgia. The first bishop of Boston, Jean-Louis Lefebvre de Cheverus, came as pastor to that city's hitherto troubled parish in 1796; in Carroll's words, he was "of great eminence & exceedingly beloved." Some of the men who arrived in the 1790s would return to France—to Carroll's dismay—once Napoleon came to power, believing themselves obliged to assist in rebuilding their nation's parishes and especially its seminaries. But others arrived in their wake. More than one hundred French priests were working in the United States on the eve of the Civil War, a majority in the South, by which time eleven Frenchmen had served or were serving as bishops of American dioceses.[21]

For all the Sulpicians' essential service as missionaries, Carroll most valued them or their work as seminary faculty. The first to arrive in 1791 established St. Mary's Seminary in Baltimore, where the first students were five seminarians who had fled France along with their teachers. More students arrived in subsequent years, including French-born Stephen Badin, who in 1793 became the first Catholic priest to be ordained in the young United States. St. Mary's struggled in its early years, perennially short of funds and students, especially the American-born. Although Carroll had founded an equally struggling academy in Georgetown—part by then of the newly created District of Columbia—in 1791, which was also intended to serve as a preparatory seminary, few youths evinced interest in a clerical career. "Of the few who have," Carroll noted gloomily, "some did not persevere & the best among them died." Carroll did ordain an American-born graduate in 1800, although the joy he surely felt was tempered by the realization that the ordination left St. Mary's with no students whatsoever. (The school had yielded at this point only five new priests for the Diocese of Baltimore.) But St. Mary's ultimately prospered, as did the struggling academy in Georgetown, ancestor of today's Georgetown University. Whatever the vagaries of funds and enrollments, St. Mary's Sulpician faculty maintained a deserved reputation for spiritual rigor and high intellectual aspirations.[22]

Carroll succeeded more readily when it came to women religious: the first convent in the former English colonies, located in Port Tobacco, Maryland, dates from 1790. Of the four sisters initially resident there, three had been born and raised in Maryland, having traveled as adolescents to join a convent in present-day Belgium, where Carroll himself had a cousin. The religious in question were Carmelites, members of a strictly cloistered order devoted exclusively to prayer. Devout Maryland Catholics rejoiced at the Carmelites' advent, and the convent's chapel soon became a popular spot for Mass and devotions. The community attracted vocations too, despite its near-desperate poverty, adding eleven new members during its first ten years. John Carroll was less enthusiastic. "I wish rather for Ursulines," he told a friend, by which he meant women religious whose vocation was teaching or nursing. Like the former Jesuits in Maryland and like their Sulpician contemporaries at St. Mary's Seminary in Baltimore, the Port Tobacco Carmelites held slaves, most of them acquired as part of the dowries required of members who came from wealthy families. This was the case, indeed, with nearly every women's order established in a jurisdiction where slavery was permitted.[23]

A second group of cloistered nuns, three Poor Clares exiled by the French Revolution, opened an academy for girls in Georgetown in 1798. Due to the nuns' inability to speak English and restrictions imposed by their rule of enclosure, the venture foundered almost immediately. It was rescued by three Philadelphia laywomen, recruited for the purpose by their pastor; relocating to Georgetown, they taught at the school and lived communally while following an improvised round of daily religious devotions. The Poor Clares having departed for France, this informal community—augmented now by new members—eventually adopted the rule of the Visitation Sisters, a French congregation dating from the early seventeenth century. By 1817, the by now canonically established community had more than twenty professed members and nearly as many novices. Visitation Academy in Georgetown, which achieved a national reputation for excellence, supplied the community with gifted new members for many subsequent generations—testimony to the female religious energy that did so much to build and shape American Catholicism.

That energy is nowhere better expressed than in the career of Elizabeth Bayley Seton, canonized in 1975 as the first American-born saint. Born in New York to an affluent family in 1774, she married a prosperous merchant at the age of nineteen and was soon the mother of five children. Seton had been raised in the Episcopal Church, of which she was a more than ordinarily devout member. But in the context of trial and grief—her husband went bankrupt in 1800 and died three years later—she entered a time of religious questing that culminated in 1805 in her conversion to Catholicism. Her extended family, on whom Seton depended for support, was predictably dismayed. Thirsting for a life of greater religious intensity than seemed possible as a widow in New York, Seton relocated to Baltimore in 1808, where she opened a girls' academy. (Her daughters, who remained with her, attended the schools she founded; her sons, funded by well-to-do Catholics, were boarding pupils at Georgetown Academy and Mount St. Mary's College.) Closely allied with the Sulpician priests at St. Mary's Seminary, Seton in 1809 moved her school at their direction to Emmitsburg, Maryland, where she presided over a nascent community of women religious. Taking vows as a Sister of Charity in that same year, she quickly attracted new recruits—enough to found communities of the Sisters of Charity of St. Joseph in Philadelphia in 1812, New York in 1817, and Baltimore in 1821, the year of Seton's death.[24]

Seton stands at the head of a long line of converts who have made significant contributions to Catholicism in the United States. Although the roots of any conversion are bound to be tangled, she appears to have been principally motivated, as others have been, by a growing conviction that

Filicchi portrait of Elizabeth Bayley Seton, ca. 1805 (Courtesy of the Daughters of Charity, Province of St. Louise Archives, Emmitsburg, Maryland)

Christ was truly present in the Catholic Eucharist. "How happy would we be," she wrote in her journal on the brink of conversion, "if we believed what these dear souls believe, that they *possess God* in the Sacrament and that he remains in their churches and is carried to them when they are sick." An intense Eucharistic piety characterized Seton's spiritual life and that of the community she founded. The Emmitsburg sisters were permitted by their rule to receive communion up to three times a week, while Seton herself at times received communion daily. The practice caused great anxiety for the order's initial spiritual director, the Sulpician William Dubourg, later bishop of New Orleans, who feared that members of the laity—as women religious are—seldom possessed the spiritual discipline it required.[25]

The Sisters of Charity, of which there are presently six branches in North America, were an order after Carroll's heart. Descended from the Daughters of Charity, a lay association founded in France in 1633 to serve the poor and dependent, Seton's sisters not only taught but nursed the sick and cared for orphans. Like Carroll, with whom she maintained a long correspondence, Seton regarded the American church as too young and impoverished to support contemplative religious life. "This is not a country, my dear one, for Solitude and Silence," she wrote to a sister who felt drawn to a cloistered community, "but of warfare and crucifixion." The rapid growth of Seton's order in the nineteenth century and that of closely related orders in the same Vincentian tradition suggests that she was right. Contemplative orders for women were rare in the United States until the twentieth century, while those engaged in active ministries drew streams of recruits. Not every recruit shared Seton's spiritual ardor or self-confident independence, which can doubtless be traced in part to her elite Protestant beginnings. "If I was a man," she wrote to her son in 1818, "all the world would not stop me, I would go straight in [St. Francis] Xavier's footsteps." But women's religious orders in the United States have nurtured some powerful personalities, as numerous bishops have discovered—often enough to their chagrin. When considering lines of authority in a hierarchical church, we do well to remember this largely hidden locus of leverage and cultural influence.[26]

The Diocese of Baltimore, coextensive at its creation with the whole of the United States, was too large to be capably governed. The Louisiana Purchase of 1803, which more than doubled the nation's territory, made the impossible even more so, causing Carroll to petition Rome for the creation of additional American dioceses—three, he thought, or possibly four. Rome was not opposed, although formal permission took time to arrive. But whom to appoint to these new posts—acceptable men, in Carroll's view, were in achingly short supply—and how to ensure their support once they had been installed? Carroll had few priests to choose from, especially eliminating recent arrivals and those with limited English. The task of church governance, moreover, had grown more demanding, due in good part to increased immigration. Ethnic variety often meant conflict, as Carroll had learned from experience—conflict exacerbated in a great many cases by poverty among the newly arrived. A successful bishop had to cope with such eventualities, which requirement might easily disqualify an otherwise competent candidate. Carroll could suggest no acceptable man for the proposed diocese of New York, scene of his onetime humiliation, which he blamed largely on poor Irish immigrants, at St. Peter's Church in the city. Best, he thought, to delay its creation.

Although Carroll had hoped otherwise, he seems to have known that the country's new bishops would not be elected by their clerical peers. All were appointed by Pope Pius VII, with the Propaganda playing a principal role. Carroll's recommendations were followed for the heads of the newly created dioceses of Boston, Philadelphia, and Bardstown, Kentucky, all of which date from 1808. Despite his recommendation to the contrary, New York received a bishop in that same year—an Irish priest, unknown to Carroll, who died in 1810, before he could reach the United States. His replacement, an Irishman long resident in Rome, was chosen with no American input, perhaps because of confusion caused by the pope's arrest and internment at Genoa during the Napoleonic wars—an excuse that Carroll was inclined to doubt. "I wish this may not become a very dangerous precedent, fruitful of mischief by drawing censure upon our religion, & false opinion of the servility of our principles," he wrote in 1815, shortly before his own death. He would not be the last American bishop to complain of what he saw as Roman high-handedness.[27]

Carroll's brand of Enlightenment Catholicism was doomed by more than what soon emerged as a trend toward the centralization of ecclesiastical control in Rome. Heavy immigration to the United States in the 1840s and after brought masses of impoverished Catholics whose lives had hardly prepared them to share Carroll's assumptions and worldview. Their Catholicism was altogether more insular and defensive. Even in Carroll's lifetime, some of his priests distrusted their bishop's embrace of American political principles. But by embracing those principles, which is to say by endorsing not just the nation's birth in popular rebellion but also the religiously neutral state, Carroll and his generation placed the American church on the side of modernity. Whatever tensions lay ahead, American Catholics never struggled, as many in Catholic Europe did, to reconcile their loyalties as citizens with fidelity to their church. The two identities fused seamlessly. Herein lies a principal source of Catholicism's remarkable flourishing in the United States and especially its success in the subsequent century at holding the loyalty of working-class men.

Part II
Growing with the Nation, 1815–1870

Samuel Mazzuchelli, O.P.

(1806–1864)

T he year is 1828. Samuel Mazzuchelli, studying for the priesthood in Rome at the age of twenty-two, has just sought permission from his Dominican superiors to depart for the American missions. Responding to a personal appeal from Father Frederic Rese, the German-born vicar-general of the recently created Diocese of Cincinnati who was touring Europe to recruit clergy, Mazzuchelli had doubtless been inspired by tales of the still numerous Indians in the northern region of Rese's diocese—Indians who have seldom seen a priest since the departure over fifty years earlier of the last French Jesuits. Mazzuchelli's prominent Milanese family oppose his missionary ambitions, as indeed they had earlier argued against his joining the Dominican order. But his superiors obviously sympathized. He left Rome for the United States in that same year, spending two months en route at a seminary in Paris, where he practiced his already serviceable French. Once in Ohio, he completed his studies at the Dominican convent of St. Rose, founded near Somerset in 1807 by English Dominicans, where Mazzuchelli did his best to master the English language. He was ordained by Cincinnati's Bishop Edward Fenwick, a fellow Dominican, in 1830 and—as if in answer to his youthful prayers—sent to the long-neglected Indian mission at Mackinac Island.

Mazzuchelli spent five years among the Indians in the northern Great Lakes, where he also ministered to a small population of French trappers and traders, most of whom had intermarried with the indigenous population.

He appeared to thrive on the physical demands of missionary labor, which in his case meant travel by Indian canoe on the treacherous waters of Lake Michigan and by foot through close to impenetrable forests. The isolation was harder to bear: with no other priest close at hand, he could only occasionally go to confession or seek spiritual counsel. "Few persons can realize the emotion of two priests who, after months of solitude, have the consolation of meeting," he wrote with regard to a visit he paid to Slovenian-born Frederic Baraga, who ministered to the Ottawa Indians near present-day Harbor Springs, Michigan. Mazzuchelli, like all frontier priests, lived almost exclusively among the laity, on whom he depended for success in his ministry. Lay catechists kept the faith alive in the various missions Mazzuchelli established; since he never gained fluency in an Indian language, he depended on lay interpreters for preaching and hearing Indian confessions. At least some of these catechists and interpreters were women, typically the offspring of French fathers and Indian mothers. On a visit to the Winnebago in Wisconsin in 1833, Mazzuchelli was grateful to "several Catholic women whose mothers were Winnebago married to Canadians. These women, having some knowledge of Christian doctrine and speaking the tribal language, would make their way into the lodges to speak of religion."[1]

Mazzuchelli's stint among the Indians ended in 1835, when he was sent by his superiors to a population of mostly Irish Catholics in the vicinity of Dubuque, where newly active lead mines were attracting immigrants. His ostensible "parish" stretched over four hundred miles along the Mississippi and up to sixty miles east and west of the river's course. The Catholic population, estimated at thirty-five hundred, was widely scattered and included longtime French settlers as well as a growing population of Germans. Over the next few years, a peripatetic Mazzuchelli visited much of his pastoral territory, lodging with families along the way and saying Mass in private homes, occasionally those of Protestants, or even taverns. He proved to be a prodigious church builder, raising funds and providing designs for more than twenty churches in Iowa, Illinois, and Wisconsin. Local Protestants, he found, were often glad to contribute to the Catholic building fund, presumably prompted by boosterism—every church added to the village skyline—and a sense that religion in general was a force for social order. Dubuque's first Catholic church—indeed the first church of any denomination in that infant settlement at its dedication in 1836—had been generously supported by local non-Catholics.

Notwithstanding such instances of practical ecumenism, anti-Catholicism was ubiquitous in the antebellum decades—an increasingly potent factor in the nation's politics and culturally resonant for many Americans. But Mazzuchelli's personal relations with non-Catholics were generally amicable. An evidently powerful preacher, he attracted Protestants to many of his services and took care to make them welcome. He was a popular speaker on civic occasions too, due in good part to his fluency in the language of patriotism. "May the American Republic be lasting, glorious and powerful," he toasted the guests at an 1836 Independence Day banquet in Dubuque. Nor were such sentiments merely rhetorical: the young United States, Mazzuchelli once wrote, "would seem to be, in the designs of Divine Wisdom, a means, first of granting perfect freedom of religion, and secondly, of promoting the emigration of many Catholic families from Europe." Mazzuchelli never doubted that his was the one true church; Protestantism, as he saw it, led ultimately to either indifference or fanaticism. But immersed as he was in the voluntary world of the American frontier, Mazzuchelli had also learned that Protestants could be sincerely devout and charitable. "Therefore any Catholic would be imprudent if he should condemn without distinction or regard for circumstances or the inscrutable judgments of God a person who appears to be outside the Catholic Church."[2]

Most of Mazzuchelli's pastoral territory was incorporated in 1837 into the newly created Diocese of Dubuque. Dubuque's new bishop—French-born Mattias Pierre Loras, serving at the time of his appointment in the Diocese of Mobile—was stunned to discover that his new diocese had only a single priest. Loras soon left Alabama for Europe to recruit additional clergy, arriving in Dubuque in 1839 with two French priests in tow, having left four French seminarians in Baltimore to complete their training and acquire facility in English. Mazzuchelli's pastoral burdens were substantially lightened by these developments, as was his isolation. (He had been traveling by steamboat to St. Louis two or three times a year in order to go to confession.) He still rode a mission circuit but under less strenuous conditions than had previously been the case. The local supply of priests was such by 1843 that Mazzuchelli, in increasingly fragile health, could embark on a journey to Europe—in part to recruit additional priests but also to visit his family. He traveled first to Baltimore, accompanying Bishop Loras as his theologian to the Fourth Provincial Council of the American bishops. Mazzuchelli was impressed by the size and ceremony of the gathering, which was indeed indicative of a maturing institution, but proud too of the simple life his own bishop led in faraway Dubuque. The frontier church, in Mazzuchelli's telling, resembled that of apostolic times, when "the first bishops acted as zealous and energetic parish priests."[3]

Mazzuchelli returned to the United States in 1844, having published his *Memoirs* in Italy to encourage support for the American missions, which depended heavily on European contributions. Previously celebrated for the numerous parishes he had founded, he now turned his hand to Catholic schools. After establishing what proved to be a short-lived college for men in Wisconsin in 1846, he presided in 1847 over the founding of the Sinsinawa Dominican Sisters, which grew from an initial four members to be one of the principal teaching orders in the upper Midwest. In 1848, the sisters opened a school for girls at their southwestern Wisconsin motherhouse, which was soon a flourishing enterprise—the remote ancestor, in fact, of today's Dominican University in suburban Chicago. Not long thereafter, Mazzuchelli became the founding pastor of St. Patrick's parish in the nearby village of Benton, where he died in 1856—the result, or so it is said, of pneumonia contracted on a foul-weather sick call to a rural parishioner. Long cherished as a saint in regional Catholic memory, Mazzuchelli was declared venerable—the first step in the official canonization process—by Pope John Paul II in 1993.

Mazzuchelli's American life seldom brought him to the nation's major cities, which especially after the mid-1840s were home to a majority of Catholic immigrants and where the Catholic future rested. Mazzuchelli's career, indeed, can be read as a study in evanescence: the Indian missions he initially served were decimated by federal removal of the Great Lakes tribes to lands west of the Mississippi in the 1830s and 1840s, while the frontier ethos he celebrated—the simplicity of clerical life, the priest's intimacy with the laity—could not survive the growth in Catholic wealth and numbers. Midwestern Catholicism did retain certain "frontier" characteristics, most notably a tradition of lay initiative and openness to ecumenical cooperation in the civic sphere. But in the Midwest, as elsewhere on the waning frontier, Catholic life was increasingly characterized by a growing distance between priest and people and a greater degree of Catholic institutional separateness. The "frontier" chapter in American Catholic history in which Mazzuchelli played so notable a role is nonetheless worthy of examination. It reminds us of an important truth: that Catholic life varies in its rhythm, mood, and texture according to the environment in which a church takes root.

The Frontier Church

E ven at the time of the Civil War, Catholics were more urbanized
than their fellow Americans. But Catholics also settled on the nation's rapidly expanding frontiers, hundreds and sometimes
thousands of miles from the principal nodes of Catholic institutional life. As many as a third of Maryland's Catholics left the state in the
antebellum decades, migrating initially to frontier Kentucky and then in
growing numbers to points west and south. The building of roads and canals
drew Irish immigrants westward in the 1820s and after; they were numerous
as well in mining communities, initially east of the Mississippi but then across
the West. Far more likely than the Irish to settle outside of cities, German
immigrants on the frontier typically went into farming. Their numbers were
especially great on the prairies and eastern plains, where the Catholics among
them often supported a vibrant liturgical life. A much smaller population
of French Catholics was already resident when the lands along the Mississippi became an American frontier; the same was true in the Great Lakes
region and portions of the Pacific Northwest. When the United States annexed the former Republic of Texas in 1845 and more than five hundred
thousand square miles of western territory formerly claimed by Mexico in
1848, thousands of Hispanic Catholics found themselves living on an American frontier.[1]

Frontier Bishops and Their Priests

Priest-poor and starved for cash, even the most zealous bishops could not supply the religious needs of most frontier Catholics, whose very existence was sometimes unknown to their distant shepherds. Carroll's successors in Baltimore repeatedly prodded Rome to create additional dioceses as a first step toward solving the problem. From the five dioceses in existence as of 1808, the number grew to eleven in 1830, twenty-one in 1844, and forty-one in 1854, including seven archdioceses. San Francisco was the seat of an archbishop by then. The Diocese of Galveston dates from 1847, that of Santa Fe from 1853. Even the thinly populated Plains came into the episcopal fold, with Apostolic Vicariates—the first step toward establishing a diocese—created for Kansas and Nebraska in 1857 and jointly for Idaho and Montana in 1858. By the eve of the Civil War, most of the estimated three million Catholics in the United States, including those living in remote locales, could reasonably expect to see a bishop at least once in their lives, most likely when he toured his diocese to administer the sacrament of confirmation.

Nearly all frontier bishops were intrepid travelers, negotiating the wilderness by foot and on horseback and its sometimes turbulent rivers by none-too-reliable vessels of every description. Their strenuous itineraries— some traveled thousands of miles in a typical year—could undermine the health of even fairly vigorous men. Samuel Mazzuchelli, alone at Mackinac, was delighted to welcome Cincinnati's Bishop Edward Fenwick on pastoral visits in 1831 and again in 1832, when the bishop preached a two-week mission—akin to a decorous Protestant revival—and heard hundreds of confessions. Fenwick, whose diocese encompassed the states of Ohio, Michigan, and Wisconsin at its creation in 1821, had several times traveled to the Indian missions in the vicinity of Green Bay and had planned to do so again in 1832. But afflicted by "extreme weakness," in Mazzuchelli's words, the bishop cut short his journey. He died on the return trip, perhaps of the cholera then raging in Detroit, attended in his final hours not by a priest—there were none to hand in Wooster, Ohio—but by a female teacher from the area, one of his converts, who "prayed and strove to make him sensible by reciting the Litany and some words of the Psalms."[2]

Each of the dioceses created in the antebellum years was acutely short of clergy. A diocese encompassing several states might have only one or two priests at the time of its institution. When a bishop was sent to the newly created Diocese of Nashville in 1837, he found no priests there whatsoever. The Catholic population might be widely dispersed; it was almost certainly poor. Early bishops sometimes struggled to house themselves adequately, let alone build churches and schools. Most eventually turned to Catholic Europe for funds as well as priests, usually traveling there in person—an added burden to a ministry already marked by frequent bouts of itinerancy. Simon Bruté, first bishop of Vincennes, having reluctantly decided in 1834 on a begging trip to Europe, first rode on horseback some six hundred miles to visit Catholics on the periphery of his very large diocese. At home in Vincennes he was equally vigorous, caring "for about 1,500 impoverished Catholics, primitive and illiterate"; preaching and catechizing; visiting the sick and dying, "often at great distances"; and tending single-handed to diocesan administration.[3]

Despite the proliferation of dioceses that looked at the time of their creation like administrative fictions, the American bishops as a group in the antebellum years moved toward something like nationwide organization. The bishops gathered at Baltimore for provincial councils on seven occasions between 1829 and 1847, mostly at three-year intervals, and at plenary councils—the creation of two additional archdioceses in 1846, one in the Oregon Territory and one at St. Louis, meant that many dioceses were no longer part of the Baltimore province—in 1852, 1866, and 1884. Bishops at the various councils discussed mutual problems—safeguarding a bishop's ownership of church property dominated concerns in 1829—and issued ambitious directives with regard to such varied subjects as the liturgy ("uniformity in following the Roman Ritual" was repeatedly stressed), clerical conduct, and Catholic education. The Baltimore meetings were objectively burdensome for many frontier bishops, given the cost and hardships of travel. But the psychic rewards were potentially great. No matter how poor and ill organized one's own diocese, a man was reminded at Baltimore that he belonged to something larger—certainly to a universal church but also to its peculiarly American incarnation, where rapid growth in the Catholic population seemed to promise a bright future.[4]

The bishops who assembled triennially in Baltimore were of varied nationalities—French, Belgian, Irish, German, and Italian, in addition to Americans of English descent. Their priests came from equally disparate backgrounds. In the earliest years of the Diocese of Detroit, carved in 1833 from the Diocese of Cincinnati, the priests who worked there were of French, Italian, Belgian, German, Swiss, Hungarian, and Slovenian origins.

Detroit was not atypical in this regard, nor was it unusual in its lack of native-born priestly vocations. The bishop of Detroit did not ordain a man born in the United States until 1850, doing better in this regard than certain of his confreres, including the archbishop of St. Louis. Nearly every priest born abroad spoke at least two languages, with many speaking three. A linguistic prodigy like Frederic Baraga, first bishop of the Diocese of Marquette on the Michigan mining frontier, spoke seven languages, including two Indian tongues for which he devised orthographies. A working knowledge of French, German, and English was essential in most American dioceses, while Spanish was necessary in Texas, the vast Southwest, and California, sufficiently populous by 1850 to become a state. Gaelic would have been useful too, at least in the early years of Irish immigration. "There are Germans and Irish who do not know any English at all," the future bishop Edward Fenwick, fluent in French, reported from Ohio in 1818. But even the redoubtable Frederic Baraga did not speak "Irish."[5]

Ethnic variety in American Catholicism has often meant conflict, especially in those many cities where immigrants settled in large numbers. Separate parishes for the various ethnic groups quickly emerged as the urban norm. The clergy too were sometimes balkanized, with Irish, German, and, later, Polish factions vying for influence and advantage. But on the frontier, such ethnic divisiveness was far less common. Frontier churches served—indeed, were often built by—all local Catholics, no matter their ethnic origins. A French sermon might feature at one Sunday Mass and a German sermon at another. But the church belonged to everyone, and so did the burden of its support. As for frontier priests, they lived and worked in such isolation that contacts with their fellow clergy were both limited— itself a means of muting tensions rooted in differing customs—and emotionally liberating. Only a fellow priest could hear one's confession—no small matter for men who feared, perhaps above all else, the prospect of dying without the sacraments; only he could understand the spiritual dilemmas bred by frontier ministry. If urban priests knew ethnic divisions and certainly hierarchies based on age, this was far less true of their frontier counterparts. Frederic Baraga did not hesitate to call the newly ordained Samuel Mazzuchelli his "spiritual advisor," although Baraga was eleven years the young priest's senior and far more experienced.[6]

Not every frontier priest was a multilingual saint. (Baraga, like Mazzuchelli, has been proposed for canonization.) Frontier bishops probably

received more than their share of the period's numerous problem priests—
men who stayed briefly and then moved on, often after causing scandal.
Some were well-intentioned souls overwhelmed by the burdens of frontier
ministry—its isolation, physical hardships, and very real dangers. "Here I am
in this wretched country, abandoned, alone," one desperate Flemish cleric
wrote from frontier Arkansas in 1832, shortly before he abandoned his post.
"Take me from this suburb of hell." Others brought their troubles with them
in the form of alcoholism or even mental imbalance. Priests from Ireland
were particular offenders, at least according to many bishops, who feared
that their Irish counterparts were less than thorough in their vetting of men
for the missions. Where a troubled priest had an ethnic base, as in a big city
parish, he might enjoy a degree of support within his congregation. "It is
truly surprising how much authority these drunkard priests exercise among
the lowest classes of their own race," in the words of Baltimore's Archbishop
Ambrose Marechal. But few such priests lasted on the frontier, where an ethnic base was harder to come by and clerical life was far less comfortable.[7]

The record is largely silent when it comes to the impact of troubled
clergy on the laity to whom they ostensibly ministered. We know rather
more about those priests, invariably men in good standing, whose rigorous
views on morality alienated many of the hitherto faithful. A premier example is found in Stephen Badin, who came to frontier Kentucky in 1793,
shortly after his ordination in Baltimore. His was a moralism of the sternest
stripe, derived perhaps from exposure to Jansenist clerics in his native
France. Badin preached vigorously against dancing and drink and evidently
too against what he saw as excesses in the marital bed. "Old men are not
allowed the marriage act more than once a week," according to a Kentucky
Dominican, who feared that Badin's rigorism had driven many local Catholics from the practice of their religion. Most of Badin's clerical contemporaries also warned against the dangers of drink and dancing, although to
the best of our knowledge they had little to say, at least in public, about
marital sex. What set Badin apart was his unbending zeal, especially as a
confessor. "Young people are not admitted to the sacraments without a sol-
emn promise of not dancing on any occasion whatever, which few will
promise and fewer still can keep," another Kentucky Dominican informed
John Carroll in 1808. "People are taught that every kiss lip to lip between
married persons is a mortal sin." As a result, "many have not been [to con-
fession] for 3 to 12 years."[8]

Badin was not alone in his rigorism. His colleague Charles Nerinckx, a Belgian priest-refugee from the French Revolution who arrived in Kentucky in 1805, was of the same mind and, like Badin, a fierce ascetic in his private life. One could name others. As for the battle against dancing, it went on in most dioceses until after the Civil War, spurred by the growing popularity of partnered dances like the waltz that seemed, at least to a celibate clergy, to present especially grave dangers. (Badin and Nerinckx, very likely, had been doing battle in Kentucky against round or contra dancing, in which sustained physical touching is limited.) But this was a battle that the clergy lost, as Badin—unlike Nerinckx—lived long enough to realize. Resident in his final years in the Cincinnati home of Archbishop John Purcell, the elderly Badin was a frequent presence at local Catholic affairs. On one such occasion in 1850, at Cincinnati's St. Xavier's College, the college band acknowledged his presence by closing its concert "with a beautiful composition named in honor of our beloved Octogenarian, the Badin polka." The old priest apparently accepted the compliment with good grace.[9]

A long-lived priest like Stephen Badin learned other lessons from his frontier experience. Consider his stint as a missionary to the Potawatomi Indians, then resident in the vicinity of what became the University of Notre Dame, in the early 1830s. Too old, in his view, to learn an Indian language, Badin depended heavily on a lay assistant, Angelique Campeau, of French and Indian descent and slightly older than Badin, being sixty-eight. Campeau was Badin's interpreter for preaching and confession and functioned in her own right as a catechist, remaining in the mission during Badin's periodic travels. Given the ambiguities inherent in her role, it is hardly surprising that the Indians should assume that Campeau possessed priestly powers of her own. "During my absence they wanted to confess to my interpreter, who is a very pious lady," Badin acknowledged in 1831, adding that Campeau was indeed "zealous for their salvation and eloquent in expressing all that which concerns the faith, the customs, the ceremonies and the discipline of the church." Every priest worth his salt eventually learns that the human condition is more complex than his seminary textbooks appeared to allow. But frontier ministry upended the customary hierarchies of gender and ecclesial status in particularly vivid ways.[10]

Frontier priests lived far more intimately with the laity than their urban counterparts did—a principal cause of their ministry's singularity. An itinerant priest depended on the laity for food and shelter while he was on the road. A night in a humble log cabin was far preferable to sleeping rough, especially in the early days of settlement, when a lone camper was vulnerable to snakebite or even animal attack. Father Edward Fenwick, in his first years of itinerancy in backwoods Ohio, worried—not implausibly—about bears. Trekking from Maryland to frontier Missouri in 1823, a portion of the way on foot, the Jesuit Charles Van Quickenborne was grateful to the Catholic families who received him and his traveling companions "like Apostles" and whose charity often made him "shed tears." As a literal bearer of the sacred, a priest in such humble circumstances did not cease to be a man set apart and honored as such by his hosts. But he shared the lives of his people in a way that no urban priest could. (City priests were regularly cautioned against socializing with the laity.) Masses said in private homes, a common practice in the early days of settlement, had an intimacy often lacking even in small churches and further reduced the emotional distance between a priest and his flock. John Mary Odin on his missionary travels in Texas in the early 1840s found about twenty Catholic families clustered along the Brazos River about thirty miles from Houston. He heard confessions and said Sunday Mass in the most centrally located house, where the ceremonies were witnessed by a "great number" of Protestants. Good pastor that he was, Odin went one step further. "There was sickness in all the families; so I offered the holy sacrifice in each house to give everybody the consolation of attending holy Mass."[11]

Once Catholic settlers were sufficiently numerous, they almost invariably built a church, which in its first incarnation was apt to be exceedingly modest. Simon Bruté spoke in 1834 of blessing "a kind of church built of rough logs" on the frontier near Vincennes. Even a regularly itinerant priest had to have a home base, generally in the place of thickest settlement. Most lived initially in hastily constructed quarters that also served as places of worship, although some chose to board with a local family. But after fifteen years or so, the scene nearly always looked very different, with a properly appointed church replacing the earlier structure and a separate rectory for the priest. With growth in the number of clergy, more and more former itinerants now functioned as resident pastors. Most still tended a handful of outlying missions, typically within a few hours' journey, which might be visited on a weekly or bimonthly basis. But even at midcentury, many rural pastors lived close to the bone, supported inadequately or at least inconsistently by a still impoverished laity. "Many indeed considered it to[o] much to give occasional[l]y a dollar to the priest who came to see them," the normally genial Father John Cappon reported in 1867 of his parish in southwestern Michigan. "They want a very cheap and easy religion." Living in such obvious dependence on the laity might breed a kind of familial intimacy, but family life can evoke irritation as well as more positive emotions.[12]

Rural pastors like Cappon often made ends meet by tending a kitchen garden; some kept chickens or even a cow. Most seem to have had rough carpentry skills, probably gained on the job. Theirs were the calloused hands of men who worked outdoors, in striking contrast to the soft, unblemished hands of clerical stereotype, by which revolutionary priest-hunters were said to identify their otherwise-disguised prey. Like most priests in the antebellum years, they dressed simply in public—in boots, long trousers, and a midcalf coat. Since every one of these garments was black, the costume signaled that its wearer was a clergyman, although not necessarily a Catholic priest. Accustomed to priests in cassocks on the streets of Rome, Samuel Mazzuchelli was struck by "the almost secular appearance of the priest in America." But even with regard to costume, the frontier priest stood out. Detroit's Gabriel Richard owned at least one suit of buckskin clothes, according to an inventory of his meager estate, presumably for purposes of wilderness travel. Others apparently did too: Celeste de la Hailandière, second bishop of Vincennes, "appeared dressed like any other man of the Indiana woods, sunburnt, dusty, and with dry mud on his clothes," according to the Sisters of Providence, recently arrived in his diocese from France.[13]

A frontier priest's poverty brought him closer to his people, at least in terms of sharing their experience. So, very likely, did his physical appearance. Few such men could approximate the gentlemanly dress or demeanor that even in the antebellum years was the beau ideal of the urban clergy. The frontier priest's coarsened hands, weathered complexion, and often rather shabby garments may have caused him to seem reassuringly masculine—a distinct advantage at a time when religion was widely seen as the special province of women. Even his rectory might occasionally assume the guise of a family residence, with the priest as paterfamilias. A boy attracted to the priesthood might live for a time with his pastor, who would tutor him in Latin—such instruction being otherwise unavailable in most frontier locales—in exchange for help with household chores. A few priests even adopted boys in the casual mode of the nineteenth century, when orphans and "half-orphans"—those with a living parent temporarily unable to care for his or her children—were often incorporated into families who could use their labor. No hint of sexual impropriety appears to have attached to a priest's residing with an adolescent boy. A female was more problematic, although priests did occasionally hire girls or young women as domestics. Elderly spinsters and widows—every bishop's ideal of a rectory housekeeper and standard rectory issue by the later nineteenth century—were in short supply in most frontier districts.[14]

Frontier Catholics, including their priests, had closer and more regular contact with Protestants than most of their urban counterparts did—contact that could complicate ministry, especially for priests trained abroad. In the earliest days of settlement, when clergy of any variety were apt to be scarce, priests were sometimes asked by non-Catholics to baptize their infants and young children, even though the parents themselves had no interest in converting. To do so would be highly irregular, at least by the standards prevailing in Europe. But Archbishop John Carroll permitted the practice, fearing that the children in question might otherwise not be baptized at all and anxious not to alienate their parents. Most of his brother bishops agreed, albeit uneasily. The Propaganda eventually overruled them—the practice, Rome feared, would lead to profanation of the sacrament. In the interim, however, a good many priests had to wrestle internally with the question. Religious intermarriage posed a similar dilemma, being common almost everywhere among Catholics in the early decades of the century but particularly so in frontier districts, where Catholic numbers were often small. Some priests, Stephen Badin among them, refused to officiate at such weddings—a stance that the Propaganda would subsequently endorse. But many couples so refused simply married in Protestant or civil ceremonies. Was strict conformity with canon law a greater good than pastoral solicitude for souls thus lost to the church? American realities, it seemed, and frontier realities in particular, made it hard at times to be a good priest, at least by the standards a man absorbed in seminary.[15]

At the same time, many frontier priests were buoyed by hopes of converting Protestants, especially in the early days of westward expansion, when anti-Catholic sentiment nationally was at relatively low ebb. Non-Catholics in frontier regions do seem to have attended Catholic ceremonies in surprisingly large numbers, and that news featured regularly in reports to superiors and begging letters sent to Europe. Father John Anthony Elet,

S.J., his Maryland superior was proudly informed, had said Mass at the home of a Protestant in Buffalo Creek, Missouri, on an 1828 visit with well over a hundred non-Catholics present. The lone Catholic family living locally, it seems, had a house too small to accommodate the crowd. Father Elet apparently took pains with his sermon, aware that oratory of all varieties was for many Americans a form of popular entertainment. "He preached during Mass for three-quarters of an hour and after Mass was forced to yield to a unanimous request to preach another sermon, which was done to their great satisfaction." Actual conversions were probably not numerous, despite occasional claims to the contrary. But those that did occur, coupled with the apparent friendliness of many Protestants, confirmed at least some frontier priests in their optimism about an American Catholic future.[16]

Anti-Catholicism surged in the United States after the early 1830s, fueled in part by quickened Catholic immigration. Its most severe manifestations were urban, with serious violence occurring in the antebellum decades in cities like Boston, Philadelphia, and Louisville. But anti-Catholicism flourished on the frontier too, as itinerant clergy quickly learned. Traveling through hamlets in Illinois and Missouri in the early 1830s, the Jesuit Charles Van Quickenborne found scattered Catholic families too fearful of their neighbors to publicly identify as such. In one Illinois village he visited, the two Catholic households locally "did not even dare" to receive him. Why, then, did frontier priests so regularly claim that the conversion of America was a lively possibility? Their optimism reflected in part what was clearly the dominant frontier reality: communities in the early stages of development could ill afford the luxury of religious division. Every neighbor was necessary. Priests typically found that hostility waned once fearful locals heard them speak. (Most preached in a public place on their initial visits and took care to respond to what they called standard Protestant calumnies.) Even Father Van Quickenborne, as stern a moralist as Stephen Badin, was made an optimist by his missionary travels. Just a few more priests, he told his superiors, and Catholics "could in a short time with the grace of God convert a great multitude of persons in these western states."[17]

Optimism of this sort was also balm to deep priestly anxieties. Frontier ministry was difficult in the extreme and not just because of its physical challenges. Missionaries worried incessantly about the many neglected Catholics who lay beyond their reach, whose salvation might well be in doubt. Some of those to whom they did minister had drifted from the church in the course of their frontier residence, because they had either married non-Catholics or attached themselves to an available Protestant congregation. Others, still nominally Catholic, proved anything but model parishioners once a priest had arrived. Clerical rigorism alienated a not insignificant number and kept the more stubborn from confession. "The firmness of this holy minister displeases many, especially the French," wrote Mother Rose Duchesne, a Religious of the Sacred Heart in Missouri, of Father Van Quickenborne in 1825, "who say that he does not like them and that they would rather go to another." (Mother Rose, privately of the opinion that "sometimes weaknesses need to be indulged," was eventually canonized.) As to the Indians who prompted so many missionary vocations, they were mostly removed from territory east of the Mississippi in the antebellum years, while Indian missions in the West were largely the province of religious orders, the Jesuits in particular. Periodically frustrated and sometimes filled with self-doubt, frontier priests may have sought solace in their fantasies—for such they were—about a Catholic America, especially in light of sobering news from home. "Try to gain a hundred souls in America for every one who loses the Faith in Europe," Father John De Néve wrote to his Belgian successor at Niles, Michigan, in 1863, when he was rector of the recently founded American College at Louvain. "Pray for your country, but don't regret having left it."[18]

So positive a view of the American future, which rested—whether acknowledged or not—on the benefits afforded Catholicism by a religiously neutral state, endowed those frontier priests who shared it with what we might call an honorary American identity. They were different in significant ways from the men they had been in Europe. "I regard myself as one in exile," was how De Néve put it in 1863, when he wrote from his native Belgium. It also brought them closer to the immigrant people they pastored, whose movement west was largely fueled by hope. American Catholics had embraced political modernity in the years surrounding the nation's War for Independence. The frontier experience confirmed and strengthened that orientation, leaving in its wake a Catholicism open to the nation's democratic culture and even its pluralism. This openness was harder to discern by the turn of the twentieth century, with the rise of Catholic institutional separatism and a strengthened emphasis on the papacy as a locus of Catholic identity. But it was never extinguished. The American bishops at Vatican II, conservatives almost to a man, made as a group only one significant contribution to the work of that great reforming conclave—their efforts in support of its Declaration on Religious Liberty.[19]

Lay Religious Practice

Frontier Catholics in the early days of settlement nearly always lived without a resident priest. Visits from itinerant clergy came only at lengthy intervals, and some Catholics never saw a priest at all. Almost no frontier bishop, at least early on, had a remotely accurate notion of how many Catholics were in his charge or precisely where they were located. "On my trip to Baltimore I found fifty Catholic families in the State of Ohio," Bardstown's Bishop Benedict Joseph Flaget reported in 1815, when that state had no resident Catholic clergy but lay within Bardstown's jurisdictional boundaries. "I heard there are many others." Years of living without a priest, Flaget feared, had left these newly discovered Catholics in something close to a pagan state. "Many of those I met have almost forgotten their religion and they are bringing up their children in complete ignorance." Nearly every frontier bishop and priest expressed similar anxieties. But how to address the problem when clergy were so few in number?[20]

One popular strategy was the parish mission—an intense course of sermons, preached by a visiting missionary, that aimed at stirring sorrow for sin and fear of its punishment. A mission's success was invariably measured by the numbers who went to confession. Although superficially similar to the Protestant revivals sweeping the antebellum nation, the Catholic mission originated in sixteenth-century Europe and had long been a staple of Catholic practice there. Cincinnati's Bishop Fenwick, appointed to that new diocese in 1821, preached an eight-day mission at his cathedral at the close of 1826 and then, in the company of two priests, toured Ohio for the next eight months preaching missions at stops along the way. Bardstown's Flaget did the same, as did several other frontier prelates. Gratifying results were reported from such disparate locales as Alabama, Louisiana, and Missouri, along with Kentucky and Ohio.[21]

The arrival in the United States of the first Redemptorist priests in 1832—their order specialized in mission preaching—was a major assist to the frontier bishops. Those in Indiana and Michigan were the first to employ them, sending two-man teams as spiritual "shock troops" to remote areas of their dioceses. "Husbands with their wives and children devoted themselves to learning the catechism," the bishop of Detroit noted of an 1843 mission at long-neglected Saginaw, "and after an assiduous preparation of eight days, all approached the sacraments with tears of joy." The Jesuits were increasingly active as mission preachers too. An 1848 German-language mission preached at Oldenburg, Illinois, by the Jesuit Francis X. Weninger was a model of its kind: "he ... drew tears of repentance and consolation from the eyes of his hearers," according to the *Cincinnati Wahrheitsfreund*. "Often there was general sobbing and weeping throughout the church."[22]

Missions, however, were only a stopgap. Many Catholics thus "awakened" might go for months or even years before seeing a priest again. How to keep faith and a Catholic identity alive in the interim? Parents were charged with grave responsibility in this regard, as Jean Cheverus, later bishop of Boston, reminded a Maine father of his recent acquaintance in 1798 in an early example of what became standard pastoral counsel. His family should pray both morning and evening, Cheverus instructed Roger Hanly, who had emigrated from Ireland with his brother in 1770. They should keep the church's prescribed days of fast and abstinence and avoid non-Catholic worship. (Local Catholics had been accustomed, at least on occasion, to attend the only church in town, which belonged to the Congregationalists.) On Sundays, "if possible," Cheverus continued, the Hanlys should gather with their Catholic neighbors "to read in the morning the prayers & instructions of the Mass with at least one chapter in the poor man's catechism." Sunday afternoons should be given over to devotions and spiritual reading, for which Cheverus recommended Challoner's *Garden of the Soul*. "Take care to be well prepared for confession and for receiving the blessed Sacrament, against the next time that you will have a Catholic priest with you." The seed, in this instance, fell on good ground: a prayer book used in those distant days was passed down the Hanly generations and still survives.[23]

Not every abandoned Catholic was as well placed as Roger Hanly to keep faith alive in the long-term absence of a priest. Some were illiterate, while a few had been decades without recourse to the sacraments. When a group of French Catholics in Oregon petitioned in 1834 for a priest to be sent to them, the auxiliary bishop of Quebec—Oregon then being claimed by Great Britain—confessed that he had none to send them. Himself resident in Manitoba, he would try to visit once the weather permitted. In the interim, Bishop Joseph-Norbert Provencher counseled gently, "Raise your children the best way you can. Teach them what you know of religion." No talk here of Sunday assemblies or spiritual reading! Still, this probably illiterate group was eager for a priest, despite years away from the sacraments. Father John-Marie Odin, C.M., the newly appointed Vicar Apostolic of Texas, encountered a similarly abandoned group in 1841, when he arrived in San Antonio. The Mexican population there had not seen a priest in years—not, in some cases, since suppression of the local Franciscan missions in 1812. But Odin was greeted with tears of joy. "Some among them cried out that they did not fear death any longer now that heaven had sent them Fathers to assist them in their last moment."[24]

There were certainly Catholics in priest-poor locales who drifted away from the church. Others, still nominally Catholic, clung to lax religious habits even after a priest had come to live in their midst. Jesuits ministering to a long-neglected French population in Missouri commented sourly in 1837 on the males among them, most of whom never received the sacraments and some of whom seldom attended Mass. "Unless the mothers, for the most part pious enough, bring the children to church, the bad example of the fathers will spoil them." Complaints of this sort were common in the antebellum years, with the French an especially popular target, although priests complained bitterly too on occasion about the Irish and even the Germans. Men like these were not likely to have been unbelievers in any meaningful sense, theirs being a world where theism in some form was the near-universal default. Nor were they necessarily unremittingly hostile to the church. If staying home on Sunday morning was a badge of male privilege in their communities, the church nearly always had the final word. "All are glad enough to receive the last sacraments," according to the Missouri Jesuits with specific reference to the more troublesome of the male laity.[25]

The historical record is mostly silent when it comes to the lay perspective on life in a priest-poor world. Hence the value of surviving correspondence between an antebellum Michigan couple who lived in a rural community that seldom saw a priest. James Birney, born in Vermont to Irish immigrants in 1821, and Bridget McClear, born in County Tyrone in 1820, met in Bunkerhill, Michigan, in 1840 when their families relocated there—James's from Ohio, Bridget's from Connecticut—to try their hand at farming. The couple was quickly betrothed, although Bridget returned to Connecticut for several subsequent years to work in the carpet mills. Finally flush with cash, James and Bridget were married by a Catholic priest in 1845, having traveled a good many miles for the privilege. Bunkerhill had only a handful of Catholic families at midcentury and was distant from the nearest community with a resident priest. A Mass was not said in Bunker-hill until 1845, after which the village was occasionally visited by itinerant clergy. From 1858 until 1867, a priest came at three-month intervals from Jackson, weather and the roads permitting. The parish gained a resident pastor in 1868 but reverted again to mission status between 1873 and 1905.

Thus for more than twenty years of their marriage, James and Bridget Birney lived in a village where Mass was at best an occasional event. Their daughter Jane, born in 1846, wrote to her father after her confirmation at Jackson in 1859, "saturday knight was the first time i ever was in a catholic church." If the Birneys gathered with their Catholic neighbors for Sunday prayer and spiritual reading, the surviving record does not say so. Local Catholics did organize a Sunday school, although it met intermittently, perhaps because local roads were impassable for portions of the year. Bridget herself, professing unease, prepared two of her three children for first communion and confirmation, sacraments usually received on the same day when the candidate was twelve or thirteen. "You know children ne[e]ds a great deal of instructions. More than I am capable of giving them." Bunkerhill had a Cath-olic cemetery by the 1850s—graveside services, conducted by a layman, pre-sumably proceeded according to a recognizably Catholic ritual—and local Catholics in the mid-1860s built a modest church.[26]

Bunkerhill was deep in Protestant territory, and the 1840s saw an up-surge in Protestant militancy and millenarian movements in particular. There were disciples of William Miller, who famously predicted the Second Coming for 1844, in both Bunkerhill and the Connecticut village where Bridget was then working. "Miller and his desipels have got people so far persuaded into his doctrine that many have give up work and are preparing to leave this world on or before the first or third day of April," Bridget in-formed James. Both James and Bridget at the time were afflicted by religious doubts, which they had apparently discussed at length prior to Bridget's de-parture. Although the exact nature of those doubts is unclear, they appear to have centered on specifics of Catholic doctrine—hardly surprising, given the couple's immersion in a suddenly ebullient Protestant environment. Neither had access to a priest for counsel, Bridget's Connecticut village be-ing just as bereft in this regard as Bunkerhill. And yet both opted ultimately for their inheritance as Catholics, aided perhaps by revulsion at the warring claims of Protestant sectarians, anti-Catholic to a man. "The[y] cannot all be right," as Bridget put it. "There is but one way to heaven."[27]

The Birneys were Catholics for the rest of their lives, passing a lively faith on to their children. Subsequent family generations produced a priest and two women religious. But the austerity of their religious imaginations, at least as revealed in letters exchanged by the couple at a time of crisis, seems anything but conventionally Catholic. In the year between the summers of 1859 and 1860, when James was in California prospecting unsuccessfully for gold, epidemic disease—including malaria—repeatedly swept the Bunkerhill region. Large numbers died, including James's brother Charles. Grief-stricken, anxious, and lonely, James and Bridget each struggled with faith in a merciful God. But the language with which they did so, at least in their letters, was nowhere peculiarly Catholic. Neither mentioned the saints or the Virgin Mary or the virtue of praying for the dead. The Birney's God was wholly transcendent—a God whose providence was sure but whose ways were mysterious. Save for Bridget's assuring James that Charles had received the last sacraments, this particular cache of letters might have been written by Calvinists. Their private prayers may well have been different—more emotively Catholic in tone and substance. Still, the years of infrequent priest's visits and limited exposure to communal devotions do seem to have left their mark.

Most frontier regions grew up quickly. As nodes of settlement expanded and the supply of clergy grew, more and more former frontier Catholics found themselves living near a church with a resident priest. The small-town parish differed in certain ways from its big-city counterpart, at least in the mid-nineteenth century. It was seldom the exclusive property of a single ethnic group and, given its pastor's likely obligations to a mission church or two, its devotional life was apt to be less extensive. But small-town Catholicism at its best possessed genuine vitality. Father John De Néve's parish at Niles, in rural southwestern Michigan, was apparently a model. "I have here already a well-organized community, a real Flemish parish," he wrote in 1859 to a friend in Flanders. (His parishioners, in point of fact, were mostly Irish.) "On Sunday, masses, instruction, vespers, the rosary—everything is fixed as among you." Even the parish church at Niles was authentically "Belgian," despite being built of wood, with an elaborate high altar and a fine engraving of the Immaculate Conception—the latter a gift from a Belgian Marian sodality. The church itself was named in honor of Mary's Immaculate Conception, the distinctively Catholic dogma—declared as such by Pope Pius IX in 1854—that Mary was born untainted by original sin.[28]

De Néve, like most of his fellow priests, doubtless encouraged his parishioners to confess and receive communion more frequently than their forebears had done—perhaps four times a year for the lukewarm and monthly for the devout. Only a minority would have complied, most of them women. Old habits die hard, and many adults continued to receive the sacraments only once or twice a year. Tensions over standards of conduct may have played a role as well. De Néve, like many of his confreres, inveighed against strong drink and dancing; some period priests even preached against such innocuous pastimes as parish picnics, with predictable results. But in parishes with a resident priest, a substantial majority of Catholics do seem to have been regularly present at Mass—an outcome that certain frontier clergy had despaired of achieving. All but a stubborn remnant, overwhelmingly male, fulfilled their "Easter duty" to confess and receive communion annually during the Easter liturgical season. That stubborn remnant, in De Néve's view, needed constant but tactful monitoring, and the project was close to his heart even after he left the United States. "Has James Finnegan been to his Easter duty?" he inquired from Belgium of his successor at Niles in 1860. "Would you deem it advisable for me to write to him, not mentioning anything, but inquiring?" But De Néve's hopes, like those of his confreres, rested mainly with the parish children. A resident priest meant regular catechetical instruction through which the young could be socialized to a more exacting standard of sacramental practice.[29]

Lay practice among rural and small-town Catholics varied widely at midcentury, with the presence of a resident priest seeming to make a critical difference. Two examples illustrate what might be called the extremes. Nearly 40 percent of the congregation at St. Charles Church in Newport, Michigan, failed to make their Easter duty in 1868, although a priest was by then saying Mass there bimonthly after a long history of neglect. "About fifty mans and fifty womans" had not received the sacraments "for years," according to the visiting missionary, a Frenchman like many in the congregation, and local Catholics continued as in frontier times to marry before a justice of the peace. A mostly German parish in Jasper, Indiana—one blessed early on by a resident priest—provides a striking contrast, as described in 1843 by Mother Théodore Guérin of the Sisters of Providence, only recently arrived from France. "The congregation is a very fervent one," she wrote. "During the six months that the pastor had been absent the good Germans who composed it were wont to come seven or eight miles to sing hymns in the church." On the Feast of the Ascension, which is celebrated on a Thursday, the entire parish participated in a ten-mile procession, after which all attended Mass and listened to two lengthy sermons, the first in English and the second in German. "I confess I was much fatigued myself," Mother Guérin acknowledged, "and I will add to my shame, that my fervor was put to the blush when I saw those true and sincere Christians begin again their pious procession." The entire congregation "set out on their homeward course, chanting hymns and sacred songs."[30]

Women Religious

On the frontier, as in more settled portions of the nation, women were far more willing than men to embrace a religious vocation. Frontier Kentucky, poor in priests, gave birth to no fewer than three religious communities for women. Early in 1812, three young women who had been teaching school in Kentucky's first Catholic settlement asked for and received a rule of religious life from Father Charles Nerinckx. The Sisters of Loretto at the Foot of the Cross, as the infant community was known, was devoted mainly to teaching. Just months thereafter, upon hearing a sermon on the religious life from the Sulpician John Baptist David, another two women—soon joined by a third—sought permission from him to live as religious. The three formed the nucleus of the Sisters of Charity of Nazareth, which grew in the space of a generation to 145 members. A similar sermon, this one preached by the Dominican Samuel Wilson, resulted in 1822 in the birth of the Kentucky Dominican Sisters, who opened a second convent in Ohio in 1830. These indigenous congregations did not labor alone. In 1818, Religious of the Sacred Heart came from France to frontier St. Louis, where they founded the city's first school.

Especially in the early years of women's communities on the frontier, their recruits were often very young. It was not unusual for a girl to enter as a postulant at the age of sixteen; the Sisters of Loretto had entrants who were as young as twelve. Catherine Spalding, the distinguished first superior of the Sisters of Charity of Nazareth, was elected to that office in 1813 at the age of nineteen. Few early entrants, in all likelihood, had much in the way of formal schooling, opportunities for such being limited in frontier districts. A few were clearly illiterate. (The same was apparently true of students at the earliest frontier seminaries. Bardtown's Bishop Flaget noted in 1815, with regard to a seminary he had opened four years earlier, that "very many of the pupils had to be instructed . . . in the very elements of reading and writing.") Every woman's community in the antebellum years suffered from appalling poverty, with sisters sometimes subjected to conditions of life that were seriously detrimental to health. Most orders experienced a high incidence of tuberculosis, an affliction greatly exacerbated by overcrowded quarters, spartan diets, and inadequate heat in the winter. The Sisters of Loretto, on whom Nerinckx had imposed a rule of unusual severity, lost twenty-four members under the age of thirty to disease in the space of eleven years.[31]

Poor though they were in material resources, women's communities on the frontier attracted a steady stream of recruits, many of them fired by missionary zeal. Horrified by the lodgings provided her sisters at one of her order's Indiana schools—the "log house open to every breeze" had neither bedding nor a door lock—Mother Guérin proposed removing them. But "these poor dear children pressed me so urgently and extolled so highly the happiness of their position and the good they could do and had already done that I decided upon leaving them there until the retreat." Ill-prepared sisters, fired by the same spiritual energy, somehow acquired sufficient learning to staff a growing number of schools, a few of which acquired national reputations. Every order established at least one "female academy," which accommodated boarders as well as day students. The academies were frankly aimed at the affluent—they charged tuition and supplemented their academic offerings with instruction in such female ornamentals as embroidery—and for this reason a majority of their boarding students prior to the Civil War were Protestants. Revenues generated by the academies—tuition plus fees for private instruction in music—enabled each community to staff "free schools" as well, where day pupils were taught the academic basics. Such schools were the first tuition-free educational institutions in a number of frontier communities.[32]

Every frontier community also cared for orphans, housing them at their boarding academies and sometimes their convents. Several freestanding orphanages were founded in the then-frontier states in the 1830s, in the

wake of the decade's great cholera epidemics. The Sisters of Charity of Nazareth, for example, staffed St. Vincent's Orphan Asylum at Louisville after
its establishment in 1832. Very little is known about St. Vincent's early years
or indeed those of its counterparts elsewhere. An 1849 letter from Sister of
Charity Margaret George does sketch the daily program at St. Vincent's,
which in August 1849 housed 137 children, almost half of them under the
age of six. Even the youngest were expected to follow a convent-like daily
routine—morning prayer at 5:30 a.m., Mass at 6:30, breakfast at 7:00, followed by lessons for those aged three and older, midday prayer and dinner,
and additional lessons in the afternoon. "The only chance these poor children have for education is while they are with us, therefore, we should do all
we can for them." Each sister "fine-combed" about twenty children every
day in order to stem an apparently chronic infestation of lice. A few of the
younger children had recently been adopted, according to Sister Margaret,
and others had been "placed out," which meant that a child went to live with
a family in exchange for domestic or other labor. All of the children, it was
hoped, would be "placed out" by the time they arrived at early adolescence.[33]

Cholera returned to the United States on a number of occasions after
the initial epidemic in 1832, generating ever more orphans and creating
short-term crises with regard to medical care. Every woman's community on
the frontier provided nurses during cholera and other epidemics, as did their
counterparts in more settled parts of the country. Such service commanded
the admiration of even hitherto-hostile Protestants. Many antebellum sisters
worked at least occasionally as nurses, but relatively few orders staffed hospitals on a permanent basis prior to the Civil War. Those that did often labored
under primitive conditions, as suggested by an 1845 account of the opening
of St. Mary's Hospital in frontier Detroit by the Emmitsburg Sisters of Charity. The local bishop, according to Sister Rosaline Brown, "tried to impress on
the minds of the people, that their duty was to help us, by bringing bedding
and articles to furnish the wards. They brought us a few bedticks, somewhat
longer than pillow-ticks, with a little straw in them." Still, St. Mary's was the
city's first permanent hospital and as such a major contribution to civic welfare. A subsequent donation of land and generous response to the sisters'
efforts to raise a building fund resulted in a new "St. Mary's House for Inva-
lids" late in 1850, with space for more than one hundred patients.[34]

Women religious occupied an ambiguous status everywhere in the
antebellum United States but perhaps especially on the frontier. In their

Log cabin hospital in St. Louis, founded by the Sisters of Charity, ca. 1840s
(Courtesy of the Daughters of Charity, Province of St. Louise Archives,
Emmitsburg, Maryland)

distinctive habits, they embodied Catholic otherness in a particularly visible
way. (Many sisters donned "civilian" clothing when obliged to travel beyond
their home territory.) Their lifelong celibacy challenged cultural assumptions about woman's supposedly dependent nature and her God-ordained
destiny as wife and mother. The various institutions the sisters established
challenged gender norms as well, since they were governed by female authority. That authority could be seductive, at least in the eyes of certain Protestants, who cited the growing ranks of Catholic "female academies" as
particularly menacing. A majority of those schools in the antebellum
decades—there were over two hundred by 1860—were located in recently
settled regions of the South and Midwest, where public education was still
poorly developed. Probably a majority of their pupils were Protestants—the
principal cause for alarm. Admiring their sister-teachers, as they were bound
to do, Protestant girls might be tempted to convert—no matter that every
academy assured non-Catholic parents that its teachers would not prosely-
tize. At the very least, such a starstruck youngster would, in the words of one
Protestant critic, "defend the Sisters all her life and on all occasions."[35]

At the same time, a great many non-Catholics admired the sisters' contributions to education and social welfare—again, especially on the frontier, where civil society was being built from scratch. Those contributions multiplied as the number of sisters grew. There were fewer than one thousand women religious serving in the United States as of 1835 but almost five thousand on the eve of the Civil War, by which time the nation was home to as many as sixty communities of women. Many had been recruited from Europe, especially after 1840 and the advent of mass immigration from Ireland and Germany. Ireland was a particularly fertile source of sisters, but France and Germany were important too. For some Protestant critics, the sisters' growing numbers simply amplified the threat they represented. But for many others, gratitude tempered fear and often conquered it. "What citizen is there who will not hail the coming of these Sisters of Mercy as among the choicest of blessings for our city?" asked the *Chicago Daily Democrat* in 1846 with regard to a recent announcement that sisters from Ireland would soon open a local school. Sisters, like Catholics generally, remained "other" in many respects, and Catholic leaders worked hard to shore up communal boundaries, even in recently settled places. Frontier conditions, however, placed a premium on what might be called an ecumenism of necessity, of which Catholics were the principal beneficiaries.[36]

An Urban Stronghold

The antebellum decades saw the beginnings of mass immigration to the United States—a development of immense and enduring importance for American Catholicism. Roughly one and a half million immigrants from what would soon be the nation of Germany arrived prior to the Civil War, most of them after 1830. Perhaps 30 percent were at least nominally Catholic. The Irish arrived in even larger numbers: more than 260,000 between 1820 and 1840, followed by a flood— some one and a half million between 1845 and 1854—of desperately poor refugees from a massive famine in Ireland. An additional million had arrived by 1870. Prior to the 1830s, a majority of Irish immigrants were Protestants, many of them Ulster Presbyterians—a good fit, religiously speaking, for a host nation whose history had been so profoundly shaped by Calvinist Christianity. But over the course of the 1830s, growing numbers of Catholic peasants joined the migrant stream; they probably made up a majority of those arriving from Ireland by the early 1840s. The outflow from Ireland occasioned by the Great Famine of the mid- to late 1840s was almost entirely Catholic, as was post-Famine emigration in the 1850s.

The arrival of so many Catholic immigrants gave a hitherto marginal church—marginal, at least, with regard to the American landscape—a startling new visibility. Whether accurately or not, the Catholic Church was generally reckoned by the 1850s to be the single largest denomination in the United States. That visibility was heightened by the tendency—overwhelming in the case of the Irish—of Catholic immigrants to settle in cities. By 1850, Irish-born residents made up roughly a quarter of the population in both New York and Boston and were nearly as prominent a presence in Philadelphia. With Irish immigrants heavily concentrated along the eastern seaboard, German immigrants often moved west, where many hoped to farm. But significant numbers of Germans also settled in such burgeoning cities as St. Louis, Cincinnati, and Milwaukee, which together defined an area known as the "German triangle." Along with visibility, concentration in cities meant Catholic political power—something new on the American scene and predictably alarming to custodians of the established order.

The leaders of the American church were ill prepared for the immigrant influx, given the dearth of clergy and a severely limited number of urban churches. But numbers were the least of their problems. Many of the Catholics arriving from Ireland in the antebellum years had hardly been catechized at all. Nor had they been habituated to anything approaching the regular practice of their religion. (Ireland's storied religious discipline mostly postdates the Famine.) Close to half the arriving Irish were illiterate, and a sizable minority had at best a limited mastery of English. Those who fled the Famine were for the most part desperately poor; all were deeply traumatized. The Germans, including the Catholics among them, were better equipped for American success, being notably more prosperous than the Irish upon their arrival and typically possessing marketable skills. Unlike the Irish, many of whom arrived as lone individuals, most Germans came in family groups—a balm for immigrant loneliness and, in the eyes of their American neighbors, a reassuring sign of social stability. Few of the Germans spoke English, however, and nearly all hoped—indeed, expected—to retain their ancestral language and customs and hand them on to the next generation. What this meant for the future of an ostensibly American Catholic Church was by no means clear.[1]

Catholic leaders, then—and here we speak mainly of the nation's bishops—faced a daunting agenda. They had somehow to recruit enough priests to tend their vastly expanded flock and see to the building of sufficient churches to accommodate the literal hordes of the faithful. They had somehow to catechize an unlettered people whose principal focus was survival and accustom them to an alien mode of religious discipline. Bodies as well as souls needed help: even large cities in the antebellum years made scant provision for the hungry, sick, orphaned, and otherwise dependent.

And immigrant children needed schooling, all the more so in those many cases in which their parents were illiterate. Public schools were increasingly available by the 1830s in most of the nation's cities, although southern cities lagged in this regard. But those schools nearly always bore a distinctively Protestant stamp with regard to their ethos and curricular content, which posed yet another problem for the nation's bishops. The bishops were also troubled by ethnic divisions among the faithful—hardly a new phenomenon but greatly exacerbated by the explosion in immigrant numbers.

Especially in the nation's cities, the bishops confronted their daunting agenda in an increasingly hostile environment. Anti-Catholicism, bred in the Anglo-American bone, had been at relatively low ebb since the days of the Revolution. But rapid growth in the population of Catholic immigrants in the 1830s triggered its resurgence, which grew in reach and intensity until the Civil War and occasionally gave rise to violence. Anti-Catholic propaganda—quasi-pornography, in a good many cases—circulated widely in these years, featuring sexually voracious priests who seduced young women in the confessional and ravished nuns who were allegedly imprisoned in convents for precisely this purpose. The best-known example of the genre, *Awful Disclosures of the Hotel Dieu Nunnery* by the pseudonymous Maria Monk, was a runaway best-seller from the time of its publication in 1836 until the eve of the Civil War. When a mob composed mostly of Scots-Presbyterian bricklayers torched an Ursuline convent in the Charlestown section of Boston in 1834, the rioters justified the action—in the words of a witness at the subsequent trial—by claiming that "bishops and priests pretended to live without wives, but that the nuns were kept to supply the deficiency in this particular." The popularity of "convent inspection" measures, which became law in several states, was rooted in the same assumption.[2]

Such a climate greatly complicated the exercise of episcopal leadership. Even matters internal to the church—disciplining a fractious priest or attempting to secure at law episcopal ownership of parish properties—could easily generate a popular backlash. Matters touching on public questions were even more explosive. Should a bishop demand public funding for Catholic schools as a matter of right or simply attempt to prevent the "Protestant" King James Bible from being read in the public schools, he risked stirring popular violence. Rioting in two of Philadelphia's working-class suburbs triggered by the "Bible question" killed scores in 1844 and resulted in the burning of two Catholic churches. Similar, if less lethal,

URSULINE COMMUNITY,
MOUNT BENEDICT—CHARLESTOWN, MASSACHUSETTS.

Sketch of the Ursuline convent, Mount Benedict, Charlestown,
Massachusetts, undated (Courtesy of the American Catholic History
Research Center and University Archives [ACUA], the Catholic University
of America, Washington, DC)

clashes occurred elsewhere, most notably at Louisville in 1855, where the probable death toll stood at twenty-two. At the same time, a climate so hostile to Catholics seemed to a great many bishops to require institutional separatism—not just Catholic schools but colleges too, along with orphanages, hospitals, and reformatories. (Irish Catholics at the time constituted a grossly disproportionate share of the urban prison population.) But how to achieve so ambitious a goal when so many Catholic immigrants lived in dire poverty?

Against these seemingly insuperable odds, the bishops achieved remarkable progress in the antebellum years with regard to both institutional development and consolidation of their own authority. When John Hughes arrived in New York in 1837 as coadjutor bishop to John Dubois, the city had just seven Catholic churches. Over the course of his episcopal reign—he became bishop in his own right in 1839 and died in office in 1864—Hughes oversaw the building of over one hundred churches, twenty-five of them in his See city, and laid the foundation for what would eventually be a full-fledged system of Catholic schools. Most of the churches were heavily indebted; a few congregations were forced into bankruptcy during the era's recurrent recessions. But the achievement stands. Unlike his hapless predecessor, Hughes ruled his diocese—archdiocese after 1850—with an iron hand, tolerating no dissent among the clergy or claims to authority on the part of lay trustees. "I will suffer no man in my diocese that I cannot control," Hughes allegedly told journalist Orestes Brownson, perhaps the most prominent convert of the day. Hughes wielded power in the secular sphere as well, particularly with regard to public funding for Catholic schools, around which issue he mobilized Catholic voters in frankly aggressive fashion. Never a team player, he was not popular with his fellow bishops, the more influential of whom intervened with Rome to prevent his being named a cardinal. But he stood nonetheless for the future. If bishops in subsequent generations were not generally cast in his flamboyant mode, they shared his assumptions about the episcopal office.[3]

Cities other than New York also recorded dramatic gains in the number of churches, schools, and Catholic charitable institutions. But urban Catholicism on the eve of the Civil War was still an ecclesial work in progress. Immigrant numbers and need dwarfed even ambitious building programs, and a good many urban Catholics remained only loosely connected to the church. New York's new St. Patrick's Cathedral, its gothic splendor even today dominating its stretch of fashionable Fifth Avenue, provides an apt metaphor. (The original St. Patrick's, dedicated in 1815, was tucked away on Mott Street in lower Manhattan.) Archbishop Hughes blessed the cornerstone of his new cathedral in 1858 before an exultant crowd of more than sixty thousand. But in 1860 building tradesmen at the site struck for higher wages, and work was suspended for the next five years. The cathedral was not completed until 1878, some twelve years after Hughes's death; its famed spires date only from 1888, when their addition made St. Patrick's for a time New York's tallest structure.

St. Patrick's stood at its completion not simply for immigrant pride and sacrifice but for a Catholicism far removed from the genteel interiority of colonial Maryland's Catholic elite. Immigrant Catholicism was simultaneously more defensive than the Maryland variety and far more aggressive in its self-presentation. St. Patrick's flamboyance and massive size both trumpeted Catholic power and embodied a fortress mentality. The devotional ethos of the immigrant church preached a bleak view of the human condition: morally incapacitated by original sin, individuals journeying to-ward death and judgment were constantly endangered by contact with a hostile world. Hence the heavy emphasis on intercessors—the Virgin and a panoply of saints—for help and protection, on communal rather than pri-vate devotions, and on the hierarchical nature of the church. Popular inter-est in the miraculous quickened, as did the appeal of indulgenced devotions, with their intimate link to the papacy. Piety of this sort could easily under-gird tribalism. But it provided comfort too and cohesion for a Catholic people divided by class and ethnicity.[4]

Trusteeism

Prior to the 1830s, urban Catholic populations were fairly inconspicuous. Catholics invariably constituted a small minority in the local population, and some were modestly prosperous. Every city, moreover, had at least a sprinkling of high-status Catholic families whose visibility afforded their church a certain social protection. Philadelphia's Matthew Carey, to pick a conspicuous example, was both a leading Catholic layman—the young na-tion's most prominent publisher, he produced the first American edition of the Catholic Douai-Rheims Bible—and an indisputable member of the city's social elite. (His grandson, not raised a Catholic, was Henry H. C. Lea, a distinguished historian whose still useful work is informed by a deep-rooted anti-Catholicism.) The first generation of American bishops was also cast in a gentlemanly mode. Boston's John Cheverus moved as easily in Boston society as John Carroll did in Baltimore, and both men had their portraits done by Gilbert Stuart. Speculating in 1813 on the future of inter-confessional relations in the United States, Harvard's president John Thorn-ton Kirkland could imagine a time when "it may be lawful for us to believe in the compatibility of the Romanish faith with a capacity for salvation and admit the possible, nay more, the presumptive Christianity of a virtuous and devout Roman Catholic."[5]

Urban Catholicism did cease to be inconspicuous—a generally happy condition—when parishes were wracked by conflict. This happened on typically protracted occasions prior to the 1830s in New York, Philadelphia, Baltimore, Norfolk, New Orleans, and other locations as well. The cause, nearly always, was "trusteeism." Almost every American parish in these years had a board of lay trustees that held title to and managed parish properties; in the absence of a resident priest, trustees might also serve as lay religious leaders. Trouble arose in those instances—few in number but explosive in outcome—when local trustees claimed the right to hire and fire the parish clergy, a claim that put them at odds not just with the bishop but usually with a faction in the congregation too. When John Carroll was prevented from saying Mass at New York's St. Peter's Church in 1788, his assailants were parishioners—mostly "people of little importance and Irish," in Carroll's words—who supported a pastor opposed by the board of trustees. The pastor's removal from his post—an outcome, in this instance, favored by Carroll—was finally secured by the trustees going to court. The priest in question, an Irish Capuchin, subsequently left the country.[6]

Philadelphia Catholicism was bedeviled by conflict for many of the years between 1788 and the early 1830s. Ethnic rivalries were a principal cause. Philadelphia's German Catholics seceded from the city's St. Mary's parish as early as 1788, when they established Holy Trinity Church as a distinctively German entity. Trinity's trustees, themselves elected, insisted from the first on the right to choose their pastor—an insistence that over the years gave rise to lawsuits, excommunications, threats of violence, and lurid newspaper headlines. Apparently radicalized in the course of battle, Trinity's trustees eventually championed the creation of a separate diocese for German Catholics in the United States, who would then elect their bishop. St. Mary's, founded in 1765, was quiescent in its early years. But from 1812 until the early 1830s, the parish plunged repeatedly into conflict, with trustee elections in the early 1820s precipitating violent clashes between rival factions in the congregation. St. Mary's was mostly Irish, and its troubles were fueled in good part by class antagonism. But ethnic rhetoric still featured, with one side accusing the other of being veritable Orangemen, which is to say Irish Protestants. At St. Mary's, as at Holy Trinity, dissenters asserted the laity's right to elect the local bishop.[7]

Conflicts like these were occasioned by more than class and ethnic hostility, important as those factors were. The period's radical shortage of priests played an often critical role. Although priests in a mission country like the young United States had virtually no rights in canon law, their limited numbers gave them leverage in contests with a bishop. On more than one occasion, a priest chosen as pastor by parish trustees and subsequently ordered by his bishop to vacate the post simply refused to do so. Nor could a bishop easily discipline a man who divided his parish by cultivating a particular class or ethnic base. With whom would the bishop replace him? American bishops prior to the 1830s, moreover, seldom possessed legal title to parish properties—a distinct disadvantage when disputes with trustees went to court. The example of local Protestant congregations, many of which chose their own clergy, was a factor too, along with period expansion of the suffrage to ever larger numbers of adult white men. Trustees and their supporters regularly invoked republican principles. The dissenting factions at St. Mary's in Philadelphia issued a call to the nation's Catholics in 1821 to establish "some general system": "an uniform system—whereby our rights can be secured."[8]

The republican rhetoric deployed by trustees and their supporters often drew the approval of non-Catholic observers, who interpreted intrachurch conflicts in terms of their own revolutionary heritage and its putative Protestant roots. But their sympathy was a double-edged sword, since the tyrant against whom the trustees struggled was nearly always the local bishop. Nativists also invoked these conflicts as evidence of the inherently autocratic nature of the church. The trustees, for their part, were doubtless sincere in their talk of inalienable rights. But if they were democrats, the democracy they endorsed was a limited one. Nearly every parish that elected its trustees confined the suffrage to those adult male members who rented a pew, which limited the parish electorate to as little as 10 percent of the congregation. (The annual renting of pews, with those at the front of the church commanding the highest prices, was a common mode of parish support in the United States for much of the nineteenth century.) Some parishes, Philadelphia's St. Mary's among them, explicitly limited the suffrage to white pewholders; it goes without saying that no women could vote. Trustees, in consequence, were typically prosperous men of property who enjoyed long tenure in office.[9]

The incidence and severity of "trusteeism" conflicts ebbed in the 1830s and 1840s. The bishops meeting at the First Provincial Council in 1829 decreed that no new churches should be built unless deeds to the property were first consigned to the local bishop. Such legislation could not always be enforced. But individual bishops subsequently petitioned the various state legislatures to secure this right at law. The archbishop of Baltimore was made owner as a "corporation sole" of all church properties in his jurisdiction by the Maryland legislature in 1833, and most other states eventually followed suit. The bishops also resolved at their 1829 meeting to impose a uniform standard of discipline on the parish clergy. In this respect too, enforcement was not always easy. But especially with regard to urban priests, bishops by the 1840s had far more control than had earlier been the case. Perhaps most important, the Catholic immigrants who arrived in the 1830s and 1840s, many of them poor and unlettered, evinced little interest in parish governance or their putative rights as laity. In the event of parish conflict, they were likely to side with the bishop. As immigrant numbers grew, therefore, the trustees' power waned. By the eve of the Civil War, trustees in city parishes were generally appointed by the pastor or bishop rather than elected by the pewholders.[10]

The Immigrant Church

The quickening of Catholic immigration in the 1830s made urban Catholics a far more visible population than they had previously been. Irish Catholics outnumbered Germans in each of the East Coast's principal cities, and the Irish as a group were significantly poorer. Thus the church's new visibility came with an aura of social danger—a palpable threat to the Anglo-American ideal of cities as composed primarily of the "middling sort." That immigrant ships brought cholera to the United States for the first time in 1832 simply magnified the unease. But the Irish who arrived prior to 1846, poor though they typically were, were not the traumatized victims of famine. Some achieved a degree of respectability by dint of hard work and sober living. Temperance was a popular cause among them: more than five thousand Philadelphia Catholics had taken the pledge within months of the founding of the city's Catholic Total Abstinence Society in 1840, and each of the city's predominantly Irish parishes had established a temperance organization before the year was out. "Respectables" like these not infrequently looked on the Famine Irish—the flood that arrived between 1846 and the early 1850s—as threats to their own security.[11]

Immigrant numbers do much to explain the resurgence of popular anti-Catholicism in the 1830s and after. The instability of the U.S. economy, then in the early stages of industrialization, was a factor too. Immigrant numbers were simply more threatening in the context of economic depression, such as characterized the years between 1837 and 1843—precisely the years when "Native American" political parties proliferated in the nation's cities. (Most such parties were short-lived, but anti-immigrant forces coalesced in the 1850s to form the nativist American Party, which functioned— if briefly—on close to a national level.) Working-class fears and resentments clearly fueled rioting in 1844 between Irish weavers, most but not all of them Catholic, and Protestant workers in Kensington, then an industrial suburb of Philadelphia. Although Catholic as well as Protestant elites denounced the violence on both sides, Philadelphia's nativist party swept local elections late in 1844 in each of the city's working-class districts. In that same year, nativist parties enjoyed success in Boston and elected a mayor in New York.[12]

Famine immigration from Ireland intensified nativism and largely explains its emergence as a national political movement. Nearly every Famine immigrant was desperate, and the poorest and sickest invariably settled in the port where they entered the country. Boston and New York, especially, but other East Coast cities too were soon overwhelmed by the needs of their new populations. Once-respectable districts were transformed, seemingly overnight, into congested immigrant slums, as single-family houses and commercial buildings were subdivided into tenements and shoddily constructed rooming houses sprang up in former back gardens. With municipal sanitation still in a primitive state, the immigrant districts were potent breeders of disease. Successive cholera epidemics were incubated in the immigrant slums, while tuberculosis took a fearful toll among the immigrants themselves. The slums bred crime as well, and urban crime soared as the immigrant flood intensified. Irish Catholics were disproportionately represented in the jails of nearly every city, with public drunkenness and prostitution looming large among their offenses. They were overrepresented too in municipal institutions for the radically dependent. Sixty-four percent of those admitted to New York's Alms House in 1858 were Irish.[13]

If the nation's bishops were dismayed by the physical needs of their immigrant flock, the spiritual state of these putative Catholics was even more troubling. Substantial numbers of the newly arrived Irish were ignorant of basic Catholic beliefs and unaccustomed to regular attendance at Mass. "Most of the two million Irish who emigrated between 1847 and 1860 were part of the pre-famine generation of non-practicing Catholics," according to historian Emmet Larkin, "if indeed they were Catholics at all." Surprising numbers of German immigrants were also lax Catholics, although on the whole they were better catechized than the Irish and more disciplined in their religious practice. Still, many attended Mass infrequently—some never went at all—and significant numbers in the antebellum years failed to marry in the church. Although clerical numbers were growing in every eastern diocese, with most new priests coming from abroad, no city in the antebellum years had enough clergy to serve its exploding Catholic population. Nor were there sufficient churches. On the basis of the Catholic population of New York at the time of the Civil War, the seating capacity of its churches, and the number of Sunday Masses, historian Jay Dolan concludes that probably 40 to 50 percent of the city's Catholics were present at church on any given Sunday.[14]

Given the extreme poverty of many immigrant Catholics and their propensity—common even today among the poor—to move frequently, even 40 percent attending Mass might plausibly be read as an achievement. Most Protestant churches did not do as well when it came to working-class populations. The enhanced ethnic consciousness that came with emigration gave Catholic leaders an advantage in this regard, which they typically used to good effect. Although committed in principle to a church that transcended ethnic divisions, most antebellum bishops permitted the creation of German-language parishes once German immigrants arrived in large numbers. Even New York's Hughes, firmly opposed to such "national" parishes, blessed the establishment of the city's first German-language church in 1833. With the church now a locus of ethnic pride and an increasingly central focus of ethnic communal life, more and more Germans embraced a regular religious practice. As for the Irish, their tribal identity as Catholics—true even of those who seldom attended Mass—was deftly exploited by the growing number of Irish bishops in the United States, who endorsed the cause of Ireland's freedom and vigorously defended the much-maligned Irish now resident in the country. Here too the effect over time was to bind the immigrant population more tightly to the church.

Following the example of their frontier brethren, bishops in the more populous dioceses also made use of the parish mission. Even Catholics who seldom went to church could often be induced to attend when a celebrated preacher was on offer. The increasingly numerous Redemptorist order, whose members specialized in the preaching of missions, decided in the late 1840s to devote its efforts primarily to the nation's cities, and orders like the Jesuits and Augustinians followed suit. Many urban pastors also preached missions in their own and occasionally in colleagues' churches. By the 1850s, missions were so frequent in Philadelphia that the city, in the words of historian Dale Light, "experienced something approaching a perpetual revival." The same could be said of every heavily Catholic city along the eastern seaboard and growing numbers in the nation's interior.[15]

Urban missions followed the same general program as missions preached on the frontier: the cycle of sermons typically stretched over eight days and nights, with a graphic emphasis on sin and eternal punishment. Elaborate props were increasingly used to heighten the element of fear—a casket surrounded by candles might feature at the sermon on death, and funereal hymns might be sung. Given the massive population of most urban parishes, missions preached in city churches had the added drama of dense crowds and the heightened emotions they generated. Missions always concluded with the congregation collectively renewing its baptismal vows, at which time the preacher often held up an infant's baptismal robe, symbolic of baptismal innocence. "Simply holding up the white robe of baptism set the people almost frantic," New York's Father Richard Burtsell noted of one mission in the city. "All the preacher said after drowned in the uproar." A mission at the Jesuits' St. Francis Xavier parish in Manhattan in 1863 saw more than twenty thousand people queuing for confession; up to twenty confessors were on duty each day from early morning until late at night.[16]

Nearly every mission yielded a crop of men, and even the occasional woman, who returned to the fold after years away from the sacraments. But how could their ardor be kept alive once the mission had ended? If missions vibrated with emotion, the same could hardly be said of the Sunday liturgy in most parishes. The typical Sunday "low Mass" was a bare and hurried affair, lasting not much more than half an hour, with no music and often enough no sermon. The midmorning high Mass offered greater drama: there was organ music and a choir, and a sermon always featured. But the high Mass was lengthy—sermons in those rhetoric-loving days often stretched to an hour—and since pewholders usually attended this Mass, their elegant dress set a standard that many parishioners could not meet. Some priests tried to address the problem by preaching regularly at low Masses too—usually a brief instruction on aspects of the catechism. Paulist Father Walter Elliot remembered his childhood pastor in Detroit being the first priest locally to preach such sermons back in the 1850s, when close to half the city's population was foreign-born. The Dutch-born Father Peter Hennaert was also notable, at least as Elliot remembered it, for a sermon on the condition of labor and the worker's right "to fair hours and honest pay"—a rarity indeed at a time when social Catholicism was understood exclusively in terms of personal charity.[17]

A proliferation of devotions also helped bind immigrants to the church. Marian devotions grew in number and prominence, as they did in

Catholic Europe, where apparitions of the Virgin were increasingly common. The Miraculous Medal devotion, the fruit of a vision in 1830 on the part of a young French nun, spread rapidly in the United States in the 1840s and after, while Catholics in this country were eager consumers of news about a series of Marian apparitions in the remote French village of Lourdes in 1858. Sacred Heart devotions grew in popularity too. But the typical urban parish in the years of heavy immigration offered additional options: novenas to particular saints, various modes of Eucharistic piety, Stations of the Cross during Lent. Devotions had a participative quality that was absent for many Catholics in the Latin Mass—the set prayers were usually in the vernacular, hymns were often sung, and one's desires as well as one's fears could be brought before a powerful intercessor. Saints, after all, were popularly regarded as specialists—one prayed to St. Anne to find a spouse, while St. Joseph was the patron of a happy death—and devotions made room for the frankly instrumental aspects of religion.

The communal dimension of devotions was important too, contributing as it did to the shoring up of social bonds in uprooted immigrant populations. Devotions brought neighbors together to pray in the parish church, with the good of others—both the living and the souls in Purgatory—uppermost, at least ideally, in their minds. "Each Member labors not for himself alone," according to a pamphlet promoting the Bona Mors Society, a devotion meant to ensure that its practitioners died in a state of grace, "but to supply the necessities of the other Members." One prayed, then, not simply for the grace of a "happy death" but that others too might die with the sacraments, and one counted on the prayers of others to shorten one's own probable time in Purgatory. The Forty Hours devotion, rare in the United States prior to the 1840s, summoned the entire parish to an extended period of prayer before the consecrated Host, solemnly exposed on the altar, bracketed by Masses and Eucharistic processions. Under the leadership of Bishop—now Saint—John Nepomucene Neumann (r. 1852–60), the Diocese of Philadelphia became the first in the nation to establish the devotion in all of its churches, scheduled so that the Blessed Sacrament was constantly being adored by a portion of the faithful.[18]

Except for devotions like Forty Hours, in which an entire parish was urged to participate and men alone could keep the vigil once night had fallen, the devotional world was largely female. Women seemed more at home in its floridly emotional atmosphere and perhaps less threatened by its

emphasis on human helplessness in a fallen world and the need for obedience to church authority. Although the clergy bemoaned the situation, they
recognized women's influence on the recalcitrant males with whom they
lived. When missions were preached to congregations segregated by sex, as
was nearly always the case in urban parishes, the opening days of the mission belonged to the women. Wives, mothers, and daughters would then
persuade their husbands, sons, and fathers to make the mission in their
turn—or so the clergy assumed. When men were attracted to parish organizations and through them to a closer church connection, it was usually
through such practically oriented entities as benefit societies—insurance
pools, usually lay initiated, that provided modest benefits should a working
man fall sick or a more substantial benefit in the event of his death, which
was frequently spent on a lavish funeral. Parish temperance societies, steeped
in the rhetoric of self-improvement, might attract the more ambitious.

Immigrant loyalty to the church may also have been stimulated by the
visible intensity of the urban Catholic building program, no matter that the
results of the program were still at midcentury inadequate to the needs of
the urban Catholic population. Even those who seldom attended Mass
could regard a splendid new cathedral as testimony to immigrant achievement and the claim of these newest Americans to membership in the national community. Early in the century, Catholic cathedrals were generally
built in a chaste neoclassical mode, with particularly fine examples rising in
Baltimore, Cincinnati, and St. Louis. A shift in architectural fashion, which
coincided with the dramatic upsurge in Catholic immigration, resulted in
more flamboyant offerings—the soaring gothic of New York's St. Patrick's,
the Renaissance eclecticism of Philadelphia's Basilica Church of Saints Peter
and Paul, the exuberant German baroque of Milwaukee's St. John the Evan-
gelist. Growing numbers of parish churches were also distinguished by their
size and imposing architecture, and even modest urban churches were increasingly furnished with statues, paintings, and elaborate altars.

Less immediately visible to most of the laity but still indicative of institutional consolidation was the proliferation of colleges and clerical seminaries. In most American dioceses, the first "seminary" was located in the
bishop's residence, itself a typically modest affair, with the bishop as principal teacher. Since most of the earliest seminarians had already completed a
portion of their training in Europe, the curricular limits of the "house seminary" was not an immediate problem. But in order to recruit and train an

American-born clergy, something more ambitious was needed. Most bishops eventually established a diocesan college-cum-seminary, in which those
enrolled as seminarians did much of the teaching and the lay students' fees
kept the enterprise afloat. (As was the case with Catholic female academies,
many of the lay students in the antebellum years were Protestants.) Nearly
every bishop disliked the arrangement, despite its practical value: such close
contact with their lay contemporaries, the bishops feared, would distract
the seminarians and endanger their vocations. But the seminary-college did
serve as an economical stopgap, producing a number of reasonably well-
prepared priests—close contact with the laity was perhaps an advantage in
this regard—and a growing, if still inadequate, number of American-born
vocations. It also gave birth to more than a score of Catholic colleges or—
more accurately—what would one day be colleges, the level of instruction
in the antebellum period typically approximating that of today's middle
schools. Many students at the time entered "college" in their early teens.[19]

Freestanding seminaries, the beau ideal of every bishop, emerged
mostly after the Civil War. Even before the war, however, three institutions
had been founded in Europe to train aspirants to the American priesthood
in a sheltered seminary setting: the Missionary College of All Hallows in
Ireland, established in 1842; the American College at Louvain, founded in
1857; and the North American College in Rome, established in 1859. These
institutions provided the American bishops with a welcome level of "quality control" with regard to imported clergy. Improved clerical education,
coupled with the enhanced ability of bishops to discipline their priests,
meant a diminution of clerical scandals in the years of heavy immigration
and fewer explosive conflicts at the parish level. Urban priests, in particular,
were as a result more remote from the people they served—legislation in
most dioceses prohibited their attendance at most public amusements and
confined their socializing to clerical circles. But an orderly church had its
attractions, perhaps especially for immigrant Catholics. Marginal people
themselves, they may well have found consolation in their link, however
tenuous, to a clearly hierarchical and increasingly powerful institution.

Catholic institutional visibility—an essential aspect of the urban
church's aura of power—was also enhanced by the building of hospitals, the
expansion of existing orphanages and the founding of new ones, and the establishment of institutions to care for such vulnerable constituencies as the
aged poor, immigrant women arriving alone, and women "rescued" from

prostitution. All such institutions were primarily the work of women religious. Catholic periodicals also increased dramatically in number, from seven
in 1840 to twenty-one in 1860, and improved—if less dramatically—in quality. A disproportionate number were produced by converts—an early sign of
the outsized role that converts would play in the intellectual life of the American church. No institution, however, enhanced Catholic visibility more than
the Catholic primary school, which as an urban institution had its roots in
the 1840s and 1850s. Made possible by the close-to-unpaid labor of women
religious, those schools—along with their sister-teachers—were a principal
focus for organized anti-Catholicism, a phenomenon that peaked in the mid-
1850s. If many immigrants held aloof from such schools, at least initially, the
schools ultimately played a major role in promoting an intense Catholic consciousness in an ethnically diverse Catholic population.

The School Question

A limited number of Catholic parishes supported a school prior to 1840,
generally on the initiative of an ambitious pastor. But no American bishop
by that date had embarked on the building of a Catholic system of primary
education in his diocese. Public schools altered the equation, however, once
they began to appear in significant numbers, as was happening by the 1830s
in areas outside the South. Those schools reflected the nation's dominant
culture, which was strongly inflected by Protestantism. A reading from the
King James Bible and recitation of the "Protestant version" of the Lord's
Prayer were typically part of the school day, while textbooks promoted
Protestant Christianity as the source of enlightenment and human freedom. If mass education was rapidly becoming the American norm, at least
through the primary grades, even the poorest Catholic child would have to
be educated. But could this happen safely in the public schools as they
stood?

The occasional American bishop was a quiet supporter of the public
schools. How else, such men asked, could impoverished immigrants afford
to educate their children? Boston's John Fitzpatrick (r. 1846–66) was the
most prominent. Himself educated in the city's public schools, which
evolved in Boston far earlier than elsewhere, he invested little effort in the
building of Catholic schools and avoided conflict with local authorities
over public-school curricula. But the great majority of his episcopal peers

regarded the public school as a danger to faith and even morals. (In the eyes of most bishops, Protestantism was but a way station on the road to unbelief and its notorious consequences.) At the very least, the public school would have to be purged of its Protestant content. But better by far would be Catholic schools, where true religion could not only be taught but also infuse the institution's culture. Catholics were too poor, however, to fund schools of their own. Hence the demand, raised by a number of bishops in the 1840s and 1850s, for a portion of tax dollars to be spent on exclusively Catholic schools.[20]

New York's Bishop, later Archbishop, Hughes was among the first to move in this direction, which he did with his storied aggressiveness. Demanding a share of public educational funds to support a system of Catholic schools and encountering resistance from New York's Common Council, Hughes then attempted to secure his goal by means of state legislation. In the course of this latter campaign, Hughes publicly promoted a slate of candidates who were favorable to the Catholic funding cause—an unprecedented flexing of political muscle on the part of a Catholic prelate. "If I did not go beyond my episcopal sphere I went at least to the farthest edge of it," as Hughes himself acknowledged privately. Hughes did not succeed with regard to public funding. But the legislature did impose on New York City its first elected school board, which enabled Catholics—given their numbers—to exert some control over public-school curricula. By the mid-1840s, the city's Jews had joined Catholics in opposing mandatory religious exercises in the public schools, and by the 1850s, those schools were emerging as nonsectarian institutions. By that time, however, Hughes had embarked on a school system of his own.[21]

Catholic demands of this nature provoked vigorous opposition. Did Catholic immigrants not intend to assimilate? the critics wondered. Did they reject the democratizing norms that, as the critics saw it, defined the public school? Such demands also reminded non-Catholics of an uncomfortable reality: in many of the nation's cities, Catholic numbers meant Catholic political leverage and even eventual political dominance. Nearly every outbreak of anti-Catholic violence in the antebellum years occurred at or near election time and was justified on the grounds of Catholic enmity toward public education or its Protestant, and hence democratic, ethos. Other factors were at work as well: class tensions in a newly industrializing society, the political instability generated by the slow collapse of the

Whig Party, even displaced tensions over slavery and its place in American life. But anti-Catholic and anti-immigrant—largely anti-Irish—sentiment was sufficiently strong by the 1850s to fuel a national political movement, which endorsed a twenty-one-year residency requirement for citizenship and, in some places, restriction of officeholding to the native-born. The American Party, as the movement's political wing was known, reached its apex in the mid-1850s, when it controlled at least seven state legislatures and elected eight governors, close to one hundred members of Congress, and mayors in Boston, Philadelphia, and Chicago.

The Catholic schools that ostensibly triggered such widespread anxiety were no more than a work in progress prior to the Civil War, even where the local bishop had made schools his first priority. In Hughes's New York, some sixteen thousand children were enrolled in the Catholic schools as of 1865—a remarkable achievement in institution building. But that number represented only 16 percent of the total school population in a probably majority-Catholic city. A good many Catholic children, moreover, were not enrolled in school at all or attended only irregularly. "They run the streets whole days as thieves," Mother Caroline Friess wrote in 1853 of the immigrant children in the vicinity of her New York school, some of whom appeared sporadically in class. The "thievery" to which she referred was mostly scavenging: "they collect rags, bones, coal and old iron and sell these things for money which they must bring home to their wicked parents who use it for alcoholic drink." But drink was by no means the only cause: the poorest immigrant families needed the labor of young children simply to survive. The need for child labor depressed even public-school enrollment among Catholic youngsters in every U.S. city, in many of which the Catholic schools reached proportionally fewer children than in New York.[22]

Since public funding for Catholic schools was nowhere forthcoming after 1840, those schools depended for their survival on the low-wage labor of women religious. Many of the schools they staffed were, by present-day quality standards, appalling. Classes of sixty and upward were common, and the teachers themselves often had only limited formal education. (Similar conditions, to be fair, prevailed in the public schools as well.) Many of the early Catholic schools were sandwiched into quarters not originally built for the purpose, with the sister-teachers often housed in equally primitive accommodations. And many of their pupils suffered from the ravages of poverty. The just-quoted Mother Caroline, serving with the School Sisters of

Notre Dame in New York, complained of the children in her school who "could not sit still because of bites and itches" from lice and fleas. "The majority of children have bugs not only in their hair but also in their clothes." Discipline was a problem too, perhaps especially for those many sisters who in less economically straitened circumstances would have taught only girls, such being the rule in their communities. Sister Ancaria, who came from the Emmitsburg convent of the Sisters of Charity in 1848 to open a school in Buffalo, recalled its opening days with dismay. "The children began to pour in—over one hundred and twenty five were counted. To keep them in some kind of order was all that could be done; they would not kneel for prayers, just squat back on their heels; run in and out without order."[23]

Despite the daunting circumstances, however, Catholic schools were widely regarded as effective educators of the poor. Certainly they were seen as orderly places, thanks largely to a determined corps of sister-teachers. The beleaguered Sister Ancaria not only survived her difficult early days of combat with "the Buffaloes," as she called them, but swiftly gained the upper hand. "They soon became studious and docile," she tells us. "In the course of time, we taught them Sewing and Tapestry-work; that pleased them wonderfully!" In strictly academic terms, schools in the poorer immigrant districts probably imparted little more than basic literacy, although the print orientation of nineteenth-century culture meant that even those with minimal schooling often developed into competent readers. But the sisters also conveyed, via a heavy focus on religion, both basic catechetical knowledge and a conviction of their students' dignity—their inherent worth as individuals, the pride attendant on being Catholic. The Catholic schools also provided youngsters from non-English-speaking families with a chance at bilingual education—a rarity then in the public sector. The earliest German parish schools were usually taught in German only. But parental demand often resulted in English being added as a medium of instruction—a pattern that subsequently characterized the schools of other ethnic groups. How else could immigrant children thrive in an English-speaking country?[24]

It was anything but certain, on the eve of the Civil War, that American Catholics would go on to build a nationwide system of parochial schools. By the close of the century, however, the commitment had been made. The Third Plenary Council of Baltimore, meeting in 1884, marked a symbolic turning point: noting that only 40 percent of parishes in the United States

supported a primary school, the council fathers urged every pastor to establish one forthwith and all Catholic parents to enroll their children. That was
clearly impossible, as the fathers knew. But the number of Catholic schools
did multiply rapidly thereafter and soon came to include a raft of secondary
schools as well. The commitment to Catholic education, made possible by
dramatic growth in the ranks of women religious, both reflected and intensified an inward turn on the part of the American Catholic community,
even as that community grew in wealth and political power. It also meant
that the vast majority of women religious in the United States would be
teachers and gave those anonymous women an influence on American
Catholic culture rivaling that of the clergy.

Converts

The converts who entered the antebellum church were notable less for their
numbers than for their occasional prominence. Enough high-profile Americans embraced the Catholic Church in the pre–Civil War decades to cause
alarm among anti-Catholics, especially those of elite status. The best-
known converts were from New England and heirs to its reformed Protestant tradition, which was widely regarded as the bedrock of American
democracy. By embracing a church firmly linked in the public mind with
autocracy, those converts seemed dangerously disloyal to many of their fellow Americans and a worrisome portent for the future. Those same Americans also worried about increased religious intermarriage among the
nation's elites, generally seen as another means—and a typically authoritarian one—of producing high-status Catholics. William Tecumseh Sherman
provides a prominent example. His marriage to a Catholic did not result in
his conversion—seldom a churchgoer, he seems to have professed a fairly
vestigial form of theism. But he did agree—most reluctantly, with regard to
his sons—to the Catholic education of his children. Had he refused to do
so, no priest would have married the couple. When his eldest son entered
the Jesuits, Sherman was so distressed that he temporarily separated from
his wife, who was delighted by the young man's vocation.[25]

Those who converted for purely interior reasons had a number of motives, few of which can be certainly known. A perceived erosion of Protestant
theological rigor seems to have played a role, as Calvinism's American heirs
attempted to humanize a theology that had come for many to seem bleak and

coercive. The highly subjective theologies that resulted, in the view of critics, lacked a firm principle of religious authority and left would-be believers too much on their own, veritable prisoners of their class and culture. Many converts sought certitude, in short, and a warm, communal life of faith that to certain wistful outsiders seemed uniquely available in the Catholic Church. Attending a lecture by Theodore Parker, a prominent reformer and Unitarian minister, soon-to-be Catholic convert Eliza Allen Starr "found him demolishing every foundation-stone of my religious faith, and even hope." Her subsequent search for "an authorized faith" led Starr to embrace Catholicism. Many high-status converts apparently had little contact with the gritty realities of Catholic life prior to entering the church, embracing instead what might be called the idea of Catholicism. Rubbing elbows with actual Catholics could be a shock. "*Inter nos* I do not like in general our Irish population," Orestes Brownson confided to Isaac Hecker, some years after both men had converted. "They have no clear understanding of their religion."[26]

Brownson and Hecker, who entered the church in 1844, were the most notable of the antebellum converts with regard to their impact on American Catholicism. Both had modest origins. Hecker was born in New York to German immigrant parents and left school at the age of thirteen to go to work, while Brownson was the son of impoverished farmers in Vermont. Both were spiritual seekers. Brownson moved in the late 1820s from Presbyterianism to the Universalist ministry, which he subsequently abandoned for utopian socialism and the New York Workingman's Party, followed by advocacy of a reform-minded but apparently non-Christian "church of the future." Hecker seems to have been unchurched prior to an intense mystical experience in 1842, although he was deeply committed to moral purpose and social reform. Profoundly shaken by the aforementioned spiritual encounter, he retreated to the newly established Brook Farm—a communal experiment founded by the Unitarian George Ripley—to puzzle out his future. Months of prayer and study led him ultimately to the Catholic Church. His conversion, like Brownson's, was accomplished in part by Boston's Bishop John Fitzpatrick, friend to that city's Brahmin elite.[27]

Neither Hecker nor Brownson found in the church an initially congenial environment. Even Hecker, lacking though he was in formal education, was troubled by what he saw as Catholic parochialism and the perfunctory quality of the liturgy in New York's Irish parishes. Both lost friends as a result of their conversions: "we break with the whole world in which we have hitherto lived," as Brownson explained the condition of a Protestant-turned-Catholic. Brownson coped by donning the mantle of the nation's preeminent Catholic intellectual, converting the journal he had founded in 1838 into *Brownson's Quarterly Review,* easily the most sophisticated of American Catholic publications in the mid-nineteenth century, and producing a flood of books and essays in addition. Hecker escaped, if that term be allowed, into the Redemptorist novitiate. Trained in Belgium, he was ordained a priest in London in 1849. After a stint of mission preaching in the parishes of that city, he returned to the United States in 1851, part of an English-speaking mission band made up of four American-born converts. He was thirty-one at the time—junior to Brownson by some sixteen years.[28]

Hecker lasted fewer than ten years as a Redemptorist. Zealous for the conversion of American seekers like himself, he unsuccessfully sought permission from his religious superiors to preach missions to non-Catholics. (Among the many former associates whom Hecker tried personally to convert was a bemused Henry David Thoreau.) Tension over the issue resulted in Hecker's being summarily dismissed from the Redemptorist order in 1857, although he and four like-minded Redemptorist colleagues were subsequently permitted to offer their priestly services to an American bishop. The five then established the Missionary Society of St. Paul, based in New York, in 1858, with Hecker as the first superior. The Paulists, as the group was informally known, was the first religious community of men to be founded in the United States. Headquartered at New York's St. Paul the Apostle Church, which was soon renowned for its preaching, music, and parish library, the Paulists devoted themselves primarily to mission preaching. The community was too small at midcentury to preach before as many non-Catholics as Hecker would have liked. Still, he estimated that he had addressed over twenty thousand non-Catholics during the community's first decade.

Hecker's commitment to social reform, along with his optimism with regard to human nature and freedom, were constants during his ministry. He never flagged in his conviction that Catholicism and democracy were fully congruent or in his love for the United States and what he regarded as its singular mission in the world. After his death in 1888, his ideas generated a good deal of controversy, since they came to stand—accidentally, in part—for one of the parties embroiled in a struggle over Rome's response to modernity. During his life, however, Hecker was seldom criticized, due largely to his winsome personality and irenic mode of discourse. Orestes Brownson, by contrast, grew militantly conservative with age. While Hecker was privately opposed to the 1870 declaration of papal infallibility at the First Vatican Council, Brownson was vigorously in favor. A sinful world, he argued, required an absolute moral authority. Religious liberty and the secular state, providential developments to Hecker, were for Brownson, in the words of historian David O'Brien, "simply revivals of pagan absolutism, now in the name of the people." Brownson was particularly alarmed by the nascent movement for women's suffrage, which he called the most dangerous reform initiative ever undertaken in the United States.[29]

Sunday Morning at St. Stephen's

Early one wintry Sunday in 1868, a reporter for the *Atlantic Monthly* visited New York's St. Stephen's Church for the 6:00 a.m. Mass. About one thousand women were in attendance, he estimated, and perhaps one hundred men. (The church, one of the city's largest, seated four thousand.) Nearly all the women, according to the reporter, appeared to be domestic servants, while the men were mostly "coachmen and grooms." Nearly everyone present was Irish. The Mass itself did not impress the visitor, being—to his ears, at least—almost entirely inaudible and lasting only half an hour. But the prayerful attentiveness of the congregation did. Unlike Protestants, who in the visitor's telling were crippled by self-consciousness when praying in public, the Catholics present were fully at ease. "A Catholic appears to be no more ashamed of saying his prayers than he is of eating his dinner, and he appears to think one quite as natural an action as the other." Catholic faith was communal, the visitor pointed out—a frequent theme in period conversion narratives. "Among Catholics there is not the distinction (so familiar to us) between believers and unbelievers. From the hour of baptism, every Catholic is a member of the church, and he is expected to behave as such."[30]

That Sunday morning at St. Stephen's spoke of remarkable progress on the part of the immigrant church. One of thirty-two churches in the city of New York, St. Stephen's was not only vast but sumptuously decorated. Among other things, the visiting reporter noted "the new blue ceiling and its silver stars." If there were Catholics in its immediate vicinity who would not be present at any of the Sunday Masses, the throngs who did attend

were evidently devout. If the city's immigrant slums still pulsed with misery, there were numerous Catholic institutions now that helped, however
inadequately, to alleviate it. As of 1868, moreover, Catholics had greater reason than at any time since the late 1820s to feel confident about their American future. The recently concluded Civil War, horrific though its casualties
were, had muffled the anti-Catholic sentiment that had surged so mightily
in the 1850s and denied the compatibility of Catholicism with democratic
citizenship. The admiring tone of the *Atlantic Monthly*'s account of Mass at
St. Stephen's reflected this brief interlude of interconfessional calm.[31]

S • I • X

Slavery and the Civil War

In 1838, the Jesuits of the Maryland Province sold most of their slaves—
the total came to 272 men, women, and children—to a Louisiana
planter. It was not the first time the order had parted with slaves: 14
had been sold from the Jesuits' St. Thomas plantation in 1835 and 11
from the St. Inigoes plantation shortly thereafter. But the scale of the sale in
1838 attracted broad notice and widespread disapproval, even among the
many Americans who were hostile to the growing movement for the immediate abolition of slavery. The reaction was sufficiently negative that the
Jesuit provincial who ordered the sale, Thomas Mulledy, was removed from
his office by the order's superior general and transferred to Rome. Mulledy's
exile did not last long. He returned to the United States in 1843 as founding
president of Holy Cross College in Worcester, Massachusetts. His services
were specifically requested by Boston's Bishop Benedict Fenwick, himself a
Jesuit and one who had been deeply distressed by the 1838 sale. "Poor Negroes!" he wrote at the time to his brother. "I pity them."[1]

Some eighteen months after the 1838 sale, Pope Gregory XVI issued an
apostolic letter condemning the slave trade and seemingly by implication
the institution of slavery itself. The letter, apparently prompted by Gregory's interest in the evangelization of Africa, had nothing directly to do with
the 1838 sale, although knowledge of the letter's existence prior to its publication may have ensured that the Jesuit's superior general would call Mulledy to Rome. Despite its explosive contents, given period tensions over

119

slavery, the letter received little attention in the United States until 1844, when it briefly surfaced in the course of that year's presidential campaign. Rome was distant in those days of slow communication, and papal statements, especially on matters of social morality, were relatively rare. Only in the reign of Gregory's successor, Pius IX, did the encyclical become an important mode of exercising papal teaching authority. The American bishops, moreover, had every reason to deflect attention from Gregory's 1839 letter. Once this was no longer possible, the bishops were quick to insist that the letter spoke only to the international slave trade and had no bearing on slavery or slave sales in the United States.[2]

Hardly any American Catholics endorsed slavery as an unambiguous good. The most prominent instance of such an endorsement came in 1861, when the bishop of Natchitoches, French-born Augustin Martin, asserted in a pastoral letter that the enslavement of Africans was divinely ordained. Martin was eventually forced by Rome to retract the letter, which in the view of the Propaganda was opposed to papal teaching and based on an erroneous reading of Scripture. But neither did any prominent Catholic prior to the Civil War publicly advocate immediate emancipation. Erie, Pennsylvania's Bishop Josue White, not insignificantly a convert, appears to have favored abolition by the early 1850s but was generally quiet about his position and had little influence on his fellow bishops. Cincinnati's Archbishop John Purcell, onetime mentor to Josue White, had embraced abolition by mid-1862 and was the lone American bishop to speak publicly in favor of the Thirteenth Amendment, which abolished slavery, in 1865. (Bishop White was near death at the time.) Despite Purcell's prominence, he stood more or less alone. When the nation's bishops assembled in 1866 at the Second Plenary Council, they expressed their collective regret that "a more gradual system of emancipation" had not been adopted.[3]

Catholic thinking on slavery, bound today to seem both alien and ambiguous, was rooted not only in tradition—prior to the nineteenth century, popes themselves had owned slaves—but also in anxiety over liberal individualism. Slavery, in the Catholic view, was among those numerous hierarchical relationships—husband-wife and parent-child provided the archetypes—that made for social order. Such relationships were not to be purely one-sided. Just as husbands had obligations to their wives as well as authority over them, so masters had obligations to slaves: masters must permit slaves to marry—a legal impossibility in the United States—and see to their instruction in the Catholic faith. Slavery was an ancient institution, Catholics argued, tolerated by the Church Fathers and even Christ himself. It was not, however, necessarily an enduring one. The Catholic Church had played an honorable role in the gradual end of slavery in medieval Europe, or so Catholics liked to assert. But immediate emancipation, in the dominant Catholic view, was sure to cause social upheaval—a far greater evil than slavery itself. Slaves, indeed, were exempt from some of the worst injustices of the current economic regime, at least in the Catholic telling. Unlike the poorest industrial workers, they did not go hungry or suffer abandonment in sickness and old age.[4]

Catholic thinking about slavery was not explicitly racial. Slavery was an institution found in every age and culture; it was not the destiny of a particular human group. Christ died to save the entire human family, Catholic theologians emphasized, to which every racial group belonged. The antebellum years, indeed, saw the establishment of two religious orders for women of African descent: the Oblate Sisters of Providence, founded in Baltimore in 1828 by mixed-race refugees from Haiti, and the Sisters of the Holy Family, canonically recognized in 1842, whose founder was Henriette Delille, born to a mixed-race mother. The early histories of both congregations were sharply inflected by race. The Oblate Sisters' spiritual needs were mostly ignored by Baltimore's clergy, and the order came close to dissolving in consequence. Neither congregation was permitted to serve any but persons of color, while the Sisters of the Holy Family initially limited membership to light-complexioned women. Still, the very existence of these congregations affirmed in a public way the full humanity of African-descended people.[5]

But race was nonetheless deeply entwined with Catholic attitudes toward slavery in the United States. Most Catholics, like most Americans, regarded Africans as inferior, and those in the nonslave states and territories were generally hostile to their presence—again, an attitude widely shared with their non-Catholic counterparts. As C. Vann Woodward has cogently noted, racial segregation was a practice born in the antebellum North. The Irish were especially aggressive in their racial hostility, presumably due to their poverty and low social status. Low-skilled Irish workers often competed with blacks for jobs, and employers used blacks on occasion to break Irish strikes. New York's Archbishop John Hughes, himself an Irish immigrant and one-time manual laborer, articulated something of their fear and loathing in an 1854 sermon that touched briefly on the obligations of slave masters.

African-descended people, he confessed, seemed to him "as dark in their spirit as in their complexion, and incapable almost of understanding." But such prejudice or even its public expression was hardly peculiar to the Irish.[6]

Abolitionists, for their part, were frequently anti-Catholic and anti–Irish Catholic in particular. That popery and slavery were parallel systems of despotism was a favorite abolitionist trope. "The Catholic clergy are on the side of slavery," as Theodore Parker asserted in an 1854 sermon. "They love slavery itself; it is an institution thoroughly congenial to them, consistent with the first principles of their church." Many northern supporters of the nativist American Party in the 1850s were antislavery, or at least opposed to slavery's extension into the western territories. Most of them voted Republican once the American Party collapsed, a victim of growing sectional tension after the mid-1850s. Although a number of prominent Republicans publicly deplored nativism, for the great majority of Catholics the new party was irrevocably tainted. Most viewed the decisive events of the early 1860s—Lincoln's election, southern secession, and the advent of war—with a near-visceral conviction that attacks on slavery were attacks on the Catholic Church. Irish Catholics, in particular, became more fervently Democratic in their voting behavior, and Lincoln lost the Catholic vote decisively in 1864.[7]

The Catholic population by the 1850s was heavily concentrated in the North, the result of mass immigration. Close to 90 percent of the nation's Catholics in 1861 lived in states that remained within the Union. Southern Catholics were not terribly likely to be slaveholders, although they—like southerners in general—do appear to have grown more protective of the institution as abolitionist attacks intensified. Slavery as an issue posed no challenge to American Catholic unity, unlike the several Protestant denominations that had divided into northern and southern entities due to bitter disagreement over its morality. But once southern troops had fired on Charleston's Fort Sumter—troops commanded, incidentally, by a Catholic officer of French descent—and civil war loomed, the prospects for Catholic unity dimmed. Southern Catholics nearly all supported the Confederate cause, and several of their bishops were prominent in its defense. Northern Catholics and their bishops supported the Union, although many dissented from Lincoln's policies once casualties soared and emancipation emerged as a principal Union war aim. But despite considerable internal tension, the American church did not suffer division in any formal sense, which in the wake of a terrible war was a source for Catholics of both comfort and pride.

Catholics in Wartime

In the early stages of the war, northern Catholics displayed enthusiasm for the Union cause and even for joining the Union army. This was especially true of the Irish. The so-called Irish Brigade, composed of heavily Irish regiments from New York, Massachusetts, and Pennsylvania, received wide and generally favorable publicity for its battlefield exploits, some of it in nativist publications. A number of additional regiments were majority Irish and publicly identified as such, but the Union army had no regiments with a majority of German Catholics, who as a group were far more conflicted about the war than their Irish counterparts. A number of prominent Union officers were known to be Catholics, chief among them General Phil Sheridan and Major General William Rosecrans, who along with his brother Sylvester—later first bishop of Columbus, Ohio—was a convert in his youth. Rosecrans's victory at Stones River early in 1863, a dark time for the Union cause, made him a northern hero. The officers of such prominent Irish regiments as the New York Sixty-Ninth (Col. Michael Corcoran) and the Ninth Massachusetts (Col. Patrick Guiney) also enjoyed a popular following, thanks to the Catholic press. The Irish-born Guiney, a prosperous attorney, defied Catholic stereotype by becoming a Lincoln Republican shortly after the war began.[8]

Many Catholics at the time believed that their coreligionists, like immigrants generally, were overrepresented in the Union army. (Southerners, for their part, regarded the Union army as the preserve of foreign hirelings.) But such was not the case. Despite the prominence of Irish names on the lists of battlefield casualties, the Irish-born were actually underrepresented in the Union army, as were German Catholics. It was probably hard for recent arrivals to feel much connection to the conflict. Immigrants who had not yet filed for citizenship, moreover, were not subject to conscription—the South had a draft as of April 1862, while the North followed suit in March 1863—and immigrants seem to have figured disproportionately among those who evaded the draft by leaving their current place of residence. Given immigrant Catholics' views on slavery and their poverty, it is somewhat surprising that they served in the considerable numbers that they did, as their countrymen seem to have recognized. Especially in the first years of the war, Catholic patriotism was widely admired in the North, and nativist sentiment went into retreat.[9]

The first wave of Catholic recruits, patriots to a man, enlisted under the illusion that the war would be short. As the war stretched into its second year and casualties mounted, the U.S. government was forced to encourage enlistment—the term of service, initially only ninety days, was now three years—by the paying of bounties, which became increasingly generous as the war ground on. Drafts to meet militia quotas were required in several states by later 1862; national conscription soon followed. Northern Democrats generally opposed the draft, with working-class Catholics especially apt to oppose it by force. Militia conscription met with violent resistance on several occasions in 1862 in both Irish and German Catholic enclaves, while antidraft violence erupted in a number of cities in the spring of 1863—violence not infrequently directed toward blameless locals of African ancestry.

Nothing, however, prepared the nation for the riot that convulsed New York for close to a week in July 1863, as officials began drawing names for the national draft. New York's mostly Irish rioters burned local draft offices and other federal property and attacked the offices of Republican newspapers. But it was the city's blacks who suffered most. The mob lynched at least six, destroyed black homes, and torched the Colored Orphan Asylum, where a child was killed. With an official death toll of 105, the riot still stands as the worst in American history. Catholic leaders were quick to denounce the New York violence, which certain of the city's priests—Isaac Hecker was one—attempted personally to halt. The Irish Brigade, fresh from heroic service at Gettysburg, was among the military units that ultimately brought the riot to an end. But the violence still raised serious doubts about Catholic loyalty, at least in Republican quarters.[10]

It did not help that Catholic leaders, in the months leading up to the riot, had bitterly criticized the Emancipation Proclamation. Lincoln, in their view, had no right to alter the goal of the war unilaterally; what had been a fight to preserve the Union and constitutional government, many Catholics argued, had become by presidential edict a fight to impose abolition—a program of the Republican Party—on an unwilling nation. Arguments like these were frequently tinged with race-based fear and anger. The *New York Freeman's Journal,* lay edited but widely regarded as a militantly Catholic paper, assured its mostly Irish readers that emancipation would cost them their jobs. Editor James McMaster, a scurrilous racist, had been briefly imprisoned in 1861 for his opposition to the war. Louisville's Bishop Martin Spalding, a Confederate sympathizer, privately regarded the Proclamation as a license for the newly freed "to murder their Masters and Mistresses!"[11]

Many Catholic soldiers shared such sentiments. "The feeling against nigars is intensly strong in this army," according to Peter Welsh, a member of the Irish Brigade, writing shortly after the promulgation of the Emancipation Proclamation. "They are looked upon as the principal cause of this war and this feeling is especialy strong in the Irish regiments." Irish soldiers, indeed, had on certain occasions actually returned fleeing slaves to nearby Confederate outposts. Welsh, an Irish American carpenter who had last lived in New York, did not criticize his comrades' racism, although he preferred to blame England for the war rather than the hapless slave. The British, hostile to republican values and jealous of American prosperity, had to Welsh's mind worked in multiple ways to exacerbate sectional tensions in the United States, with civil war as the ultimate consequence.[12]

Peter Welsh's letters do confirm the prevailing historical consensus on Irish Catholic racism. But they also betray a more complicated attitude toward the war and its meaning than that consensus might lead one to expect. Welsh was no racial egalitarian. But he did see the war—or perhaps he came to see the war—as a critical chapter in the evolution of human freedom. "This is the first test of a modern free government in the act of sustaining itself against internal enemys and matured rebellion," he wrote in 1863. "If it fail then the hopes of millions fail and the desighns and wishes of all tyrants will succeed." Should the forcible end of slavery be necessary to ensure the nation's survival, Welsh was prepared to accept it. "If slavery is in the way of a proper administration of the laws and the integrity and perpetuety of this nation then i say away with both slaves and slavery."[13]

Welsh, who enlisted in the fall of 1862, seems to have done so in part because of domestic difficulties caused by his drinking—a problem over which he appears to have gained control once under military discipline. He was attracted too by the enlistment bonus and the promise of regular pay. He doubted, as he wrote to his invalid wife at the time of his enlistment, that he would have to serve for as long as a year; "this war must be ended very soon." But a year's service would still be tolerable, since "I would be better paid th[a]n working at my trade." His unit soon saw action, first at South Mountain, then at Antietam, and most disastrously at Fredericksburg, where "we lost twelve killed and wounded out of the 37 men in our company." Fredericksburg had shaken him deeply: "the storm of shall and grap and canister was terrible[,] mowing whole gaps out of our ranks and we having to march over their dead and wounded bodies." The Irish Brigade was so decimated by these three engagements that it could hardly be called a fighting force in the early months of 1863; Welsh's regiment did not see serious subsequent action until Gettysburg.[14]

Christmas 1862 brought welcome respite. The Irish Brigade at the time was attended by three Catholic chaplains, and Mass was offered in camp on Christmas Day. Welsh had not recently gone to confession—"i will in the course of a week please God"—and was therefore unlikely to have received communion, which speaks perhaps to his practice in civilian life. Serving as he did in the Irish Brigade, Welsh had readier access to a priest than most Catholic soldiers. But in none of his subsequent surviving letters does he mention formal religious observance. Did he confess on the eve of battle, as so many Catholic soldiers were said to do? He does not say. His wife seemed worried on this score, writing early in 1863 about a sermon she had recently heard at the Paulist church in New York, in which the preacher had warned that death in battle would not save the soul of a Catholic soldier who was not in a state of grace. Welsh responded somewhat acerbically: "Shurely no Catholic is so silly or so ignorant of the teachings of the Catholic church as to believe that dying on the battle field would gain their salvation." Welsh did wear a religious medal under his uniform and in May of 1863 asked his wife to send him a prayerbook. And if his letters are oddly reticent with regard to specifically Catholic practice, they make frequent reference to the will of God and his confidence in God's protection.[15]

Peter Welsh reenlisted in January 1864, over the objections of his wife. The generous bounty attached to reenlistment was perhaps a factor, although he does not say so. Earlier letters suggest a deeper motive—a genuine conviction that the Union cause was the cause of God. Was rebellion without just reason not "a crime of the greatest magnitude?" he asked, citing St. Paul and New York's Archbishop Hughes as authorities. Did the Constitution not guarantee liberty of conscience, "the most important of all rights enjoyed by the citizen of a free nation?" ("Where on earth except in that fountain of religion Rome can anyone point out to me a spot where the [Catholic] Church enjoys such freedom as in the United States?") Was the United States not the hope of oppressed people in Ireland and elsewhere? Was its survival as a prosperous republic not essential to the diffusion of self-government? "We all know that to gain the salvation of our souls is the all important object but we have political relation with our fellow man and it is our duty to do our share for the common wellfare not

only of the present generation but of future generations." To his wife's rejoinder that the nation's priests and Catholic bishops were not of one mind
with regard to the war, Welsh responded crisply: "The clergy being devided
upon the war question does not therefore go to prove that God has nothing
to do with it."[16]

Welsh suffered what looked initially to be a superficial wound at the
Battle of Spotsylvania Courthouse in May 1864. The wound was subsequently judged to require surgery, and Welsh was evacuated to a Washington, DC, hospital, where he later died of blood poisoning. An honest eulogy
would depict him as a complicated man. Welsh was in some respects deeply
parochial. Archbishop Hughes, in his view, was "one whose abilitys as a
statesman as well as an eclisastic are second to none in the land." Lamenting
the "generally low moral standard of a very large class of the American people," for which the war might well be God's punishment, Welsh blamed the
public schools, "where there is neither releigous training nor morality
taught either by practice or precept." And yet he also thought in terms of
universal values. A working-class Irishman himself, he was horrified upon
hearing news of the draft riots in New York. The new draft law was fair, he
insisted, and likely to convince the South that the Union would fight to the
finish. "The originaters of those riots should be hung like dogs. They are
agents of jef davis and had their plans laid [to] start those riots simultanes-
ly with Lee[']s raid into Pensilvenia."[17]

Peter Welsh can hardly be called a typical Catholic of his generation or
even a typical Irish American. We know too little about him for labels of this
sort. But the brief glimpse we have of his interior life, imperfect and limited
though it be, reminds us that generalizations, however necessary, are inevitably somewhat deceptive. Welsh was a complicated man. The same could
probably be said of most Catholics in his and subsequent generations.

Catholic Chaplains

No Catholic chaplains were attached to either the army or the navy on the
eve of the Civil War. The navy, indeed, required every seaman to attend
Protestant services—a policy quickly altered by Congress once war broke
out. No Catholic chaplains were subsequently assigned to the navy, perhaps
because its Catholic numbers were relatively small, but some seventy priests
served as chaplains in both the Union and Confederate armies and in

military hospitals on both sides over the course of the war. Although a majority of chaplains served with the Union, Catholics in the Union army, given their enormous numbers, were less well supplied with priests than their Confederate brethren. Many chaplains, moreover, served only briefly, often less than a year. Every bishop was short of clergy and loath to surrender priests to the war in any significant number or for an extended period of time. The chaplains who served for several years came disproportionately from religious orders, especially those that sponsored colleges. Student numbers plummeted during the war, as young men flocked to the colors, and their would-be teachers were therefore free to follow. The most celebrated chaplain on the Union side, Father William Corby, who spent three years with the Irish Brigade, was a Holy Cross priest who had previously taught at Notre Dame.[18]

Field chaplains North and South followed a similar round of activity. When the army was on the move, chaplains marched with the troops and made rough camp at night. Older men or those in less than optimal health might easily find the regime too strenuous. They offered Mass, if possible daily, in improvised settings. His comrades had built an "enclosure" of cedar boughs in front of the chaplain's tent, Peter Welsh told his wife with regard to a Mass he attended on Christmas Day in 1862. "That forms the church with the little alter in the tent." Confessions, generally heard in the open, consumed many hours in camp, especially on the eve of a battle. "I heard confessions all that night—no sleep," according to Peter Paul Cooney, a Holy Cross priest who served as chaplain to the Thirty-Fifth Indiana, poised for battle in Kentucky in the fall of 1862. "I sat eight hours without getting out of my seat." Even lapsed Catholics, when faced with combat, often went to confession— an important reason this ministry was so gratifying to every priest who served. His soldier-comrades, according to Cooney, felt pity for him as he heard confessions for so many hours on what was a very cold night. "They little knew the joy that was in my breast, midst all these trials, when I considered how much God was doing with the hands of his unworthy son."[19]

Chaplains also provided soldiers with a nonsacramental listening ear and tried to be general morale boosters. "I find it an advantage sometimes in camp to crack a joke with them," Cooney noted. "It cheers them up and enlivens the monotony of camp life." Chaplains often helped soldiers manage their money, carrying pay packets destined for soldiers' families to the nearest post office or express facility. Peter Welsh invariably sent funds to his wife through the chaplain assigned to his regiment, although he admitted at one juncture that he did not know the name of the current incumbent. Certain chaplains, having gained reputations as preachers, offered sermons outside of Mass—a form of popular entertainment in a culture that lionized oral performance. Protestants might well attend, no "Catholic" regiment being exclusively so, and such preaching may have prompted the occasional conversion. Father Cooney baptized a number of Protestants over the course of his long service, most notably General David Sloane Stanley in 1864.[20]

Catholic chaplains in the Union army were nearly all assigned to one of the "Catholic" regiments, even though a majority of Catholic soldiers served elsewhere. Although chaplains often visited nearby units to minister to "unattended" Catholics, a good many Catholic soldiers received the sacraments only on rare occasion. Some never saw a priest at all, since certain unit commanders refused to allow Catholic chaplains to visit. Even soldiers in Catholic regiments were often underserved. The Irish Brigade, with its five regiments, always had at least one chaplain. But it never had more than three, with two the likelier number. At one point in 1863, when Holy Cross priest William Corby was the lone chaplain to the Irish Brigade, he was also the only Catholic chaplain in the entire Army of the Potomac. Even Catholic soldiers who died in a hospital did not invariably receive the last sacraments, although commissioned and volunteer chaplains tried to visit regularly. Women religious serving as nurses almost certainly ushered more Catholics into the next world than hospital chaplains did.[21]

Catholic chaplains, although troubled by their limited numbers, often found their service to be exhilarating. Those capable of withstanding the hardships of military life reported a newfound physical vigor. "It seems as if my health grows better as my hardships and fatigues increase," in the words of Father Cooney. Father Corby rejoiced at a life lived mainly out of doors, with Masses said at primitive altars. So it must have been, he mused, for missionaries to the Indians. Chaplaincy immersed the priest in a thoroughly masculine world, where—perhaps for the first time since ordination—he experienced warm and easy relations with the younger members of his sex. ("There is, it seems, a natural timidity on the part of youth as it grows to manhood to meet a priest," as a Michigan pastor explained the problem.) Father Corby, for one, saw distinct advantages to chaplaincy when compared to life in a parish: "We had no old women to bother us, or pew rent to collect." The chaplain, moreover, could expect to reap an abundant harvest of souls, with fear of death as his chief ally. Men who ignored religion when safe at home, as Father Cooney noted, "may die good Catholics in the army," if the chaplain attended to his duties. A priest, in Cooney's words, became in these circumstances "a direct instrument in the hand of God to bring these poor souls from the brink of hell."[22]

Contact with Protestant clergy, frequent on the battlefield and in military hospitals, could also boost Catholic chaplains' morale. Protestant ministers, claimed more than one priest, had nothing to offer the dying beyond words, while the Catholic chaplain could give sacramental absolution or, in the case of certain non-Catholics, the absolution of baptism. The most prominent instance of Catholic sacramental power came at Gettysburg, when Father William Corby gave absolution to the men of the Irish Brigade, who knelt before him as he stood on a boulder, with the sounds of battle— the Brigade was poised to enter the strife—surging in the background. Corby explained what he was about to do—no mass absolution, apparently, had ever previously been administered in the United States—and urged the men to make a good act of contrition. Non-Catholic onlookers, some of them kneeling, were deeply moved by the brief ceremony, which for Corby had meaning for soldiers beyond those immediately present. "That general absolution was meant for all—in quantum possum—not only for our brigade, but for all, North and South, who were susceptible of it and who were about to appear before their Judge," as Corby explained in his memoirs.[23]

At the same time, many Catholic chaplains were buoyed by increasingly friendly relations with their Protestant counterparts, which they saw as a measure of Catholicism's growing acceptance in a hitherto-hostile United States. "One good result of the Civil War was the removing of a great amount of prejudice," in the words of Father Corby, and he, like others, regarded the work of Catholic chaplains as an important cause. The occasional cross-confessional friendship could also enlarge the worlds of both men. Such was the case with Jesuit chaplain Joseph B. O'Hagan, attached to a New York regiment, and Congregationalist Joseph Twichell, who also served with a New York unit. The two young men, both highly educated and similarly burdened by their difficult work, soon became unlikely friends. One cold night shortly after the Battle of Fredericksburg, the two were forced to sleep rough and lay down together to share their blankets. O'Hagan, according to Twichell, could not help but laugh at the sight they afforded: "a Jesuit priest and a New England Puritan minister—of the worse sort—spooned together under the same blanket. I wonder what the angels would think." In a quiet victory for wartime ecumenism, O'Hagan answered his own question: "I think they like it."[24]

Catholic Nursing Sisters

If Catholic chaplains helped to ease prejudice against their church, this was even truer of the women religious who served as wartime nurses. More than six hundred sisters did so. Few American women as of 1861 had had experience of hospital nursing. It was otherwise with Catholic women religious, who on the eve of the war were staffing or administering probably thirty hospitals. Some of their hospitals, especially those in strategic locations, took in sick and wounded soldiers at the request of local military commanders. Sister-nurses also served in government-run military hospitals and sometimes on the battlefield. Not every sister who nursed the sick had had prior hospital training. But the great majority were experienced nurses who quickly gained a reputation for skill and devotion to duty. This was perhaps especially true of the Sisters of Charity, a family of orders long committed to nursing, which contributed more nurses to the war than any other of the twenty communities that lent sisters to the cause.

Although most sister-nurses worked in the North, they also served in southern hospitals and cared for the wounded of both armies. Many of their patients were non-Catholics, including some who had never before seen a woman religious and others who had been nurtured on a scurrilous anti-Catholicism. A few of their patients initially feared them, according to the sisters' reports, while others were hostile. But the sisters' selfless service—they cooked and cleaned as well as nursed—and their gentle serenity ultimately conquered most doubters. Sisters came to be seen, even by non-Catholics, as more heroic than other medical personnel. The Sisters of Charity who staffed Philadelphia's Satterlee Military Hospital were given sole charge of the smallpox tents erected at a distance from the hospital's main buildings late in 1864, no one else being willing to do the job. "We had, I may say, entire charge of the poor sufferers," one sister's journal noted, "as the physician who attended them seldom paid them a visit, but allowed us to do anything we thought proper for them." The soldiers "often said it was the Sisters who cured them."[25]

Sisters of Charity who served as nurses at Satterlee Hospital, Philadelphia, ca. 1865 (Courtesy of the Daughters of Charity, Province of St. Louise Archives, Emmitsburg, Maryland)

Sister-nurses endured great hardship on the job, for the hospitals in which they served were understaffed and sometimes so overcrowded that nursing in the usual sense was hardly possible. "After the Battle of Gettysburg, we received a large number of patients who were badly wounded—in all we had about 6,000," a sister from Satterlee remembered. "The wards were densely crowded, and there were three hundred tents on the ground." Many of their patients died, often in agony. But probably the greatest hardship, endured by surprising numbers, was infrequent access to Mass and the sacraments and suspension of their rigorous communal prayer life. In remote locations, especially in the South, no priest might be available to say Mass for the sisters for weeks at a time. The Gospel mandate to care for the suffering provided comfort to many. As the superior of the Sisters of St. Joseph of Philadelphia counseled her sister-nurses: "Offer up all the actions of the day, attend to those poor people and I think Our Lord will be satisfied."[26]

The horrendous death toll in the Civil War meant that sister-nurses presided at numerous deathbeds, both in hospitals and on the battlefield.

Although sister-nurses refrained from proselytizing non-Catholics, they did speak of many "conversions" in their patients' final hours. Probably most of these involved lapsed Catholics. But some were clearly conversions to Catholicism, at least as the church was embodied in the attending sister-nurse. The Holy Cross sisters, who despite their prior lack of hospital experience provided large numbers of nurses to hospitals North and South, performed more than seven hundred baptisms in the course of their nursing duties in 1862, according to the Holy Cross fathers at Notre Dame. (In such situations, lay Catholics are permitted by church law to administer the sacrament.) It seems unlikely that many lapsed Catholics had never been baptized. What sisters made of their newfound role as sacramental ministers—that, for all practical purposes, is what they were—is something they kept to themselves.[27]

Catholic nursing sisters received near-universal praise for their work. They were positively depicted in such hitherto anti-Catholic venues as *Harper's Weekly*, while the federal government thanked the Holy Cross sisters by presenting them with two captured Confederate cannons to be melted down in order to fashion a religious statue. As late as 1874, with anti-Catholic sentiment again on the rise in the nation's politics, two Dominican sisters were asked—allegedly by President U. S. Grant—to unveil the Lincoln monument in Springfield, Illinois. But the most telling honors came from non-Catholic soldiers like the Maine volunteer who kept a journal while languishing in a Confederate prison. "I am far from being a Roman Catholic," he wrote. "But from what I have seen during this war, I am convinced that the Roman Catholics have done more for sick and wounded soldiers North and South than any other religious sect." If Catholic loyalty had been called into question by events like the New York riot, Catholic leaders by war's end had ample reason to believe that the war had ultimately worked to endow their church with an authentically American stamp.[28]

Postwar Religious Tensions

Despite Catholic optimism, religious tensions mounted in the 1870s, with education once again the principal bone of contention. Barely five years after Appomattox, Republican leaders were levying charges of Catholic disloyalty and hostility to democratic norms. President Grant, whatever his respect for the war's sister-nurses, in 1875 endorsed a proposed constitutional amendment prohibiting government aid to sectarian schools. The amendment, in his view, would shield Americans from despotism, "whether directed by the demagogue or by priestcraft." That the postwar era of interconfessional good feelings was so brief is partly explained by Republican fears about national cohesion in the wake of the war. The public school, in the view of Republican leaders and allied opinion makers, was an essential tool for nation building, while sectarian schools and Catholic schools in particular actually threatened the enterprise. Did Catholic schools not teach submission to an authoritarian church and loyalty to a foreign potentate? Such was the view of their liberal critics.[29]

Such fears were exacerbated by developments in papal Rome, which over the course of the 1860s came under increasing military pressure from the new Italian nation. The Papal States, which once encompassed a significant portion of central Italy, had shrunk by 1860 to Rome and its environs, where a beleaguered Pius IX still ruled by courtesy of French military protection—a precarious state of affairs, as the pope clearly knew. When the French began to reduce their garrison, as happened in 1866, the pope's days as a secular ruler were numbered. The end came in 1870, when Italian forces breached the walls of Rome and claimed the city as Italy's capital. Pius retreated to the Vatican, where he remained for the rest of his long life, presenting himself to the world as a prisoner of the new Italian republic. If American Catholics were often moved by the pope's plight, seeing in it something of their own marginality, they were hardly well placed to appreciate his response to it. As Pius lashed out against the forces of secular modernity, he gave voice to sentiments that were wholly at odds with basic American values.

The first blow came in 1864 with the "Syllabus of Errors," in which the pope denounced such liberal mainstays as freedom of speech, press, and worship and the separation of church and state. Baltimore's recently named Archbishop Martin Spalding, understood to be speaking for the American hierarchy, told the nation's Catholics—and, more importantly, the nation's non-Catholics—that the document referred only to certain European radicals and not to American principles and arrangements. He was right in the limited sense that the document's authors were responding directly to anticlerical Italian nationalists. But when Spalding begged several high Vatican officials for a statement assuring Americans that the pope's condemnations did not apply to their Constitution, he failed to get results. American liberals, for their part, seized on the Syllabus with something like glee, as did their European confreres. Here was proof—should proof be needed—that the Catholic Church stood athwart the tide of historical progress.[30]

A second blow came in 1870, when the First Vatican Council defined the doctrine of papal infallibility. Although the pope's headship of the church was nowise in doubt, American Catholics had long been taught that papal infallibility was merely a theological opinion. "No enlightened Catholic holds the pope's infallibility to be an article of faith," Archbishop Purcell assured a multiconfessional audience in 1837. "I do not; and none of the brethren, that I know of, do." Even New York's Hughes, whose devotion to Rome was never in doubt, authorized a catechism for use in his diocese that called papal infallibility "a Protestant invention." Papal decrees were binding only when "received and enforced" by the church's bishops. American Catholics, for the most part, evinced little interest in the question. Republican government, after all, had meant freedom for the nation's Catholics, and their church was in a flourishing state. It was otherwise in Catholic Europe, where the rising tide of liberal nationalism threatened the church in manifold ways—a situation neatly symbolized by the Italian army's entering Rome while the council was in temporary abeyance. (It was never resumed.) Vatican I, in short, was a council dominated by fear. The council's formal definition of infallibility should be understood in this essentially reactionary context.[31]

Most of the American bishops in attendance at the council's final sessions voted with the majority, albeit uneasily. Few regarded a formal definition as well timed, and all were concerned with political backlash at home. A smaller number, led by Rochester's Bernard McQuaid and Patrick Kenrick of St. Louis, had theological objections. They did not see adequate grounding in Catholic tradition for a formal definition of infallibility and worried, quite rightly, about diminution of their own authority as leaders of the church. Kenrick and McQuaid were among the bishops who tactfully departed Rome prior to the final vote. Kenrick, indeed, continued for a time thereafter to speak candidly about his reasons for opposing the council's decision, although under pressure from Rome he eventually made his public submission. They were joined in departure by Cincinnati's Purcell, already under suspicion in Rome for his aggressive wartime advocacy of the Union cause. Little Rock's Edward Fitzgerald cast one of the two negative votes when the final tally was taken, for reasons that are still unknown.[32]

Most American Catholics, in all likelihood, were but dimly aware of these events. Their liberal antagonists paid far more attention. Pius IX was personally popular and even reputed to be a saint. But he was still a distant figure in the lives of most American Catholics, very few of whom—shades of Al Smith!—knew what an encyclical was. For the vast majority of Catholics, the most immediate impact of the aforementioned events was the further fueling of anti-Catholicism on the part of liberal elites. The effect was to strengthen among Catholic leaders an already lively disposition in favor of Catholic separatism. The bishops assembled at the Third Plenary Council in 1884 were prompted by such when they instructed every Catholic pastor to establish a school in his parish. That the bishops were also responding to a Roman directive, which perhaps made it easier to ignore the enormous financial commitment at stake, was also linked to recent Roman developments. Pius IX is rightly regarded as the first modern pope. A cultic celebrity in his own right, thanks to the rise of mass communication, he achieved in the course of his long reign an unprecedented centralization of ecclesial authority in Rome.

The War's Long Shadow

Few Catholic leaders at war's end devoted much attention to the plight of the newly freed slaves. Southern bishops, presiding over an impoverished church, were typically short in the extreme of priests and women religious. Northern bishops fared better when it came to wealth and personnel but were distant from the problem and, as postwar immigration quickened, soon confronted by new claims on their resources. As the sources of immigration diversified in the 1880s and after, the Catholic Church outside the South entered an era of unprecedented heterogeneity. Supplying a polyglot Catholic populace with priests and sisters who spoke its languages, mediating intergroup conflicts, facilitating immigrants' integration into a disciplined American church—such tasks preoccupied the majority of bishops into the 1920s. Some of the most prominent were also distracted by serious division within the episcopate—division stoked in part by ethnicity but having more fundamentally to do with disagreements over the church's orientation to an increasingly secular world.

Was race therefore of no account in explaining Catholic neglect of the hapless former slaves? In so frankly racist a culture, race could not help but play a role. Like other white Americans, most Catholics chose to remember the war without reference to slavery and therefore without reference to justice claims on the part of the newly emancipated. It was Catholic wartime heroism that dominated Catholic memory, which sharpened group resentment at persistent anti-Catholicism. Thus emancipation caused little change in Catholic racial attitudes. Most Catholics remained staunch Democrats even as Democratic regimes in the South kept black men from the polls, imposed legal segregation, and turned a blind eye to mounting violence against an increasingly isolated black population. Catholic churches in the South nearly always relegated blacks to segregated pews, while some northern parishes barred them entirely, as did Catholic schools and hospitals throughout the nation.

But individual Catholics sometimes swam against this dispiriting tide. Augustus Tolton, born a slave, was ordained to the priesthood in Rome in 1886, thanks to his Irish-born pastor in Alton, Illinois, who saw to his Catholic primary schooling, mostly via private tutoring. Local German Franciscans then educated him through college and aided in his subsequent admission to the Urban College of the Propaganda in Rome. Although Tolton had expected to serve in the African missions, the Propaganda sent him instead to work in the United States, despite—or possibly due to—no American bishop's having been willing to accept him as a seminarian. With Rome decisively on his side, he ministered first in Alton and then in Chicago, where he founded the city's first "national" parish for Catholics of African descent. Tolton's parish got financial aid from Mother Katharine Drexel, the Philadelphia heiress who in 1891 founded the Sisters of the Blessed Sacrament, a congregation exclusively devoted to teaching black and Indian children. Drexel's sisters taught in Tolton's St. Monica's parish once it established a school, a 1912 triumph that Tolton did not live to see. He died in 1897, apparently of a stroke—mute testimony to a life of struggle. Pope Francis declared him "Venerable" in 2019—the first step toward canonization.

A second black priest, Charles Randolph Uncles, was ordained in 1891. Uncles was a founding member of the Society of St. Joseph of the Sacred Heart, the Baltimore-based offshoot of an English order devoted initially to missionary work in Africa. Unlike Tolton, Uncles attended an American seminary—St. Mary's in Baltimore—and was ordained in the United States. The Josephites ordained two additional men of African descent, John Henry Dorsey and John J. Plantevine, in 1902 and 1907, respectively. But although the Josephites in the United States ministered primarily to African Americans, the order's commitment to ordaining black clergy was put on hold between 1907 and 1941. As for the Blessed Sacrament Sisters, they refused to accept black candidates until the early 1950s. One would not wish to impugn the generosity and compassion of Katharine Drexel, who was canonized in 2000, or of such lesser-known worthies as Tolton's boyhood pastor. Still, black Catholics remained a small and generally segregated minority in the American church until at least the 1950s, when white Catholics began— slowly, hesitantly, and often incompletely—to embrace the liberationist implications of a now-distant Civil War. In this respect, they did not differ greatly from most of their fellow Americans.[33]

Part III

A Turbulent Passage, 1871–1919

Mother Frances Xavier Cabrini, M.S.C.

(1850–1917)

T he year is 1889. A steamship en route from Le Havre has just docked at New York's Castle Garden, the city's teeming reception center for newly arrived immigrants. Along with its cargo of impoverished laborers from Italy's southern provinces, the ship carries Mother Francesca Saveria Cabrini, superior of the recently founded Missionaries of the Sacred Heart, and six members of her order. Born near Milan in 1850, Mother Francesca had even in childhood nursed missionary aspirations. She hoped to evangelize in China, which had long since supplanted the New World Indian missions in the religious imaginations of devout European Catholics. But Piacenza's Bishop Giovanni Battista Scalabrini, an early patron of Cabrini's order, had a different vision of missionary labor, as attested by his founding in 1887 of the Missionaries of St. Charles, whose priests served the Italian diaspora in the United States and Latin America. At Scalabrini's initiative, Pope Leo XIII—himself deeply worried by the spiritual condition of Italy's numerous emigrants—ordered Mother Cabrini to New York, where an orphanage for the city's Italians was to be her first order of business. That Cabrini had already booked her passage by the time she met with the pope suggests that no order was necessary.[1]

Although New York's Archbishop Michael Corrigan had consented to Cabrini's coming and had serious need of her services, he received her coldly. There was no chance of founding an orphanage for Italian children, he told her brusquely. She might as well go home, especially since no provision had been made by the city's Scalabrinian priests to house and support Cabrini's sisters. Cabrini was probably the unwitting victim of a quarrel between Corrigan and a wealthy New York convert who hoped to sponsor an Italian orphanage in her fashionable Manhattan neighborhood. Corrigan, well known as a zealous defender of his episcopal prerogatives, opposed the proposed location and therefore—he was not always prudent—the project itself. Fortunately for the nation's Italians, Mother Cabrini stood her ground. The pope had sent her, she pointed out, producing her credentials—a deft move, indeed, given Corrigan's Roman training and ardent support of the papacy. But she surely played her trump card gracefully. Even her adversaries conceded that Cabrini was a woman of vast personal charm and an astute reader of character—qualities that help to explain her achievements in an ecclesial world where, formally at least, only ordained males wielded authority.[2]

Cabrini's first weeks in New York were marked by confusion and insecurity—an experience she shared with the immigrants she came to serve but with whom she had otherwise little in common. Had it not been for the generosity of other New York women religious, Cabrini and her sisters would initially have been homeless. Cabrini spoke almost no English upon her arrival—it sounded to her like "the language of geese"—and found the language hard to learn, although she eventually gained something approaching competence. She was shocked by New York's noise and congestion and the poverty of its immigrant slums. New arrivals from Italy, she quickly discovered, were among the city's poorest residents and were held in particular contempt, even by their fellow Catholics. "They cannot bear the sight of the Italians," as she put it, half suspecting that the collection of "seat money" at the doors of the city's Catholic churches was meant to keep the Italians at bay. And she was simply bewildered by the city's religious variety, the likes of which she had never witnessed. "Here it is a desolation to see so many Protestants, so many Hebrews, so many sectarians."[3]

Whatever her initial disorientation, Cabrini was still capable of action. Within weeks she had opened a catechetical center in St. Joachim's parish on Manhattan's Lower East Side, only recently established for the city's Italians. In the charge of two Scalabrinian priests from Italy, the parish was so poor that successive pastors were obliged to rent the church's lower floor to a rag-picking concern. Cabrini's "school" was desperately poor as well, hardly more than an overcrowded child-minding center. Nothing daunted, she and her sisters also established an orphanage for Italian girls, aided by the monied convert whose independence had so enraged Archbishop Corrigan. That first orphanage, shortly to be replaced, was wholly inadequate to the need. "We have found that many children are abandoned shortly after they reach this city. Their parents, who have come here expecting to be rich immediately, now learn their mistake, and being unprovided with money, they set the children adrift to care for themselves," Cabrini told the *New York Sun,* apparently via a translator. She and her sisters had learned this unfortunate truth by visiting every Italian family in the vicinity of St. Joachim's—a pastoral strategy that the group would employ wherever they established a convent.[4]

After this burst of activity, Mother Cabrini returned to Rome, having been resident in New York for a scant four months. Such would be the pattern for the rest of her career. Between her initial arrival in New York in 1889 and her death in Chicago in 1917, she spent just over thirteen years total in the United States. The rest of her time was spent either in Europe, where she established houses of her order in France, Spain, and England, or in Latin America, where she opened houses in Argentina, Nicaragua, and Panama. She traveled widely too while in the United States, eventually founding houses in New Orleans (1892), Newark (1899), Scranton (1899), Chicago (1899), Denver (1903), Seattle (1903), Los Angeles (1905), and Philadelphia (1912), as well as visiting numerous Italian colonies in the nation's mining districts. Her sisters invariably opened at least one school and an orphanage wherever they settled and engaged as well in a program of home visiting— an emphasis that came to include regular visits to local prisons. They also staffed hospitals, each with a nursing school attached, in New York, Chicago, and Seattle. Cabrini, in short, was managing something akin to a multinational corporation—a role for which at the time there was for women no secular equivalent.[5]

When Cabrini left New York for the first time in the summer of 1889, she was accompanied by three young recruits to her order, who were to spend their novitiates in Italy. All three were Irish American, as were a number of subsequent recruits. Probably a quarter of Cabrini's sisters in the United States at the time of her death were non-Italians, most of them Irish surnamed. Why were such women attracted to Cabrini's order, given that few if any of them were initially able to speak Italian? Cabrini's person was a principal part of the answer. Adept at publicity and indisputably charismatic, she was even in her early years in the United States a widely admired public figure. That her sisters ministered to the poorest of the poor was probably a factor as well, at least for the most idealistic of young Catholic women. The order's varied ministries may also have played a role. Some of Cabrini's sisters were teachers, as was the case with the vast majority of women religious at the time, but they also worked as nurses, catechists, and friendly visitors—as social workers, in effect. Few orders at the close of the nineteenth century afforded their members such relative freedom with regard to what we now call ministry.[6]

Perhaps most important, the Irish sisters in Cabrini's order signal a maturation of consciousness among a portion of the nation's Catholics. Theirs was a generous view of the church, one that transcended the ethnic tribalism so often found in the immigrant generation. A shared Catholicity and a shared commitment to the poor was what made for sisterhood, rather than a common ethnic inheritance. Cabrini herself came to understand that Catholic immigrants in the United States were destined eventually to redefine what it meant to be Catholic—to move beyond the local or regional or national loyalties that had conditioned their faith in the old country. For this reason, her schools in the United States employed English as the principal medium of instruction, with Italian taught as a foreign language—as indeed it was for those from the Italian south who spoke a variety of dialects. And perhaps it was for this reason that Cabrini herself became a U.S. citizen—she did so, as Frances Xavier Cabrini, in 1909—and instructed the foreign-born members of her order to do the same.

Cabrini's death in 1917 was quickly followed by calls for her canonization. Even in her lifetime, Pope Leo XIII had referred to her as a saint, and Pius X had publicly praised her virtue. She was beatified in 1928, the canonically prescribed fifty-year waiting period having been waived by Pope Pius XI, and honored as the patroness of immigrants at a lavish ceremony in Rome. (Ten Chinese postulants from her order, which had recently established two houses in their country, were present in the congregation—a posthumous realization of Cabrini's initial missionary aspirations.) She was canonized in 1946, the first American citizen to be so honored. Her principal resting place—portions of her body are housed at shrines in Rome and Chicago—is on the grounds of the former St. Frances Cabrini High School in northern Manhattan. Founded in 1899 as an elite boarding academy, the school at the time of its 2014 closure was serving a primarily Dominican population. Although immigrant need remains, Cabrini's order—in common with other women's orders in the United States and Europe—now lacks sufficient younger members to respond to that need with its former enterprise and vigor.[7]

Immigrant need is a major theme in the chapter of American Catholic history through which Cabrini lived. The volume of immigrants arriving in the United States increased sharply in the 1880s and remained at high levels until Congress passed restrictive legislation in the early 1920s. With growing numbers now originating in southern and eastern Europe, the new immigration was more varied than the old with regard to language and culture. It was also more heavily Catholic, which posed a major burden for the nation's Catholic bishops, most of them of Irish descent but at least a generation removed from their own immigrant past. How to provide for an immigrant horde that was not only poor and uprooted but spoke dozens of different languages? How to maintain at least a façade of Americanness for a church newly riven by ethnic tensions and feared as ineluctably foreign by a significant portion of the nation? Was Americanness in fact a goal to which the church should aspire? Some bishops had their doubts. The issue would eventually fuel a major crisis in the American hierarchy.

Even as new immigrants poured into the country, however, the descendants of earlier Catholic arrivals were rapidly assimilating. Although most Catholics remained working class, a growing Catholic middle class was evident in towns and cities throughout the nation. Even working-class Catholics in the American-born generations spoke American English as a first and often only language, while interethnic marriages, primarily between Irish and German Catholics, became increasingly common. American-born Catholic women, especially those from more affluent families, evinced a hunger in these years for extended schooling and aspired, often successfully, to white-collar occupations. At least a third of Chicago's public-school teachers in 1910 were estimated to be Catholic women, and similar numbers prevailed in other heavily Catholic locales. American-born Catholic males, by contrast, tended to achieve mobility within the blue-collar ranks. Given that young Catholic women were often more "refined" than their brothers, a prominent Catholic author noted in 1900, it was often hard for them to find appropriate Catholic marriage partners. What such disparities might have meant for Catholic domestic life—most Catholic women, after all, did eventually marry other Catholics—must remain the stuff of speculation.[8]

Despite their evident ambition, few Catholic women at the time would have called themselves feminists. Indeed, as American-born Catholics became increasingly similar to their non-Catholic fellow citizens, they favored a rhetoric of Catholic difference—a difference that was particularly apparent when it came to matters of gender. No matter how talented or ambitious a Catholic woman might be, her allegiance to Catholic tradition meant rejecting autonomy as an appropriate female goal. Cabrini embodied the Catholic ideal: a woman of remarkable independence, initiative, and authority, she was also—Catholics would have said primarily—a spiritual mother whose life was devoted to others. That the Catholic Church was history's greatest champion of women's rights was for several generations the standard rejoinder of educated Catholics to feminist critics of their church. A career like Cabrini's could be offered in evidence: she had surely achieved far more within the church than she could have done as a woman in the secular world. It was only when women's opportunities outside the church underwent a dramatic expansion, as began to happen in the 1960s, that feminist criticisms gained new bite and the Catholic Church in the United States developed a woman problem.[9]

Institutional Growing Pains

The half-century between 1870 and 1920 saw the maturation of the United States as a nation, both institutionally and with regard to popular consciousness, and its birth as a nascent global power. Knit together by the world's most extensive railroad system—the first transcontinental route was completed in 1869—and increasingly by the telephone, domestic distances shrank. Frances Cabrini could travel with relative ease over terrain that previous missionaries had plied by horseback. Toward the end of the period, the automobile helped shrink distances too, especially after its mass production got under way in 1910, a critical moment in what is sometimes called the second industrial revolution. The United States became the world's leading producer of steel in the 1890s, signaling its new global stature in the realm of heavy industry. The country was not yet a leading military power. But it acquired a modest empire, including Puerto Rico and the Philippines, via a brief war with Spain in 1898, and in 1917 intervened decisively on the side of the Allies in the First World War. In the latter conflict, a newly activist federal government drafted not only soldiers but also public opinion via a propaganda campaign unprecedented in the nation's history.

Catholics were integral to this national story of growth and consolidation. Probably a majority of the nation's immigrants in these years were at least nominally Catholic. Most of them settled in the nation's cities, where their labor fueled the country's industrial transformation. Catholics were prominent too in the period's labor movement, which largely due to employers' recalcitrance generated disturbing amounts of violence. An increasingly standardized consumer culture encouraged immigrants' assimilation, as did a growing emphasis on compulsory education for the nation's children. With growth in Catholic numbers—the roughly six million Catholics in the country as of 1880 rose to just under twenty million by 1920—came enhanced political leverage, itself an additional force for cultural integration. Boston elected its first Catholic mayor in 1884, Massachusetts its first Catholic governor in 1914. Two wars provided stages on which Catholics could demonstrate patriotism, with the happy effect of a temporary diminution in anti-Catholic sentiment. If the clash with Spain was brief, most Americans saw the enemy as a corrupt Catholic power, and American Catholics received due credit for their generally robust support of the war.

Rather in the spirit of the period's secular reformers, the nation's Catholic bishops took steps in these decades to bring greater discipline and uniformity to the institution over which they presided. The Vatican under Leo XIII endorsed their aspirations, approving the creation of forty-six new dioceses in the United States between 1880 and 1904, by which time there were thirteen archdioceses, seventy dioceses, and four vicariates apostolic—the latter essentially missionary territory governed by a bishop. Few bishops any longer presided over territory so vast that it could not at least in theory be effectively governed from the top. But the flood of new immigrants complicated matters, given their ethnic and linguistic variety. So did the proliferation of religious orders, whose members' first loyalty was owed to their superiors, and in many locales a continued shortage of clergy. Thus progress was often slow. A majority of dioceses in these years remained loosely governed; a few were barely governed at all. Such was the case in Detroit, where an aged bishop's compromised health—episcopal retirements were rare in those days, with bishops expecting to die in office—brought the minimally staffed chancery to an administrative halt for some years prior to his death in 1918.

The Third Plenary Council of 1884 was the last such gathering of the nation's bishops until 1919. For many of the intervening years, the U.S. hierarchy was riven by conflict, principally but not exclusively over the question of just how accommodating of American values the Catholic Church in the United States could be. The nation's archbishops, it is true, did meet annually after 1890 to discuss internal church affairs. But theirs were low-keyed gatherings that had little apparent impact on their fellow bishops and even on some of their own number. San Francisco's Archbishop Patrick Riordan had occasion to speak in 1911 of the isolation he felt in his still quite remote location: "We are so cut off from the great life of the nation, by two ranges of Mountains, the Rockies and Sierras, and a vast desert intervening, that we seem to belong to a Foreign country."[1]

The result was an absence of Catholic leadership on the national level. The church's titular leader for the whole of the period was Baltimore's James Gibbons, named a cardinal in 1886—the second U.S. prelate to be so honored, New York's John McCloskey having been the first in 1875. Gibbons, American-born and possessed of a winsome personality, was known beyond his archdiocese as the author of the best-selling *Faith of Our Fathers* (1876), an accessible and surprisingly irenic exposition of Roman Catholic Christianity. (For several generations of Catholic youngsters, the book was a perennial confirmation gift.) The nation's capital then lay within the boundaries of the Archdiocese of Baltimore, and Gibbons had powerful friends among the political elite, which also enhanced his national reputation. Theodore Roosevelt was an admirer and eventually something of a Gibbons intimate. At Gibbons's death in 1921, he was eulogized by the *New York Times,* not historically friendly to Catholics, as "one of the wisest men in the world."[2]

Despite Gibbons's prominence and his status in Rome as de facto head of the American church, he could not provide leadership for a badly fractured hierarchy. Averse to conflict, he sometimes temporized in difficult situations, which grew in number as the century drew to a close. Generally aligned with what was called the "Americanist" faction among the bishops, he was distrusted by their conservative adversaries, even as his most liberal colleagues questioned his depth of commitment to their cause. Various players in this ongoing drama—New York's Corrigan was one—bypassed their brother bishops entirely as they pursued their disparate goals, cultivating allies in Rome. Not until 1919 did the nation's bishops once again have a forum for regular meetings and at least the chance of concerted action at the national level. Although Gibbons was well into his eighties by this time, he played a significant role in the establishment of the National Catholic Welfare Council (NCWC), the remote ancestor of today's U.S. Conference of Catholic Bishops. Under its auspices, the nation's bishops began to meet annually, while a standing committee of selected prelates coordinated Catholic activities nationwide and spoke for the hierarchy as occasion demanded.

His Eminence *JAMES CARDINAL GIBBONS* — The Honorable *THEODORE ROOSEVELT*
Archbishop of Baltimore, Died March 24th, 1921 — *Ex-President of the United States, Died January 6th, 1919*

THIS PHOTOGRAPH WAS TAKEN AT ORIOLE BASEBALL PARK, BALTIMORE, MARYLAND, SEPTEMBER 28TH, 1918, AT WHICH TIME
EX-PRESIDENT THEODORE ROOSEVELT DELIVERED AN ADDRESS AT THE LAUNCHING OF THE DRIVE FOR THE FOURTH LIBERTY LOAN.
THE PICTURE WAS MADE UNDER GREAT DIFFICULTY. WHEN THE CARDINAL AND THE EX-PRESIDENT MET AT THE PARK A LARGE CROWD
SURROUNDED THEM. THIS PICTURE IS AN ENLARGEMENT OF A KODAK PICTURE AND HAS BEEN COPYRIGHTED BY C. C. KNOBELOCH.

Cardinal James Gibbons with Theodore Roosevelt, 1918 (Courtesy of the
American Catholic History Research Center and University Archives [ACUA],
the Catholic University of America, Washington, DC)

If the Third Plenary Council of 1884 marked the temporary end of
relative episcopal unity, its achievements did point toward eventual Catholic cohesion. The parochial schools so emphatically endorsed by the council
fathers proved for several generations of immigrants to be effective engines
of assimilation and a source of pride and distinctiveness for the great majority of Catholic Americans. The *Baltimore Catechism,* the production of
which was authorized by the council, provided generations of young Catholics with a standard introduction to their faith and a shared store of not
invariably happy memories. Its question-and-answer format, in which
young Catholics were endlessly drilled, could be agony for children. Ten-
year-old Frankie Eardley, a midwestern farm boy, was not unusual in hav-

INSTITUTIONAL GROWING PAINS

ing no high opinion of his church's new catechism: "I would rather take a dozen kicks from the calves than to study that for fifteen minutes." But the *Baltimore Catechism* did succeed in condensing for popular consumption the complex arguments of the Neo-Scholastic philosophy that increasingly dominated Catholic intellectual life. "Thus the close proximity of the intellectual, the student, and the common man," in the words of historian William Halsey, "kept alive an essential myth for the Catholic community that truth was the possession of all men and not of an elite."[3]

The council also approved, albeit with significant dissent, the establishment of a Catholic University, to be located in the nation's capital. Accident certainly played a role: had it not been for a generous gift to the proposed university by a young Catholic heiress, a decision on its establishment would doubtless have been postponed to an anticipated Fourth Plenary Council, which was never held. (Subsequent rumors linked the heiress romantically to Bishop John Lancaster Spalding, who was the university's chief proponent and had known the woman since she was a child. The rumors, true or not, help to explain why this talented priest spent the whole of his episcopal career in the Diocese of Peoria.) The Catholic University of America, which opened in 1889 as a graduate school of theology, initially accepted as students only seminarians and the ordained. The higher education of an elite among the clergy, in the view of Bishop Spalding, would eventually raise the level of intellectual culture among Catholics generally. He was not alone in deploring his coreligionists' lack of distinction when it came to intellectual achievement—a lament that would be echoed well into the twentieth century.[4]

The Catholic University was crippled from the first by powerful opponents in the hierarchy, among whom New York's Corrigan was prominently numbered. So was Rochester's Bernard McQuaid, last encountered as a theologically informed opponent of the 1870 declaration of papal infallibility. Opposition to the project was not unwarranted: the cost was not easy to justify, given competing needs, and Washington, DC, was hardly a center of Catholic population. But opposition was more fundamentally fueled by growing division in the hierarchy over issues only tangentially related to the university itself. Personal animosities also played a role. Despite opposition, the university limped along, opening its doors to lay male undergraduates in 1904, which helped to boost lagging enrollment. Faculties in philosophy, law, and the social sciences had by this time been added, which strengthened the school's appeal. Even in its most financially troubled years, the university's faculty included some distinguished scholars and was thus a source of pride for intellectually ambitious Catholics and those who hungered for respect from the nation's opinion makers. It played a particularly important role in the interwar years of the twentieth century in the elaboration and popularization of Catholic social teaching.[5]

The American bishops in the nineteenth century were endowed, at least in the abstract, with enormous power, particularly with regard to the clergy. Until the United States ceased in the eyes of Rome to be mission territory, which did not happen until 1908, its priests had virtually no rights in canon law. Should a priest have a grievance against his ordinary, his only option—should his bishop prove unwilling to negotiate—was an appeal to the Propaganda in Rome. But even when it came to his priests, a bishop's power in practice was not absolute. Prior to the Civil War, an acute shortage of clergy had provided a certain protection to men who avoided public scandal, and this remained true for the rest of the century in priest-poor dioceses outside the regions of heavy Catholic settlement. The threat of clerical appeals to Rome, which increased in number as the century wore on, sometimes afforded protection too. Invoking Rome brought unwelcome attention, at least from a bishop's perspective, and the risk of Vatican intervention in American church affairs. When Leo XIII assigned an Apostolic Delegate to the United States in 1893, despite the opposition of nearly every American prelate, a principal justification was the need for firsthand mediation between certain bishops and their priests.

Notwithstanding such frustrations, episcopal governance in general grew in strength and effectiveness between 1870 and 1920. In nearly every diocese, the bishops' ownership of all church property was recognized in civil law and seldom contested by the laity. Certain eastern European immigrants, most notably the Poles, did sometimes challenge their bishops over just this issue, occasionally resorting to violence. But their resistance almost never had the staying power of the antebellum trusteeism conflicts, some of which went on for the better part of a generation. If a small minority of priests were willing to seek Roman redress of what they regarded as their rights, the vast majority of the clergy were docile. Urban priests in particular were closely monitored, both by the chancery and their clerical brethren, and governed by a highly restrictive code of conduct. Clerical scandals, as a result, almost certainly diminished in frequency or were at the least more quickly contained. With growing numbers of the laity achieving modest prosperity and a few accumulating wealth, most bishops were liberated from the crippling poverty of their antebellum predecessors, which facilitated the building of solid diocesan infrastructures. Obstacles did remain nearly everywhere to the full consolidation of episcopal power, which in most dioceses was achieved only in the 1920s and after. But real change had still taken place.

Priests

The number of priests in the United States grew dramatically in the latter decades of the nineteenth century and the first years of the twentieth. But the Catholic population was growing too, and most bishops continued to regard themselves as woefully short of clergy, regardless of what was often improvement in their actual manpower circumstances. Growing numbers of priests were American-born, especially in those parts of the country with significant Catholic populations—a development that pleased nearly every bishop. Irish American recruits to the priesthood were the most numerous, although German Americans figured prominently too, especially in the heartland's German triangle. But in sparsely populated dioceses, particularly in the trans-Mississippi West, the clergy continued to be mostly foreign-born. French diocesans and Italian Jesuits played a major role in the Archdiocese of Santa Fe in its early decades and in the Diocese of Denver, while the various California dioceses—San Francisco was now the West's most populous Catholic center—recruited many of their priests from seminaries in Ireland. With the advent of heavy immigration from southern and eastern Europe, coupled with an upsurge in immigrants from Quebec, numerous bishops were forced to recruit a new generation of priests from abroad.

The continuing multiethnic cast of the clerical population retarded the development of a cohesive clerical culture. The presbyterate in most dioceses was divided along ethnic lines, which even the American-born found hard to ignore. When a German-surnamed classmate at St. John's Seminary in suburban Boston was rumored to be leaving, seminarian Charles Aiken explained his departure at least partly in ethnic terms: "it is probable that the strictures of discipline and the absence of other Germans than himself, have caused him to become dissatisfied." The classmate in question may well have been born in the United States, given that Aiken's diary entry dates from 1887. He might even have had an Irish American mother. But in heavily Irish Boston and indeed in New England as a whole, from which region St. John's students were also drawn, a German surname could easily hamper a young priest's career. Irish ethnicity locally was still of the militant variety, quite capable of generating hostility to a blameless cleric who bore a non-Irish name. The newly arrived Quebecois, mostly resident in New England's mill towns, were equally suspicious of outsiders, even those who spoke French fluently.[6]

German priests had a good deal more freedom in the Midwest, even when the local bishop was not himself a German. Many priests of German origin did indeed spend their careers in German-language parishes, although there were fewer and fewer such parishes that did not require a priest who could also speak English. But in many places they were also assigned to the growing number of parishes that no longer bore a distinctive ethnic stamp. Irish ethnicity in the heartland, while still a discernible force, lacked the truculent defensiveness so evident in Boston and New York; English-language parishes there sometimes shed their Irish identity within the space of two generations. Polish ethnicity, by contrast, proved enduring, at least in the industrial centers where Poles settled in very large numbers in the 1880s and after. Polish-surnamed priests, even when American-born, typically served in Polish parishes for the whole of their careers. Many were doing so as late as the 1950s. Priests from other locales in eastern and southern Europe often faced similar restrictions in their assignments. A Lithuanian priest, initially imported to serve a congregation of his emigrant compatriots, might spend the whole of his priestly life as pastor of that parish.

If ethnicity remained a source of division, American-born aspirants to the priesthood increasingly shared a common experience of priestly formation. Growing numbers by the end of the century were trained in freestanding seminaries—institutions devoted solely to clerical formation, typically located in secluded, semirural environs. Although some young aspirants continued to enroll for their preliminary courses in colleges attended by laymen, the final years of preparation were invariably spent in the exclusive company of other seminarians and a faculty of priest-teachers. A number of the larger dioceses opened major seminaries in the later nineteenth century—institutions to which neighboring and even distant dioceses could send their students for the final years of clerical training. Among the more prominent were St. John's in the Archdiocese of Boston (1884), St. Bernard's in the Diocese of Rochester (1893), Kenrick Seminary in the Archdiocese of St. Louis (1893), St. Paul's Seminary in St. Paul, Minnesota (1894), and New York's St. Joseph's Seminary in suburban Yonkers (1896). If local church demographics endowed certain seminaries with an unofficial ethnic identity—Boston's St. John's coded Irish, Milwaukee's St. Francis regarded as German—the message of seminary education was otherwise. Every seminary preached the gospel of priestly otherness—of membership in a sacred fraternity whose bonds trumped those of family and ethnicity alike.

Most American seminaries in these years were intellectually mediocre, providing what might best be described as vocational education. Seminarians had to learn Latin for liturgical purposes but also—at least ostensibly—as a spoken language, since classes were formally required to be taught in Latin. Most were probably not, although subject matter related to sex was invariably presented in that ancient tongue—"veiled in the relative decency of Latin," in the words of novelist David Lodge. Students generally dabbled in ancient Greek as well and occasionally even Hebrew, but seldom with any application to the dangerous field of Scripture scholarship. Church history was invariably taught, but usually in cursory fashion—St. Mary's in Baltimore gave the subject a single hour per week—and rarely in a critical mode; in some seminaries, indeed, the class might best be characterized as an exercise in apologetics. Dogmatic and moral theology came in for the heaviest emphasis, with students expected to commit large portions of their textbooks to memory. Class discussion was apparently rare and debate almost unknown. "I was brought up in a system where the teachers neither directed the energy of the student, nor solved his difficulties by force of reason," as one priest put it in 1904, when self-critical impulses among Catholics were briefly in the ascendant. As a result, "I know almost nothing."[7]

Several American seminaries in the years around the turn of the century did bear marks of intellectual liveliness. Their numbers include St. John's in the Archdiocese of Boston and New York's St. Joseph's, both staffed at the time by Sulpician priests, and Rochester's St. Bernard's, where the theologically literate Bishop McQuaid was a major influence. St. John's Charles Aiken, who had been—unusually for a Catholic seminarian—an undergraduate at Harvard, spoke appreciatively of reading he had done in the seminary, evidently under the direction of Rector John Hogan. "I spent this afternoon in analyzing a chapter of 'Nature and the Bible,' an excellent book in two vols. translated out of the German. . . . It is just the kind of information we need today in order to meet the demands of our contemporaries." Cardinal John Henry Newman's "Letter to the Duke of Norfolk," with its famous paean to conscience, was for Aiken a "delicious" treat. Aiken's less gifted classmates doubtless consumed a more restricted intellectual diet. But Rector Hogan, a well-known advocate of seminary reform, championed high intellectual standards. Ours is an age of unprecedented intellectual ferment, Hogan argued, particularly in the natural sciences and the development of historical consciousness, especially with regard to Scripture. A priest should be sufficiently knowledgeable to follow current debates and respond intelligently from a Catholic perspective.[8]

Hogan's agenda for the nation's seminaries, influential in the 1890s, died shortly thereafter. The antimodernist crusade, which reached its apex under Pius X and his 1907 encyclical *Pascendi Dominici Gregis,* ushered in an era of stringent Roman control over Catholic seminaries in the United States. The result, as we shall see, was a stifling of debate and scholarly openness not just in the nation's seminaries but in Catholic institutions of higher learning generally. The Sulpicians were summarily removed from St. John's in 1911 by Boston's Archbishop William O'Connell, aptly described by historian Donna Merwick as "authority's answer to intellectual curiosity," and under rather more complicated circumstances from New York's St. Joseph's in 1906. Even in a less repressive climate, however, it seems unlikely that most of the nation's seminaries would have striven for academic distinction. Their purpose, after all, was to produce priests for a Catholic populace that was still heavily working class—precisely the social stratum from which most clerical vocations came. "The ecclesiastical seminary is not a school of intellectual culture," as John Lancaster Spalding told the fathers assembled at the Third Plenary Council, making the case for a national Catholic university, "and to imagine that it can become the instrument of intellectual culture is to cherish a delusion."[9]

If seminary reformers like Hogan were mainly concerned with curriculum, they also sought improvement in the seminary's physical environment and what might be called its psychic climate. In this regard they had lasting success. For much of the nineteenth century, seminary accommodations were spartan in the extreme. New York's diocesan seminary, opened at Troy in 1864, lost numerous students over the three decades of its existence to tuberculosis and other diseases, a problem aggravated, if not caused, by ill-heated dormitories and inadequate food. Similar conditions prevailed elsewhere, invariably justified by invoking the ideal of priestly asceticism. The most strenuous exercise typically permitted was a weekly group walk, in cassock and biretta, beyond the seminary grounds. The result, according to Father John Talbot Smith, a vigorous proponent of reform, was not simply "lowered vitality" but "scrupulousness and other forms of insanity." The American boy, in Talbot's view, was by nature active; it was cruel to consign him abruptly to "a sedentary routine."[10]

The seminaries opening toward the close of the century, which were widely regarded as models, featured much-improved facilities for students, including gymnasiums. Actual athletic programming was less common, given widespread doubt in clerical quarters as late as the 1890s that athletic pursuits were consonant with clerical dignity. Some seminaries that permitted their students to play baseball still insisted that they play in cassocks. But student enthusiasm for sport ensured an ongoing round of activity, much of it spontaneous. Charles Aiken at Boston's St. John's played handball and baseball with his classmates, rowed and skated on a pond in the seminary grounds, and even tossed around a football, despite that sport's being frowned upon as excessively violent by many Catholic leaders. A generation later, nearly every seminary in the country made regular provision for student athletics, participation in which was now seen as a mark of healthy masculinity, and featured accommodations that were sometimes significantly better than the student had known at home.

Seminary athletics proved to be a powerful source of student bonding and thus a major contributor to the increasingly cohesive clerical culture that characterized nearly all American dioceses as the twentieth century progressed. Sports probably made the strict regime of the seminary—the long hours spent in chapel, the weekly confessions, the "great silence" that prevailed for a portion of the typical day—significantly easier to bear. Perhaps regular recourse to the playing field also made it easier for young adult males to contemplate celibacy—the "putting on of the tin pants," as the students at Newark's major seminary liked to call it. Certainly it endowed seminarians, and by extension priests, with a reassuringly masculine aura, thus easing relations with males in general. "You may not interest an ordinary young American in conversation about the infallibility of the Pope," in the words of a popular manual of pastoral theology, published in 1897, "but you will have his ear and tongue on baseball and prize-fights." The young priest who could talk sports and loft a football with authority was the church's best weapon against the tendency of young males to distance themselves from religion, or so Catholic leaders came increasingly to believe.[11]

Prior to the 1920s, the work environments of the nation's priests varied markedly—something that would be progressively less true as the twentieth century wore on. Some dioceses in the later nineteenth century were still essentially mission territory, especially in the South and West. W. J. Howlett traveled from his home diocese of Denver in 1870 to attend the Sulpician seminary in Paris, followed by postordination training at a German university, only to serve for the first years of his priestly career as a peripatetic missionary to various Colorado mining camps. (Attendance at a European seminary normally signaled that a young man was destined for prominence as a big-city pastor, seminary teacher—which Howlett eventually became—or even a bishop.) Howlett's work was much easier than that of his missionary predecessors. He could travel by train to the various camps and sometimes stayed at local hotels rather than bunking with a family. But even after his assignment to the cathedral in Denver, where he assisted the pastor, local need was such that he still engaged in missionary travel. "In those days," he later recalled, "the whole of Northwestern Colorado was almost a wilderness."[12]

Dioceses centered on large cities contained remote rural areas too. As late as 1910, newly ordained priests were sometimes sent as pastors to small-town or rural parishes, while their more fortunate classmates—such was the reigning perspective—were sent as assistants to the pastors of large urban churches. Rural work was hard, if only because one's scattered parishioners were apt to be poor, which meant that the pastor was poor as well. Detroit's Patrick Cullinane was sent to organize a parish in Yale, a mostly Protestant village in the Michigan Thumb, shortly after his ordination in 1898. "I had never heard of the town," he later confessed, "and did not know in what part of the state it was situated." Although he took meals with a local family, he lived initially at the town's hotel, where he said his first Mass on Christmas morning. "The altar was the kitchen table." His parishioners, although few in number, soon raised sufficient funds for him to rent a modest house; the farmers among them contributed oats and hay to feed their pastor's horses. Building a church took longer; although parishioners did much of the labor, the church at Yale was not completed until 1903. Cullinane himself helped to build the rectory, having acquired construction skills in the course of his rural boyhood, and together with his brother, Eugene, who was also a priest, wired the church for electricity.[13]

If a rural pastor was not a self-starter, his job could be exceedingly lonely. Farm families came to church only on Sundays and only when the roads were passable. It was hard for a priest to raise funds in a rural population, which tended to be cash-poor; his salary "had to be coaxed, persuaded, and fought for," according to one rural veteran. Resentment, that most isolating of emotions, could easily result. Father Cullinane, however, was a self-starter par excellence, regularly traversing his very large parish—it included two missions as well as Yale—and getting to know his parishioners, from whom he learned much of pastoral utility. Having preached a Sunday sermon on the Rosary to a seemingly appreciative congregation at one of his missions, Cullinane subsequently discovered via meal-time conversation that few of them knew what the Rosary was. Nearly all had been raised in heavily Protestant parts of the state that were seldom visited by Catholic clergy. "I could readily understand their situation," Cullinane acknowledged, apparently wise beyond his years. "These were good-living people and Almighty God gave them grace according to their need."[14]

Most young priests, not surprisingly, regarded a rural assignment as something to be endured. But for men of a certain temperament, a rural assignment had real advantages. Patrick Cullinane, for one, reveled in the freedom of his early years of ministry. Largely ignored by a distant chancery, he mingled more freely with his parishioners than a city priest could do and got to know many non-Catholics as well, it being his policy to attend all public events in the district. He hunted with the men of the parish and frequented the racetrack, although diocesan regulations prohibited a priest from doing either. On at least one occasion, he embarked on a distant late-night sick call carrying both the Blessed Sacrament and a revolver—the latter a probable violation of canon law. Heartily masculine in his public persona, Cullinane seems not to have suffered from the acute self-consciousness said to afflict the newly ordained—a self-consciousness that had to do not simply with a priest's visibility but with his ambiguous sexual status as a vowed celibate. Transferred to Detroit in 1914, where he subsequently founded two parishes, Cullinane was, he tells us, made almost physically ill at the prospect of leaving Yale.[15]

With the Catholic population growing steadily more urban, most priests could expect to spend at least a portion of their careers in a city parish. Except in the poorest immigrant enclaves, a city assignment normally meant that a priest would receive his full salary and often additional fees besides. Urban rectories were usually substantial structures, affording comfort and privacy to the priests who lived there. The rectory, indeed, was often larger and invariably better appointed than the neighboring convent, with its numerous complement of teaching sisters. A city priest almost always had the services of a cook-cum-housekeeper and was seldom obliged to do manual labor around the church plant. For all of these reasons, a city assignment conveyed a certain status. Men assigned to the most prosperous urban parishes were widely regarded by all but the saintly among their peers as members of a favored elite. With living standards for priests still markedly unequal in virtually every diocese, bitterness could bedevil those priests who were less well-off, especially as the years of priesthood wore on.

Every newly ordained priest who received a city assignment went as a curate—or, to use the more common American term, an assistant to the pastor. The role was not always easy. Even where relations were amicable, pastors almost invariably regarded their assistants as priests-in-training—men to be monitored and instructed. The newly fledged priest was apt to bristle. Some pastors, moreover, were objectively difficult men, incapable of dealing tactfully with even the most docile of their junior colleagues. Pastors should take care not to "show themselves unkind, cold and unfriendly toward their curates," a popular pastoral manual counseled in 1909. They should not "find fault with everything" or treat their assistants like "children in the nursery." Assistants, for their part, were warned against "haughtiness" and advised to be discreet, considerate, frugal, and punctual. Happily for the men ordained in the years around the turn of the century, the term of assistantship in most dioceses did not last long—from three to five years in most cases. Priests ordained in the middle decades of the twentieth century often spent upward of twenty years as assistants.[16]

A curate in a large urban parish was apt to be a busy man. The pastor generally functioned as a kind of CEO—"more superintendent than actual worker," in the words of one observer. "He directs his assistants, employs teachers, builders, and tradesmen." The assistant—or assistants, there sometimes being more than one—said the early morning Mass, heard most of the confessions, taught catechism in the parish school, supervised the parish youth groups, visited the sick and dying, presided over numerous funerals, counted the Sunday collections, and made himself generally available. Contact with parishioners often made the work rewarding, although priests were regularly cautioned against cultivating lay friendships. But in a large city parish, even the most energetic priest could know only a fraction of his parishioners. "For the most part he gets to know only those who come to him," according to New York's Father Edward Moore, "and all too often spends his time saving those already saved." An idealistic young priest, overworked but certainly aware of the problem, risked feeling like a failure. In that regard, a rural priest like Patrick Cullinane was probably better off.[17]

Being pastor of a large urban parish meant heavy responsibilities. The pastor was often a builder, since parishes regularly outgrew their existing facilities. He was almost certainly a manager of considerable debt—debt that did not disappear during economic downturns or in the event of a radical change in neighborhood demographics. He oversaw, and was ultimately responsible for, the parish school or schools, a plenitude of social and devotional organizations, and all forms of charitable outreach—the need for which was great in almost every parish. The Abbé Félix Klein, visiting from France in 1903, was dazzled by the activity he encountered in American urban parishes, citing as an example St. Patrick's in Washington, DC. St. Patrick's supported two schools, two orphan asylums, a St. Vincent de Paul Society and a Ladies of Charity for visiting and aiding the poor, various devotional groups, a Sunday school, a choral association, and a dramatic club. Despite its relatively modest size—St. Patrick's had only about five thousand members—the parish also boasted a gymnasium, library, and lecture hall.[18]

In a miniprincipality like St. Patrick's, the pastor was king. If he did not know all of his people, as indeed he could not do, he was nonetheless known to them. For the devout, he was a spiritual leader; for those less closely tied to the church, he stood for the community and embodied its aspirations. The pastor of a large parish was typically a public figure, recognized as such by city officials and the local press. The deference he commanded from outsiders, the honors he might receive—these were widely understood as tributes to the group he represented. Accustomed to the intense anticlericalism of French liberal culture, Abbé Klein was impressed by the evident devotion of American Catholics to their clergy, which he attributed mainly to the separation of church and state and the clergy's consequent dependence on free-will offerings from the faithful. But in a pluralistic society where Catholics still occupied the lower ranks of the social hierarchy, the symbolic function of the clergy was a factor too. If the pastor was not exactly a tribal chieftain, his role encapsulated many of the same functions.

Women Religious

The number of women religious in the United States exploded in the final decades of the nineteenth century, growing far faster than the number of priests. Almost forty-seven thousand sisters were working in the country as of 1900, up from roughly five thousand at the time of the Civil War. By 1920, their numbers had soared to north of ninety thousand. Some of the more than three hundred religious communities nationwide in 1920 had deep roots in the American nineteenth century. Others were recent arrivals, many from southern and eastern Europe. The Felician Sisters—Polish Franciscans who staffed the schools in a number of Polish immigrant parishes—were among the more prominent. Like many communities from eastern Europe, the Felicians even in the 1920s remained ethnically homogeneous, with some of their members unable to speak much English. By the turn of the century, however, most religious communities in the United States included sisters from more than one ethnic background. No community could flourish in this country if it did not recruit American-born vocations, and those vocations came increasingly from a population in which ethnic consciousness of the immigrant variety was fast disappearing.

That said, it must also be conceded that Irish American women accounted for a vastly disproportionate share of vocations to the religious life. Demographics provide part of the explanation: the Irish are the only major immigrant group in our history in which women regularly outnumbered men, something that was especially true in the decades after the Civil War. Among Irish arrivals in 1900, about 53.8 percent were female, most of them young and unmarried. They brought with them a culture profoundly altered by the Famine of the mid-1840s. The post-Famine Irish—and to a surprising extent their American counterparts—were significantly less likely to marry than were members of other ethnic groups; when they did marry, they tended to do so relatively late in life. Irish American communities, then, typically included a large population of single women accustomed to earning their own living and not necessarily expecting to marry. A religious vocation in these circumstances might appeal for more than spiritual reasons. It provided a lifelong substitute for family, both economically and emotionally, and might permit an ambitious if ill-educated girl to achieve professional status.[19]

No religious vocation, of course, can be understood without reference to the spiritual. The disparate souls who made up individual religious communities were bound together by shared religious assumptions and a daily round of religious observance that bordered on the strenuous. In this regard too, the Irish possessed a certain advantage, having inherited a Catholicism suffused with asceticism and yet oriented to action in the world—the latter quality derived in good part from their church's intimate connection to the struggle for Irish nationhood. Few women religious of any ethnic background have bequeathed to us reflections on the roots of their vocation, the essence of which was self-abnegation in the service of God and neighbor. "Let your actions be hidden in time, and known only to God," the Sisters of St. Joseph of Carondelet were quite typically instructed. "Rejoice more when in the eyes of the world His glory is promoted by others rather than by yourself." But the nature of religious life is such that its taproot is necessarily spiritual. A woman could hardly bear its discipline, toil, and physical hardship were her motivations purely self-interested.[20]

The work undertaken by sisters in the decades around the turn of the century continued to be varied, albeit less so than in the decades prior to the Civil War. If many sisters taught school, there were also sister-nurses and sisters who staffed such institutions as orphanages, old-age homes, and, after the late 1890s, the Catholic version of social settlement houses. By the 1890s, however, the various orders had come under intense pressure from the nation's bishops to produce teachers for an ever-expanding network of Catholic schools, which now included a small but growing number of high schools. Some orders abandoned other ministries to concentrate solely on education, thereby severing their communities' links to a cherished past. The demand for teachers was such that the youngest members of the order often had to go into the classroom with only minimal training. (The tallest girl in the novitiate was frequently tapped for classroom duties, according to the Felician Sisters' convent lore.) Relatively few recruits to religious life even in the early twentieth century had much in the way of formal education: among those who entered Philadelphia's Sisters of St. Joseph between 1909 and 1916, for example, 78 percent had an eighth-grade education or less.[21]

Societal standards with regard to education rose rapidly in the early twentieth century, and pressure grew for states to certify teachers in private as well as public schools. Although under intense pressure to produce ever more teachers, the various women's orders had little choice but to institute a longer and more rigorous period of education for their newest members. By 1915, if not before, most orders required the equivalent of a high school

diploma before a sister entered the classroom. The most intellectually promising were often sent for further study, sometimes to Washington, DC's Sisters' College, affiliated at its founding in 1911 with Catholic University, and
sometimes to a local teachers college, which at the time would probably have
been a secular institution. These highly trained women would then staff the
equivalent of a normal school for members of their order, who even after
they began to teach would continue their education via summer study. This
remarkable effort to improve sisters' educational credentials generated tension with pastors impatient for teachers and even with bishops, despite its
evident necessity. But the leadership of the various orders nearly always held
firm when it came to their educational priorities and continued to do so in
subsequent generations.

Teacher training in the various orders reflected each order's particular
ethos and traditions, which frustrated efforts at the diocesan level to standardize teacher preparation. But if Catholic schools lagged behind their public counterparts in this regard, the pedagogy of most orders was remarkably
astute. Sister-teachers were indeed taught to be firm disciplinarians—a necessity, given the very large classes that featured in most Catholic schools.
But they were also taught to be gentle and compassionate. The "course of
studies" for the Sisters of Notre Dame de Namur, a sizable teaching order,
counseled teachers to "rule by kindness rather than severity": "For some of
your pupils their school days may be the only happy period of their lives;
therefore, make them all sunshine." Teachers should never use corporal punishment, the Notre Dame sisters were told—a stricture found in the teaching
manuals of many orders. In the context of an overcrowded classroom, gen-
tleness might sometimes go by the boards. But sister-teachers were typically
trained in a humane and surprisingly child-centered pedagogy and bound to
its precepts by both conviction and peer pressure. An order's most admired
teachers were invariably those who "ruled by kindness."[22]

Sister-teachers received little more than subsistence pay for their service in parish and diocesan schools, where pressure was fierce to keep tuition minimal. Teaching brothers, far fewer in number, typically earned
twice as much. Had sisters not worked for so little, the nation's Catholic
schools—by far the largest system of schools in the world not funded by the
state—could not have existed in anything like the numbers that they did.
(In 1920, the nation's approximately six thousand Catholic schools enrolled
some 1.7 million children.) Most orders continued to earn additional funds

from their elite academies and high schools; growing numbers also founded colleges, especially in the 1920s and after, for which tuition was routinely
charged. The larger orders, especially, also benefited from private benefac-
tion, with wealthy donors contributing to such projects as the building
of commodious motherhouses. But on the job, most sisters lived close to
the bone—a reality that probably enhanced their cultural authority. If self-
sacrifice was universally understood to be the essence of true motherhood,
the poverty of the parish sisters bolstered their status as spiritual mothers.

With growing numbers of young Catholics now enrolled in school for
an extended period, women religious came to exert even greater influence
on the nation's Catholics, especially those resident in heavily Catholic locales. But they were evocative figures too for those who seldom saw sisters
and certainly for non-Catholics, for whom sisters had long been objects of
mystery, eliciting fear along with the inevitable fascination. Much of that
fear had dissipated by the later nineteenth century, when anti-Catholic propaganda no longer focused obsessively on nuns. Largely for that reason,
women religious had long since abandoned their earlier practice of traveling in civilian clothing. But the fascination lingered. Father Peter Cullinane
brought two Holy Cross sisters from Indiana to his rural Michigan parish
for a three-week visit in 1910. "Business was at a stand still during the time
of the Sisters' journey through town," he reports, "and they were the topic
of conversation for days." Cullinane's parish was still too small to support a
school, and most of his parishioners had had little exposure to women religious. But they greeted the sisters as powerful symbols of Catholicity.
"When we were leaving a certain home in the country the 'haus frau' knelt
and asked for their blessing," an amused Cullinane relates. The startled sisters recovered their wits sufficiently to ask "Father" to do the honors.[23]

Organizing Nationally

The reform movements of the so-called Progressive era, which had its roots
in the mid-1890s and ended in 1917, evinced a passion for bureaucratization,
order, and efficiency—all of which were notably lacking in the period's
immigrant-thronged cities. Most Catholic leaders held aloof from such
movements, which were almost invariably led by Protestants and which
tended, as Catholics saw it, to endorse unduly secular remedies for the
problems they addressed. But Catholic leaders were still concerned with

period social problems—hence the numerous programs to assist recent immigrants and institutions to house the dependent—and seldom indifferent to the benefits of centralization and administrative efficiency. Most bishops were anxious to impose more stringent controls on charities and schools in their dioceses, ideally by means of a central command, and to generate a greater sense of unity among their clergy. Still, the Catholic Church in the United States was a markedly decentralized institution as late as the First World War, even at the level of most dioceses. Only with the organization of the National Catholic War Council in 1917 can it be said to have achieved a national presence, or at least the potential for such, in an administrative and leadership sense.

The bishops were not the first to organize on a national level. The Catholic Educational Association, which dates from 1904, provided a venue for educators throughout the country to consult on mutual problems at annual meetings and via the association's regular publications. High on the organization's agenda was the centralization of school administration in the various dioceses. Every diocese should have a school superintendent— he would invariably be a priest—with sufficient authority to standardize curriculum and textbooks, oversee teacher training, and develop measures to assure educational quality. Although progress was uneven, most dioceses had moved in this direction by the 1920s. The National Conference of Catholic Charities, founded in 1910, also stressed the importance of centralized administration, efficiency, and professional standards, in this case for Catholic charitable endeavors. Under the influence of Monsignor William Kerby, a longtime member of the faculty at Catholic University, the conference promoted a more systemic analysis of poverty, and thus of its remedies, than had hitherto characterized Catholic charity. Support for fair wages and restrictions on child labor, in Kerby's view, was as much the obligation of the social worker—and indeed of the conscientious Catholic—as was personal assistance to the poor.

U.S. entry into the First World War, which occurred in April 1917, occasioned the creation—initially as a temporary body—of the National Catholic War Council. Its immediate purpose was to coordinate Catholic war-related activities, ranging from provision of military chaplains to financing the Knights of Columbus in its near-herculean effort to provide recreation and support to Catholic soldiers in training camps domestically and abroad. The council also served to assure the public of Catholic patriotism—something called into question, even for otherwise-tolerant Americans, by the large number of recent immigrants in the Catholic population. Few of the bishops were closely involved with the wartime workings of the council, but those who were—Cardinal James Gibbons, in particular—quickly recognized its value in protecting Catholic interests when it came to national legislation. (Organized at Catholic University in Washington, DC, the council was initially headquartered there.) This advantage, coupled with the prominence that the council afforded the nation's Catholic leaders, argued for a permanent body, at least in the view of Gibbons and his episcopal allies.

That permanent body, initially christened the National Catholic Welfare Council, came into being in 1919, with a standing executive committee that oversaw five departments, the two most important of which dealt with education and social action. Although supported by a substantial majority of the nation's bishops, the council was vigorously opposed by several prominent prelates, including Boston's William O'Connell and Milwaukee's Sebastian Messmer. The council, in their eyes, represented an extralegal challenge to a bishop's authority in his own diocese, where he was answerable only to Rome. Subsequent actions by the staff of the Social Action Department, headed by Father John A. Ryan, further fueled the resistance. Ryan, an outspoken advocate of liberal reform, was the principal author of the "Program for Social Reconstruction," a document released by the department late in 1919 and popularly seen as reflecting the views of the nation's bishops, although they never voted to approve it. The document's endorsement of a living wage, an end to child labor, and public provision of health care for the indigent made Ryan a popular man in New Deal Washington in the 1930s. But it did not endear him or the council that employed him to certain conservative members of the hierarchy in 1919.[24]

Several of the council's opponents were well connected in Rome and almost succeeded in destroying it. A Roman congregation actually issued a decree of suppression against the council in 1922—a decree ultimately overturned by vigorous action on the part of the council's episcopal supporters. The council's survival—it was called the National Catholic Welfare Conference after 1923—meant triumph for the national consciousness that increasingly characterized its supporters and signaled a new chapter in American Catholic history, in which the church, via its organized leadership, was a growing presence in the nation's civic life. It took time for the conference to emerge as an assertive lobbying presence. But once the Democrats became the nation's majority party in the early 1930s, it represented, at least in the eyes of most politicians, a potentially formidable political player. Bishops then and in subsequent generations grew accustomed to having their views solicited on a wide variety of policy questions.

One of the first pieces of national legislation on which the council took a position and deployed a lobbying effort—in this case, in vain—was the Johnson-Reed Act of 1924, which established an immigration policy heavily weighted against would-be arrivals from southern and eastern Europe. The new law, which remained substantially in effect until 1965, marked a definitive end to the era of mass immigration that began in the 1830s. It had long-term effect on the composition of the nation's population, including the number of Catholics and Jews, which would almost certainly have been larger had mass immigration continued. At the same time, the law afforded a breather of sorts to the nation's Catholic leaders. With immigration from southern and eastern Europe slowing to a trickle, recent immigrant communities in this country moved more rapidly toward assimilation, which helped to ease ethnic tensions among Catholics and facilitated the centralization of diocesan administration. The nation's bishops by 1920 had presided for some forty years over a church more varied in its ethnic makeup than any in the modern world. Their lot had not been easy.

A People Numerous and Varied

etween 1870 and 1920, immigrants constituted a relatively constant proportion of the U.S. population, ranging from just over 13 percent in 1860 to 14.7 percent in both 1890 and 1910, the highest figure ever recorded. But the *numbers* of immigrants entering the country in these same decades soared. Close to nine million arrived between 1901 and 1910, the largest decadal total prior to legal restriction in the 1920s. Beginning in the 1880s, moreover, the sources of American immigration underwent a profound shift, from northern and western Europe to the continent's South and East. Irish immigrants, who in the 1840s had made up close to half the nation's new arrivals, constituted about 4 percent of those arriving between 1901 and 1910. Immigration from Germany declined in similar fashion. In place of what now were regarded as the "old" and generally superior immigrants came a flood from Italy and a dismembered Poland and a smaller but still significant stream from eastern Europe, Greece, and Turkey. Emigration from a severely overpopulated Quebec transformed the population of many New England mill towns at just about the same time.[1]

The so-called new immigrants were no poorer or less equipped for American life than their Irish Famine predecessors had been. But they were in many respects more visible than those earlier arrivals and provoked far more resistance to the nation's lenient policies with regard to immigration. The new arrivals were even more likely to settle in cities than their Irish predecessors and constituted a far more urbanized population than that of the native-born. As such, they were associated with, and often blamed for, the disorder and corruption that many Americans saw as endemic to the nation's rapidly growing cities. Most new immigrant populations were heavily male—Italian immigrant males outnumbered females by a factor of three to one—and included many transients. At least a third of Polish immigrants and an even larger percentage of Italians are estimated to have returned to Europe, although an unknown number subsequently remigrated to the United States. The footloose foreign male, adrift in a normless city, elicited fears in the native-born that were not easily assuaged. Finally, the new immigration was even more Catholic than the old and also included large numbers of Jews.[2]

Catholics already resident in the country greeted their newly arrived coreligionists with pronounced ambivalence. A heavily Catholic immigrant stream meant spectacular growth for the church—the nation's Catholic population doubled between 1884 and 1914—and greater Catholic political leverage. But a good many Catholics also feared the otherness of this new population—its myriad languages; its maleness, transiency, and alleged criminality; its seeming indifference to American norms. They worried especially about anti-Catholicism, which even in relatively tolerant times lurked just below the surface of American political life. Their fears were soon realized: the depression-ridden 1890s saw an upsurge of anti-Catholicism akin in many respects to that of the 1850s. Like that earlier episode, the anti-Catholicism of the 1890s was fueled by a kind of panic over recent immigration. So was the heavily rural surge of anti-Catholic agitation that marked the years leading up to the First World War.

For Catholic leaders, the new population meant a drain on already stretched resources. Immigrants needed priests who could speak their language, as well as churches, schools, and social welfare institutions. In many immigrant populations, the laity took the initiative when it came to fundraising and parish founding. But despite their generosity, which was sometimes close to heroic, they often needed additional help, whether from affluent lay Catholics or the local bishop. Some immigrants also recruited priests, or at least attempted to, but most bishops opposed this particular manifestation of lay initiative. Only a bishop was equipped to verify a priest's credentials, especially if he came from abroad. Securing a supply of reliable clergy from Europe's remoter corners was an ongoing burden for many prelates into the 1920s. So was mediating the intragroup conflicts that all too often accompanied the creation of the immigrant parish.

The two largest by far of the new immigrant groups came from Italy's southern provinces and partitioned Poland. The Italians, like the Irish before them, settled mainly in New York City, New England, and the mid-Atlantic states, where—again, like the Irish before them—they worked primarily as manual laborers. Italian workers paved the streets, built the subways, and eventually dominated the construction trades. Significant concentrations of Italians were also found in Chicago, New Orleans, and San Francisco. Polish immigrants, by contrast, settled mainly in the industrial cities of the north-central states. Chicago quickly emerged as the leading Polish city, with large numbers also locating in Buffalo, Pittsburgh, Milwaukee, and Detroit. Poles worked mainly in heavy industry, almost invariably at the least skilled and most dangerous jobs. "In America Poles work like cattle," in the words of one disgruntled immigrant. They were less inclined than the Italians to be geographically mobile, at least once permanently settled in the United States, and more inclined to defend their turf aggressively. If Italians were often criticized by American clerics for their neglect of church support and indifference to the parochial school, Poles raised ecclesiastical eyebrows with their frequent assertions of ownership when it came to the local parish.[3]

Immigrant Catholicism: The Italians

The first arrivals from southern Italy were overwhelmingly young and male; many did not expect to remain in the New World permanently. Most were infected by the anticlericalism so common to their native place, where the church and its functionaries were often viewed as allies of the aristocracy. For some, indeed, the local bishop had also been the landlord. Few of these men, in all likelihood, had been accustomed in Italy to regular attendance at Mass, that sort of observance being widely regarded as the province of women and the old. Theirs was not a Catholicism centered on the sacraments, save on those rare occasions that marked life's major transitions and sometimes not even then. Men in the Italian South might neglect annual confession and reception of the Eucharist for many years running and even in the United States were likely to opt for a civil marriage. These immigrant males, in short, were hardly the stuff from which an ethnic parish might be built. In most cities where southern Italians settled, it took several years to organize even a skeletal Italian congregation and often much longer to build a church.

But those same immigrants, or at least the great majority, still regarded themselves as Catholics. They typically brought their saints along as they journeyed abroad. A statue or painting of a local or regional wonder-worker or, more commonly, the Virgin Mary could be found in communal apartments or tenement courtyards wherever Italian immigrants settled. The benefit societies regularly organized in Italian immigrant communities, which provided assistance in times of sickness and burial money in the case of death, were often placed under the patronage of such saints, some of whose images eventually migrated to the newly established parish church. These holy helpers connected immigrants to the distant villages of their birth and the moral world those villages represented—a world made vulnerable by immigrant loneliness and the frequent absence of a family anchor. The saint who accompanied immigrants to a place where they were poor and despised was often the sole reminder of their innate human dignity. "Our Italians, and I mean the old folks, feel that without the guardianship of their former patron saint, life would be next to impossible," according to an Italian American raised in immigrant New York.[4]

Nearly every Italian parish honored its resident saint—or saints, as was sometimes the case—with an annual *festa,* which typically entailed a parade and sometimes a street fair. (Prior to the organization of an Italian congregation, local benefit societies often staged more modest versions of such celebrations.) Even Catholic observers were often repelled by this mode of immigrant piety. "In those parades there were no prayers and no religious songs," according to a priest from northern Italy, for whom southerners were an alien breed, "but only some yelling or disorderly exclamations. Some women in their ignorant simplicity, were holding candles and walking barefooted." The males who paraded, he was careful to note, were rarely present at Mass. "Everything begins and everything concludes exteriorly," which is to say outside the sanctuary. But immigrant men did sometimes follow their saints into church. Men were particularly apt to attend Mass on the feast day of a patron saint, and they occasionally frequented novenas. Visiting an Italian parish in the slums of New York, where the lower floor housed a rag-picking shop, a journalist in 1905 witnessed a touching act of devotion. "On one occasion, while the writer was present one of the rag-pickers in the basement sang a hymn to the Virgin ... and his voice was of rare sweetness and purity."[5]

Much in Italian immigrant piety disturbed, even scandalized, the nation's bishops and clergy, especially the Irish Americans. For all the Italians' professed devotion to the saints, according to Father Bernard Lynch, writing in the *Catholic World,* they did not understand "the great truths of religion." The ubiquitous *feste* were regularly criticized as irreligious, even semipagan. A number of bishops banned them, although seldom with vigorous enforcement. Italian anticlericalism was a particular irritant, given period papal politics. Italian independence, so recently gained, had come at the expense of the pope, now a self-styled prisoner of the Vatican. Celebrations of Italy's national day, an annual occurrence in Italian immigrant communities, were often regarded by other Catholics as demonstrations against the papacy. The "Italian problem," as it was regularly labeled, was increasingly thought to require separate parishes for the group. "They cannot well be mixed with other nationalities on account of their filthy condition and habits, even if they were willing to come to our churches themselves," in the blunt assessment of an Irish American pastor in New York.[6]

Separate parishes were expensive, however, and Italian immigrants were notoriously reluctant to contribute to the church. In most locales, the first Italian congregations were housed in the basements of existing churches, often those of Irish Americans. Although such congregations were always served by an Italian-speaking priest, many immigrants saw the basement location as an insult. Father Nicholas Odone, whose congregation worshiped in the cathedral crypt in St. Paul, Minnesota, solicited funds from his people for a church of their own by appealing to their wounded pride: "What humiliation for us, here, numerous as we are . . . to have come here in this low and humid hall, placed under the feet of a dissimilar people who sometimes look down on us. . . . Let us reawaken in us the national pride. We are Italians and let us remember we are children of Dante Alighieri." Odone's appeal was not immediately successful. But as Italian communities grew and especially as families proliferated, Italian parishes began to appear. Sometimes the immigrant population managed to build a church of its own, often with help from outsiders. Sometimes Italians were heirs to a church whose original members had fled an increasingly Italian neighborhood.[7]

Some bishops were initially reluctant to endorse juridically ethnic parishes for new immigrant groups like the Italians, fearing that such parishes would retard assimilation to the American Catholic norm. Being housed in a "mixed parish," even in its basement quarters, was assumed to have beneficial effect on a group like the Italians, widely regarded as "the worst Catholics that ever came to this country." (The words are those of Father B. J. Reilly, pastor of New York's Nativity Church.) But such experiments were seldom successful. Immigrant "guests" in such parishes, along with their priests, resented their seemingly inferior status and regarded parishes of their own as a symbol of group achievement. The lay and clerical "hosts" in such parishes were often contemptuous of their "guests" and less than patient with their foibles. The pastor at New York's St. Patrick's Church, the city's onetime cathedral on the Lower East Side, finally closed his basement to its Italian congregation, apparently frustrated beyond endurance by that congregation's failure to contribute financially to the parish.[8]

The Propaganda eventually spoke to the "ethnic parish" question, ruling in 1887 that the American bishops should permit their various immigrant groups to form such parishes when numbers and resources made it possible. Somewhat ironically, given the fears of certain prelates, the ethnic parish proved to be a remarkably effective engine of assimilation. Immigrants nearly always arrived with a local or regional rather than a national identity. The Irish had come as Kerry or Killarney folk; the Italians came as Pollese (from the village of Polla) or, in a more cosmopolitan take, as Calabrese (from the province of Calabria). Varying dialects reinforced such divisions within groups whom Americans saw as unambiguously "Irish" or "Italian." Newly arrived immigrants typically formed their benefit societies on a village or regional basis. But an immigrant parish had of necessity to include as broad a population as possible, given the shortage of clergy and the enormous cost of supporting a priest and a church. In the context of parish building, then, immigrants shed their local identities and acquired membership in what Americans called a national group. Pollese and Calabrese became "Italians," although not invariably without struggle.

The ethnic parish provided a protective environment for the immigrant generation—a place where traditions were preserved, loneliness was assuaged, and the immigrant's dignity was affirmed, along with that of the group. Italian parishes typically boasted a rich social life, usually orchestrated by the various societies that had existed prior to the parish but now moved within its orbit. These societies mounted the annual festa, staged parades, and tendered a seemingly endless round of banquets. A marriage or baptism might merit a banquet; so did the feast of the patron saint and even—in the words of an Italian visitor to Philadelphia—such events as "the departure of a barber who goes to spend a couple of months in Italy." The societies also ensured that the typically lavish funerals of parishioners were well attended. "For funerals one spends fabulous sums," according to our Philadelphia informant. "One has even seen processions of forty carriages for the funeral of a new-born baby."[9]

Italian immigrants were generally reluctant to support parochial schools, which exposed their children early on to the assimilative effects of public education. Often more fluent in English than their parents' dialect Italian, the American-born increasingly married across village and regional lines and even occasionally took non-Italian spouses. Their allegiance to the ethnic parish, partly in consequence, was fleeting. Italian Americans, as the second generation nearly always regarded themselves, stood out among period ethnic groups for their unusually high rate of geographic mobility. As they moved of their own volition into parishes dominated by thoroughly assimilated Catholics, their religious practice moved closer to the American Catholic norm. One might return to one's childhood parish to attend the annual festa. One's private prayer might still be addressed to the Virgin or the saints. But Italian American Catholicism was increasingly centered on regular reception of the sacraments. Even men conformed to the emerging pattern, albeit very slowly.[10]

With the abrupt end of mass immigration from Italy in the mid-1920s, most Italian national parishes went into decline. Each of Chicago's twelve Italian parishes, to pick a representative example, lost membership between 1920 and 1927. But Italian American Catholicism did retain certain distinctive characteristics. The intense familialism of Italian culture made celibacy a difficult ideal, and the group produced few priestly vocations. (Italians were said to prefer religious-order to diocesan priests for service in their parishes, apparently regarding the former as products of a quasi-familial environment.) Southern Italian assumptions about sex—its explosive force, its necessity for "normal" men—undermined efforts to impose on the group the asceticism so central to Irish Catholicism. Even in the American-born generations, Italian Catholicism was more sensual and emotive than the Irish American norm and more oriented to the tradition's consoling elements. The all-forgiving Virgin Mary remained a dominant presence, as did the ever-helpful saints. Thus beneath a growing surface conformity, American Catholicism retained its various ethnic flavors, of which the Italian was among the most piquant.[11]

Immigrant Catholicism: The Poles

The initial wave of Polish immigrants to the United States began arriving in the 1850s. This migrant stream came almost exclusively from present-day Germany, which included a substantial population of stateless Polish speakers. Many arrived in family groups, intending to stay in America permanently. German Poles also accounted for almost all of the Polish immigrants—roughly 10 percent of the total—who settled in rural areas. Poles from the Austrian province of Galicia began arriving in large numbers in the 1890s, followed by Poles from the Russian empire, who constituted the largest of the three migrant streams and came mainly after 1900. Like the Italians, Polish immigrants from Russia and Austria were disproportionately male and prone to remigrate. Like the Italians, they arrived with a strong regional identity. But immigrants from every region spoke a mutually comprehensible Polish and identified strongly as Roman Catholics. Deprived of a political nation—the Polish state did not exist between 1795 and 1919—Poles channeled their national aspirations into a distinctively Polish Catholicism. Few Polish Catholics regarded Jews from the territory that had once been Poland as their compatriots.

This potent fusing of religion and nationalism made Poles prodigious church builders. The first immigrants to arrive in an American locale usually worshiped at a nearby German parish, the early arrivals nearly always coming from a German-speaking region. But tensions soon flared: local Germans looked down on the new arrivals, or so the Poles claimed, and indeed in some churches the newcomers were relegated to segregated pews. Once a sufficiency of Poles had arrived, perhaps two hundred at the most, the community took steps to establish a parish of its own. A lay committee typically raised funds and bought land for an eventual church, sometimes prior to consulting the local bishop, and even on occasion attempted to import a priest. The result in a good many cases was conflict with the local ordinary, whom Poles tended to regard, whatever his actual ethnic origins, as an autocratic Irishman. No immigrant group in these decades challenged episcopal authority more frequently or more energetically than they.[12]

Conflict notwithstanding, Polish achievements in the realm of institution building were truly astonishing, given the group's poverty. Many of their early churches were not only large but lavishly decorated. Chicago's St. Stanislaus Kostka, opened in 1869, offers one such example; Detroit's

St. Albertus, dedicated in 1872, provides another. Both churches were built by German Poles, a group possessing certain advantages, but subsequent waves of immigrants built sumptuous churches too. Within ten blocks of Detroit's St. Albertus are Sweetest Heart of Mary Church, opened in 1893 for a temporarily schismatic congregation composed mainly of Galicians, and St. Josaphat parish, founded in 1889, which eventually served a predominantly Russian one. Both churches, even larger than St. Albertus, were built of brick and expensively decorated, with Sweetest Heart boasting two massive stained-glass windows from the Tiffany studios in New York. Like St. Albertus, both of these newer parishes supported schools, Poles being the period ethnic group most committed to Catholic education. Of the 762 Polish parishes nationwide by 1921, 511 included at least an elementary school. Roughly two-thirds of Polish American youngsters in that year are estimated to have been enrolled in a Catholic school.[13]

Poles' heavy commitment to parish education retarded group assimilation—an outcome consciously sought by the immigrant generation. Few of the sisters imported from Poland to teach in the schools—almost a dozen religious orders were involved—spoke English upon their arrival. Parish schools were taught exclusively in Polish, at least in the early years, and partly in Polish for many years thereafter. The proliferation of social and devotional societies in Polish communities constituted a similarly antiassimilative bulwark, for most conducted their business at least partly in Polish. Unlike the Italians, moreover, Polish immigrants and even their children were inclined to remain in the area of first settlement, which is to say in a distinctively Polish environment. Slow to be socially mobile—in this they were like the Italians—Poles were laggards too when it came to geographic mobility. Even after the Second World War and the subsequent rush to the suburbs, cohesive Polish neighborhoods survived in many Rust Belt cities.

No institutional barrier, however, could keep American culture totally at bay. The American-born nearly always learned English. "Not two boys out of twenty employ Polish in their conversation with one another," wrote Father J. A. Burns in 1908 of a typical Polish community, "and in all probability the two boys, could they be found, would be newly arrived immigrants." Burns attributed the boys' facility in English primarily to their passion for sports, noting that "girls are slower at abandoning Polish as a medium of conversation." But girls learned English too and increasingly with parental encouragement. Eager for their children's success in the world of work—the wages of adolescent sons and especially daughters were often essential to family survival—Polish parents increasingly called for English instruction in the parish schools. The schools responded for the most part, albeit slowly. Only in the 1920s, with the abrupt cessation of mass immigration and increasing pressure from state governments, did reliance on Polish as a medium of instruction begin to wane significantly.[14]

If the immigrants' children became Polish Americans, they still displayed an unusual loyalty to the immigrant parish. The vitality of Polish parish life helps to explain why. Most such parishes were very large—forty thousand souls in some cases—and boasted an astonishing variety of social and devotional groups. Some were aimed specifically at adolescents and with apparent success. St. Stanislaus Kostka parish in Chicago sponsored a cadet corps, a youth choir, and various athletic teams, all of them popular with parish boys. The Living Rosary Society at the same parish claimed an active membership of four thousand young women, who played a prominent role in Marian devotions during the month of May. (Despite the society's overtly devotional agenda, it also sponsored social activities.) As educational aspirations among the American-born began to rise—something that was especially true of girls—Polish parishes banded together to underwrite high schools with distinctively Polish curricula. Even the young, in short, could lead reasonably satisfying lives within the confines of the ethnic group, which greatly increased the chances of marrying a fellow Polish American.[15]

The intensely communal nature of Polish religious observance also bolstered ethnic identity among the American-born. Most Poles, even the men, regularly attended Mass, where congregational singing often featured. The liturgical calendar was all-encompassing: Advent devotions were crowned by a family feast on Christmas Eve; January brought Three Kings Day and the clergy's blessing of parishioners' homes; February meant the feast of St. Blaise and its protective blessing of the throat; March brought the feast of St. Joseph and distinctively Polish Lenten liturgies; April usually meant Easter and the blessing of food baskets; May was Mary's month, when the Living Rosary was enacted by candlelight in the church; June brought Corpus Christi processions and the feast of St. John the Baptist, when certain innovative pastors blessed local swimming places; parish children brought flowers to Mary on the Feast of the Assumption in August and celebrated her birthday at school in September; October was a popular month for Forty Hours devotions, while November's feasts of All Souls and All Saints turned hearts and minds, however briefly, toward death and the world to come.[16]

The immigrant generation was usually served by priests born in Poland. But despite its poverty, the immigrant community soon produced vocations of its own. In this regard too the separatist impulse so strong among the Poles was evident. Prompted by a long campaign on the part of Father Joseph Dąbrowski, Polish-born but serving in the United States, the American bishops in 1884 approved the founding of a national seminary for clerical aspirants of Polish origin. Located initially in Detroit, Saints Cyril and Methodius Seminary trained several generations of Polish American priests, virtually all of them destined for service among their people. (The seminary's clerical students today are mostly men born in Poland.) As late as the 1950s, in dioceses with significant Polish American populations, a Polish-surnamed youth who aspired to the priesthood could expect to attend the "Polish" seminary and spend his career in whole or in part on the Polish parish circuit.

A principal reason for the bishops' support of a separate seminary for the Poles was the conflict that all too frequently characterized Polish parish life. Detroit's Bishop Caspar Borgess, an ardent supporter of the proposed seminary, spoke in 1887 of "riots, scandals, murders, etc. among the Polish Catholics in the United States, caused by the bad priests of their nationality." Only a carefully monitored seminary on American soil, in his view, could stem the tide. Such conflict was sometimes an intraparish affair, with the priest and his supporters ranged against a dissident faction in the congregation. Seminary founder Dąbrowski nearly lost his life when an angry group in his rural Wisconsin congregation stocked his woodpile with explosive-packed logs. His "offense" was choosing to build his new church at a prudent distance from the local saloons. Other conflicts, frequently more enduring, pitted priest and congregation against the local bishop. Having contributed both money and labor to build a church and school, many Poles were loath to grant their bishop the title to parish properties—something that church and frequently civil law required. If the matter was not handled tactfully, a bishop might find himself with a rebellious or even schismatic congregation. Should a bishop remove a popular pastor for what he believed were financial or sexual indiscretions, he might also face a parish revolt. The long-suffering Dąbrowski was dragged from the altar of St. Albertus Church in Detroit by a mostly female crowd as he tried to say Mass. His offense in this case was attempting to replace an immensely popular priest whom the bishop had removed for amply documented cause.[17]

The violence that attended certain Polish parish disputes is truly startling. Partisans sometimes came to blows; shots were fired on occasion; a smattering of fatalities occurred. There is nothing uniquely Polish at work here. Trusteeism conflicts in the early nineteenth century sometimes degenerated into violence too. But of all the "new" immigrant groups, the Poles were clearly the most conflict-prone, at least when it came to matters ecclesial. The intimate tie between Catholicism and Polish nationalism is part of the explanation. The same phenomenon had prompted the first wave of Irish immigrants to defend their putative "rights" as laity in occasionally violent fashion. Because of Poles' reluctance to leave the area of first settlement, they were also more likely to dominate their urban neighborhoods in a numerical sense than other ethnic groups could do. With parish and neighborhood virtually synonymous, at least in the immigrant mind, the sense of parish ownership was intensified. The immigrant generation, moreover, both founded the parish and built the church. Held in contempt by many Americans and relegated to the dirtiest and most dangerous jobs, immigrants were psychologically primed to regard the parish as a literal extension of the self. In no other institutional setting was immigrant worth and dignity so tangibly affirmed.

Polish parish rebellions were much less frequent after the turn of the twentieth century. The many immigrants still arriving came to cities where numerous Polish parishes were already extant, and other communal organizations had proliferated too. Quickly absorbed into the ethnic community, the newly arrived were protected, at least to a degree, from the alienation experienced by those who came earlier. But tensions persisted, especially with the nation's bishops, none of whom prior to 1908 was of Polish descent. That 1908 appointment—Father Paul Rhode was named auxiliary bishop of Chicago—came as the direct result of a vigorous campaign by Polish leaders around the United States, who continued their agitation until after the First World War. Although Edward Kozlowski was made auxiliary bishop of Milwaukee in 1913 and Paul Rhode was named to Green Bay just two years thereafter, subsequent Polish appointments were slow to come, primarily due to doubts in the American hierarchy. "The Polish are not yet American enough," in the words of Milwaukee's Archbishop Sebastian Messmer, "and keep aloof too much from the rest of us."[18]

A few Polish disputes did result in schism—in parishes that rejected the authority of the local bishop and, by extension, that of Rome, at least as the bishops saw it. Some of these congregations eventually returned to the Roman Catholic fold. Others found their way, via a small but growing network of similarly situated parishes loosely affiliated with the Old Catholic movement in Europe, into the Polish National Catholic Church (PNCC), founded in Scranton in 1904 by the Polish-born priest Francis Hodur. Individual parishes in the PNCC were lay owned and governed; its liturgy moved gradually toward the vernacular, with Polish eventually displacing Latin; and PNCC priests were permitted to marry as of 1921. The breakaway church—it does not recognize papal authority—had thirty parishes by 1916, with an estimated membership of nearly thirty thousand communicants. Still in existence, if not in a growth mode, the PNCC constitutes the only enduring major schism in the history of American Catholicism.

Among the Catholic Americans

Immigrants from Ireland and Germany continued to arrive beyond the turn of the twentieth century. But their diminishing numbers were dwarfed by those of the first and second American-born generations, who increasingly set the tone of local religious life. Thus German parishes by the 1890s were offering sermons in English and taking care to welcome those who no longer spoke the ancestral language. Irish-descended Catholics sometimes joined such parishes, often after having married a Catholic of German descent. German-descended Catholics, for their part, were increasingly apt to affiliate with English-language parishes whose origins had been Irish. The expanding neighborhoods that were home to assimilated Catholics like these gave rise in turn to new parishes with no discernible ethnic flavor, save for the aura of otherness that surrounded anything Catholic in Protestant America. For many of their members, indeed, it was Catholicism itself that increasingly constituted the heart of their ethnic identity.

Assimilation was not invariably coupled with social mobility. Even in 1920, American Catholics were heavily working class. But the American-born generations typically lived in more secure circumstances than their immigrant forebears and were more attuned to mainstream norms and values. Hence the heavy emphasis in the culture of assimilated Catholics on discipline, respectability, and even, albeit to a lesser extent, civic consciousness. In the years around the turn of the century, Catholic sacramental practice grew dramatically more disciplined, as growing numbers of the faithful went more frequently to confession and communion. The change was most pronounced among middle-class Catholics, especially women. But practice among working-class Catholics changed as well, as did practice among males generally—the latter an especially remarkable development, given the norms enforced in the confessional, stringent with regard to both sex and drink. Catholic publications preached to a greatly expanded audience the virtues of sobriety, piety, and gentility. Certain clerical seminaries in these years even instituted mandatory courses on manners. And particularly after the turn of the century, middle-class Catholics in particular evinced a new interest in civic life and social reform.

Many Catholics, especially immigrants, did continue to confess and receive communion only once or twice a year. But by the late nineteenth century, standards were rising, particularly in those many parishes now dominated by the American-born. By the 1890s, if not before, monthly reception of the sacraments was widely, if wishfully, preached as the standard for all good Catholics, including those of the male persuasion. Catholic men's organizations like the Knights of Columbus and the various parish units of the Holy Name Society asked their members to confess and receive communion once a month, although their leaders sometimes conceded that four times a year was probably a more achievable goal. How many men complied is impossible to know. "In church, men are shy and timid," in the words of a popular pastoral manual first published in 1897, while women "push themselves forward in church as if they owned it." Men were also notoriously reluctant to confess. Still, genuine change did occur, as witnessed by the swelling ranks of the Holy Name Society, introduced into a limited number of dioceses in the late nineteenth century but national in its reach by the time of the First World War. That women were excluded from the monthly parish Mass at which the Holy Name men received communion was perhaps a help to the intimidated.[19]

The pontificate of Pius X (r. 1903–14) spurred even more dramatic change in sacramental practice. The pope endorsed weekly communion for the laity early in his reign, while the Propaganda in 1905 ruled that daily communion, hitherto regarded as the prerogative of a spiritual elite, "should be open to all the faithful of whatever rank and condition of life."[20] Of equal significance was the pope's 1910 decree lowering the age of First

Communion to about seven from twelve or thirteen. Many priests were initially troubled by this, since working-class Catholic parents often regarded the reception of First Communion as marking the end of their children's parochial school careers. But in fact the effect was positive, at least from a clerical perspective: so early an admission to the Eucharist enabled the nation's Catholic schools to habituate their students to monthly or even weekly reception of the sacraments. "There is an interesting race between the girls of the Children of Mary and the boys of the Junior Holy Name Society as to which has the largest number of communicants each month," ran a typical report from Detroit's Annunciation parish school in 1913. "The boys have a small margin the best of it at present." As many priests had hoped, moreover, the example of youthful piety often affected adults. The number of weekly communicants grew substantially after 1910. In a handful of parishes, moreover, a devout elite began to receive communion daily, sometimes outside of Mass—a practice that eventually became quite common.[21]

Despite the new emphasis on frequent reception of the sacraments, American-born Catholics continued to support a vibrant devotional life. Eucharistic devotion, not surprisingly, seems in most places to have gained a new intensity, with parish holy hours—a time of collective prayer before the Blessed Sacrament—growing in popularity. Boston's Archbishop William O'Connell in 1911 ordered each of his parishes to hold a weekly holy hour during Lent. The Forty Hours devotion, which centered on Eucharistic adoration, was by the later nineteenth century a staple in nearly every parish. Devotion to the saints continued to appeal, with Anne, Anthony, and Joseph high on the list of favored helpers; so did devotion to the Sacred Heart. Marian devotion, however, took pride of place. Ethnic Madonnas often featured in foreign-language parishes: Our Lady of Częstochowa among the Poles, for whom she was their lost nation's mother; Guadalupe among the Mexicans. But in more generically American parishes, the emphasis was on a kind of Marian universalism. In parishes like these, Mary was presented as queen and protector of all the world's varied peoples, although prevailing Marian imagery continued to be thoroughly European.

One of the most striking of period Marian devotions was that of Our Lady of Lourdes. Originating in 1858, when young Bernadette Soubirous had visions of a mysterious woman in a grotto near her Pyrenees village, the Lourdes cult soon assumed international proportions. By the 1870s, Lourdes had emerged as a destination of pilgrimage and miraculous healing especially but not exclusively for the French. The devotion had by then begun to spread in the United States, where the Holy Cross fathers at Notre Dame were among its most fervent promoters. In 1872, the fathers began distributing "Lourdes water," which came from the now-famous spring at the site of the apparition. A brisk traffic soon developed, with water from the tiny vials mostly requested by the sick and infirm or those who cared for them. They too were pilgrims, in a very real sense, but pilgrims for whom a journey to Lourdes was not necessary. Mary's care was freely available to her faithful in every locale—such was the message of the cult and its prayers. Profits from the water, which was not sold but for which hopeful clients nearly always remitted a free-will offering, helped to finance the imposing basilica that graces the Notre Dame campus.[22]

The Holy Cross fathers also constructed a small Lourdes shrine at Notre Dame in 1877, which was replaced in 1896 by the still extant replica of the grotto at Lourdes where the apparitions occurred. The latter site quickly became a place of pilgrimage for Catholics throughout the Midwest. Parishes in a number of dioceses subsequently erected grottoes of their own, a few of which gained local repute as sites of miraculous cures. Catholics have a long tradition of shrine replication, although Lourdes provided the American church with probably its most popular manifestation. Such replications conveyed a supremely comforting message: believers are never separated by time or geography from the sacred occasions on which the Divine breaks into history. The most famous Marian apparitions of the nineteenth century all took place in Catholic Europe. (The lone Marian apparition in the United States endorsed as authentic by the church was not so designated until 2010, although it occurred in rural Wisconsin just one year after the apparitions at Lourdes.) Mary's American shrines reminded the faithful that they too walked on holy ground.[23]

Shrines of this sort also marked boundaries, being visibly and peculiarly Catholic. Herein lay an important source of their appeal for the rising Catholic middle class. Assimilated and at least modestly prosperous, such Catholics were hungry for social acceptance. But they were also committed to a separatist ethos, prompted in probably equal measure by persistent anti-Catholicism and the waning of ethnic identities. Catholic difference— an insistence which lay at the heart of separatism—was not incompatible with full American citizenship, or so Catholics were quick to insist. Good Catholics were not only loyal and responsible citizens but actually more faithful than many non-Catholics to the nation's core values—firm believers in the supernatural elements of Christianity at a time of growing Protestant doubt, defenders of the family against those who would tolerate divorce and contraception. Perhaps Catholics were destined to be an American saving remnant, rescuing the land they loved from the scourge of indifference and hedonism. "The Puritan has passed, the Catholic remains," Boston's Archbishop O'Connell told a packed cathedral in 1908, on the occasion of his archdiocese's centenary. Neither he nor his hearers doubted that the republic remained in good hands.[24]

An upsurge in lay activism was evident among the Catholic middle class by the late 1880s, and it spoke the language of Catholic difference. A lay-initiated Catholic Congress was held at Baltimore in 1889 in conjunction with the centennial celebration of the American hierarchy, followed by a similar gathering at the World's Columbian Exposition in Chicago in 1893. The speakers at both congresses, which in 1893 included several women, outlined Catholic solutions to the problems of the day and summoned the laity to social action. That the nation's relative handful of black Catholics staged five such meetings between 1889 and 1894 suggests that a quickened lay consciousness transcended race, if not class. Here too the delegates spoke of reform, but within the church as well as beyond it, calling for additional schools and parishes for African American Catholics, along with more charitable treatment from their white coreligionists. Similar congresses had been held in Europe, where they were regarded by many bishops as signs of Catholic health. But a number of American prelates, including the usually tolerant Cardinal Gibbons, were made uneasy by what they saw as undue lay assertiveness. A lay congress planned for 1904 was quashed by backdoor episcopal action, and no further such gatherings were held.

Lay activism at the local level was generally more successful. Consider the reading-circle movement, which attracted a substantial middle-class following in the 1890s and the earliest years of the new century. The movement was almost exclusively female, although that was not the intention of its founders. But Catholic men who aspired to activism had a number of avenues open to them, including politics and trade unionism. Most women did not. The typical reading-circle member was female, young, and single, often with the kind of intellectual ambition that characterized her college-bound contemporaries. Some reading circles made rigorous demands on their members, emphasizing both reading and writing in fields like history along with discussion of current events. The reading circle at Detroit's cathedral parish, for example, took Roman history as its principal subject in 1895, along with a side excursion into the theory of evolution. (John Zahm, a Holy Cross priest and scientist who wrote extensively on "theistic evolution," was a popular speaker on the reading-circle circuit.) The movement was sufficiently popular that it prompted the founding in 1892 of a Catholic summer school, which moved to its permanent location on Lake Champlain in 1894 and flourished there until 1941. Like the Protestant Chautauqua, the Catholic summer school provided vacations-cum-study. Over seven thousand students—with women solidly in the majority—attended the Cliff Haven school in 1905, by which time additional schools had been established in Maryland and Wisconsin.

The gospel of "Catholic difference" could be costly for middle-class women who did not join a religious order. Their options were visibly more limited than those of their Protestant counterparts. Protestant women in the decades around the turn of the century were increasingly active in social welfare work, which often led to a heightened political consciousness and sometimes to political action. But on the Catholic side, women religious largely took charge of such efforts. The Protestant-dominated temperance movement was mostly female in its leadership and ranks; its Catholic counterpart was predominantly male. Relatively few Catholics were active in the women's suffrage movement, which assumed mass proportions after 1910, in part, presumably, because so many of their bishops and priests opposed it. The elite and heavily Protestant leadership of that movement was also a factor. There were certainly exceptions: Chicago's Margaret Haley, a founder of that city's first teachers' union, was an ardent Catholic suffragist, as was Leonora Barry, an organizer for the Knights of Labor and a temperance activist. Rochester's redoubtable Bishop McQuaid spoke in favor of women's suffrage as early as 1894, while independent-minded priests occasionally endorsed it too.

Catholic women also suffered when it came to higher education. The first generation of American college women dates to the 1870s, when a number of state universities embraced coeducation and well-credentialed women's colleges began to proliferate. In the view of most Catholic leaders, however, institutions like these were dangerously secular, and Catholic attendance was vigorously discouraged. "I know two young ladies who graduated at Radcliffe to have lost their faith there," in the typical words of Philadelphia's Archbishop Patrick Ryan in 1897, with regard to the "women's

Members of the first graduating class at St. Mary's Hospital School of Nursing,
under the direction of the Sisters of Charity, Evansville, Indiana, 1897
(Courtesy of the Daughters of Charity, Province of St. Louise Archives,
Emmitsburg, Maryland)

annex" recently founded at Harvard. Many Catholic women were indeed
hungry for extended schooling, as these Radcliffe graduates suggest. Twenty
women applied for admission to Catholic University in 1895, when that institution was first opened to lay students, although of the male variety only.
Happily for that resolute group, the College of Notre Dame of Maryland,
the nation's first accredited Catholic women's college, opened in 1896. It was
followed by Trinity College, near neighbor of Catholic University, which enrolled its first class in 1900. Trinity was a great step forward, according to a
fictional character in an essay by Leila Hardin Bugg, given its promise of
academic excellence. Fair enough, responds another character in the same
essay—one who presumably spoke for the author—but it would have been
better by far had Trinity been made a constituent college of Catholic University where female students could study for university degrees.[25]

A member of Trinity's first graduating class, Bugg had already made a
name for herself as a popular Catholic author, despite—or possibly because

of—her penchant for the acerbic. She was not alone. The proliferation of Catholic periodicals in the waning years of the nineteenth century permitted a number of Catholic women to support themselves as writers. Among the best known was Katherine Conway, the first woman journalist in her native Rochester, New York, who joined the staff of the *Boston Pilot* in 1883 and served as its editor from 1905 to 1908. (The advent of Archbishop William O'Connell brought her tenure to an unceremonious close.) She subsequently taught at St. Mary's College in Notre Dame, Indiana, among the best of the fourteen Catholic women's colleges accredited by 1918. Despite her record of achievement, Conway opposed women's suffrage, although this was not invariably true of her female Catholic writer-peers. Women's natural aversion to public life—something that suffrage implicitly denied—was essential to protect the family, at least according to Conway. Her own highly public career was, in her view, actually a spiritual ministry, like the work of a sister-teacher or nurse. But once the suffrage was won, Conway—along with the American bishops—urged Catholic women to vote. How else were Catholic interests to be protected?[26]

Conway, like many of her Catholic contemporaries, defended moderate trade unionism, a movement in which Catholic participation and leadership were increasingly prominent. The Knights of Labor, the single largest labor organization of the nineteenth century, was headed after 1879 by the Catholic Terence Powderly, who was also a zealous temperance advocate. A substantial majority of its members were Catholic, which complicated matters for the nation's bishops when the Vatican condemned the Canadian Knights in 1884 at the request of the archbishop of Quebec, who objected to its religiously mixed ranks and ethos of secrecy. The intervention of Cardinal Gibbons, who spoke for most of his episcopal confreres, prevented the condemnation from being extended to the United States. Even in the prosperous United States, Gibbons pointed out, workers suffered—often grievously—from low wages, long hours, and dangerous conditions on the job. The Knights were not above criticism, he conceded. But "our Catholic working men sincerely believe that they are only seeking justice, and seeking it by legitimate means." Should the Vatican condemn the American Knights, a good many working-class Catholics would almost certainly leave the church. "A condemnation would be considered both false and unjust and would not be accepted."[27]

Gibbons's successful defense of the Knights enhanced his church's American reputation as a friend of labor—a reputation it had acquired mostly because the vast majority of Catholics were working class. Very few priests and bishops in the decades around the turn of the century spoke openly in defense of unions, fearing the potential radicalism of working-class labor activism. No Catholic could be a socialist, as Catholics were regularly reminded. Those lay men and women of radical bent—and there were some—nearly always left the church. The Knights of Labor, hardly socialist, is best described as utopian, given its commitment to organizing the unskilled, including women and blacks. It did not long endure. The most prominent Catholic unionists by 1900 presided over many of the nation's skilled trades unions, nearly all of them affiliates of the recently organized American Federation of Labor. Conservative in their political outlook, such unions were mainly devoted to the welfare of their members, large numbers of whom were Catholic. Church leaders quietly approved. If they were on record as opposing the worst excesses of capitalism, the nation's Catholics were also—in the words of William Howard Taft—among its principal "bulwarks against socialism and anarchy."[28]

After 1900, however, many middle-class Catholics, in company with their non-Catholic counterparts, evinced a new interest in social reform. The appearance of Catholic settlement houses in the nation's major cities was a telling indicator. Many of the houses were founded and at least initially staffed by women religious. But laywomen played an increasingly prominent role. Mary Workman, for example, founded Brownson House in Los Angeles in 1901 to serve an Italian and Mexican clientele. Like nearly every settlement, Brownson offered classes in English, sewing, and domestic science, as well as a library and playground. By 1915 it was hosting three medical clinics a week. Brownson also sponsored catechism classes, as did all of its Catholic counterparts. As far as most bishops were concerned, the principal purpose of the Catholic settlement was religious outreach and education. Mary Workman pointedly disagreed. "When a man or woman is hungry, over-worked or exploited, you cannot teach Catechism to him, you must first remedy his condition." Unlike their Protestant counterparts, who had founded the nation's first settlement houses roughly a generation earlier, Catholic activists were seldom free of ecclesiastical oversight. Workman eventually left Brownson House over tensions with the local chancery.[29]

Catholic reformism even surfaced in politics. During the later nineteenth century, heavily Catholic political machines, most of them Irish dominated, wielded power in those many cities where Catholics had settled in large numbers. Accused with some accuracy of corruption, machine politicians served their working-class constituencies by providing access to city jobs and distributing material aid and favors to families in temporary crisis. Precisely because of their parochialism, however, they were not reformers. The Irish "never thought of politics as an instrument of social change," in the somewhat hyperbolic assessment of Daniel Patrick Moynihan. But after the turn of the century, as Catholic voters grew more sophisticated and the national political climate grew increasingly progressive, the urban machines produced a crop of sometimes distinguished reform politicians. New York's Alfred E. Smith, remembered today as the first Catholic to run for president on a major-party ticket, began his career as a reform-minded state assemblyman in 1904 under the aegis of Tammany Hall. During his multiple terms as New York's governor, an office to which he was first elected in 1918, he compiled a record of reform so extensive as to presage the New Deal.[30]

The spirit of Catholic reform was channeled most eloquently by Father John A. Ryan, the principal author of the 1919 "Bishops' Program for Social Reconstruction." Ordained in 1898 for the Archdiocese of St. Paul, Ryan first came to public attention with the publication in 1906 of *A Living Wage*, portions of which also appeared in the *Catholic World*, a weekly published by the Paulist fathers. The working man, Ryan argued, had a natural right to a wage sufficient to support a family in modest comfort and to save for emergencies and old age. A fortunate minority of workers could secure such a wage through collective bargaining, which Ryan applauded. But to protect the many who could not, Ryan endorsed minimum-wage legislation, along with the eight-hour day, unemployment insurance, and pensions for those too ill or old to work. Accused of socialism by some wealthy Catholics and speaking in a mode seldom heard in American Catholic quarters, Ryan invoked Pope Leo XIII (r. 1878–1903) in his defense. In *Rerum Novarum*, Leo's celebrated 1891 encyclical on labor and capital, the pope had endorsed state intervention when class-based injustice could not be otherwise addressed. "Only those who know the condition of American Catholic social thought before 1890," Ryan later wrote, "can understand how and why Leo's teaching on the state seemed almost revolutionary."[31]

Ryan, like the pope, assumed as a matter of course that the family breadwinner would be male. Mothers should not be employed, nor should children below their midteens. Families, moreover, ought to be large, with seven to eight children constituting an ideal average, at least in Ryan's view.

Most Catholic families at the turn of the century were nowhere near that numerous, since birthrates nearly always fell after the immigrant generation. "In many cities the number of children per family among Catholics of the middle and comfortable classes is little more than half of the average that obtained in the families of their parents," as Ryan himself acknowledged in 1916. The reason, almost certainly, was birth control, perhaps by means of condoms or pessaries—both were commercially available—or, more likely, coitus interruptus. "Some Catholics have been able to persuade themselves that contraceptive practices are not necessarily sinful, at least in certain extreme cases," according to Ryan, who blamed the example of their Protestant neighbors and the silence of their priests. Our people need straight talk on marital matters, Ryan warned his fellow clergy. Otherwise they will succumb to the reigning American ethos of self-interested utilitarianism.[32]

Ryan was right, at least with regard to clerical silence. Parish priests virtually never broached the subject of contraception in Sunday sermons or the hurried interview with the pastor that passed in those days for premarital instruction. Genteel standards forbade it. When Margaret Sanger, birth control's most famous American advocate, burst on the scene in 1914, her cause was widely regarded as radical and, in some quarters, obscene. (Ryan's summon to priestly action, which appeared in a 1916 clerical journal, was clearly prompted by Sanger's activism.) The subject was even off-limits in many confessionals, or so the evidence suggests. One should not question penitents closely about sexual sins, confessors were regularly warned; in fact, it might be better not to question at all. One did not want to alienate penitents or, still worse, inform them about sins that were hitherto unknown to them. As for those penitents whose circumstances, such as poverty or a wife's fragile health, would make right behavior extremely hard, it was perhaps best to leave them in ignorance. A confessor should not instruct a penitent in his or her marital duties, according to one prominent authority, "unless he has good reason to think that his advice will be heeded, lest what was purely a material sin should become a formal sin."[33]

Parish missions constituted the lone venue where straight talk on sex was apt to prevail, as Ryan duly acknowledged. Most missions were preached to sex-segregated congregations and, in the larger parishes, to congregations further subdivided by marital status. A greater frankness was therefore possible. Prior to 1920, however, even mission preachers sometimes failed to mention contraception, although they regularly denounced abortion and, not surprisingly, fornication. The Paulists conform to this pattern. But the Redemptorists, the largest of the mission-preaching orders, did preach regularly against birth control even in the nineteenth century and apparently asked about the sin during mission confessions. So did the Jesuit F. X. Weninger, who in his German-language sermons heaped scorn on the laity's self-professed ignorance of the moral law. "That which one never sees an animal do, and for which one would feel shame if others knew about it— that you didn't recognize as evil?" ran his forthright challenge to congregations of the married. Missions, however, were occasional affairs, as Ryan pointed out. Their message was all too easily blunted by the passage of time and the pressures of everyday living.[34]

Ryan's 1916 call to arms did not ignite an immediate pastoral revolution. Many clergy clung to their reticent ways throughout the 1920s and sometimes even beyond. But most Catholics after the First World War had at least a limited awareness of the secular politics of birth control, in which Catholic teaching—or the media's version thereof—featured prominently. Although most Protestant churches were still on record as opposing marital contraception, Margaret Sanger succeeded in persuading the press that the Catholic Church—"a dictatorship of celibates"—stood alone in this regard. Thus even before the mainstream Protestant churches made their public peace with contraception, which mostly happened in the 1930s, Catholic opposition to birth control and liberalization of the laws that limited access to it had become a principal public marker of Catholic difference. The issue would eventually prove immensely divisive among Catholics. But long before that happened, it divided Catholics from the secular liberals with whom by the 1930s they shared the Democratic Party.[35]

A Glorious Isolation

At the close of the First World War, the nation's polyglot Catholics basked in the reflected glow of their amply demonstrated patriotism. Many Catholics had initially opposed intervention on the Allied side, mostly for reasons of residual ethnic loyalty. German Americans had been frank partisans of the Central Powers, while Irish hostility to England drove many in this population toward militant neutrality. Once Congress declared war, however, Catholics rallied to the cause. They were grossly underrepresented in the ranks of the nation's conscientious objectors—a mere 4 Catholics out of

3,989—and overrepresented in the armed forces, mostly due to the youth of the Catholic population nationally. More than fifteen hundred Catholic priests served as wartime chaplains, including Father Francis Duffy of New York's "Fighting Sixty-Ninth," who was celebrated at war's end as a national hero. Catholics were active on the home front, too, supporting the various wartime loan drives and volunteering with the Red Cross, while the Knights of Columbus organized and staffed more than six hundred "huts" on military bases where soldiers might avail themselves of recreation and spiritual counsel. Cooperating in many of these endeavors with Protestants, Catholics emerged from the war with a comforting sense of acceptance.[36]

Those same Catholics, however, took pride in Catholic difference, and many embraced its protection by means of institutional separatism. Indeed, a new urgency in this regard was evident in the 1920s, as the existing network of Catholic institutions—schools, colleges, social service and cultural organizations—was strengthened and expanded. Advocates of separatism were nearly always sturdy patriots, although they might rue their country's alleged drift into a normless secularism. With so many Catholics having journeyed from immigrant poverty to respectability, there was widespread gratitude in their ranks to the nation that had made it possible. But a great many Catholics, especially the more affluent, had come to regard themselves as a people set apart. After a brief period of openness at the end of the nineteenth century, moreover, Catholic intellectuals also embraced a posture of militant otherness. Some did so reluctantly—Rome played a prominent role in the drama. The so-called Americanist crisis—generally termed the "modernist crisis" in Europe—ultimately affected many more Catholics than just the intellectual elite. The following chapter tells the story.

"They Are Afraid of Democracy at Rome"

Edward McGlynn was the kind of priest who tries the patience of even the most accommodating bishop. Longtime pastor of St. Stephen's parish in Manhattan, one of the city's largest and most prominent, McGlynn championed a number of controversial political causes. He gained a particularly loyal following through his speeches promoting the Irish Land League, which in the early 1880s campaigned for land reform in Ireland, soliciting support as it did so from the Irish diaspora. Orchestrating rent strikes and resistance to evictions among Irish tenant farmers, the league was decried by its opponents as an enemy of property rights. McGlynn was also a supporter of Henry George, an antimonopoly crusader whose advocacy of a "single tax" on the value of land brought him plaudits in certain quarters and notoriety in others. George ran for mayor of New York in 1886 on the ticket of the short-lived United Labor Party. Ordered by the recently installed Archbishop Michael Corrigan to have nothing to do with the George campaign, McGlynn insisted on delivering an already promised speech on George's behalf. The archbishop then suspended McGlynn from his priestly functions and removed him as pastor of St. Stephen's.

McGlynn's many supporters erupted in seemingly spontaneous protest. An estimated seventy-five thousand people, including a very large number of women, marched through St. Stephen's parish in support of its exiled pastor. Between two and three thousand persons attended the early

meetings of the Anti-Poverty Society that McGlynn established shortly after his suspension, where he railed against the "ecclesiastical machine" that
had attempted to silence him. Corrigan subsequently forbade Catholics under his jurisdiction to attend society meetings, refusing a Catholic burial to
one unfortunate man who died while in attendance. McGlynn's case took a
fateful turn in the summer of 1887. Summoned to Rome by the pope to
explain his allegedly heterodox views, McGlynn refused to go—and did so
publicly. Corrigan thereupon excommunicated him. McGlynn's defiance of
the pope cost him a fair degree of support, especially among middle-class
Catholics, but his case remained a source of contention among the American bishops and between those bishops and various centers of power in
Rome.[1]

Despite McGlynn's radicalism, which was theological as well as political, he had episcopal allies. Among them was Richmond's John Keane,
who attempted to intervene at the Vatican on McGlynn's behalf in 1886.
Keane, soon to become the first rector of Catholic University, was hardly a
McGlynn clone. He had little interest in secular reform and not much sympathy for the more advanced of McGlynn's views on the church, which apparently included opposition to mandatory clerical celibacy. But he did
sympathize with McGlynn when it came to democratic values and the genius of U.S. constitutional arrangements with regard to church and state.
The church, in Keane's view, ought as an ever-developing community of
faith to be open to reforming currents and to learn from the best in every
age. Catholics, and especially American Catholics, had to make their peace
with democracy and religious pluralism. They had also to grapple with
the religious implications of advances in science and the critical study of
Scripture. Like other American bishops, moreover, Keane worried that the
McGlynn affair might alienate working-class Catholics from the church.

Keane was among the most prominent of the so-called Americanist
bishops, while New York's Corrigan figured with equal prominence among
their conservative opponents. The McGlynn affair, indeed, can be seen as the
opening skirmish in a war between these episcopal factions that ultimately
had profound consequences for the church. Keane's liberal allies included
St. Paul's Archbishop John Ireland, a sometimes hesitant Cardinal James
Gibbons, Peoria's John Lancaster Spalding, San Francisco's Patrick Riordan,
and then-monsignor Denis O'Connell, rector of the North American
College in Rome. Isaac Hecker, not far from death, was an inspiration and

passive sympathizer. Corrigan's party included Rochester's Bernard Mc-Quaid, most of the German bishops, and a number of prominent Jesuits. Each faction had Roman allies, with Corrigan's including an American woman long resident in Rome—Ella Edes—who was almost preternaturally privy to ecclesiastical gossip. The fortunes of both parties rose and fell with the ebb and flow of Vatican politics. Big personalities prevailed on both sides—Ireland's and Corrigan's were probably the largest—and the ongoing conflict was driven in part by personal rivalries. But very real differences were also at work.

John Ireland was the best known of the Americanists and probably the most representative. Born in Ireland to parents who emigrated during the Famine, he was educated in France as the protégé of St. Paul's French-born Bishop Joseph Cretin. Ordained in 1861, Ireland served briefly—but, in his telling, memorably—as a Civil War chaplain. Partly as a result of his war-time experience, or so he later claimed, he was notably liberal on questions of race, advocating an end to miscegenation laws, workplace discrimination, and segregation in public accommodations. (In this regard, he was anything but representative of even his liberal episcopal colleagues.) Early in his ca-reer, Ireland gained renown as a preacher, often in the cause of temperance, a lifelong passion. He was named coadjutor bishop of St. Paul with right of succession in 1875, when he was just thirty-seven; he assumed full jurisdic-tion as St. Paul's bishop in 1884, after which he moved increasingly on a national and even international stage. He became an archbishop in 1887. At the height of his Roman influence, in 1892, he confidently expected—as did many of his confreres—that he would be named a cardinal.[2]

As befitted his rags-to-celebrity story, Ireland was an ardent patriot. He admired the openness of American society and the room it made for striving and initiative. He trusted American institutions, including the pub-lic schools, and generally favored an activist state—a principal reason for his Republican political loyalties. He favored an activist church as well. "We desire to win the age. Let us not, then, stand isolated from it," he urged his fellow bishops at a Mass commemorating the twenty-fifth anniversary of Gibbons's episcopal ordination. "Our place is in the world as well as the sanctuary." It would not be easy, Ireland conceded, for Catholics to win a world so suddenly hostile to traditional modes of authority. "Religious ac-tion to accord with the age must take new forms and new directions," as he put it in another sermon, this one before the Lay Catholic Congress of 1889.

Happy heirs to a democratic tradition, Catholics in the United States were especially well situated to claim the future for the church. "Let there be individual action!" he exhorted the delegates, all of whom were male. "Laymen need not wait for priest, nor priest for bishop, nor bishop for Pope."[3]

The Americanists as a group shared Ireland's optimism, openness to experience, and confident faith in democracy. They favored assimilative policies for the nation's Catholic immigrants and encouraged already assimilated Catholics to participate actively in American intellectual life. They championed high standards for the nation's Catholic schools, which in their view included borrowing from the best in their public counterparts. High-quality schools cost money, as every bishop knew. Attempting to address the problem, Ireland negotiated an agreement in 1891 with the school boards of two Minnesota towns, Faribault and Stillwater. In exchange for public support, the local Catholic schools—still taught by Catholic religious—agreed to follow a mandated state curriculum, with religion taught only in after-school hours. Such arrangements, he hoped, would eventually prevail in dioceses throughout the nation. Ireland's critics accused him of secularizing the schools in question and used the issue to undermine his standing in Rome—unsuccessfully, at least in the short term, since the Propaganda ruled in 1892 that Ireland's school experiment might be tolerated. By that time, however, local Protestant opposition to the arrangement had caused its demise.[4]

The Americanists' opponents were not opposed to high standards in the Catholic schools, although they might differ on precisely what constituted excellence. Nor were they opposed to American democracy or U.S. constitutional provisions with regard to church and state, which to a man they accepted as unalterable political realities. Unlike the Americanists, however, they did not think in terms of a church with a national genius or a mission to save the nation. Their orientation was more parochial. Jealous of their autonomy as bishops, they saw their principal task as keeping Catholics Catholic. For the German Americans among them, that task was best accomplished by promoting ethnic separatism. For virtually every anti-Americanist, it entailed a healthy skepticism about an increasingly secular world and its alleged intellectual achievements. Rather than encouraging Catholics to reconcile their ancient faith with a scientific and historically conscious worldview, as the Americanists were doing, their opponents warned of the project's dangers. They rightly saw the threat it posed to a certain understanding of Catholic orthodoxy and to their own authority. Their increasingly numerous Roman allies shared their fears and more.[5]

Divisions in the American episcopate began to harden in the later 1880s. From then until 1893, the Americanist faction held sway in Rome. Bishops regarded as Americanists had their way with the pope when it came to the Knights of Labor and the establishment of the Catholic University. They also succeed in deflecting two separate efforts to promote the interests of ethnic Catholics in the United States, the second of which—the so-called Cahensly memorial—asked for bishops of the same nationality to be appointed in any diocese where a particular ethnic group was numerous. (The Cahensly memorial, somewhat misrepresented in communiqués sent from Rome by Denis O'Connell, was denounced by nearly every non-German bishop in the country.) Ireland even succeeded in defending the unusual educational arrangements that briefly prevailed in Faribault and Stillwater, which had actually been modeled on a similar experiment in Poughkeepsie, New York. The high point of his Roman influence, however, came in 1892, when he artfully stage-managed the American tour of Archbishop Francesco Satolli, soon to be announced as the Vatican's first Apostolic Delegate to the United States. Early in his American tour, Satolli began the proceedings that would lift the excommunication of Edward McGlynn.

Satolli's American itinerary included the World's Parliament of Religions, held in conjunction with the Chicago world's fair of 1893. Nothing in Satolli's prior experience, in the words of historian Marvin O'Connell, "had prepared him for the spectacle of Catholic prelates mingling on professionally equal terms with all conceivable varieties of heathen." Ireland and Keane played prominent roles at the gathering; their opponents pointedly stayed away, as Satolli could not help but note and evidently appreciate. His allegiance soon shifted to Corrigan's party. Since Satolli's reports from the front carried great weight in Rome, despite the new delegate's speaking no English, the Americanists feared the worst. It was not long in coming. The initial blow fell in 1895, in the form of a papal letter to the American bishops, in which Leo XIII reminded them that U.S. arrangements with regard to church and state could not be regarded by Catholics as a model for the world. Denis O'Connell was shortly thereafter removed as rector of the North American College; John Keane was removed as rector of Catholic University in 1896 and sent in obvious exile to be archbishop of Dubuque.[6]

A sterner papal document, *Testem Benevolentiae,* followed in 1899. In far-harsher language than the earlier letter, Leo denounced certain errors that, according to the pope, often bore the label of "Americanism." The various errors enumerated were variations on the themes of individualism and ecumenism. Alleged "Americanists" demanded that the church change its teachings and discipline to reflect the values of the modern age; doing so, they erroneously believed, was especially necessary for winning converts. They downplayed the importance of external spiritual guidance, trusting instead in the workings of the Holy Spirit in the individual soul. They preferred the active to the passive virtues and lacked respect for vowed religious life. The pope even managed, albeit in passing, to denounce the unhappy social effects of an unrestricted press. Bishops like Corrigan were delighted. Men like Ireland denied that the errors so rightly deplored by the pope could be found among American Catholics. But when Ireland arrived at the Vatican just a few months later, the cold reception accorded him suggested that the pope, or at least his advisers, thought otherwise. He was asked whether he believed in the divinity of Christ, an indignant Ireland told his young priest-secretary.[7]

Testem Benevolentiae was directly occasioned by the French publication in 1897 of a biography of Isaac Hecker, first published in the United States in 1891, when it was serialized in the *Catholic World.* Written by Paulist Walter Elliot, an ardent fan of John Ireland, the book lauded Hecker's admiration for U.S. constitutional arrangements and encouragement of lay activism. Hecker emerges in the book as a man of initiative, intellect, and independence, a veritable tower of Anglo-Saxon virtue. Abbé Félix Klein, a recent traveler to the United States and prominent in liberal Catholic circles, provided a glowing introduction to the French edition. Conservative Catholics in France, many of them royalists, howled in outrage, charging Klein and the author—and, by extension, his subject—with heresy. Their Roman allies echoed the charge, which prompted a Roman investigation into the American church. *Testem* was the result. As Isaac Hecker had earlier learned, Vatican fear of the modern world—palpable even under the relatively sophisticated Leo—made U.S. political verities seem threatening indeed. "They are afraid of democracy at Rome," a discouraged Hecker had told Elliot in 1883. "One of the charges made against me in Rome was that I was trying to introduce democracy into the Catholic Church."[8]

The French explosion over Elliott's book is often said to have triggered the so-called modernist crisis, which climaxed in 1907. "Modernism," a term used mostly by its opponents, is best understood as an intellectual orientation. Modernists—or liberal Catholics, as most would have called themselves— thought historically, in terms of change and development. They hoped to rec- oncile Catholic truth with recent advances in science, evolutionary theory in particular, and Scripture scholarship, to which the more intellectual of the American clergy were surprisingly open. The Neo-Thomism now ascendant in Rome, resolutely ahistorical, was regarded by every so-called modernist as inadequate to the task. The most prominent modernists were European, among them the Irish Jesuit George Tyrrell, who wrote extensively on faith and science, and Alfred Loisy, a French priest and biblical scholar. Modernism, in- deed, was until quite recently regarded by most historians as a purely Euro- pean movement. But men like Loisy and Tyrrell enjoyed an American audience too. Tyrrell's books were recommended to readers by such relatively popular journals as *Ave Maria* and the *Catholic World*, for both of which he also wrote articles. Loisy's work was less widely read, but aimed as it was at a priestly audi- ence, it had at least potential effect on sermons and pastoral practice.[9]

The American audience for modernist scholarship was admittedly small, confined to a portion of the educated laity and an elite among the clergy. But the audience was an eager one. When Father John Zahm, a pro- ponent by 1892 of theistic evolution, published his lectures on the subject in 1894, the *Catholic World* termed the volume "a veritable Godsend" for be- lievers "who wish accurate information concerning current controversies regarding Science and Faith." Believers of this description thronged Zahm's lectures and provided a readership for the five books and numerous articles he produced in the mid-1890s. His 1896 *Evolution and Dogma* attracted par- ticularly wide attention. Zahm's popularity was such that conservatives in the American church tried to banish him from the summer-school circuit, the venue where he reached his largest audiences. The Holy Cross order, to which Zahm belonged, prudently transferred him to Rome in 1896, where he remained for more than a year. It could hardly have been a congenial stay, given ecclesiastical rumors that the pope was about to condemn the theory of evolution itself. Fortunately for Catholic posterity, he did not. But Zahm's *Evolution and Dogma* was placed on the Vatican's Index of Prohib- ited Books in 1898. Having made his submission to the pope, Zahm aban- doned the subject of evolution for the rest of his career.[10]

Theistic evolution, as Zahm described it, meant accepting human evo- lution with regard to the body. Humans had indeed evolved from the primates. But the soul was directly infused by God. (Zahm relied heavily on the work of St. George Mivart, a distinguished British biologist, excommunicated shortly before his death in 1900.) By challenging traditional interpretations of the biblical account of creation, Zahm aligned himself with period Scripture scholars, whose work—much of it highly speculative—informed the intellectual trajectories of most of his liberal Catholic contemporaries. Zahm himself preached a critical reading of Scripture; certain passages in the Bible had greater authority than others, he argued, and little in Scripture had validity when it came to science. He was also regarded in Rome as an Americanist, perhaps especially for his championing of free inquiry, a cause to which his work as a popularizer was devoted. His conservative opponents, whose worldview assumed a static deposit of revealed truth, quite understandably found Zahm's mode of thinking dangerous.

Liberal Catholic intellectuals faced implacable hostility in Rome by the very first years of the twentieth century. George Tyrrell, probably the most widely read of the European liberals in this country in the 1890s, was dismissed from the Jesuit order—still a principal conservative force at the Vatican—in 1906. Apart from the silenced Zahm, however, liberal Catholic intellectuals continued their work in the United States, albeit in very small numbers. The most distinguished of the faculty at Catholic University were devoted to liberal scholarship and active in that institution's production of the *Catholic Encyclopedia,* a monumental compendium of Catholic learning published in fifteen volumes between 1907 and 1915. New York's St. Joseph's Seminary, for its part, achieved something close to distinction with its venturesome faculty appointments. In 1905, the seminary began to publish the *New York Review,* which during its brief life—it was halted by episcopal fiat in 1908—was marked by true intellectual liveliness. Tyrrell's last American article appeared in the *Review,* as did a number of well-informed pieces on recent developments in biblical studies.

The years of modest intellectual ferment ended abruptly in the fall of 1907, when Pope Pius X (r. 1903–14) issued *Pascendi Dominici Gregis.* Bitterly denouncing modernism as "the synthesis of all heresies," the encyclical imposed stern policing measures on Catholic dioceses worldwide in the form of local vigilance councils to ensure orthodoxy among the clergy and especially seminary faculty. Shortly thereafter, the pope prescribed an oath against modernism to be taken by all priests and bishops. First required in 1910, the oath remained in effect until 1967. The encyclical trafficked in

The biblical scholar Henry A. Poels, appointed to the Catholic University
faculty in 1904 and subsequently dismissed for his allegedly heterodox views
on the authorship of the Pentateuch (Courtesy of the American Catholic
History Research Center and University Archives [ACUA], the Catholic
University of America, Washington, DC)

something close to a parody of modernist thought. But crude though it was,
it accurately limned the fears of the antimodernists, who regarded notions
of development as fatal to Catholic doctrine. "Dogmas have no history," in
the words of French Cardinal Louis Billot, a passionate defender of *Pascendi*.[11] Networks of ecclesiastical spies were soon active in most European dioceses, reporting alleged offenders to Rome. The recently ordained Angelo
Roncalli, later Pope John XXIII, was a near casualty of the hypervigilance.

Spies were active too in the United States, although their targets were fewer in number. The rector of New York's St. Joseph's Seminary lost his job, as did Henry Poels, a distinguished professor of biblical studies at Catholic University. But most liberal Catholic scholars in the United States responded to *Pascendi* with prudent silence, thereby keeping their employment. Almost none criticized the encyclical publicly or subsequently published work that could qualify as provocative. Nearly all became Neo-Thomists, in some cases seemingly overnight. American Catholic intellectual life suffered accordingly, especially with regard to philosophy, theology, and biblical studies. The exceptions to the general silence can literally be counted on the fingers of one hand. The excommunications of George Tyrell in 1907 and Alfred Loisy in 1908 were presumably sobering, given their influence on American liberals. "I can compare the crisis to nothing but a cyclone during which people must simply make for the cellar," the rector of St. Joseph's wrote shortly before his dismissal.[12] The metaphor aptly summarizes the American liberal Catholic mood in the wake of *Pascendi*.

The more liberal of the American bishops maintained at the time that the modernism denounced by the pope was an exclusively European product—a conclusion embraced for decades by historians of American Catholicism. In recent years, however, scholars have identified significant links between the so-called Americanists—very definitely a product of the United States—and the modernist movement, whose most distinguished proponents were in fact European. No one argues that a man like John Ireland was a venturesome theologian. He was not. But like his fellow Americanists, he encouraged Catholics to intellectual achievement, which could only mean serious grappling with new developments in history and evolutionary science. He endorsed democracy and the separation of church and state—a position one could only reach by assuming development in Catholic teaching. He believed that the church should engage the world, rather than erecting a fortress against it. "Despite its defects and its mistakes, I love my age," he announced, quite characteristically, in 1889. "I love its aspirations and its resolves." Thus the church could learn from, as well as guide, a world in the throes of new birth. Pius X would have had no difficulty in calling such views modernist.[13]

Catholic intellectual life in the United States did not collapse in the wake of *Pascendi*, although this is sometimes asserted. Intellectual energies were instead rerouted, primarily into the social sciences, church history, and medieval studies. Catholic University developed surprising strengths, for its small size, in sociology, anthropology, and psychology; in the person of Msgr. Peter Guilday, cofounder in 1919 of the American Catholic Historical Association, the institution made pioneering contributions to the still nascent field of American Catholic history. The American Jesuits, signaling a break of sorts with their conservative brethren in Europe, founded *America* in 1909 as a vehicle for thoughtful commentary on politics and culture. But despite these achievements, Catholic intellectual life lost much of its former joie de vivre—the energy, optimism, and pioneering spirit that had all too briefly infected the American Catholic culture of inquiry. Scholars now did their work unobtrusively, nuancing findings that might cause trouble, and in isolation for the most part from the wider currents of intellectual life.

Anchored in a now-pervasive Neo-Thomism, Catholic intellectual life in its broadest sense—including, for example, the culture and curricula of Catholic colleges—did provide American Catholics in the post-*Pascendi* decades with an integrated worldview that was inherently optimistic. A few of the many Americans disturbed in the wake of the First World War by an intellectual climate where complexity, uncertainty, and cultural fragmentation took center stage found Catholic certitude sufficiently attractive that they converted. Catholics themselves displayed immense confidence in their beliefs and an almost overweening pride in Catholic identity. "We are so SURE," as Indianapolis journalist Mary McGill put it in 1927. "That characteristic would hurt me, if I didn't believe. I think I would hate people who are so certain and set apart." Considering the creedal debates that divided a number of Protestant denominations in these same years, one might be tempted to see in *Pascendi* an ironic gift to the nation's Catholics. But deferred questions seldom disappear, and Catholics could not keep the world at bay forever. Once the Catholic subculture had collapsed, its former inhabitants would arguably have been better off had their intellectual formation been less insulated.[14]

What about lay Catholics at the turn of the twentieth century—the men and women who lived through the twin upheavals of Americanism and modernism? To what extent were they even aware of the struggles that seem in retrospect to have been so important for the future of the church? Awareness would not have been hard to come by. The various battles of these years were often covered by the secular media, with some partisans leaking stories to favored journalists. When John R. Slattery, founder and general superior of the American Josephites, left the priesthood and married in 1906, he announced his departure in the mass-circulation *Independent,* where he attributed his loss of faith to his study of church history. The Paulist Walter Sullivan, who left the church in 1909 as a direct result of *Pascendi,* chronicled his alienation in a subsequent book and an autobiographical novel. Educated Catholics, moreover, were apt to have regular contact with non-Catholics at work or perhaps in school—an estimated 480 Catholics were enrolled at Harvard in 1907—and thus likely to field questions about their church's newsworthy turmoil.[15]

Some Catholics were clearly interested in the work of the modernist popularizers. Their small numbers should not detract from the potential urgency of their concerns. Most American Catholics, moreover, endorsed democracy and the religiously neutral state and regarded these achievements as models for the world. In that sense they were unrepentant Americanists. But lay Catholics seem to have weathered the storm with their faith intact, perhaps because even the educated experienced church primarily in terms of the parish. A compassionate pastor, a reverent liturgy, a sense of communal rootedness—such things nearly always mattered more than pronouncements from Rome. Al Smith, after all, was reliably reported at the outset of his presidential campaign to have been genuinely puzzled by the term "encyclical." Matters were otherwise for the clergy, who lived after 1910 with vigilance committees, antimodernist oaths, and an ossified seminary curriculum. But apart from Slattery and Sullivan, we know of only one other priest—Brooklyn's Thomas Mulvey—who resigned as a direct result of the modernist crisis. The post-*Pascendi* years, indeed, saw steady growth in vocations to the priesthood and religious life.

By 1920, the American church, so recently embroiled in conflict, appeared more vibrant and unified than at any time in the previous century. Tensions still existed among certain of the nation's bishops, but these played out behind the scenes and seldom broke into the headlines. That the bishops now had a national organization, weak though it initially was, created a welcome public impression of episcopal unity. The First World War had permitted a polyglot Catholic population to demonstrate its patriotism, with the happy effect of quashing, at least temporarily, the worst excesses of anti-Catholicism. Catholic institutions were thriving, thanks largely to the generosity of a growing Catholic middle class. If a resurgent anti-Catholicism loomed, in the form of a revivified Ku Klux Klan, it would not last long. The Democrats, unable at their convention in 1924 to muster the votes to condemn the Klan by name, chose a Catholic candidate for president just four years later. If anti-immigrant sentiment would soon result in a national policy openly biased against Catholics and Jews, the resulting decline in immigration had positive effects on Catholic unity and institutional consolidation. The American church, in short, had successfully navigated its most turbulent passage to date. Calmer waters lay ahead.

Part IV
Exuberant Maturity, 1920–1962

John C. Cort

(1913–2006)

The year is 1935. In a Boston still suffering from Depression-level unemployment, a recent Harvard graduate has just converted to Catholicism. John C. Cort is an unlikely convert. Raised in middle-class comfort on suburban Long Island and the product of elite private schools, Cort has hitherto encountered few Catholics and knows little about the church in its American incarnation. His father, whom Cort describes as "a sort of twentieth-century deist," threatened to withhold his son's college tuition should he go ahead with his announced intention of converting. (The pastor at St. Paul's in Harvard Square, invoking prudence, has advised Cort to delay his entrance into the church until after graduation.) Like nearly every convert, Cort is seeking spiritual certitude. "A proper church ought to have some teaching authority that commands respect," as he summed up his late-adolescent dismissal of the liberal Episcopalianism in which he was nominally raised. But unlike Dorothy Day, the best known today of the era's notable converts, Cort seems not to have been attracted to Catholicism as the church of the nation's impoverished working class. The poor show up anyway. The lone witnesses to his formal reception into the church are the rectory housekeeper and the sexton, "who put down his broom for a few minutes to stand beside me."[1]

Lonely in his new religious identity, Cort gravitated to the local headquarters of the Catholic Worker movement in Boston's South End, rather fruitlessly hawking the group's newspaper, also called the *Catholic Worker*, outside churches after Sunday Mass. "Because of the word *worker* in the name of the paper, we were denounced as Communists from time to time." The movement was of recent vintage, having been founded in 1933 by Dorothy Day and an itinerant Frenchman of peasant origin named Peter Maurin. The paper, devoted to the founders' religiously based pacifism and their radical gospel of charity, dates from that same year. By 1936, Day—she was the activist of the founding duo—was running two houses of hospitality in the slums of lower Manhattan, where the homeless were housed in makeshift quarters and the hungry were fed. She also oversaw a struggling communal farm, the would-be site of an "agrarian university." Her example was infectious: over thirty Catholic Worker houses and communities had been established in various U.S. cities by 1941, along with several Worker farms, none of which proved successful. The *Catholic Worker* by the mid-1930s had press runs of close to 150,000, while Day herself was a hero to a new generation of Catholic idealists.[2]

Hearing Day speak in Boston in 1936, John Cort resolved on the spot to quit his job and join the movement in New York. After a brief stint at the already failing farm in Easton, Pennsylvania—"we didn't have enough tools even to hoe the corn by hand"—Cort took up residence in the Worker house on Mott Street. Plagued by bedbugs, lice, and the occasional ravings of unbalanced fellow lodgers, Cort struggled at first with the psychic demands of voluntary poverty. "But there was something there that held you," as he later remembered. That something centered on community, the enthusiasm of the mostly young volunteers, and the sense of addressing social needs that New Deal programs could not fill. Many of those on the Worker bread line, in Cort's words, "needed a look in the eye, a word, some sign of human recognition, even more than the coffee and bread." Dorothy Day, for all her reserve and the hard life she had embraced, struck Cort as possessing "a quality of *joy*," rooted in her Gospel commitment. "She, in fact, could see the face of Christ in the least, the poorest, the most desolate and unattractive of our brothers and sisters. This was her gift, this was her message and her example, in word and deed." Her evident joy had brought Cort to New York; some taste of it seems to have kept him there.[3]

A socialist prior to her conversion, Day rejoiced in the industrial union movement of the 1930s, to which she gave generous coverage in the *Catholic Worker*. For John Cort, exposure to industrial unionism, particularly in the form of the New York seamen's strike of 1936–37, prompted a kind of second conversion. The sometimes violent struggle to organize the nation's mass-production workers, in Cort's view, was nothing less than "a just war": "I never questioned for a moment which side I was on." Aware that many of the nation's unskilled and semiskilled workers belonged to his church, Cort in 1937 helped to found the Association of Catholic Trade Unionists (ACTU), the immediate goal of which was promoting unionization among unorganized Catholic workers. (A subsidiary goal, which eventually came to dominate the ACTU agenda, was combating Communist power in the various unions affiliated with the Congress of Industrial Organizations, better known as the CIO.) Cort served as ACTU's president for the next five years and contributed to its national newspaper for almost two decades. The organization was never large. But it played an essential role for many Catholic workers in legitimizing the union cause. Via its popularization of the social encyclicals, ACTU tried, with some success, to endow industrial unions with a papal stamp of approval.[4]

Cort worked briefly as an organizer for the International Ladies' Garment Workers' Union in 1941 before being hospitalized with a recurrent case of tuberculosis, which rendered him unfit for military service during the Second World War. Dorothy Day maintained her pacifist stance despite the attack on Pearl Harbor, which cost the Catholic Worker movement much of its popular support. Probably a majority of the nation's Catholics had been fervent isolationists in the 1930s, when Day's pacifism was much less controversial. But once war was declared, Catholics served with their usual robust patriotism. Cort himself had never agreed with Day's absolutism when it came to nonviolence. Jesus did not say to turn your neighbor's cheek, he pointed out. "If your neighbor cries to you for protection against attack, how could you refuse it?" Most ACTU activists were of the same mind, and many served in the military. Cort spent much of the war in the hospital, saved from despair by writing for various Catholic publications. By 1946, his disease in remission, he returned to ACTU as managing editor of its paper and married Helen Haye, herself an ACTU activist. The first of their ten children was born in 1947.[5]

Cort's rapidly growing family, emblematic in its own way of postwar Catholic idealism, soon required a more generous paycheck than ACTU could provide. As of 1949, moreover, ACTU could no longer afford even his exceedingly modest salary, since the organization had supported a strike of cemetery workers whose employer was the Archdiocese of New York and thus lost an annual subsidy hitherto provided by Cardinal Francis Spellman. Cort took a job in 1950 with the Newspaper Guild as business agent for its Boston local. He continued to write for Catholic publications on matters pertaining to labor and politics, making a name for himself beyond Catholic circles as a bitter critic of Senator Joseph McCarthy. Building on his new ecumenical connections, Cort began hosting a discussion group in 1955 for faculty from Harvard, non-Catholics all, and the Jesuits' Boston College. "Among the subjects discussed were censorship, federal aid to education, adoption problems (a perennial headache around Boston then), freedom of the Catholic press, anti-Catholicism as the anti-Semitism of liberals, tensions between Jews and Catholics, Catholic in politics . . . and, of course, birth control." John Courtney Murray, a Jesuit widely known for his work on church-state relations, spoke to the group. So did Protestant theologian Paul Tillich.[6]

As Cort's interests in ecumenism and social justice would suggest, he was delighted by the papacy of John XXIII (r. 1958–63) and the near-simultaneous election of the nation's first Catholic president. Cort knew John Kennedy personally, if not intimately—a connection that probably explains his 1962 appointment as head of a Peace Corps educational project in the Philippines, where he served until 1964. He subsequently administered the Commonwealth Service Program in Massachusetts, partially funded by Lyndon Johnson's war on poverty, and then worked with the Model Cities program, also a product of the Johnson years. Like other liberal Catholics, he was buoyed in the mid-1960s by the near revolution accomplished at the Second Vatican Council (1962–65) and the seeming triumph of social democracy at home. Ten years later, with the country "sinking into a swamp of unemployment, inflation, and aggravated poverty" and the American church beset by factionalism, Cort moved beyond his New Deal orientation to embrace democratic socialism, even as he worried—mostly in private—about erosion of the church's teaching authority. He died in 2006, still a socialist and very much a Catholic, gratified that "fair portions" of his ten children were regular Mass-goers as adults.[7]

John Cort was hardly a typical Catholic of his own or any other generation. But his brand of tolerant, socially engaged Catholicism did grow progressively stronger after the First World War and especially in the wake of the Second. That growth reflects rising levels of education among lay Catholics and their growing sense, despite the debacle of Al Smith's defeat in 1928, of confident belonging in America. Catholics enjoyed a new prominence in national politics in the 1930s and after; they were also major beneficiaries of the New Deal. Industrial unions gave many Catholic workers a new sense of political efficacy and introduced them to a more active mode of citizenship. The rising generation of Catholics after 1945 experienced remarkable social mobility, thanks in good part to the GI Bill, which underwrote college education for legions of veterans and encouraged heightened aspirations on the part of their younger siblings. Popular culture by the 1930s was depicting Catholics in an attractive light, while anti-Catholicism as an organized movement was relegated to fringe status after the 1920s. Anti-Catholic sentiments could still be found among academics and other liberal professionals, but by the later 1950s—due in part to the Kennedy candidacy—such sentiments were frowned upon even in liberal circles.

More insular modes of Catholicism did not disappear, even in the 1950s. Certain ethnic subcultures had surprising tenacity, with Polish Americans in particular often occupying a socioreligious world quite distant from that of their fellow Catholics. Catholic fears and resentments helped to fuel the careers of Father Charles Coughlin and Wisconsin's Senator Joe McCarthy, although both men also had Catholic critics. Issues of race proved especially divisive, prompting certain Catholics to cling to a species of religious tribalism. The struggle for open housing in northern cities, acute in some places by the late 1940s, was waged primarily between African Americans and white Catholics, many of them working class. Although they often shared the workplace with African Americans, white Catholics in the nation's cities frequently opposed, and sometimes resisted, the integration of their neighborhoods. Catholic racial liberalism was accelerating in these same years, but its exponents, most of them relatively affluent, typically lived in neighborhoods far from the racial frontier. (John Cort, to give him his due, moved his family into Boston's Roxbury district, by then overwhelmingly black, for a two-year stint in the later 1960s, but few of his fellow liberals did the same.) Intra-Catholic polarization was often the result.

Despite very real differences based on ethnicity and class, however, American Catholics by the 1950s looked to be a remarkably cohesive group. Surveying the nation's religious communities at mid-decade, theologian-cum-sociologist Will Herberg was impressed by Catholics' "communal solidarity," which he attributed to "a strong emphasis on a common faith and tradition, and . . . a pervasive system of ecclesiastical control." Catholics were thus well situated, at least as Herberg saw it, to resist the corrosive effects of the nation's unprecedented affluence. Herberg did acknowledge that Catholics were experiencing rapid social mobility and opting in substantial numbers for the nation's burgeoning suburbs. "By and large, however, American Catholicism seems to be successfully coping with the difficulties and perils that its changed position in American society has brought." Catholics' "strong sense of self assurance," in Herberg's view, provided a striking contrast to the "growing minority consciousness" of the nation's Protestants.[8]

Other observers shared Herberg's assessment. The evidence, after all, was formidable. Suburban parishes built parochial schools in the years after 1945 with an enthusiasm often outstripping that of the immigrant generation. Catholic colleges, hospitals, and social service agencies proliferated or underwent expansion. Vocations to the priesthood and the religious life stood at impressive levels, especially once one took into account the very low birthrates of the 1930s, which limited the pool of recruits. Catholics attended church more regularly than the nation's Protestants and evinced a higher level of doctrinal orthodoxy than either Protestants or Jews. If religious intermarriage was a growing problem—as many as 40 percent of the nation's Catholics may have married non-Catholics in the immediate postwar years, according to the Jesuit sociologist John Thomas—those marriages often resulted in the conversion of the non-Catholic spouse.[9]

For all Herberg's perspicacity, however, he failed as a prophet. The communal solidarity he so admiringly evoked was giving way by the later 1960s to ideological polarization, while Catholic religious practice then was entering a long period of decline. Herberg was not wholly at fault. He could not possibly have predicted the reforms of the Second Vatican Council, which had the effect in the United States of greatly accelerating the collapse of the Catholic subculture. Nor could he easily have predicted, at least in the mid-1950s, the explosion in civil rights activism that in many locales heightened intra-Catholic polarization in the turbulent years after Vatican II. But he did miss certain indicators that over the course of the 1950s suggested a fundamental restiveness in the seemingly solid Catholic ranks. (In fairness, most Catholic observers missed them too.) High rates of religious intermarriage were a particularly troubling sign, which Herberg took far too lightly. And he paid no attention whatsoever to mounting doubts among lay Catholics about their church's now virtually singular ban on the use of contraceptives in marriage.

The forty years prior to the Second Vatican Council did indeed see remarkable Catholic progress. A heavily ethnic population as late as the 1920s and majority working class as late as 1945, Catholics by the early 1960s were among the nation's better-educated groups and widely respected for their disciplined religious practice. Their church enjoyed a national standing comparable to that of the mainline Protestant denominations. "The new status of the Catholic Church, and its openness to the outside world, is reflected in the fact that today it speaks to, and is heard by, the entire nation, and not merely its own community," as Herberg put it—prior, it should be noted, to both the Kennedy election and the Second Vatican Council. John Cort's father might have opposed his conversion less vehemently had it occurred in 1958. Many Catholics today look back on those years as a kind of ecclesial golden age. But there were shadows on that sunny landscape, the significance of which would soon be apparent. Maturity, no matter how exuberant, always contains the seeds of decline—or, to employ the language of faith, a transition to something new.[10]

T • E • N

This Confident Church

Immigration restriction in 1921 and, in more draconian fashion, 1924 slowed Catholic population growth for more than two decades. There were just over nineteen million Catholics in the United States in 1930, up from eighteen million in 1920—a lower rate of increase than had prevailed in previous decades. The Great Depression of the 1930s brought immigration to a virtual halt, with more people leaving the country than entering it between 1932 and 1935. Catholic birthrates plummeted in the early 1930s, when the national birthrate dropped below replacement levels, and remained at low ebb for much of the decade. But even in the 1920s, a mostly prosperous time, Catholic birthrates looked to be slowing. A Wisconsin study concluded that the Catholic birthrate in the state had declined more rapidly than that of non-Catholics between 1919 and 1933, a pattern evidently found in every Catholic ethnic group. More tentative data suggested that the same was generally true of Catholics in cities outside the South. "Birth control is now a practice with Catholics," Joseph Nevins warned his fellow priests in 1928, "and it is on the increase."[1]

The American birthrate rose significantly during the Second World War and came close to exploding afterward. The postwar baby boom did not peak until 1957 and then declined only gradually. Birthrates did not resume their downward trajectory until the mid-1960s. The Catholic birthrate in these same years was probably about 20 percent higher than the national average, with the differential rising to as much as 40 percent in certain affluent locales. In flat contradiction of demographic precedent, Catholic women with college degrees expressed preference for the largest families of all. Fueled by this astonishing procreativity, the Catholic population soared from twenty-one million in 1940 to forty-two million in 1960, when Catholics accounted for just over one-quarter of the U.S. population. Catholics' confidence surged with their numbers, as did Catholics' political influence. That influence prevented the public funding of most birth-control services prior to the mid-1960s, even as Catholic teaching in this regard was increasingly productive of tension in the Catholic ranks.[2]

With greatly diminished immigrant numbers, ethnic Catholics assimilated more rapidly than ever before. Ethnic parishes that did not adapt to the new reality often lost population, and few such parishes were established after 1930. Immigration from Mexico did quicken in the 1920s, the restrictive laws of that decade having imposed no quotas on the nations of the Western Hemisphere, while migrants from Puerto Rico began streaming to the U.S. mainland after the Second World War. Mexican immigrants settled mainly in Texas, southern California, and, albeit in much smaller numbers, the vast area in between, joining a Hispanic population whose roots were centuries old. By 1929, Los Angeles was the world's second-largest Mexican city. Others traveled north to industrial centers like Chicago. In the early 1930s, however, close to half a million Mexicans—some of them American citizens—were forcibly deported from the United States. Legal immigration from Mexico rose again after the Second World War, with roughly 275,000 arriving in the 1950s. Spanish-speaking Catholics were for the most part underserved by the American church, due largely to a dearth of priests who spoke their language. But many bishops did try to meet their needs, and genuine progress was evident by the 1950s.

American Catholics continued throughout the period to live primarily in New England, the mid-Atlantic states, and the industrial North Central heartland, although rapid population growth after 1945 in the nation's West and South did signal a coming regional realignment. Fittingly, the trans-Mississippi West received its first cardinal-archbishop in 1953, when Los Angeles's James Francis McIntyre—himself a transplanted New Yorker—received the honor. Prior to the 1950s, Catholics remained a mostly urban people. Affluent Catholics in the 1920s often moved to the sylvan precincts of outlying city neighborhoods and sometimes into the suburbs, then mostly upper income, although geographic mobility of all sorts slowed in the 1930s. Even in the late

1940s, the typical Catholic parish was urban and working class. By 1960, however, so many Catholics had moved to the rapidly proliferating suburbs that the modal parish of the near-term future would clearly be suburban. It would also serve a primarily middle-class congregation, many of whose members would have college degrees. Suburbanization imposed a huge financial burden on Catholics in the form of new churches and schools. In every urban diocese, moreover, the chancery worried about the future of the many center-city parishes whose dwindling congregations could hardly afford their upkeep.

The Consolidating Bishops

The forty years following the First World War saw the nation's Catholic bishops assume greater prominence and exercise greater ecclesial authority than ever before. Their numbers also grew: there were 111 dioceses nationwide by 1957, along with 27 archdioceses. The men who presided over the most populous and important of these had generally been appointed at the behest of a Roman patron. Boston's William O'Connell (r. 1907–47) was a protégé of Pope Pius X, Chicago's George Mundelein (r. 1916–39) of Pius XI, and New York's Francis Spellman (r. 1939–67) of Pius XII. All three were elevated to the cardinalate. During the First World War, moreover, the process of nominating bishops was altered by Rome to give greater authority to the Apostolic Delegate in Washington at the expense of local priests and the American hierarchy. The bishops thus appointed, not surprisingly, tended to be extravagant Romanists who celebrated papal triumphalism as a principal touchstone of the Catholic faith. They also tended to focus their considerable energies on their own dioceses rather than the national bishops' conference, which a number still regarded as a threat to their autonomy. To a man, such bishops strove to establish episcopal dominance over every aspect of local Catholic life.

Priests were the most directly affected by the trend toward centralization. Save in the most remote and sparsely populated dioceses, their lives were more minutely governed than ever before. Not every cleric welcomed this development. From the lay perspective, the effects were largely positive. Centralization meant such reforms as a standardized curriculum in the local parochial schools, along with uniform textbooks. Residentially mobile parents were bound to be appreciative. Most lay Catholics also delighted in their bishop's enhanced visibility and his image as what historian James

O'Toole has called a "manager shepherd." Like many prominent business-men, consolidating bishops often regarded themselves as champions of public morality, in which guise they addressed a larger-than-Catholic audi-ence, often on less-than-ecclesial topics. Boston's O'Connell, who pioneered the role, issued denunciations not just of the movies, card games, and jazz but also of such unlikely targets as psychoanalysis and the theory of relativ-ity. Every bishop, moreover, was cloaked in the aura of papal Rome, which endowed the least prepossessing with cosmopolitan polish. The exalted sta-tus of their bishop could be balm to those many Catholics who even in the late 1940s often felt marginalized. Hence the frequently elaborate public ceremonies, invariably thronged, that memorialized such events as the golden jubilee of a bishop's priestly ordination.[3]

Although most bishops did tend to focus exclusively on their dioceses, the National Catholic Welfare Conference also came to maturity in these decades. It worked mainly behind the scenes to affect legislation of interest to Catholics but with increasing sophistication and success. Leadership came primarily from midwestern prelates, especially Cincinnati's John Mc-Nicholas (r. 1925–50), Detroit's Edward Mooney (r. 1938–58), and Chicago's Samuel Stritch (r. 1940–58), who alternated the conference chairmanship from 1937 to 1950. Lay Catholics, for the most part, knew little about its ac-tivities, although national Catholic organizations were sometimes recruited by the conference to generate letters or other support for or against particu-lar policies. In the postwar years, however, the bishops' annual letter, which was issued under conference auspices, sometimes drew national notice. Such was the case with their 1951 letter on secularism ("God's Law: The Measure of Man's Conduct") and their 1958 missive on race relations, in which they called segregation a sin. That non-Catholic elites had so positive a response to such publications was a source of pride for many Catholics, confirming their sense—as aptly noted by Will Herberg—that the Catholic Church now occupied a respected place in the national life.

The consolidation of church governance, along with the heightened public presence of Catholics, reinforced for many observers a long-standing belief that the Catholic population was an impermeable monolith. Subser-vient to their all-powerful bishops and especially the pope, Catholics could not think for themselves. Or so the story ran, at least in its more extreme variants. The reality was rather different. Despite the unified front the bish-ops invariably presented to the public, they were not of one mind. Indeed, it required an order from Pius XII, then close to death, to secure the agreement of certain southern bishops to publication of the letter on race in 1958. Nor did they exercise total control over the priests of their dioceses, perhaps especially when it came to an explosive issue like race. It was not unheard-of, prior to the mid-1960s, for a pastor to defy his bishop when ordered to integrate the parish school. Although priests were now mostly American-born and trained in a similar way, generational tensions among the clergy, while hardly new, were reaching worrisome levels by the later 1950s. And there was nothing monolithic about the laity, despite the inroads of assimilation. If ethnic divisions were muted, the class divide was growing—and with it conflicting views of the world and the role of the church therein.[4]

Given the variety in the Catholic population and its conflicting interests, the unity that so impressed observers was indeed remarkable. For that unity was real in some very important respects. Catholics of all social classes attended weekly Mass in the 1950s with remarkable frequency, if their self-reporting can be credited. Relatively few persons raised in the faith appear to have left it as adults. Nor was the American church in these decades remotely threatened by schism. That religion in the American context had historically been an accepted mode of ethnic expression was one source of Catholic unity. Irish or German, Italian or Pole—most eventually assimilated to an American Catholic identity. The American tradition of anti-Catholicism also played a role, shoring up a shared sense of outsiderness. So did the Catholic liturgy, which bound Catholics together by its increasing uniformity and the exoticism of Latin, along with the practice of auricular confession—an experience for all practical purposes unique to Catholics—and the many devotions that transcended class as well as ethnic lines. "We grew up different," as Garry Wills once reminisced. But note that he employs the past tense. Even as he wrote these words, in 1971, Catholic difference and Catholic unity appeared to be things of the past.[5]

Sacramental Practice and Devotional Life

Catholic difference was on splendid display in the summer of 1926, when the twenty-eighth world Eucharistic congress was held in Chicago. A crowd of 150,000 assembled at the city's Union Station to greet the "Cardinals' Special"—an exclusive train of bright red coaches that, courtesy of the Pullman corporation, brought several European cardinals and New York's Cardinal

Patrick Hayes to the city, where their host was Cardinal George Mundelein. Philadelphia's Cardinal Dennis Dougherty, jealous of his midwestern rival, arranged for his own special "cardinal's car" with the Pennsylvania Railroad. The crowd then processed, cardinals in tow, to the city's Holy Name Cathedral, where thousands more onlookers waited and additional numbers filled the pews. The Mass that followed formally opened the five-day congress, an event that featured daily sung Masses, including one at Soldier Field, where even a late-June heat wave could not diminish the capacity crowd. The Masses and other congress ceremonies were widely publicized, to the delight of many Catholics but with less certain effect on a broader national audience. " 'The Church Universal' was a comment heard more than once as the ranks marched past," according to a non-Catholic journalist, who watched with pronounced ambivalence as hundreds of clergy, some of them obviously born abroad, processed toward the altar. "It is a proud boast—but not an American boast."[6]

Previous international Eucharistic congresses, the first of which occurred in 1881, had with only three exceptions taken place in Catholic regions of Europe. That an event so redolent of Catholic otherness could by 1926 be held in the United States suggests a perhaps-surprising level of Catholic confidence. The Ku Klux Klan, then militantly anti-Catholic, had marched some thirty thousand strong down Washington, DC's Pennsylvania Avenue less than a year before. The Eucharistic congress phenomenon also spoke to the growing emphasis in Catholic devotion on the Mass, of which Pius X's decree on frequent communion in 1905 was an integral part. Eucharistic devotion among American Catholics had quickened substantially toward the end of the previous century, when it helped to forge a shared Catholic consciousness that transcended ethnic lines. After the 1926 congress, it flourished mightily. The Forty Hours devotion remained a staple of parish life, as did Benediction of the Blessed Sacrament, usually offered weekly. Nocturnal Adoration Societies, all-male preserves, gained markedly in popularity. Nearly every parish scheduled a regular holy hour during Advent and Lent, when parishioners prayed before the Blessed Sacrament. By the 1940s, some dioceses were sponsoring such events in local sports stadiums—remarkably public displays of Catholic singularity.

American Catholics by the mid-1920s had heard more than their share of exhortations to receive communion frequently. Pastors in many dioceses were required to track their communion numbers and report them to the local chancery, where steady improvement was expected. A good many sermons, accordingly, were devoted to the subject—and some were apparently vigorous. "It pays to yell," according to Father Thomas Carey, who in 1925 was newly assigned to a parish in Michigan's heavily Protestant Thumb, where it had been customary to receive the sacraments only at Christmas and Easter. Religious instruction in the Catholic schools emphasized the need for frequent communion, which also featured prominently in Catholic publications. Frequent reception of the Eucharist, according to the latter, kept young people chaste, ensured marital happiness, and even— although this was more problematic—led to material benefit. When "Bill," a communist, returned to the church and the sacraments, his family life improved, and he soon inherited property, at least according to a 1926 story in the *Sentinel of the Blessed Sacrament.* Frequent reception of the Eucharist would make Notre Dame's undergraduates "better men, better students, and better athletes," according to Father John O'Hara, then prefect of religion at the school and later archbishop of Philadelphia. Indeed, it was a "pious tradition"—the words are O'Hara's—for students to commune on game-day mornings with the football team in mind.[7]

The number of frequent communicants does seem to have grown impressively in the 1920s and even more thereafter. Father Carey's laggard parish in Lapeer, Michigan, had by the end of 1927 more than met his goal of ten thousand communions annually. Notre Dame's students were notably devout, presumably for reasons that went beyond their football team's winning ways. A survey done on campus in 1925 reported that 86 percent of respondents self-identified as frequent communicants, by which a significant number apparently meant daily. Father O'Hara regularly distributed the Eucharist to students outside of Mass, a practice that was increasingly common in many urban parishes. It spoke powerfully to the value that the clergy now assigned to lay reception of communion—a dramatic change from just thirty years earlier, when their chief concern had been to keep the laity from receiving unworthily. The practice, somewhat ironically, was profoundly individualistic—a quality not otherwise associated with the Catholic faith, at least by its critics. Growing numbers of liturgically sensitive Catholics opposed it on precisely these grounds.[8]

The trend toward more frequent communion accelerated in the 1930s and 1940s. Depression and war proved powerful spurs to devotion, perhaps especially among men. Detroit's Father John Vismara took advantage of the altered climate by organizing the boys of his parish into "Eucharistic gangs,"

First communion breakfast, Altoona, Pennsylvania, 1940 (Courtesy of the
American Catholic History Research Center and University Archives [ACUA],
the Catholic University of America, Washington, DC)

the members of which pledged to receive communion weekly during the
summer months when they were out of school. He had decent success in 1937,
the first year of the experiment. But interest picked up notably after Pearl
Harbor, when Vismara asked each "gang" to bear the name of a serviceman
from the parish and offer their communions for his safe return. Schooled by
their teachers and inventive pastors like Vismara, young Catholics by the 1950s
were the group most likely to be frequent communicants. Probably a substantial majority by then were receiving communion at least once a month. Catholics over the age of sixty behaved quite differently, at least according to a 1951
study of a New Orleans parish, where a distinct minority of the older laity
received that often. Married Catholics in their thirties also tended to commune infrequently, according to this and other studies. Couples in this age
group, still fertile but already apt to have several children, were assumed by
most priests to be staying away from the sacrament because they were practicing birth control.[9]

As those thirty-something couples knew, Catholics could not receive the Eucharist in a state of mortal sin. Confession and communion remained intimately linked in Catholic thought and practice, and few Catholics would have received the Eucharist without confessing first. Daily communicants, always a devout elite, did not confess daily. Attempting to do so would have been regarded by nearly every priest as a sign of neurotic scrupulosity. But weekly communicants, most of them women, often went to confession every week. Few of them, in all likelihood, had mortal sins to confess on anything like a weekly basis. Theirs were mostly what were called "confessions of devotion," and such were increasingly commended to even the unremarkably observant by priests and teaching sisters. "The very fact that we go to confession means we increase the grace in the soul," in the words of Chicago's Reynold Hillenbrand, the much-admired rector of the archdiocesan seminary from 1936 to 1944. "We are holier in God's sight and our Heaven will be happier." Every good Catholic, according to Hillenbrand, ought to confess weekly. Such advice was increasingly standard in Catholic schools and parishes throughout the United States.[10]

Even in the 1950s, when American Catholics approached the sacraments more frequently than ever before, most Catholics did not confess that often. But a good many did confess monthly or close to it. Did more frequent confession result in a heightened consciousness of sin and a livelier awareness of its dangers? So the clergy hoped. That Catholics were less and less apt to be found in the nation's jails was perhaps a source of reassurance. Tellingly, or so it would seem, confessors' manuals in the late nineteenth century devoted far more space to penances for theft than did those published forty years later. But sexual sin, on which most confessions centered, was in seemingly endless supply. Indeed, the confessors of the 1940s and 1950s very likely heard more about it than their nineteenth-century predecessors had done. More frequent confession was accompanied, especially after 1930, by franker talk about sexual sin on the part of both priest and penitent. In that important sense, frequent confession probably did have profound effects on the consciences of many lay Catholics, especially when it came to the putative sin of contraception. Most confessions did not last long—two minutes is a reasonable estimated average, including recitation of the ritual formulas that framed the sacrament. But the frequently charged nature of their content gave this brief encounter an outsized emotional resonance for even the less-than-wholly devout.

Despite the drive for frequent communion, devotional life outside of the Mass continued to thrive well into the 1950s, although that decade also saw the first signs of its flagging. Marian devotion, perennially popular, assumed a new public dimension, with novenas in the Virgin's honor drawing crowds to centrally located churches, especially in the 1930s and during the Second World War. The novena to Our Lady of Sorrows at the Servites' church in Chicago drew an estimated seventy thousand Catholics weekly after its inauguration in 1937, with seven services held every Friday, while novenas to Our Lady of Perpetual Help attracted throngs to Redemptorist churches in a number of cities. Marian rallies in public venues appeared in the troubled 1930s, as did radio rosaries, with celebrities sometimes leading the prayers. Depression-era novenas were often promoted in frankly instrumental fashion: the Dominican fathers in hard-hit Detroit offered a novena "especially to obtain employment, for financial assistance, for help in paying debts and for sale of property." Wartime devotions and their Cold War successors emphasized safety—that of loved ones overseas and of the nation itself. The Marian apparition at Fatima, Portugal, in 1917 gave rise in the late 1940s to a vigorous American cult, which aimed to protect the United States from Communist subversion and the threat of nuclear war.[11]

Devotion to the saints was typically characterized by an especially intense instrumentalism. The older favorites continued to draw clients, while other venerable figures enjoyed episodic popularity. The Jesuits, for example, had some success in the 1930s with novenas to St. Francis Xavier, a reassuringly masculine intercessor for the desperate unemployed. Two promising newcomers also soared to enduring favored status: St. Thérèse of Lisieux, canonized in 1925, and St. Jude, a saint by tradition from antiquity but newly rediscovered in the early days of the Depression. St. Jude, the "saint of the impossible," was an especially evocative figure, not only for his reputed ability to work miracles when all hope was gone but also for his lack of ethnic connections. Forgotten for centuries, Jude had no history and no tradition of veneration by any national group. One could not have invented a more resonant figure for an economically devastated population beginning to move beyond ethnic particularism. The cult originated in Chicago, where the "national" St. Jude shrine is still located, and quickly spread to cities across the nation. Jude's clients "visited" the Chicago shrine by mail—a devotional innovation well suited to a far-flung Catholic populace. Surviving letters to the shrine dwell heavily on petitioners' fears about illness, unem-

THIS CONFIDENT CHURCH 227

ployment, and the heavy drinking of husbands and sons, most of the petitioners being women.[12]

Even as they prayed for specific favors, most Catholics understood that
devotion to the saints and especially to Mary ought to transcend the narrowly instrumental. The devout should strive to emulate the virtues of these
holy figures, denying the self out of love for God and neighbor. The enormously popular Sodalities of Our Lady, directed from a national office in St.
Louis but based in the parishes and Catholic colleges, linked Marian devotion
to charity. The sodalities' mostly female members offered their services to local hospitals and orphanages, assisted in catechetical work, and raised money
for the foreign missions. Other devotional groups followed suit. For most of
her clients, moreover, Mary embodied God's tenderness and infinite capacity
for forgiveness—a necessary respite from the fear engendered by Catholic
insistence on the reality of hell, a staple of catechesis and especially mission
preaching. No mission was complete without graphic depictions of the fiery
torments awaiting an apparently substantial population of "birth-controllers,
adulterers, fornicators, prostitutes, drunkards, [and] Mass-skippers." Mary's
devout thus restored, at least for themselves, an essential spiritual balance.
Devotion to Mary was also a principal marker of Catholic difference and
hence of Catholic identity. At a time of rapid assimilation, she was embraced
by many Catholics for precisely this reason.[13]

The devotional mentality remained at something close to fever pitch
into the early 1950s, when the Cold War sparked such innovations as the Block
Rosary movement—neighbors gathered to pray the rosary for world peace in
one another's homes or even in public—and the Blue Army of Fatima, a militant women's organization, which popularized the apocalyptic message conveyed to the Portuguese seers. By mid-decade, however, signs of decline were
increasingly evident. Such events as holy hours and Marian rallies in local
sports venues were drawing smaller crowds and in some locales were quietly
discontinued. A careful study of Pittsburgh's Catholics demonstrates that attendance at devotions of every variety began to fall after the early 1950s, while
more fragmentary evidence from elsewhere points in the same direction. Mission preaching by mid-decade was also drawing smaller numbers. Many factors contributed. Earlier marriage and rising birthrates kept many younger
women at home, while less burdened older wives were increasingly apt to be
employed. Television represented a formidable competitor for the evening
hours. Suburbanization also played a role, distancing many families from

public devotional events in center-city locations. Perhaps rising prosperity and medical triumphs—the Salk polio vaccine, announced in 1953, removed an especially black cloud—were factors too. With science regularly producing miracles, the need for the saints may have seemed less urgent.[14]

Perhaps most important, highly educated Catholics, on the whole a younger group, criticized many devotions on spiritual grounds. Catholic prayer should be more Christocentric, they argued, with devotions geared not to seeking favors but to deepening one's spiritual life. Marian piety, kept within proper theological bounds, could fill the bill, given Mary's intimate connection to Jesus. But the Mass should be central for every Catholic, who ought to participate in this great act of worship as fully and intelligently as possible. Rather than saying the Rosary during Mass, a common practice as late as the 1950s, Catholics should "assist" the priest by following the Latin in a missal and uniting their prayers with his. (*My Sunday Missal,* the most popular of the genre, was first published in 1932.) "Participation in the liturgy naturally produces in us the consciousness of our union with Christ and of our dignity as sharers in the divine nature," in the words of Virgil Michel, a Benedictine priest who did more than anyone else to promote the cause of liturgical revival in the United States. Such participation strengthened the bonds of solidarity with humankind and hence a commitment to charity and social reform. The Mass, Michel insisted, was profoundly communal. Thus one should receive communion, as the priest did, within the Mass itself—not privately outside the liturgy or, as was quite frequently done, at its very beginning or end.[15]

The liturgical movement, which pioneered such sentiments, made modest progress in this country in the 1930s and 1940s. Its leaders inaugurated an annual "Liturgical Week" in 1940, during which interested priests and laity assembled in various locales to hear talks on the liturgy and strategize as to movement building. Model liturgies often featured. A 1948 gathering in Chicago saw the establishment of the Vernacular Society, a group devoted to the cause of liturgy in the local language—something that triumphed at Vatican II. More mainstream reformers pinned their hopes on the "dialogue Mass," in which the congregation spoke or sang the Latin responses normally voiced by the choir or altar boys. Even in the mid-1950s, however, few American parishes offered dialogue Masses on anything like a regular basis, although they were quite common by then on Catholic college campuses. Midwestern dioceses, with their large German-descended populations, were the most receptive, the movement itself being of German origin. In Germany, by the mid-1950s, a substantial majority of Catholic churches were offering dialogue Masses more or less routinely.[16]

If many bishops still held aloof, highly educated Catholics in the 1950s embraced the liturgical movement with new ardor, as did growing numbers of younger priests. Catholic colleges and many high schools offered courses in the liturgy, with Notre Dame instituting a degree program in liturgical studies in 1947. Subscriptions to *Worship* magazine, the principal organ of the movement, grew significantly after the late 1940s and with it exposure to the movement's more daring advocates, who championed not just the vernacular but also such innovations as the priest saying Mass mostly facing his congregation. Founded in 1927 as *Oratre Frates*, the journal adopted its English name in 1952 as a concession to the vernacular. Liturgical "pilgrims" journeyed to churches like Holy Cross in St. Louis, pastored by Monsignor Martin Hellriegel, where the dialogue Mass was a regular feature, complete with Gregorian chant. Catholic bookstores, the most prominent of which were founded by women, often served as local movement centers, connecting interested laity to others of like mind. Catholic organizations, especially those for women, sponsored numerous liturgical study groups. The Grail, an international women's movement of Dutch origin, was especially prominent in this regard, running bookstores in San Francisco, Detroit, and Cambridge, Massachusetts, and encouraging local clergy to offer the dialogue Mass.[17]

The liturgical movement's appeal lay partly in the realm of aesthetics. Sunday Mass in a great many parishes was a hurried affair, where the celebrant might mumble the Latin. Even the high Mass might be marred by the sentimental renderings of an inadequately trained choir. Sermons were typically brief and not always well delivered, diocesan priests in particular having received little training in homiletics. The content was seldom compelling. "From the point of view of the listener . . . it was frequently difficult to discern the 'leading idea' in the sermons," according to a Jesuit sociologist who studied a New Orleans parish in the late 1940s. "Most of the sermons showed a lack of unity and cohesion, touching on three or four main concepts and mixing together both doctrine and admonition." Mission preaching came in for particular criticism, not only for the sometimes crude showmanship of the mission preacher but also his preoccupation with sin, fear, and hell. With birth control now a principal focus of mission sermons, such criticism conveyed a message about more than simply good taste.[18]

For a many of its advocates, liturgical reform had most fundamentally to do with a hunger for authenticity, which is to say an experience of worship congruent with their sensibilities and worldview. For the highly educated young, traditional devotions often seemed almost comically sentimental. "I hate to say most of these prayers written by saints-in-an-emotional-state," as Flannery O'Connor confided to a friend in 1956. "You feel you are wearing someone else's finery." Nor did the average parish Mass escape sometimes scathing criticism. If the church was indeed the Mystical Body of Christ, as most young Catholics had been taught, how effectively did a lackluster rite express this great truth? College-educated Catholics had typically had experience of the dialogue Mass at campus chapels or Newman Clubs, where substantive sermons were also on offer. Parish masses by contrast could seem wanting—the laity passive and often distracted, the celebrant distant and sometimes inaudible. Whatever their dissatisfactions, however, few such Catholics left the church or retreated to its margins. Highly educated Catholics were among the nation's most devout. But their spiritual hungers do much to explain the course of American Catholic worship in the wake of Vatican II.[19]

The Parish and Beyond

Even as Catholics were an increasingly assimilated population, the parish continued for many to be a primary focus of social life. Nearly every parish boasted a roster of social and devotional organizations, most with roots in the nineteenth century, and these continued to thrive. At the same time, growing numbers of Catholics began to engage in activities that took them beyond the parish and prompted a wider view of the world. A man might march in the annual parade of the Holy Name Society, where he would rub elbows with Catholic men from every parish in the diocese and presumably rejoice in a vigorous display of Catholic solidarity, such parades nearly always enlisting thousands. He would also be expected, as a Holy Name man, to engage in local political action. Campaigns against allegedly salacious movies and indecent literature were especially popular in Holy Name circles and sometimes included boycotts of offending theaters and stores. Catholic women, the more affluent of whom often gravitated to diocesan-wide organizations, frequently took part in such campaigns but, in the 1920s at least, in a clearly subordinate role. When the National Council of

Catholic Women gathered for its 1921 convention—the group, like its male counterpart, dates from 1920—the delegates obligingly passed a resolution against liberalization of the nation's birth-control laws; the resolution had not only been proposed but written by then-father John A. Ryan.

Adolescents and young adults were especially apt to move beyond the parish both literally and in their consciousness. The growing numbers now enrolled in high school often attended an institution that served multiple congregations. Catholic athletic leagues, which increasingly included teams for girls, sometimes embraced parishes from throughout the diocese. The Catholic Youth Organization (CYO), founded in Chicago in 1930 by Bishop Bernard Sheil, fostered competition between black and white Catholics in sports like boxing, basketball, track, and even swimming at a time when the YMCA was still segregated. The CYO's racially inclusive program soon spread to other northern dioceses. Participating in or cheering on an inter-racial all-star squad may not have converted white Catholics to the racial liberalism of which Sheil was so singular an exponent. But it did give an existential dimension to the notion of Catholic universality and made the world a bit more complex. Boxing was the CYO's most popular sport into the 1950s, when tournaments in Chicago drew as many as forty thousand fans. CYO boxing by then was increasingly dominated by boys from the African American parishes. Over 40 percent of the finalists in the 1952 tournament were black.[20]

If young women were also-rans when it came to the CYO, where their teams attracted only modest attention, they dominated the sodality movement, which achieved mass proportions in the 1920s and after. Prior to the First World War, the sodality movement was parish based and largely devotional in its purposes. But when the Jesuit Daniel Lord revived the organization in 1925, he gave it an activist thrust. While sodality members continued to focus on prayer and spiritual development, their mission now included what Lord called "active Catholicity." As individuals and collectively, in the parish and beyond it, sodalists should study the problems of the day, reflect on these in the light of church teaching, and then apply Catholic solutions. ("See/judge/act" was the oft-repeated formula for many varieties of what by the 1930s was being called "Catholic Action.") Too many young Catholics, as Lord saw it, knew little about their religion and had but a weak sense of Catholic identity. Catholic social activism was a means of remedying both deficiencies.

Boxing lessons at Fides House, a Catholic Worker community in Washington, DC, probably 1940s (Courtesy of the American Catholic History Research Center and University Archives [ACUA], the Catholic University of America, Washington, DC)

In most sodality units, "active Catholicity" was largely confined to the neighborhood. Sodalists might assist with catechetical instruction or staff the parish library. But especially after 1930, sodality projects increasingly edged toward the political. Sodalists were frequent participants in Catholic efforts to censor popular amusements, especially the movies. They might pressure local libraries to carry more books by Catholic authors or distribute Catholic pamphlets in public places. A number of groups campaigned against Franklin Roosevelt's policies in Mexico and Spain, which many Catholics saw as hostile to their church. Growing numbers of local activists, moreover, were attending the various "summer schools of Catholic action" sponsored, beginning in 1930, by movement headquarters in St. Louis. Together with the annual sodality conventions, the summer schools taught leadership skills to an elite among young Catholics and inspired in them a kind of buoyant militancy. "Our hearts are pure / Our minds are sure," in the words of the movement's rousing anthem. That so many of the most active sodalists were female gave special import to this development.[21]

Sodalists often raised funds for the missions, an activity widely promoted in the Catholic schools and perhaps the most evocative sign of an expanding Catholic consciousness. The American church had sent few missionaries overseas prior to the First World War. But interest in the foreign missions quickened in the 1920s, when a number of religious orders—women's orders as well as men's—sent missionaries abroad. China was then the missionary field that loomed largest in the Catholic imagination, due in good part to the work of the Maryknoll Society, an order devoted to missionary labors that sent its first priests to China in 1918. Maryknoll sisters quickly followed, arriving in Hong Kong in 1921. China soon attracted priests from other religious orders—Franciscans and Jesuits were especially prominent—as well as sisters from twenty-seven American congregations, who worked variously as teachers, catechists, and medical personnel. Maryknoll publications and mission education programs, along with those of other religious orders, introduced large numbers of American Catholics to Chinese culture and social realities in surprisingly sympathetic, if highly romanticized, terms. The effect for growing numbers was to broaden their vision of the church.[22]

Most Catholic schools by the mid-1920s were teaching what was popularly known as "mission consciousness." Students read missionary magazines, over forty of which were in circulation by the 1930s; attended talks by visiting missionaries; and competed with classmates to raise funds for mission support. Younger pupils were often encouraged to "ransom pagan babies": in return for a certain contribution, the donor could choose a baptismal name for an infant surrendered to a mission orphanage and receive a certificate of adoption. Catholic high schoolers and collegians were steered toward the Catholic Students' Mission Crusade (CMSC), founded in 1918, whose members engaged in serious study of the missions, along with prayer and fund-raising. The CMSC, which claimed over five hundred thousand members by the early 1930s, was suffused by a popularized form of the romantic medievalism then current among Catholic intellectuals: its Cincinnati headquarters were housed in the "Crusade Castle," while annual conventions featured allegedly medieval pageantry. The aura of heroism that surrounded the missionary enterprise was thus reinforced, and mission supporters themselves were encouraged to ever-greater militancy.[23]

A majority of the most active members of the CMSC were young women, as was indeed the case for nearly every organization promoting

"Catholic Action." In most such organizations and certainly in the CMSC, young women often found themselves in what for their Catholic cohort were unorthodox roles: speaking publicly before mixed audiences, exercising leadership in an organization that included males as well as females, even interpreting the Gospel. "Mission consciousness" by the 1930s had come for many in the CMSC to include a concern for Americans of African descent, and the organization took progressively bolder stands against racial discrimination, particularly in Catholic institutions. "The problem is not what to do with the Black man, so much as what to do with the white man," a high school girl from Detroit told her fellow Crusaders in 1935, when Catholic schools and hospitals in the city were still mostly segregated. "Remember, 100,000 Detroit Negroes look to us for a demonstration of the charity of Christ." A brave voice of conscience, young Margaret Murray typified a growing elite of devout and outspoken laywomen, whose spiritual progeny would increasingly shape the American church.[24]

The American Catholic missionary enterprise reached its apex in the wake of the Second World War. Missionary numbers more than doubled in the 1940s, a decade that also saw the establishment of Catholic Relief Services, soon to be a major player in global relief and development efforts. Most missionaries were expelled from China after its communist revolution in 1949, although a few managed to remain. Among them was Maryknoll Bishop James A. Walsh, who was arrested by Chinese authorities in 1958 and imprisoned for the next twelve years—a martyr of sorts to his many Catholic admirers. But new mission fields proliferated, among them Japan, Korea, the Pacific Islands, and, if to a lesser extent, the various nations of Africa. The U.S. missionary presence in Central and South America grew rapidly: almost a third of the U.S. Catholic missionary force was stationed there by 1958. American missionaries in these same years increasingly spoke out against racism and ideologies of cultural superiority; by the 1960s, many—especially those serving in Latin America—were denouncing repressive governments that were often supported by the United States. Lay missionaries also came to the fore in the postwar years, with ninety-six serving abroad by 1958. The Grail opened a school of missiology in 1950 to train American laywomen for overseas work, sending the first graduates as nurses to Africa in 1952.[25]

American Catholics were exceedingly generous when it came to mission support, especially after 1945. They did not necessarily share the global perspective increasingly found in the mission community. But support for the missions did enlarge the world for a great many Catholics and generated a more vivid sense of transnational human solidarity. Even those many Catholics whose horizons were still mostly bounded by the parish were in many respects more cosmopolitan than their counterparts thirty years earlier. Generally reckoned in the 1950s to be staunch supporters of the United Nations, American Catholics took visible pride in the global church on display at the Second Vatican Council. Having struggled for over a century to be seen as fully American, at least some in this onetime immigrant tribe now aspired to global citizenship.

Birth Control

The 1930s was a pivotal decade for the religious politics of birth control. In the waning days of 1930, as a global depression was in its first stages, Pope Pius XI issued *Casti Connubii,* an encyclical on Christian marriage. The pope denounced both divorce and contraception as grave sins—"mortal" sins, in Catholic parlance. He was responding primarily to a recent decision by the Anglican Church to tolerate marital contraception in certain difficult circumstances. By the mid-1930s, a number of other Protestant churches had followed suit, some in language far less cautious than that employed by the Anglicans. The cultural climate had shifted sufficiently by then that mainstream women's magazines were speaking favorably of birth control, albeit for the married only. Even Margaret Sanger was now widely regarded as a reformer rather than a radical. Catholics, in short, stood increasingly alone when it came to contraception, which shocked a good many older Catholics and especially priests. Public discussions of birth control, in the agitated words of the Paulist John J. Burke, "almost take our feet from under us, so that we wonder if we are strangers in a strange land."[26]

Casti Connubii, to complicate matters, included a summons to action. The pope called on every priest to do vigorous battle against contraception, especially in the confessional. Too many Catholics had been led astray by their clergy's hitherto-reticent ways. Chicago's Cardinal Mundelein instructed his priests in 1931 to question female penitents about contraception "when a family is small or apparently spaced." Having to ask every adult woman penitent about her marital status and the number and age of her children would have been quite a burden, given the quantity of confessions heard by the typical priest. But apparently some priests complied. When

Mundelein broadened his order to include male penitents in 1932, he cited information from various confessors to the effect that husbands were sometimes "the real offenders." Questioning men would be challenging, the cardinal warned. "The man will answer back, will try to argue. . . . A man is not quite so religious as a woman, he will not so likely be frightened by the danger of sudden death in sin." No other bishop seems at the time to have gone as far as Mundelein, although all expected their clergy to inform erring penitents that birth control was always a sin and elicit promises of reform. With *Casti Connubii* near universally regarded as infallible teaching, even hitherto-reticent confessors had to change their ways.[27]

The new regime in confession coincided with the depths of what is still the nation's worst depression, when the national birthrate sank for a time below replacement levels. More than half of Catholic married couples employed contraceptives, according to a Chicago pastor in 1933, although his was almost certainly an overestimate, given relatively low levels of education in the Catholic population. Many offending penitents may have practiced coitus interruptus, a not terribly effective contraceptive strategy most widely found among the less educated, or even have turned to backstreet abortions, the numbers of which soared in the early 1930s. With unemployment at record levels and little in the way of public aid to sustain the destitute, what was a confessor to do? "Every priest who is close to the people admits that contraception is the hardest problem of the confessional today," according to Joseph Reiner, a Jesuit based in Chicago. Some hardpressed penitents did talk back, justifying their conduct on the grounds of poverty, at least according to the clerical literature. At the same time, growing numbers were apparently confessing the sin of contraception or at least providing an obvious opening for clerical questions in this regard. *Casti Connubii* had been the stuff of front-page news, and preachers at missions and retreats now addressed the sin of birth control in clear and uncompromising terms. Good-faith ignorance was increasingly hard to come by.[28]

Happily for all concerned, the early 1930s marked the advent of what subsequent Catholic generations called the "rhythm method." Hard-pressed couples had since the mid-nineteenth century been permitted to limit or space their children by confining intercourse to those days in a woman's menstrual cycle when she was apt to be infertile. But it was not until the 1920s that the female reproductive cycle was sufficiently understood to correctly identify the time of a woman's probable fertility, and that information reached the public only gradually. When confessors recommended the "safe period" to penitents prior to the 1930s, they nearly always gave advice that would have made conception likely to occur. Not surprisingly, the laity had little faith in the method. That a physiologically plausible method of "natural" birth control was now available—the key publication in the United States was *The Rhythm of Sterility and Fertility in Women* by Dr. Leo Latz, first published in 1932—seemed literally providential to a good many priests. It was not long before certain mission preachers were distributing "how-to" pamphlets on rhythm—the name comes from Latz's title—to penitents facing marital stress. Some bishops attempted to suppress such literature, at least in the confines of their dioceses, but popular demand was so great that commercial publishers, immune to episcopal sanction, rushed to meet it.

The rhythm method was not terribly reliable as a mode of family limitation, even after refinements to the method were introduced in the 1950s—hence Catholic jokes about "Vatican roulette." It did often work as a means of spacing children at wider intervals, albeit at the frequent cost of a greatly reduced incidence of sexual intercourse. In the early days of rhythm, its ascetic demands fit neatly with the prevailing Catholic sexual ethic, which can only be called repressive. Catholics then were sometimes told that too much sex in marriage had a coarsening effect. But by the 1950s, the atmosphere was very different. With the nation suffused by a popularized neo-Freudianism, the younger clergy—and especially those engaged in nascent family-life ministries—spoke a language of sacralized sex. "Our bodies are good and beautiful; using them as God intends us to is wholesome and indeed sacred," according to the outline for the priest's presentation at Chicago's Pre-Cana conferences, where the soon-to-be-married were instructed in Catholic particulars. The sex so earnestly celebrated was emphatically noncontraceptive, as every Pre-Cana event made clear. But what to do when excess fertility made regular sexual communion impossible?[29]

American Catholics responded generously to the postwar emphasis on sacralized sex. Catholic birthrates boomed, and reported adherence to Catholic teaching was high. According to a national fertility survey done in 1955, only 30 percent of Catholic wives in their childbearing years had ever used a means of family limitation other than abstinence or rhythm. Those Catholics who did turn to forbidden modes of contraception typically stayed away from communion for many months at a time—another way of acknowledging the church's authority in the matter. Not every Catholic agreed with the teaching.

A 1952 poll commissioned by *Catholic Digest* found that 51 percent of the Catholics queried did not regard "mechanical birth control" as inherently sinful—a finding so distressing to the magazine's editor that he declined to publish it. Public dissent, however, was rare prior to the late 1950s and was even then typically couched in appeals for further refinement of the rhythm method, often described in its present state as subversive of marital happiness. But beneath the calm surface, dissent was swelling. A national fertility survey done in 1960 reported that 38 percent of Catholic wives in their childbearing years— and some 46 percent of those in their later thirties—were employing a means of birth control forbidden by their church. By 1964, lay dissent had gone public, with consequences that continue to echo in American Catholic life.[30]

"America's Church"

The largest Catholic church in North America was thronged with the faithful at its formal dedication in November 1959, with the crowd rejoicing in both its completion and the Catholic celebrities present. Monsignor Fulton J. Sheen, erstwhile radio luminary and now a television star, generated a particular buzz. The church was the Basilica Shrine of the Immaculate Conception, located on the campus of the Catholic University in Washington, DC. The basilica's origins date to 1920, when ground was broken for a crypt church, which was completed in 1926 and is still an active place of worship. Our Lady of the Catacombs, as the crypt church is called, bore the stamp of immigrant Catholicism: its dark, enclosed Romanesque spaces bespoke a church still under siege, while women played a dominant role in its largely decentralized fund-raising. Depression and war delayed the start of the planned upper church, whose dimensions would dwarf the crypt; construction did not begin until 1953. This time around the funds were raised under centralized auspices, with the bishops' conference imposing a quota on every diocese in the country, which 90 percent of them met. The male laity was well represented when it came to contributions: the basilica's soaring tower was funded by the Knights of Columbus, one million strong by the 1950s and emblematic of the masculine piety that increasingly marked an assimilated church. Of the roughly three hundred thousand Catholics annually in the mid-1950s who made a religious retreat, a majority were men.[31]

The basilica's interior décor was still a work in progress as of 1959. Even so, the contrast with the crypt church was evident in its soaring, well-lit spaces and bright mosaics, each of which staked a claim to Catholicism's place in the nation's life. So did the sculptural program for the basilica's east wall and porch, which establishes the church's temporal priority in the New World by memorializing Columbus and missionaries like Eusebio Kino and celebrates Maryland's Catholic founding and the bishops' 1846 placing of the United States under the protection of Mary Immaculate. The Washington, DC, location made the point as well. The basilica's massive, polychromed dome, visible for miles around, echoed the dome of the not-too-distant Capitol. Many Protestant denominations had already established "national" churches in the capital, most notably the so-called National Cathedral built by the Episcopalians. If Catholics were latecomers, at least in Washington, to the religious claiming of civic space, the size of the basilica announced that theirs was a presence to be reckoned with.[32]

The Catholic confidence evident in the basilica's size and its iconographic program seemed at the time to be warranted. A polyglot church, once deeply divided, had matured by 1959 into a cohesive body remarkable for its piety and seeming uniformity. (The original program for the church's interior décor made only passing reference to ethnicity; the ethnic side chapels that now line both the upper church and the crypt level were nearly all built after 1965, when reform of the nation's immigration laws ushered in a new chapter in its immigrant history.) The Catholic hierarchy, once rent by conflict, had worked as a single body to make the basilica possible and spoke with one voice when it came to ecclesial discipline and relevant issues of national policy. Vocations to the priesthood and religious life remained surprisingly strong, despite the unprecedented opportunities now available to young Catholics. The almost ritual bemoaning of a "vocations shortage" that featured in sermons and Catholic periodicals mostly reflected the outsized personnel demands caused by a rapid expansion in Catholic schools, colleges, and specialized ministries—another index of Catholic vigor. Perhaps most important, Catholics were now widely accepted as fully, even admirably, American. A prime prospect for the Democrats' presidential nomination by 1959, after all, was a Catholic senator from Massachusetts, already generating excitement with his tousled good looks and articulate wit.

John F. Kennedy, however, did not attend the basilica's dedication. Indeed, there is no record of his ever having visited the church, which he certainly did not do as president. Nor was his funeral Mass held there but at Washington's St. Matthew's Cathedral. Kennedy may have intuited that a monument to Catholic consolidation, for such the basilica was, might stir residual fears in certain Protestant quarters. Perhaps the basilica's grandiosity was simply alien to his religious tastes. Or perhaps this consummate politician knew in his bones that the building, while a grand achievement, marked the end of a dispensation in American Catholic history. That is unlikely, of course—Kennedy, according to his intimates, was at best a lukewarm Catholic, who evinced little interest in matters ecclesial, save as these bore on politics. Even observers far more qualified than he seldom came at the time to so startling a conclusion, which seemed to defy an abundance of evidence. But as subsequent developments would make clear, the basilica's opening did in fact coincide with the end of an era.

The basilica has continued to evolve, particularly via the proliferation of chapels funded by various ethnic organizations, whose members seek affirmation of their membership in the American Catholic family. It attracts a million pilgrims annually, many of them recent immigrants. But the upper church has become, for many disaffected Catholics, a principal symbol of Catholic intransigence on matters of sex and gender—it is, in fact, the official church of a hierarchy that grew notably more conservative after 1980—and thus of their alienation. Such Catholics can always visit the more intimate spaces of the crypt church, where Dorothy Day prayed in 1932 "that some way would open up for me to use what talents I possessed for my fellow workers, for the poor." But even if the visit brought comfort, it could not erase the stubborn reality of Catholic polarization—a principal legacy of the turbulent years that followed the Second Vatican Council.[33]

Catholic Minds

Education and Intellectual Life

The First World War, which famously produced a "lost generation" of disillusioned American youth, "precipitated within Catholicism a new sense of identity, an enthusiasm for ideals, and a rather disconcerting confidence in their beliefs," in the words of historian William Halsey. Catholic education bore witness to this transformative development, as did Catholic intellectual life. The number of Catholic schools and colleges grew dramatically in the 1920s, with an even larger surge of growth in the wake of the Second World War. The numbers alone fueled communal pride. So did significant improvement in the quality of most Catholic schools. Catholic leaders regularly claimed that their schools were superior to those conducted by the state—more efficiently run, more successful academically, and infinitely more potent with regard to moral formation. In the Catholic telling, secular schooling had by its very definition no moral content at all. If such claims were not necessarily accurate, they were balm nonetheless to the communal ego. Better-educated Catholics took pride as well in the sudden visibility of a Catholic intellectual elite, cloistered for the most part in Catholic institutions of higher learning but sufficiently numerous to command at least occasional national attention.[1]

As Catholics saw it, their thinkers and indeed their schools had a providential mission: to uphold for their disillusioned compatriots the certainties that the First World War had seemingly undermined. The universe was indeed orderly and knowable; human existence had meaning and purpose;

faith and right reason—which could never conflict—invariably issued forth in confident optimism. From the Catholic perspective, the postwar world and especially the United States still shone with bright promise. Undergirding this sunny perspective was the growing dominance of Neo-Scholastic philosophy, which by the 1930s had permeated nearly every aspect of Catholic intellectual life. As a body of thought, the American version of Neo-Scholasticism made scant room for complexity or openness to experience, although this was hardly true of the works of St. Thomas Aquinas, on which Neo-Scholasticism was based. But it did undergird a faith in reason and human responsibility at a time when such was arguably needed and provided a powerful source of ideological unity among Catholics. In the long run, however, the dominance of Neo-Scholasticism proved excessively constricting. As Catholic critics were arguing by the mid-1950s, the system was better suited to keeping the world at bay than to understanding its exceedingly complex realities.[2]

If doubts about Catholic intellectual achievements, and indeed the quality of the Catholic schools, were beginning to surface among Catholics in the 1950s, the prevailing mood in the community was still complacent—and understandably so. No people in the history of Christianity, as the Jesuit Walter Ong pointed out in 1957, had built and sustained "an organized educational program which even remotely compare[d] with that [of Catholics] in the present United States, with its 3,500,000 elementary school pupils, its nearly 700,000 secondary-school pupils, and its 500,000 students in Catholic universities and other institutions at the university level." If Catholics were not yet producing their share of nationally recognized scholars, especially in the sciences, as John Tracy Ellis pointed out in 1955, current rates of Catholic upward mobility confirmed for most that their schools were up to intellectual par. Growing numbers of bright young Catholics, in fact, were enrolling by then in Ivy League graduate programs, while Catholic undergraduates were increasingly found in the nation's best secular universities. The Catholic demand for college was such in the years after 1945 that the nation's Catholic institutions could not begin to meet it.[3]

Highly educated Catholics, not surprisingly, often turned a critical lens on the religious world that had nurtured them. The schools were a principal target, as was the life of the Catholic mind. The Catholic intellectual world was too rigid, according to the critics—too insulated from the world's complexities, too hostile to doubt and dissent. That a number of leading priest-intellectuals in Europe, along with the American Jesuit John Courtney Murray, had been silenced by papal fiat at various times in the 1950s had deeply embarrassed many educated Catholics, as had their core-ligionists' seemingly widespread support of Senator Joseph McCarthy. By the early 1960s, Catholic critics were calling for something akin to a revolu-tion in Catholic intellectual culture. Freedom and openness to experience, they insisted, were essential to the cultivation of truly Catholic minds. George Shuster, a Catholic journalist and literary scholar long critical of Catholic parochialism, was startled by the abruptness of this development. "The scene is now abuzz with young Catholic writers, philosophers and even theologians whose utterances I would have found, even in my most outspoken days, rather venturesome and challenging," he wrote in 1961.[4]

Catholic Education: The Years of Triumph

High school attendance in the United States soared in the 1920s, when many states raised the legal age of school leaving and employers required at least some high school for a growing number of jobs. As public high schools proliferated, Catholics rushed to keep up. Many extant Catholic high schools were still quite small, with most students leaving well before gradu-ation. (Graduation rates were notably higher at the elite academies staffed by the various teaching orders, some of which were of excellent quality and all of which charged fairly hefty tuitions.) By the 1920s, however, the favored model was the central high school, which served multiple parishes and of-fered, by dint of its expanded enrollment, a more diverse curriculum. Many such schools included "commercial" as well as academic courses, which is to say classes in typing, shorthand, and bookkeeping. Philadelphia was a lead-er in this regard, having established a central high school in the early 1890s. But it was only in the 1920s that the model triumphed. Not many bishops prior to that time had the necessary wealth to build such schools or the abil-ity to command the kind of cooperation—from pastors and especially the teaching orders—that their establishment required.

The central high school was usually placed in the hands of a single teaching order, although the occasional school did employ teachers from more than one community. Teaching at such schools, which were built and ultimately controlled by the diocese, was less lucrative for a religious order than running a private academy, given pressure to keep tuition low. But the

central high schools quickly proved to be fruitful sources of vocations, particularly among girls, many of whom entered religious life immediately
upon graduation. Central high schools were invariably sex segregated, although some of the earlier parish-based high schools had been coeducational out of economic necessity. Sisters taught girls; priests or brothers
taught boys. The same-sex environment arguably intensified the emotional
bond between teacher and student, making it easier to generate among students an admiration not just for the religious life but also for a specific order's ethos and spirituality. Curriculum at the central high schools typically
followed diocesan guidelines and, given enhanced state control of education, increasingly resembled—save for classes in religion—that of the local
public schools. But a school's emotional climate matters too, and in the case
of the Catholic school this reflected both its teachers' particular mode of
pedagogy and their order's distinctive devotional practices. Not surprisingly, young aspirants to the religious life usually entered the order to which
their teachers belonged.

Attendance at Catholic secondary schools rose rapidly in the 1920s.
The Great Depression, however, brought a decade of decline. Relatively few
Catholic schools closed in those years, whether at the primary or secondary
level, largely because their teachers were paid so little. On occasion, indeed,
even the pittance owed to the sisters was deferred—something that happened far less often to the better-paid priests and brothers. But parochial
school attendance in many locales decreased in the 1930s, sometimes quite
substantially. Catholic school enrollment in Chicago and its suburbs fell by
some twenty-two thousand students between 1930 and 1939. A significant
portion of the decline was caused by plummeting birthrates—first-grade enrollment in Chicago-area Catholic schools was 30 percent lower in 1939 than
it had been ten years earlier. But high school enrollment suffered too, although mostly in low-income neighborhoods. Hard-pressed parents could
not afford even nominal tuition, and some were apparently too proud to accept a parish tuition subsidy. Many Catholic adolescents did continue their
studies at the local public high school, with girls especially likely to do so.
White-collar employment during the Depression generally recovered faster
than that in blue-collar occupations. It thus made sense to working-class
parents, who still expected to share in a portion of their children's earnings,
for daughters to qualify for clerical jobs by completing at least some high
school grades.[5]

The Second World War brought prosperity, perhaps especially to a Catholic population still disproportionately working class. Catholic school enrollments again began to grow, albeit slowly, due to wartime restrictions on building. But once those restrictions were lifted, enrollment surged in unprecedented fashion at both the primary and secondary levels. By 1960, it was estimated that two-thirds of Catholic youngsters in Chicago and its burgeoning suburbs were attending a Catholic school, although in many other dioceses that figure hovered at just above 50 percent. As in the past, most students were enrolled in the elementary grades. But Catholic high school enrollment in the Archdiocese of Chicago more than doubled between 1950 and 1965, with demand for such schooling especially strong in the more affluent suburbs. The rapid expansion outstripped the resources of every teaching order, which were simultaneously struggling to ensure that every new teacher entered the classroom with a bachelor's degree in hand. Filling the gap were lay teachers, costly though they were. Only 4 percent of the teachers in the primary schools of the Archdiocese of Chicago in 1950 were lay—a figure that rose to 38 percent just ten years later. The percentage of lay teachers at the high school level more than doubled in this same decade, rising to 36 percent by 1960.[6]

Catholic higher education expanded in parallel fashion. Significant growth and development took place in the 1920s, as numerous new schools were founded and existing ones expanded and brought up-to-date. By 1926, there were sixty-nine colleges and universities that had been accredited by the Catholic Educational Association, many of recent vintage. Twenty-five were institutions for women—a number that rose to forty-five by 1930. The women's colleges were generally small, with many of their students preparing to be teachers. Indeed, rising standards for teacher certification had spurred the founding of many such institutions. Colleges for men placed a heavy emphasis by the 1920s on undergraduate vocational programs, such as business and prelaw, although hardly any had done so at the turn of the century. The Jesuits, who had moved reluctantly toward modernization of their classical curriculum, loomed large by the 1920s as purveyors of professional training, including at the graduate level. Such programs were enormously popular with college-bound Catholics, a reality that no tuition-dependent institution could afford to ignore. That most Jesuit institutions were located in large cities, where the hunger for professional training was concentrated, was a factor as well.[7]

Catholic colleges did not prosper in the Depression-ridden 1930s. But their enrollments suffered less than those of the Catholic secondary schools, largely because they drew their students from a more affluent sector of the population. Indeed, Catholic college enrollments increased more rapidly than those of their secular counterparts during the Depression decade. As had been the case in the 1920s, it is probable, though by no means certain, that half of all Catholic collegians in the 1930s were enrolled in Catholic institutions. The Second World War brought stasis, however, given wartime reductions in the available population of college-age males. Few Catholic colleges for men were free, because of the rules that governed the various teaching orders, to recruit female students as a temporary expedient, although a number of institutions did benefit from hosting government programs for specialized military training. But the war was followed by an enrollment explosion, thanks in good part to the GI Bill. By 1960, there were 231 accredited Catholic colleges and universities in existence, with enrollments that had increased since 1940 by 164 percent. By this time, however, the number of college-bound Catholics was so great that a growing majority were opting for other-than-Catholic institutions.[8]

Prior to the 1950s, nearly every Catholic college was a single-sex institution. Only Xavier University in New Orleans, founded in 1915 for African Americans, was coeducational at its inception. (Because no other Catholic college at the time would accept black students, Xavier had of necessity to accommodate both sexes.) Popes had inveighed against coeducation since its advent in the nineteenth century, with Pius XI denouncing it in a 1929 encyclical. But American realities gradually intervened. As women's religious orders began to establish colleges, where the sisters themselves provided most of the faculty, more and more women religious needed graduate degrees. A small but growing minority of laywomen also expressed an interest in graduate education. The need was initially met via summer-school programs on those Catholic campuses that offered graduate training, all of which were schools for men. But the practical difficulties involved—earning a graduate degree in this fashion would take a very long time—led some institutions to quietly admit the occasional woman, usually a sister, to the regular graduate program. These "firsts" often paved the way for graduate coeducation more generally. Sister Mary Hilger, a Dominican from St. Paul, Minnesota, was admitted—with the active support of her bishop—to Catholic University's graduate program in sociology and social work in 1924.

Three years later, a laywoman was permitted to earn her master's degree in Greek and Latin—a decision followed shortly thereafter by the university's trustees deciding to open every graduate program, save those in theology and philosophy, to qualified female applicants.[9]

Undergraduate coeducation advanced much more slowly. The Vincentians' DePaul University in Chicago was the first, in 1911, to admit women to an undergraduate degree program, but its example was seldom followed. Catholic University was unusual in the 1930s in its gradual admission of women to various undergraduate classes in the arts and sciences—a policy made necessary by the 1932 establishment on campus of a School of Nursing, whose female students needed such courses to fulfill their degree requirements. By the end of the decade, women were students and even teachers in a variety of undergraduate subjects. By the 1950s, a number of formerly all-male institutions—most of them commuter schools located in big cities—were coeducational too. But even in the 1950s, roughly 80 percent of Catholic colleges were open to one sex only, which helped to undergird among Catholics a strong ideology of gender complementarity. Sisters who staffed colleges for women, nearly all of which were smaller and financially weaker than those for men, championed single-sex education with particular vigor. Any trend toward coeducation, they rightly feared, would pose a threat to their institutions' very existence.[10]

Catholic colleges and universities varied widely when it came to academic quality, although critics—even Catholic critics—maintained that all were seriously deficient, if only in this regard, compared to the stronger secular institutions. The smaller schools often had limited library resources and inadequate provision for instruction in the sciences. Many faculty, especially prior to the Second World War, had not yet completed a doctoral degree or even, in some cases, a master's. Given heavy teaching loads and extracurricular obligations, a significant number never would. Faculty intellectual development was of necessity a low priority at the less affluent colleges, while even the larger and wealthier ones did not invariably prize scholarship in the usual academic sense. Father John O'Hara, the Holy Cross priest who served as president of Notre Dame between 1934 and 1939, was said to police the shelves at the university library and personally destroy any books he regarded as dangerous to faith or morals. He had done so, as prefect of religion, in the early 1920s to a novel assigned by George Shuster, who was then teaching English. The offending text was D. H. Lawrence's

The Rainbow, to which Shuster had already affixed a seal that prevented the book's being borrowed by any but students enrolled in his class. Shuster soon left the faculty to pursue his doctorate at Columbia. As president, O'Hara had a particular animus against books assigned by a certain priest-professor of sociology, at least according to Thomas McAvoy, himself a Holy Cross priest and a member of Notre Dame's history faculty.[11]

That Shuster, a 1915 Notre Dame graduate, had elected to teach *The Rainbow* suggests that intellectual sparks could fly even in a repressive setting. Indeed, he went on to a distinguished career as an independent-minded Catholic journalist and author, eventually serving as president of New York's Hunter College. The dearth of scholarly distinction on Catholic faculties did not necessarily mean an absence of intellectual curiosity and certainly not of a passion for teaching. Even a curmudgeon like O'Hara, moreover, understood that a credibly scholarly faculty had its uses when it came to enhancing Catholic prestige and defending the faith against critics. Notre Dame played host to a number of prominent Catholic intellectuals from England and the Continent during the O'Hara years, and their presence drew generally positive notice to the institution. The flight of Catholic scholars in the 1930s from countries threatened by fascism was dwarfed by that of their Jewish compatriots. But sufficient numbers arrived that the faculties at the larger Catholic universities, Notre Dame in particular, were strengthened as a result.[12]

A growing emphasis nationwide on graduate education after 1945 also spurred significant improvement at the larger Catholic institutions, where new resources were devoted to building up graduate programs. By 1960, Notre Dame could claim something approaching distinction in chemistry, while Georgetown was gaining notable strength in political science and international studies. Graduate programs were expensive, however, and progress in this regard was slow at even the best-endowed schools, whose most-talented graduates were usually advised to pursue their further studies at secular institutions. But the growing emphasis on graduate programs meant an influx of faculty at the larger Catholic universities with solid records of scholarly achievement or at least the potential for such. Bright undergraduates were apt to benefit. Graduate programs also meant an intensified alertness to secular standards when it came to academic excellence, which helped to fuel a surge in self-criticism among Catholic educators and intellectuals. Why have Catholics produced so few scholars of genuine distinction? they asked, decrying the alleged provincialism and intellectual complacency of American Catholic culture. John Tracy Ellis, a distinguished priest-historian at Catholic University, gave definitive voice to the argument in a 1955 essay, initially appearing in the Jesuit-published journal *Thought* but many times reprinted.[13]

Catholic colleges for women, most of them small and underresourced, seldom sponsored ambitious graduate programs. But the better ones still achieved a significant degree of academic excellence. The first Catholic institution permitted by Phi Beta Kappa to establish a chapter on its campus was the College of St. Catherine in St. Paul, so honored in 1938. Washington, DC's Trinity College, in the words of historian Philip Gleason, "produced more Ph.D. candidates in the humanities and the social sciences between 1936 and 1950 than any other institution of its size in the country." (Heading Trinity's surprisingly long list of prominent alumnae is Nancy Pelosi, the first female Speaker of the U.S. House of Representatives.) Madaleva Wolff, the Holy Cross sister who was president of St. Mary's College in Indiana from 1934 until 1961, staked a quiet claim to women's equality when she established a full-time graduate program in theology in 1943. The subject, hitherto studied only by priests and seminarians, had even in Catholic women's colleges been taught by members of the clergy, who were often the only males on the faculty. Open to both lay and religious women, the program initially aimed at preparing its students to teach theology at the college level, although provision was eventually made for those who intended to teach religion in Catholic high schools. Catholic women were heirs to a tradition of female ecclesial activism, according to Sister Madaleva, citing Saints Catherine of Siena and Teresa of Avila. St. Mary's School of Sacred Theology stood in this grand tradition.[14]

Relatively few graduates of Catholic women's colleges went on to graduate study. Nearly all of those colleges, indeed, assumed that they were preparing their students to be exemplary wives and mothers. Many featured domestic science courses, along with an often compulsory course on marriage and the family. But the example of the sister-teachers, who invariably constituted a large majority of the faculty, preached a different sermon. Many were women of keen intelligence and endowed with strong personalities. Sister Madaleva was a force for reform in Catholic educational circles from the early days of her long career. A poet, essayist, and scholar of medieval literature, who had earned her doctorate at the University of California–Berkeley, Madaleva represented a level of female achievement that must have been revelatory for her students. Presiding over a college and living in community with other women, she also embodied a startling degree of feminine independence. Perhaps it is not terribly surprising that an estimated 10 percent of Catholic women's college graduates went on to join a religious order. For the vast majority who did not, it still seems likely that their college years disposed them to a broadened vision of female possibility.

The Education of Women Religious

As states increasingly raised their standards for public-school teacher certification, pressure grew on the various teaching orders to keep pace. It helped that young recruits to the religious life in the 1920s and after were more and more likely to arrive with at least a high school diploma in hand. Some were still sent directly into the elementary school classroom once the novitiate was over, with experienced teachers assigned to serve as their mentors. But the norm in growing numbers of communities in the interwar years was the so-called twenty-year plan, by which a sister completed the first two years of college prior to entering the classroom and then pursued her bachelor's degree by means of summer study. What this meant in practice, given the sisters' very slow progress toward college completion, was that even in the 1950s a great many sister-teachers still had less formal education than their local public school counterparts. Their long-delayed degrees, moreover, were usually being earned at normal schools run by their orders, which were not necessarily accredited.[15]

Many such teachers were accomplished classroom veterans. Indeed, Catholic schools were widely regarded as unusually successful when it came to inculcating the academic basics. But rapid Catholic upward mobility after the Second World War led to heightened parental expectations with regard to education, especially at the high school level. The postwar years, in fact, were marked by rising anxiety among Americans generally with regard to the quality of their schools, which doubtless intensified Catholic concerns. School spending soared in the public sector, due in part to booming enrollments but also to ambitious efforts to tighten standards and upgrade curricular content. Advanced placement classes, especially in math and the sciences, increasingly featured in the better suburban high schools, where more and more teachers now possessed advanced degrees. Such developments posed a formidable challenge not just to the future of the Catholic schools—would heavily taxed suburban parents continue to support such schools if they believed them to be subpar academically?—but also to the self-understanding of the sister-teachers who had made nearly all of them possible.

The redoubtable Sister Madaleva Wolff fired the opening shot in what soon emerged as a full-fledged movement on the part of women religious for educational reform. Addressing the 1949 convention of the National Catholic Educational Association, she sketched the plight of "Sister Lucy." Like many of her peers, the fictive Sister Lucy had joined a teaching order with hardly more than a high school diploma. Bright and wholeheartedly committed to teaching, Sister Lucy was nonetheless fated to begin her career with wholly inadequate preparation, given prevailing practice. Anxiety and discouragement on Lucy's part was the all-too-predictable result. She might even come to doubt the integrity of religious life: "Nothing can so disillusion her ... as the dishonesty of assigning her to do in the name of holy obedience what professionally she is unqualified to do." It was time to stop wasting the promise of Lucy's generation, Sister Madaleva told her audience. "We must not frustrate the magnificence of their qualities by our lower-geared Victorian traditions and training." Every teaching order should immediately pledge to complete the college training of its new recruits prior to their entering the classroom.[16]

Sister Madaleva's call for reform was quickly endorsed by other women religious. Pope Pius XII himself appeared to champion the cause, calling in 1951—almost certainly with direct regard to Catholic education in Europe—for women religious to be fully prepared to carry out their teaching ministry. But reform would come at a cost, as bishops and pastors were quick to point out. Catholic-school enrollments were booming by the early 1950s. Withholding young sisters from the classroom while they completed their degrees would require the hiring of numerous lay teachers, who would necessarily command far higher salaries. The proposed reforms would also require that sisters' minuscule salaries be raised to cover the costs to their orders of young recruits' extended schooling. Some pastors were genuinely enraged by the sisters' calls for reform. Were women religious not bound to an ethos of self-abnegation? How, then, could they ask hard-pressed lay Catholics, especially those in working-class parishes, to subsidize what some men saw as a prideful program of self-cultivation?

The reformers persisted, however, founding the Sister Formation Conference in 1954 to oversee implementation of the changes for which they

Teaching catechism in San Antonio, Texas, 1954 (Courtesy of the American
Catholic History Research Center and University Archives [ACUA], the
Catholic University of America, Washington, DC)

had called. Given widespread support among the teaching orders, progress
was not long in coming. Only 16 percent of sister-teachers in 1955 had entered the classroom having finished at least three years of college. That figure had risen to 80 percent by 1964. Through meetings, workshops, and
publications, the conference also promoted an unprecedented degree of cooperation among the leaders of the various religious orders. The *Sister Formation Bulletin,* which appeared regularly, brought news of developments
within the various communities to a broad audience of sisters, as well as
articles that conveyed a more activist vision of religious life. The strictures
of convent life, it was argued, cut sisters off from the world and the work of
social renewal that was central to their vocation. "Skimming through issues
of the first few years of the *Bulletin,*" in the words of two sister-historians,
"one is struck by the repeated use of words like 'new,' 'current,' 'contemporary needs of sisters,' 'modern times,' 'present-day conditions.'"[17]

Perhaps most important, the leaders of the Sister Formation Conference stressed the individuality of its sister-members and the need to develop their particular talents. Articulation of this perspective sometimes came
with feminist overtones, as in a ringing address to fellow Catholic educators
in 1954 by Mary Emil Penet, an Immaculate Heart of Mary sister who served
as the first conference president. "We have never looked upon our Sisters as
a human resource to be used to the utmost intellectual capacity of each
one—perhaps because they are women, perhaps because things go slowly
in the Church . . . and perhaps because we have so many of them. Which is
all a bit like saying that we have been thinking that Sisters are expendable."
Sister Mary Emil, like nearly every conference founder and leader, had a
doctoral degree—hers was in classics from St. Louis University—and had
taught at a well-regarded Catholic women's college. Few of her peers would
have spoken so boldly. But faced with overcrowded classrooms and besieged
by the critics of Catholic education, even the most docile sister-teacher
could understand Sister Mary Emil's sense of grievance.[18]

Stirrings in the Priesthood

The pall cast by the modernist crisis still shrouded Catholic seminaries in the
1920s. Students followed a rigid course of instruction, the core of which remained unchanged from that of the later nineteenth century, save for an increasingly heavy emphasis on Neo-Scholastic philosophy. Even many of the
most commonly assigned textbooks had been in use in previous generations.
Students were still subjected to years of Latin language study and often to
more cursory study of Greek and biblical Hebrew. Rote memorization remained the seminarian's principal intellectual task, while class discussion,
much less debate, was still mostly off-limits. The seminary library, such as it
was, was apt to be either closed to students or accessible on only a limited
basis. Discipline was stringent and seemingly arbitrary: a student might be
expelled as readily for a minor violation like smoking as for a far more grievous offense like visiting the room of a fellow seminarian. Newspapers and
radios were prohibited, while students' mail was read and sometimes confis-
cated. "The general idea is to have the boy away and retired from the world,"
in the words of a priest from Detroit, making the case for his diocese's new
college-level seminary being built—as many such facilities were—in a rural
location.[19]

Seminary education did not change fundamentally until after the Second Vatican Council, although minor efforts at reform were bearing fruit by the 1950s. But American realities did make a difference, even in the 1920s. Many seminarians, especially those from working-class families, took summer jobs to help pay the costs of their schooling, which immersed them—if only for a time—in the world as most Catholics knew it. Those in their final years of study were often obliged to seek employment in church-related endeavors—one might assist one's pastor by conducting a parish census or mentor youngsters at a Catholic camp for boys. But even in these more cloistered venues, the seminarian still had generous exposure to the laity. Athletics were a principal focus of seminary life by the 1920s, and seminary athletes often competed against teams from local Catholic schools and colleges, whose spectator-fans almost certainly included a bevy of teenage girls. American seminarians, in the view of certain Roman authorities, had entirely too much contact with the world and its manifold temptations. A handful of American bishops did accommodate Roman priorities by sending at least their more senior seminarians to secluded "summer villas." Most bishops, however, could not afford to do so.[20]

Nor could an increasingly turbulent world be kept completely at bay, despite the continued ban in most seminaries on newspapers and radios. The labor wars of the 1930s, which involved large numbers of Catholics, resonated within the walls of many seminaries. Most seminarians, after all, came from working-class families, while the rise of "labor priests"—men who publicly defended the union cause, presided over "labor schools," and even marched on picket lines—embodied a dynamic new model of priesthood. The surge in Catholic lay activism in the 1930s offered a similar challenge to the prevailing emphasis in nearly all seminaries on personal holiness and detachment from the world. A number of seminaries in that decade began to provide at least occasional instruction on contemporary social problems. Reynold Hillenbrand, the innovative rector of Chicago's major seminary from 1936 until 1944, invited such luminaries as Dorothy Day, John A. Ryan, and Amarillo's Bishop Robert Lucey—a vigorous advocate of labor's cause—to address his students. More venturesome seminarians might seek out a local labor priest on a seminary free day or visit a Catholic Worker community. The Catholic Workers in Detroit dazzled seminarian Henry Offer with their almost monastic round of devotions and zealous care for the poor. "It is almost too immense to grasp in its entire significance," he subsequently wrote of the movement, certain that the Workers would have a transformative effect on the church. "And these people, we must not forget, are lay people."[21]

Domestic social problems elicited fewer passions among seminarians during and after the Second World War, although interest in the liturgical movement remained strong among an activist minority, and most seminaries continued to provide at least occasional instruction in Catholic social teaching. Growing numbers also offered elective classes in sociology and Spanish—the latter in belated recognition of continuing migration from Mexico and the Caribbean. New York's Cardinal Francis Spellman, whose diocese saw an influx of Puerto Ricans in the postwar years, sent half his ordination class in 1956 to Georgetown University for intensive instruction in Spanish, while half of those ordained in 1957 were sent to the Catholic University in Puerto Rico to study the island's language and culture. Seminarians studying Spanish in other dioceses often strengthened their language skills by means of summer fieldwork. Given the circumscribed lives of nearly all seminarians, some of whom had entered a preparatory seminary in early adolescence, the experience could prove transformative. "I think the last week has been one of the most rewarding ones I have so far lived," enthused a seminarian who was taking a religious census among Mexican migrant workers in rural Michigan in 1954. So charmed was he by the warmth and graciousness of these long-neglected Catholics that young Jerome Fraser subsequently chose to spend a summer of Spanish-immersion study in Mexico.[22]

Rising levels of education among the laity in these same years also placed new pressures on the nation's seminaries. More and more faculty evinced concern about their students' too-frequent want of intellectuality. "One problem which is of concern to the fathers of the faculty is a general lack of intellectual interests on the part of many students," the Sulpician rector of Detroit's major seminary reported in 1955. Like many seminary faculty, Father Lyman Fenn was impressed by his students' piety and generous commitment to the priestly calling. Theirs, after all, was the first generation of American seminarians for whom the priesthood was not, for the great majority, the most promising ticket to status and financial security. But an educated laity was bound to have heightened standards with regard to professional competence, which suggested that piety and goodwill alone were no longer sufficient for success in the priestly role. Highly educated

Catholics would presumably judge the Sunday sermon by the standards of the college classroom and expect their confessors to possess a fair degree of psychological acuity.[23]

Partly because of such concerns, growing numbers of seminarians and young priests in the postwar years received an education beyond the seminary's limited curriculum. Many were sent to Rome to earn degrees in theology or canon law. As in previous generations, this happy elite nearly always returned with enhanced devotion to the papacy. "The Vice-Rector recently talked to us about the reason for an American College in Rome," one seminarian rather artlessly related. "It's not to acquire culture, or Italian, or travel but primarily to acquire a very deep-rooted allegiance to the Holy Father." But in a relatively new development, seminarians and the newly ordained were also sent for graduate study, sometimes at secular institutions, in such subjects as education, history, sociology, and economics. Men like these were destined for careers within a strictly Catholic world, mostly as teachers and administrators. Their advanced degrees, however, still fostered a sense that the ideal priest was a man in touch with contemporary intellectual currents. During the Second World War, it should be noted, no students could be sent to Rome. Most were rerouted to the Catholic University in Washington, DC, where students of theology and canon law rubbed elbows with those who were studying more secular subjects—a development that, however short-lived, helped to strengthen the link between priesthood and contemporary learning.[24]

Few seminarians in the postwar years had high aspirations when it came to intellectual culture. The brightest among them, however, do seem to have grasped that a rapidly changing Catholic world required a new kind of priest—a man who, for all his cultic otherness, could hold his own among credentialed professionals. The up-to-date priest ought to specialize—to distinguish himself as a marriage counselor, perhaps, or an expert on youth work. "Have you selected your field of specialization?" seminarian Edward Farrell, then a student in Rome, demanded of a stateside classmate in 1957. He envisioned the future of priesthood in terms of teamwork and expertise. "One fruitful technique I have come across is that each member of a group takes a particular field, e.g. psychology, literature, art, politics & makes it his specialty and each man receives the benefit of the team's work." Farrell's own extracurricular reading had focused on psychology, which field he regarded as "very pertinent" for confessors. "One of the problems that has always intrigued me is the question of human motivation. . . . Especially the moral question of why do we sin & how we can remedy our weakness. . . . Moral theology classifies all the sins & virtues but it sort of neglects the dynamics of breaking the habits of sins & initiating the practice of the virtues." Catholic priest-psychologists Thomas Verner Moore and Charles Curran—not to be confused with the moral theologian of the same name—had, in Farrell's view, "done the most in tackling these problems." While unquestionably orthodox, both men were criticized in certain Catholic circles for conceding too much to a naturalistic understanding of the psyche.[25]

Farrell's vision of priesthood, generous though it was, conflicted in fundamental ways with period pastoral realities. In most large urban dioceses, the newly ordained in the postwar years waited more than twenty years before becoming pastors—a far-longer period of so-called assistantship than ever before in U.S. history. Even in his midforties, a priest might still be conspicuously junior in status and subservient to the will of a pastor who could, if he chose, be a tyrant. Even a "good assignment" nearly always meant following someone else's agenda, in part because assistants were typically moved from one parish to another at roughly five-year intervals. Farrell's vision of a collaborative priesthood echoed the ethos of the secular professions that young Catholics were increasingly entering. It made status and influence contingent on expertise rather than seniority alone. But while Catholic professionals could expect to enjoy autonomy in their middle years, their priest contemporaries were often confined to a painfully extended apprenticeship. Small wonder that growing numbers, many of them among the best educated, were complaining by the mid-1960s about lack of respect for their status as "professionals"—a term that previous generations had seldom applied to the priestly calling.

Ordained in 1957, Edward Farrell attended seminary at a time of booming enrollments. American seminaries were filled to bursting in the postwar years, when new seminaries were opened and existing ones being expanded at a rate never previously equaled. But over the course of the decade and particularly toward its close, those seminaries also experienced unprecedented attrition, including attrition in the final stages of preparation for the priesthood. "It used to be quite an occasion when someone left the seminary in theology," a worried seminarian noted in 1956. "Now the increase in fellows leaving [has] many wondering what could be the problem." Young Catholics by the 1950s had multiple options when it came to

professional employment, which presumably made it easier for the dissatisfied to leave. It was probably no accident that the largest ordination classes
in most dioceses date from the Depression-ridden 1930s. The romance of
domesticity so prominent in the 1950s, when even certain Catholic clergy
spoke of marital sex as a quasi-sacrament, almost certainly made celibacy
harder to contemplate. With adolescence increasingly a time of freedom
and experimentation even for the Catholic young, the strictures of seminary life may also have come to seem more than usually irksome.[26]

Despite rising rates of attrition, which rightly alarmed a good many
bishops, most men who enrolled at the nation's major seminaries in the postwar years persevered to ordination. Those ordained in the 1950s were almost
certainly better educated than any previous clerical cohort. But no matter
how extensive their schooling, few priests at the time of the Second Vatican
Council were prepared for the changes that came in its wake. "We were per-
fectly trained to serve in a world that disintegrated as soon as we stepped into
it," according to a priest from Baltimore. Like Edward Farrell, the newly ordained were sometimes men of almost breathtaking idealism. Prompted by
their own education and the example of their professional peers, they hoped
to engage a world beyond the Catholic subculture and function as leavening
agents there. At the same time, their formation was premised on a high cultic
vision of priesthood. When the social and theological supports for that vision
were abruptly eroded, as happened in the wake of the council, such men
could not avoid hard questions. What did priesthood mean in a world where
Christian witness was more and more understood in terms of tangible service to humanity? Why be a priest rather than a physician or lawyer or even a
community organizer? Why was the confessor's role self-evidently superior
to that of the psychiatrist? The resulting confusion, as we shall see, prompted
both an unprecedented wave of resignations from the active priesthood—
something to which the best educated of the younger clergy seem to have
been especially prone—and an abrupt decline in seminary enrollments.[27]

Catholic Intellectual Life

Reflecting on his years as an editor at *Commonweal,* a lay-edited and generally progressive periodical dating from 1924, George Shuster betrayed a certain sympathy for the anti-Catholicism of many well-educated Americans.
"This was a mood into which they had more or less been born; and it seemed

to me highly improbable that a change would take place unless Catholics stopped sounding like a blend of the D.A.R., Bruce Barton and a random devotee of Torquemada." His own career as a Catholic intellectual, especially in the interwar years, had resulted on occasion in "isolation ... as grimly complete as that of a lone sailor clapped in the brig." Shuster's problem was partly political: his neutral position in the mid-1930s on the Spanish Civil War elicited hostile criticism from Catholic leaders, all of them ardent supporters of Francisco Franco, and prompted his departure from *Commonweal*. But his problem also had to do with his sophisticated literary tastes and openness to contemporary intellectual currents—qualities shared by only a handful of his fellow Catholic thinkers. Shuster's closest intellectual companions came from the ranks of prominent converts, most notably philosopher Jacques Maritain, in exile after 1940 from his native France.[28]

Shuster was not wholly wrong: Catholic intellectual life in the interwar years and even into the 1950s was indeed parochial. But it was also remarkably ambitious in its aspirations and not without its achievements. Catholic intellectuals in these years envisioned their work in terms of national redemption: employing the riches of the Catholic tradition, Catholic thinkers would resuscitate American innocence, badly damaged by the First World War, and restore the nation's birthright optimism and sense of providential destiny. Unlike a decadent Protestantism, the argument ran, Catholicism provided assurance that the world was governed by a higher law known intuitively to every well-disposed person. Despair was therefore irrational, as well as un-American. Indeed, Catholic thinkers contrived to root the American experiment in the Catholic past—a project that flourished especially in the tribal 1920s, when anti-Catholicism surged. "The heart of the Middle Ages was the Catholic Church; and it was from the heart of the Middle Ages that America was born," in the 1926 words of historian Peter Guilday. Medieval political theory, with its emphasis on natural law and limited government, was the taproot of democracy, according to Guilday and many others. The Founding Fathers, in other words, had been Scholastics without quite knowing it.[29]

Catholic intellectuals, many of whom were priests, inhabited a separate world from their Protestant, Jewish, and secular counterparts. They taught mostly in Catholic colleges, belonged to their own professional societies, and published in their own learned journals. Theologians and philosophers, nearly all of them clerics and thus vulnerable to Roman sanction,

were the most insulated, occupying something close to a hermetically sealed
sphere. The modernist controversy shadowed their fields even in the 1950s,
as evinced by the silencing in 1954 of John Courtney Murray, a formidable
Jesuit theologian whose work commanded attention beyond the usual
Catholic circles. (He taught as a guest at Yale in the early 1950s and in 1960
graced the cover of *Time* magazine.) Murray's principal passion was church-
state relations and the closely related problem of religious pluralism. The
Anglo-American West, Murray argued, had gradually come to a deeper understanding of human dignity, rooted in natural law. That deeper understanding was premised on the rights of conscience in the realm of religion
as quite literally sacred. Freedom of religion, along with church-state separation, was thus an essential attribute of good government—a conclusion
directly opposed to reigning Roman orthodoxy. Forbidden to publish on
the topic, Murray continued to write privately—preparation, as it happens,
for his ultimate vindication at the Second Vatican Council, where he was a
principal force behind its 1965 declaration on religious liberty.

Greater freedom accrued to Catholic scholars in economics and the
social sciences, even when those scholars were priests. In fields like these,
the occasional Catholic made valued contributions to his or her chosen
field of expertise. Priest-anthropologist John Montgomery Cooper, who
taught at Catholic University, offers a conspicuous example. His extensive
fieldwork among various North American Indian groups in the 1920s and
1930s provided invaluable data to the field at large. Others of a more activist
bent helped to shape the national discourse. John A. Ryan came into his
own during the 1930s, as various New Deal programs began to implement
many aspects of the Program of Social Reconstruction that Ryan had drafted in 1919. Catholic journalists and even scholars did much to legitimize
those programs for a Catholic audience whose cultural heritage entailed
deep suspicion of the centralized state. One of Ryan's students at Catholic
University, Father—later Bishop—Francis Haas, helped to implement them
as a highly visible Roosevelt appointee. Haas, whose PhD was in sociology,
served in various capacities in the National Recovery Administration, the
National Labor Relations Board, and the Works Progress Administration,
and he briefly chaired the Fair Employment Practices Committee in 1943.
He was also a prominent labor mediator.[30]

Perhaps the most durable achievements in a purely academic sense
were those of Catholic historians. Histories produced in the 1920s and 1930s

sometimes bordered on the apologetic and were often excessively defensive. That democracy was of medieval origin was a popular theme, as was the unimpeachable patriotism of Catholics in the American past. No Catholic alive at the time of the American Revolution, according to Father Peter Guilday, then dean of the Catholic historical profession, was known to have been a Loyalist. But the best of these productions were thoroughly re-searched and thus of value to subsequent scholarly generations. Catholic historical scholarship after the mid-1940s was marked by greater profes-sionalism, as seen in the work of Fathers John Tracy Ellis and Thomas T. McAvoy. Both produced impressive work on the Americanist controversy, a subject hitherto ignored by American Catholic historians. (Ellis's contribu-tion came via a lengthy biography of Cardinal James Gibbons.) "The his-torical recovery of the Americanist episode," in the words of historian Philip Gleason, "indirectly nurtured [among Catholics] a more positive at-titude toward the modern world."[31]

Like the Americanists, growing numbers of Catholic intellectuals by the 1950s were decrying both Catholic separatism and their coreligionists' alleged want of intellectual culture. It was time to abandon the siege men-tality that had come so naturally to an immigrant church and participate fully in the national life—a project requiring, in the 1958 words of Fordham sociologist Thomas O'Dea, "that a genuinely creative tradition should be developed among American Catholics." The Second World War does much to explain this, having involved far more interdenominational cooperation than the First and teaching a far grimmer lesson about the dangers of trib-alism. The dramatic surge in Catholic upward mobility after 1945 also played a role, although many of its beneficiaries were still quite young at the close of the 1950s. With growing numbers of Catholics attending secular colleges, it was natural that many should aspire to a life less bounded by the separatist impulse. Those who attended graduate or professional school were almost bound to internalize something approaching an ecumenical ethos. The professional workplace placed a far-stronger premium on har-monious relations with colleagues and clients, no matter what their reli-gious background, than did labor in the nation's factories.[32]

No account of Catholic intellectual life in the United States can fail to acknowledge the major role played by converts to Catholicism. As in the nineteenth century, converts contributed disproportionately in the precon-ciliar twentieth century to the ranks of American Catholic intellectuals.

Consider the early years of *Commonweal,* a journal described by one historian "as arguably the most vital and enduring vehicle of a Catholic commitment to the intellectual life." Its founders included Michael Williams, a lapsed Catholic who returned to the practice of his religion after an intense experience of conversion in his midthirties, and Carleton J. H. Hayes, a prominent historian at Columbia University who had converted to Catholicism in 1906. *Commonweal's* first issue in 1924 featured no fewer than three convert authors, all of them British: Bertram Windle, G. K. Chesterton, and Theodore Maynard. That none were clerics was telling: *Commonweal* was a lay-run enterprise and a self-proclaimed venue for lay contributions to Catholic intellectual life. That a non-Catholic also numbered among the first issue's contributors was telling too, *Commonweal* being from its inception far more ecumenical in spirit than other Catholic publications.[33]

Convert intellectuals, whether foreign- or native-born, were often the products of elite secular universities. Confident as to social status and exposed to a wider range of ideas than most of their fellow Catholics, they generally brought to their work a greater breadth and sophistication than was commonly found in Catholic intellectual circles. A surprising number were women, among them Dorothy Day, historian Elizabeth Kite, journalists Katherine Burton and Carol Jackson, and sociologist Eva Ross. Foreigners, not all of them converts, loomed especially large, traveling in growing numbers to the United States to teach at Catholic universities and ply the lecture circuit. G. K. Chesterton was especially popular in the latter regard, along with Frank Sheed, an Australian journalist and raconteur who with his British wife, Maisie Ward, established a branch of their London-based publishing house in New York in 1933. Sheed and Ward, as the house was known, published numerous titles by Catholic authors from Britain and the Continent, exposing American Catholics to fiction and scholarship of genuine distinction. As late as 1958, sociologist O'Dea could write, with only the faintest hint of exaggeration, that "a genuine Catholic intellectual life is still dependent upon translations of European works and books of British origin."[34]

French Catholic writers and intellectuals appeared on the American scene in the 1930s and remained important thereafter. Among the most influential were philosopher Jacques Maritain, himself a convert, and medievalist Etienne Gilson. A skilled and subtle exponent of Neo-Thomism, Maritain achieved academic celebrity in the United States, teaching at Notre Dame, Columbia, the University of Chicago, and finally Princeton. His work played a role in many notable conversions, including those of Jesuit philosopher Avery Dulles, Canadian media analyst Marshall McLuhan, and Thomas Merton, the Trappist monk and poet whose spiritual autobiography, *The Seven-Storey Mountain,* was a best-seller upon publication in 1948. Gilson, whose New World career included Harvard but was passed primarily at the University of Toronto, was also an influence on numerous converts, Merton among them. The prestige enjoyed by both men, especially in the 1950s, did much to enhance the intellectual respectability of Catholicism in the United States. So, for the cognoscenti, did the work of French theologian Henri de Lubac and French philosopher-cum-playwright Gabriel Marcel, yet another convert.[35]

Toward *Morte D'Urban*

Prior to the 1950s, Catholic intellectual life was at its weakest in the realm of literary fiction. The interwar years were particularly dismal, despite a proliferation of Catholic authors, reading groups, bookstores, and publishing houses. Not a single Catholic writer in these years could claim anything like distinction, largely because their work was governed by extraliterary purposes. According to the guardians of Catholic literary culture, art ought to dramatize religious truth, celebrate ideals, and limn the boundaries of moral conduct— an agenda wholly at odds with the ethos of literary modernism, where pessimism, skepticism, subjectivity, and sexual frankness were the order of the day. Lapsed Catholics might win respect in such a cultural climate—Theodore Dreiser, Eugene O'Neill, and F. Scott Fitzgerald were the most prominent—but never a writer who spoke from the heart of the Catholic subculture. This did not prevent educated Catholics from feverish promotion of literary achievement or inhibit their search for the first great American Catholic novel.[36]

That the interwar years in Europe witnessed a Catholic literary renaissance suggests that American Catholics adhered to unusually provincial standards when it came to fiction. So did the ambivalence with which educated Catholics greeted the growing number of critically acclaimed European imports. Historian Paul Messbarger, who graduated from St. Benedict's College in Atkinson, Kansas, in 1956, recalled meeting monthly with fellow members of the campus literary guild to discuss the works of Georges Bernanos, François Mauriac, Paul Claudel, Sigrid Undset, Evelyn Waugh, "and most especially Graham Greene": "All of these writers caused greatly mixed reactions in us. Their power—confirmed even by secular critics—offered a convenient validation of our confidence in the superiority of Catholic culture. But these works were greatly troubling for us as well, especially for the deep gloom, even pessimism of their environments, the abundance of human failure, the 'decay' of all social institutions," and their candid acknowledgment of sexual desire. Messbarger and company quite rightly saw themselves as budding intellectuals, admirably up-to-date in their interests. Their literary tastes suggest that they were also among the last Victorians.[37]

The American Catholic literary scene had begun to stir by the 1950s, although Messbarger and his literary companions were apparently unaware of it. By his own admission, the group had never heard of J. F. Powers, whose critically acclaimed short stories appeared in venues like the *New Yorker* and who published short-story collections in 1947 and 1956. Nor, evidently, did they know the work of Flannery O'Connor, although her well-received first novel had appeared in 1952, followed by a short-story collection in 1955. The Georgia-bred O'Connor's work was set almost exclusively in the American South and peopled mainly by Protestants, many of them fundamentalists. Even "literary" Catholic collegians might well have doubted that hers were truly "Catholic" productions, especially as O'Connor's protagonists were often profoundly damaged individuals. O'Connor herself was wearied by criticism, much of it Catholic, that her fiction was excessively sordid. "The stories are hard ... because there is nothing harder or less sentimental than Christian realism," she rather tartly responded. Powers, by contrast, wrote almost exclusively about Catholics—priests in particular. But he too discomfited many in his limited Catholic readership, for whom his mordant wit and keen eye for hypocrisy were unaccustomed flavors. Like O'Connor, he wrote—in the words of William Halsey—"of the rather large area between despair and moralism."[38]

Powers, despite a long life, produced only two novels, the first of which, *Morte D'Urban,* won the National Book Award in 1963. (Catholic convert Walker Percy had won the prize for his first novel in 1962.) Powers's protagonist, Father Urban Roche, is a glad-handing wheeler-dealer who, for all his commitment to the priesthood, hankers after success in the American mode— recognition by the powers that be, chumminess with men of affairs, popularity with the masses. His various worldly initiatives, as Urban sees it, are undertaken solely to benefit the "Clementines," the poor and almost comically mediocre preaching order to which Urban belongs. He cultivates wealthy donors on its behalf, despite their obvious moral shortcomings, and in the course of his pursuit dines at Chicago's Palmer House and perfects his near-professional golf game. "Charity toward all, even when a few sharks get in among the swimmers, is always better than holier-than-thou singularity. That, roughly speaking, was the mind of the Church." A series of disasters, analogous to the temptations of Christ in the desert, culminates in Urban's conversion to a chastened vision of the priesthood. His radically reduced ambition and seeming ineptitude in his new office as the Clementine's provincial—his conversion is decisively effected by a bishop's errant golf drive, which causes a concussion with lasting effects—gained Urban a "reputation for piety he hadn't had before, which, however, was not entirely unwarranted now."[39]

Is Urban's a story of spiritual triumph? The text provides few reasons to think so. The postconversion Urban, while appropriately humbled, is a diminished man. He seems fated to steer his hapless order even farther down the road toward oblivion. "I write about priests for reasons of irony, comedy, and philosophy," Powers once said. "They are officially committed to both worlds in a way that most people are not. This makes for stronger beer." Powers's own history spoke to the tension, given his calling—in the words of his wife—as a "divinely inspired gadfly." One of the few Catholic conscientious objectors during the Second World War, he refused upon his marriage in 1946 to work at a conventional job—the sort that demanded "eight hours out of my life daily so that the system may prosper and the crapshooters running it"—and thus exposed his growing family to enduring penury and more than twenty changes of residence. That his literary output was so small—three collections of short stories in addition to the novels—made matters considerably worse. "The decision will not be rendered in this ring," Powers once said of Father Urban and undoubtedly also of himself—not to mention the rest of us.[40]

Powers, a notorious contrarian, was hardly a representative Catholic. Nor has *Morte D'Urban* ever attracted a substantial Catholic readership—or indeed a substantial readership of any variety. But published as it was in 1962, just as the Second Vatican Council was convening in Rome, the book is eerily prophetic. Rather like Father Urban, American Catholics after the council rushed to embrace the world and its manifold contradictions, as in fact they were encouraged to do by the council's progressive majority. The Catholic ghetto, after all, had contradictions of its own. But as Urban ultimately learns, the world is full of traps. Postconciliar Catholics would encounter painful ambiguities in their efforts to negotiate it.

Public Catholicism

Politics and Social Movements

F
or all the confidence they evinced in the wake of the First World War, Catholics were marginal to national politics for most of the 1920s. A solidly Republican decade, the 1920s were also scarred by virulent anti-Catholicism. If Catholics' growing importance to the Democratic Party led to a Catholic's being that party's standard-bearer in 1928, Al Smith was still defeated on the grounds of his religion—or so Smith's coreligionists firmly believed. Everything changed with the coming of the Great Depression, when the Democrats emerged for the first time since the Civil War as the nation's majority party. Massive Catholic support was critical to Franklin Roosevelt's successive victories, as the president duly acknowledged by appointing Catholics to a record number of federal positions. A heavily Catholic labor movement, forged in the mid-1930s, introduced many working-class Catholics to active citizenship and raised their expectations with regard to government's welfare functions. Catholics' support for labor and the New Deal meant a rapprochement of sorts with the secular liberals with whom they shared the Democratic Party. But those same liberals were also troubled by a concomitant Catholic enthusiasm for policing sex and popular culture.

The Second World War proved more powerfully integrative for the nation's still heavily ethnic Catholics than any previous conflict—a development with obvious political import. During the prosperous years that followed, an increasingly affluent Catholic population displayed growing political independence, particularly at the national level. A good many Catholics "liked Ike," especially in 1956, when probably a plurality of Catholic voters cast Republican ballots for president. If Catholics did return in huge numbers to the Democratic fold in 1960, it was largely because one of their own was running for the nation's highest office. This time around, the Catholic won. But the Catholic unity so essential to Kennedy's narrow victory was mostly an illusion. His tragically brief presidency was followed by an era of Catholic fragmentation, fueled especially by issues of race and gender, which had enduring repercussions in the nation's political life.

From the Margins to the Center: The 1920s and 1930s

Briefly mired in recession after the end of the First World War, the U.S. economy boomed for the rest of the decade. Like other Americans, with the signal exception of the nation's small farmers, Catholics saw their living standards rise, often quite significantly. A draconian law restricting immigration and heavily biased against recent Catholic arrivals did cast a pall. So did resurgence of the Ku Klux Klan, at this juncture in its history as anti-Catholic and anti-Semitic as it was antiblack, at least outside the South. Briefly under Klan domination, Oregon passed a law in 1922 compelling all children between the ages of eight and sixteen to attend a public school, while Michigan tried but ultimately failed to do the same. Anti-Catholicism by the 1920s was more rural in its appeal than earlier outbreaks, which probably comforted a heavily urban Catholic population. So did the abrupt collapse of the Klan in the mid-1920s following a leadership scandal. In 1925, moreover, Catholics triumphed at the nation's highest court, which ruled with regard to the Oregon school law that no state had the power to "standardize its children by forcing them to accept instruction from public teachers only." That the ruling was unanimous made it all the sweeter.[1]

In these relatively benign circumstances, Catholic political quiescence hardly comes as a surprise. In heavily Catholic cities and states, Catholic candidates continued to win public office with strong Catholic support. But voter participation, including that of Catholics, was at low ebb nationally in 1920 and 1924, when conservative Republicans triumphed. Progressive movements in general withered in this time of conspicuous prosperity, and few voters paid much attention as the nation's income distribution grew progressively more unequal. Indeed, one of the few strong reform initiatives nationally was defeated in part by Catholic opposition. In 1924, a constitutional amendment empowering Congress to regulate child labor was introduced in the House of Representatives, where it was promptly ratified. The Senate quickly followed. But the amendment then languished, due in probably equal measure to employers' opposition and that of various religious leaders. A majority of Catholic voters probably favored the amendment's ratification, even if tepidly. But it had some prominent Catholic opponents, most notably Cardinal William O'Connell and Baltimore's Archbishop Michael Curley, who maintained that parents and not the state had the sole right to govern their offspring. When Massachusetts held an advisory referendum on ratification of the amendment late in 1924, O'Connell ordered his priests to preach against it and instruct their parishioners to vote. The amendment's defeat in Massachusetts helped to halt its momentum nationwide, and it was never ratified.[2]

Catholic numbers were growing in the 1920s. So, in consequence, was their importance to the national Democratic Party, historically attractive to Catholic voters. With anti-Catholicism as a popular movement apparently in retreat, it seemed safe by 1928 for the Democrats to nominate a Catholic for president. Governor Al Smith was popular in New York State, despite its Republican leanings, which appeared to strengthen the case for his candidacy, as did the endorsement of prominent liberals. Smith was known as a reformer, and his candidacy for many non-Catholic liberals stood for "tolerance in American life—racial, religious, and social tolerance," according to the decidedly secular *Nation*. But even the prospect of Smith's nomination stirred anti-Catholic rumblings, especially but not exclusively in the South and rural Midwest. Smith's opposition to Prohibition, imposed nationwide in 1919, troubled many Protestants, as did his New York working-class accent—both emblematic of big-city otherness. It was Smith's religion, however, that elicited the greatest hostility, fueled in part by ignorant bigotry but also by very real fear.[3]

That fear was often articulated in crude and absurdly exaggerated form. The pope, according to one favored rumor, was even now sequestered in New York, waiting for Smith's victory to take up residence in the White House. But it was most famously presented in the genteel pages of the *Atlantic Monthly* in 1927. Was it not the case, asked attorney Charles Marshall, citing recent papal encyclicals, that Catholics were opposed in principle to religious freedom and the religiously neutral state? Smith was genuinely bewildered by the charge. "I had never heard of these encyclicals and bulls and books that he writes about," he is said to have told two close advisers, both of them Jewish. Although Smith believed himself incapable of producing a rebuttal, having left school at the age of fourteen, a rebuttal was clearly necessary. Smith's formal response to Marshall, which also appeared in the *Atlantic Monthly*, was drafted in close consultation with Father Francis Duffy, the celebrated chaplain of New York's "Fighting Sixty-Ninth." Smith spoke from the heart, albeit with Duffy's considerable assistance. Should any pope attempt to interfere in matters civil or political, Smith's conscience would oblige him to say, "Back to your own sphere of rights and duties, back to the things of God." (The words, doubtless provided by Duffy, are those of John Ireland.) Smith pledged to protect the sacred rights of conscience for all Americans and to defend "the absolute separation of Church and State."[4]

Smith's statement, which probably secured his nomination, was widely applauded by leaders in both parties and by the nation's press. The campaign was another story. Probably no Democrat could have won in 1928—the nation was prosperous, and Herbert Hoover was by far the most qualified of the decade's Republican presidential candidates. Still, Smith's defeat shocked and embittered Catholics. Smith had in fact drawn many more votes than the Democrats' presidential candidates in 1920 and 1924, due in good part to enhanced voter turnout. But he carried only eight states, six of them in the Deep South, where anti-Catholicism was trumped by an even-deeper commitment to white supremacy, still associated in the southern mind with the Democratic Party. The anti-Catholic rhetoric that punctuated the campaign, moreover, was all the more shocking for being unexpected, at least in Catholic circles. Most Catholics experienced the outcome in deeply personal terms—as a rejection of their claim to membership in the national community. Smith's defeat, according to Leonard Feeney, then a newly ordained Jesuit priest, was "the night of six million tragedies."[5]

Economic disaster soon obscured the election's bitter aftereffects. With unemployment soaring, especially among blue-collar workers, Catholics worried less about status and more about survival. Their church, moreover, was newly visible due to the national crisis. In many cities, Catholic charities did more to aid the destitute than the hapless Hoover administration, and a number of priests served on boards that coordinated local relief. Priests and even bishops sometimes spoke of the crisis in startlingly radical terms. The surplus wealth of the rich, Cincinnati's Archbishop John

McNicholas told one public gathering, "belongs to the poor." Thus "a con-
fiscation of excess wealth" would be just if such a measure were necessary to
keep people from starving. Catholic journalists and even certain Catholic
mayors made names for themselves by their fierce commitment to public
relief. Detroit's Frank Murphy, elected in 1930 to govern a city already devastated by mass unemployment, invoked *Rerum Novarum* in support of his
local welfare initiatives. Detroit-based Father Charles Coughlin, then a
Murphy confidant, blossomed as a radio star with a growing national audience. Not yet discernibly ideological, Coughlin mesmerized listeners with
his fervid condemnations of widespread want amid natural plenty.[6]

Having bested Al Smith for the Democratic nomination in 1932,
Franklin Roosevelt courted the Catholic vote in unusually vigorous fashion,
most notably by quoting from *Quadragesimo Anno*, the 1931 social encyclical issued by Pius XI. The encyclical was "one of the greatest documents of
modern times," he told a crowd in Detroit, and was "just as radical as I am."
Roosevelt easily defeated Hoover with the help of a massive Catholic vote.
He reciprocated by naming two Catholics to his first cabinet—there had
been only four Catholic cabinet appointments prior to 1933 in the whole of
the nation's history—and nominating a number of Catholic judges to the
lower federal courts. A Catholic appointment to the Supreme Court would
come in 1940, when Frank Murphy became an associate justice. Several of
Roosevelt's closest advisers were Catholics, and the White House cultivated
close relations with a number of Catholic bishops. Of even greater importance were the president's innovative efforts to promote employment and
provide relief to the long-term unemployed. The National Industrial Recovery Act, passed in 1933 but declared unconstitutional in 1935, enjoyed
particular Catholic support, given its seeming harmony with the corporat-
ism endorsed by the pope. John A. Ryan served on one of the National Recovery Administration's numerous administrative boards, as did a number
of priests at the regional level.[7]

Strong Catholic support of the New Deal—the Catholic vote for
Roosevelt in 1936 is variously estimated at between 70 and 81 percent—gave
rise to a new sense of Catholic confidence when it came to public life. Not
every prominent Catholic was a New Deal advocate. Al Smith, troubled by
the growing size of the federal government, was among the president's
strongest critics. The increasingly controversial Father Charles Coughlin, a
passionate Roosevelt supporter in 1932, had emerged by 1935 as a vitupera-

tive critic. But Catholics grew accustomed to their leaders endorsing various New Deal programs and even endowing the president with a kind of
honorific Catholicity. Roosevelt received honorary degrees from Catholic
University (1933) and Notre Dame (1935), the latter in the midst of his dispute with a number of Catholic leaders over the administration's policy
with regard to Mexico, where an anticlerical government was openly perse-
cuting the Catholic Church. Chicago's Cardinal George Mundelein, a Roosevelt intimate, bestowed the Notre Dame degree. John A. Ryan, popularly
known by this time as the "Right Reverend New Dealer," gave the benediction at Roosevelt's inauguration in 1937. Whatever the depths of their alienation at the close of 1928, Catholics by the mid-1930s appeared to themselves
and others to have "reached a position of respect and integration" in the
national life.[8]

President Franklin Roosevelt and his wife, Eleanor, visiting Catholic
University, 1933 (Courtesy of the American Catholic History Research Center
and University Archives [ACUA], the Catholic University of America,
Washington, DC)

Buoyed by a new sense of citizenly belonging, lay activism flourished, especially among the more affluent young. Some of that activism spoke directly to the nation's economic crisis, although not invariably in terms that secular liberals would applaud. Catholic Workers sheltered the indigent in bare-bones communal settings and fed much larger numbers on seemingly eternal bread and soup lines, while the movement's eponymous newspaper preached social justice as an essential Catholic commitment. But Dorothy Day thought almost exclusively in terms of radical personal charity, declining to vote and indifferent or even hostile to the welfare state. Catholic social workers, most of them women, were generally partisans of the New Deal but concerned nonetheless with protecting Catholic interests when it came to social policy. Birth control was a particular sticking point. Growing numbers of professional social workers by the 1930s regarded access to contraception, or even its free provision, as essential to mitigating working-class poverty. Catholics insisted that a living wage was the only solution to the problem. When the bishops at their annual meeting in 1932 called for a "family wage" and endorsed the right to collective bargaining, they linked these positions with their opposition to birth control. Numerous lay witnesses at hearings in Washington, DC, and various state capitals, recruited for this purpose by the National Catholic Welfare Conference (NCWC) or individual bishops, duly repeated the argument.[9]

A good deal of Catholic activism, moreover, focused on cultural issues, particularly the content of movies and popular magazines. The Jesuit Daniel Lord in 1930 called on members of the massive sodality movement to boycott the numerous movies he blacklisted in its nationally circulated journal. Volunteer critics from the National Association of Catholic Alumnae were essential to the effort. By 1934, the NCWC had established an office devoted to the vetting of movies, which sponsored an allegedly popular movement known as the Legion of Decency. Every bishop soon required that Catholics in his diocese take the "Legion pledge" on an annual basis, publicly promising not to attend any but films approved by the office. Philadelphia's Cardinal Dennis Dougherty made headlines by forbidding Catholics in his archdiocese to attend any movies at all—a prohibition that ultimately proved unenforceable. Catholics were sufficiently numerous that Hollywood paid attention. Daniel Lord was instrumental in drafting the code that governed American movies from 1934 well into the 1950s. The code, whose enforcement office for its first twenty years was headed by a

Catholic layman, required that films be an unalloyed force for good. Extra-marital sex, not to mention divorce, should not be portrayed in a sympa-thetic or attractive way, nor should movies' content arouse prurience. Criminal activity should always be punished. Authority figures were to be portrayed as legitimate, the clergy were to be accorded special respect, and interracial romance was strictly prohibited.[10]

Prior to the 1950s, would-be Catholic censors enjoyed considerable Protestant support. Cardinal Dougherty's ban on movie attendance was en-dorsed by many Protestant clergy in his heavily urban diocese, while Protes-tant leaders throughout the nation applauded the work of the Legion of Decency and urged their coreligionists to boycott offensive films, which sometimes included those that offended for reasons of ideology. A movie sympathetic to the Spanish Republicans was withdrawn from a Detroit the-ater after vigorous protests by local Catholic organizations and the American Legion in 1938. (Happily, an equally ecumenical effort did not result in the destruction of Diego Rivera's stunning murals, pilloried at the time as Marx-ist, at the Detroit Institute of Arts.) Catholic campaigns against allegedly sala-cious books and magazines also drew Protestant support and sometimes Protestant cooperation. But if Catholics built bridges to other Christians through their efforts at policing culture, they alienated a good many intel-lectuals and other partisans of free speech. Such tensions intensified in the prosperous years after 1945, as educational levels rose and sexual norms be-gan to change.

The Labor Movement

Given the heavily Catholic composition of the nation's industrial working class, Catholic participation in the industrial union movement of the 1930s must rank as the decade's most consequential instance of Catholic social activism. Most Catholic workers, of course, joined a union for largely mate-rial reasons—for better pay, shorter hours, and a degree of job security. But Catholic leaders worked hard to endow the infant labor movement with religious meaning. Priests in unprecedented numbers publicly defended the union cause, offered prayers at union meetings, and even showed up on picket lines. Invoking the social encyclicals, labor priests nearly always ar-gued that active union membership was for Catholic workers a religious obligation. "If Christ Who 'had compassion on the multitudes' were to walk in our midst today," in the words of one pastor, "we would find Him in the march with Labor, and He would ask you: 'Why are you not in my ranks.' " Such sentiments were even articulated by the occasional bishop. With employers monopolizing money and power, according to Amarillo's Bishop Robert Lucey, Catholic workers had "a duty to join a labor union for their own good, the welfare of their families, and the peace and security of human society." Most bishops did not go quite this far. But many did give public support to labor's cause, if only because so many Catholics belonged to the working class.[11]

Efforts to unionize the nation's mass-production workers had scant success prior to 1935. The problem was twofold. Despite apparently prounion language in the National Industrial Recovery Act, the right to unionize was not yet protected by federal law. Employers could and did blacklist workers who were union advocates. Most existing unions, moreover, were craft unions, whose leaders had little interest in organizing mass-production workers. Matters changed fundamentally in 1935, with the founding of the Congress of Industrial Organizations (CIO) and passage of the Wagner Act. Catholics were prominent among the founders of the CIO, especially Philip Murray, who served as its second president. Head of the Steelworkers' Organizing Committee and later the United Steelworkers union, Murray was a committed Catholic who liked to quote the social encyclicals. Close to several American bishops, Murray helped to ensure strong Catholic support of the CIO even as it came under attack for the indisputable presence of communists in its ranks. The Wagner Act, which gave strong federal protection to workers' right to organize, also enjoyed strong Catholic support. The NCWC sent a representative to Congress to testify in favor of its passage— the first time the conference had done such a thing.

Unions benefited greatly from strong Catholic support. But the success of the industrial union movement—membership peaked in 1954 at just under 35 percent of all wage and salaried workers—also benefited a great many Catholics and their church. The higher wages and fringe benefits enjoyed by unionized workers made upward mobility possible for the rising generation in numerous working-class families. Soaring Catholic numbers were made possible too, since these rested on early marriage and generous fertility, both of which in the postwar years were facilitated by economic security. Union membership introduced many working-class Catholics to a greater cosmopolitanism: one's union brethren were so because they were workers and not because they were fellow members of an ethnoreligious tribe. That message was vigorously conveyed by both labor priests and those members of the Association of Catholic Trade Unionists who were staffing Catholic "labor schools" by the end of the 1930s. The social encyclicals were integral to the curriculum at such schools, but so was parliamentary procedure, knowledge of which was essential for participation in union meetings and assuming positions of leadership.

Benefits to the church went beyond the happy fact of soaring Catholic numbers. More affluent Catholic workers tended to be closer to the church—more regular in their attendance at Mass and more generous when it came to church support. Roughly 74 percent of working-class Catholics in heavily unionized Detroit reported weekly attendance at Mass, according to a survey done in 1958—fewer than the 82 percent of their white-collar coreligionists who reported the same but still impressive. A more assimilated Catholic population cooperated more readily in diocesan projects and was less inclined to ethnic turf and status wars. Perhaps most important, Catholic support of the labor movement muted whatever anticlericalism might have been spawned by the hardships of the 1930s, especially among Catholic men. Father Neil O'Connor "would never forget the looks of gratitude and respect" he and another priest received when they showed up unexpectedly at a local union meeting in the late 1930s. Some thanked him for his presence "with tears in their eyes." Many priests in turn were grateful for the vital new model of priesthood—less cloistered, more visibly masculine—that the labor movement had made possible.[12]

The Strange Career of Father Coughlin

The ultimately infamous Charles Coughlin was blessed with a golden radio voice. That voice, coupled with Coughlin's knack for leavening his florid oratory with homely anecdotes, made for a singular radio presence. There was simply no one like him in the early days of the medium, as his always diverse audience attests. Coughlin began his career in modest fashion, broadcasting sermons locally from his suburban Detroit church. Prompted by the Depression's ravages, he turned to politics in 1930, when he signed an agreement to broadcast over the Columbia network. Coughlin's broadcasts in 1930 and even 1931 were impassioned but not particularly ideological. Given soaring unemployment and paralysis in Washington, however, his palpable anger at injustice was compelling. "It is unique in the history of Christian civilization that such widespread starvation has existed when our granaries are choking with wheat; that such noticeable privation has existed when our banks are bursting with gold," Coughlin roared in a typical broadcast. His audience was sufficiently large by 1931 that he was able to assemble a network of his own when Columbia refused to renew his contract.[13]

A more ideological Coughlin emerged in 1932 with a new and somewhat eccentric focus on monetary policy. He also raged against Herbert Hoover as the November election drew near—a step that greatly troubled the Apostolic Delegate in Washington. Despite, or perhaps because of, these developments, Coughlin's audience continued to grow, probably peaking in 1933 and the first half of 1934, when the priest was a fervent Roosevelt booster. "The New Deal is Christ's Deal!"—or so Coughlin assured his listeners. His audience, as noted, was remarkably diverse: disproportionately Catholic, very likely, but including large numbers of Protestants and Jews. Whatever his private sentiments, Coughlin's public rhetoric betrayed no hint as yet of anti-Semitism. Indeed, he frequently celebrated the ecumenical nature of the putative movement he headed.[14]

Coughlin grew increasingly critical of the New Deal in the latter half of 1934, although he refrained for a time from attacks on Roosevelt himself. By the end of 1935, a visibly frustrated Coughlin—frustrated in good part by his lack of influence at the White House—was attacking the president as well as his policies. Matters came to a head in 1936, when Coughlin orchestrated a third-party challenge to Roosevelt's reelection. His increasingly intemperate rhetoric and subsequent attacks on the industrial unions that belonged to the CIO alienated many of his erstwhile followers. By the summer of 1936, there is ample evidence that the priest's once enormous and disproportionately lower-middle-class following had eroded, leaving him with a poorer, less articulate, and more heavily Catholic constituency. Coughlin's descent into overt anti-Semitism and fascist apologetics reflected in part the increasingly marginal nature of his following.[15]

The nadir of Coughlin's career occurred in November 1938 with his infamous broadcast comments on Kristallnacht, a night of concerted violence by the Nazi government against the Jews of Germany. Two weeks prior to Coughlin's broadcast, three Catholic bishops, joined by Al Smith and the priest-rector of Catholic University, had delivered a ringing condemnation of the Nazi attacks as un-Christian violations of the right to life and religious liberty. Catholics too had been victims of such persecution, they reminded their audience, citing recent events in Mexico and Spain. Although the anti-Nazi broadcast has been largely ignored by historians, it was carried by two national networks and made the front page of the *New York Times*. The publicity was such that Coughlin devoted a portion of his own broadcast to criticism of the earlier program, which he claimed showed greater sympathy for the Jewish victims of violence than their far-more-numerous Catholic counterparts. Jews had been principally responsible for the Russian Revolution, Coughlin told his audience, and bore major responsibility for the spread of communism throughout the world. Nazism, however deplorable it might be, had to be understood "as a defense mechanism against the incursions of Communism."[16]

Although the November broadcast was unusually vile, Coughlin's anti-Semitism was on frequent display for the rest of his public career. So was his sympathy for Italian and even German fascism, from which governments he may have received indirect funding. His audience did continue to shrink, along with the reach of his radio program, which fewer and fewer stations were willing to carry. Coughlin was forced to cancel his 1940–41 broadcast season, ending his radio career. But there were still Catholics and a good many others—Coughlin's radio audience late in 1938 was estimated to be about 40 percent Catholic—who continued to find the priest compelling. (The diehards after his radio demise could stay in touch by reading *Social Justice*, a lay-published periodical whose content was effectively dictated by the priest.) Anti-Semitism, a sentiment then found in even the most respectable circles, was for certain disaffected Catholics a natural outgrowth of religious tribalism. Fervent anticommunism on the part of many Catholics, coupled with their fears of involvement in a second European war, made Coughlin's apologies for fascism seem less shocking than might otherwise have been the case.[17]

Catholic Coughlinites could also point out that Coughlin's continued public activity implied a kind of approval on the part of church authorities. He was, after all, a diocesan priest who was subject to his bishop. Michael Gallagher, Coughlin's bishop until Gallagher's death in 1937, was indeed a Coughlin supporter, resolutely ignoring appeals from Rome to censor or silence the priest. Gallagher's successor in Detroit, Archbishop—later Cardinal—Edward Mooney, was decidedly not a supporter, as he took pains to make clear. But Mooney's various efforts to muzzle Coughlin—appointing a censor for his radio program, insisting that Coughlin sever his connection with *Social Justice*—had little immediate effect. The notorious Kristallnacht broadcast was actually vetted by the chancery's censor, who was evidently lulled by Coughlin's distinction between "religious" Jews, who were genuine victims of Nazi atrocities, and those who were secular leftists. Mooney obviously feared the anger of Coughlin's diminished but increasingly militant supporters, hundreds of whom had written the chancery protesting Mooney's initial attempt to silence their champion. He worried particularly about so-called Christian Front activity in Brooklyn and Boston, where Catholic street toughs harassed and sometimes assaulted Jews. With Coughlin's audience visibly waning, Mooney—a socially progressive but innately cautious man—opted for reasons of prudence to play a waiting game.[18]

War and the federal government eventually came to Mooney's rescue. Even after Pearl Harbor, *Social Justice* continued its scurrilous criticism of Roosevelt and the war aims of the Allies, prompting interest at the Department of Justice in suing the paper's publisher and editors. Although Coughlin had by this time disassociated himself from *Social Justice,* his well-known influence over the paper's content suggested that, in the event of indictments, he too might be in legal peril. Working in concert with the Roosevelt administration, Mooney used the threat of indictment to at last bring Coughlin to heel. *Social Justice* ceased publication, and Coughlin agreed, under pain of suspension from the priesthood, to refrain henceforth from political activity of any sort. This time around, almost no angry letters arrived at the Detroit chancery. "Apparently he has alienated the major portion of the simple Catholics who followed him so blindly," a grateful Mooney wrote to Roosevelt. "For that, at least, it may have been worthwhile to be patient." Subsequent generations have been less generous in their judgment of Mooney's choices.[19]

The Second World War and Postwar Prosperity

Prior to Pearl Harbor, a majority of Catholics were ardent isolationists. Once war was declared, however, Catholic support for the war was unflagging, despite widespread unease about the nation's wartime alliance with the Soviet Union. The war was preeminently a theological struggle, according to Monsignor Fulton J. Sheen, a radio fixture since the early 1930s, and the enemy was the Anti-Christ. If the nation's bishops were troubled by the wholesale promotion of condoms on military bases and training camps as

a means of combating venereal disease and by the extent of the Allied
bombing campaign, they kept those grievances behind the scenes. (As far as
the bishops were concerned, the two issues—seemingly so disparate—were
intimately connected.) Their public statements on the war, like those of
most Protestant and Jewish leaders, endorsed it as a holy cause. That leaders
across the confessional divide shared a wartime language suggests the extent of the war's homogenizing impact. Both intellectually and emotionally,
wartime Catholics came to feel at home in a proudly pluralistic nation.[20]

The war's duration and its totality do much to explain its integrative
effects. Catholic soldiers, most of them draftees, served for months at a time
in units with Protestants, Jews, and the religiously unaffiliated. Soldiers of
every variety took their leisure at centers staffed by the ecumenical United
Services Organization (USO). Catholic women in unprecedented numbers
joined others of their sex in industrial work, while Catholic males in defense
plants had often to share both the workplace and the union hall with African
American men. That long-standing barriers to employment on the basis of
gender and race were breaking down had obvious import for a Catholic mentality rooted in self-segregation. Catholic chaplains, for their part, routinely
lived with clergy of other denominations and sometimes ministered to soldiers who were not members of their church. Relations with their Protestant
counterparts were often surprisingly amicable. "Some of them are very nice
chaps, sincere and zealous," in the words of a Polish American priest who had
never previously known any Protestant clergy. Contacts with rabbis were
fewer and more freighted with uncertainty. But at least the occasional Catholic chaplain came to a sense of shared spiritual patrimony. Finding himself
behind enemy lines while driving a group of Jewish soldiers from Yom Kip-
pur services, Father Hubert Maino attributed the group's safe return to an
unlikely trio. "Abraham, Isaac, and Jacob must have been the patron saints on
duty that day," he told his archbishop, not entirely in a jocular vein.[21]

The most visible Catholic chaplain of all was New York's Archbishop
Francis Spellman, appointed vicar of the Military Ordinariate by Pius XII in
1939. A Roosevelt intimate and the primary conduit between the White House
and the Vatican, Spellman traveled extensively throughout the war, visiting
troops and functioning as a quasi-diplomat. Generous publicity followed.
"There were newsreels, radio reports, and reams of newspaper and magazine
articles about his travels," in the words of a Spellman biographer. "Press pho-
tographers captured him saying mass in ruins and on runways, visiting the

wounded in hospitals, and blessing doughboys in the trenches as well as their bombs, tanks, machines guns, and bullets." Spellman had been instrumental in securing Roosevelt's appointment in 1939 of Myron C. Taylor as the president's "personal representative" at the Vatican—another wartime "first." Taylor's appointment, along with Spellman's wartime prominence, confirmed for Catholics both the war's ecumenical dimensions and their own acceptance as full partners in the American crusade.[22]

As had been the case after the First World War, anti-Catholicism resurfaced in a major way following the Allied victory. But this time around, the anti-Catholicism was largely an elite phenomenon. As journalist Paul Blanshard explained in a 1950 address at Harvard, "the new movement against Catholic aggression is rising not on the fringes, the lunatic fringes of religion and fanaticism, but right in the hearts of American University leaders." Blanshard's *American Freedom and Catholic Power,* an unlikely bestseller upon its publication in 1949, was the movement's principal scripture. Catholicism was inherently authoritarian, according to Blanshard, and thus a threat to the nation's future. Genuine democracy depended on fully autonomous citizens—men and women of a skeptical bent, capable of growth and intellectual independence. American Catholics might give lip service to democracy and the Constitution, Blanshard conceded. But Catholic separatism—the parochial schools were a particular bugbear—and Catholic views on authority were incompatible with a truly democratic culture. A good many liberals, both secular and Protestant, endorsed his arguments.[23]

Although tensions of this sort were not new, they intensified in the postwar years for two principal reasons. The first had to do with public funding for Catholic schools—a perennial source of tension in many localities but revitalized after the war by the nation's growing investment in education. With students at Catholic colleges now receiving aid through the GI Bill, Catholic leaders were able not only to cite a precedent for federal aid to their schools but also to argue that public aid of any sort was best understood as assisting the individual student rather than the institution he or she chose to attend. That argument appeared to triumph in the Supreme Court's *Everson v. Board of Education* decision in 1947, when a divided court upheld a New Jersey township ordinance that subsidized school bus fees for students at local parochial schools. (Indirect assistance to Catholic schools, like public provision of transport or textbooks, was not uncommon by the mid-1940s.) The *Everson* decision, one of the decade's most debated, dismayed a good many liberals. But *Everson* proved to be a Pyrrhic victory for Catholics, since the court in that decision invoked, for the very first time, a "wall of separation between church and State." If five justices in 1947 had found the New Jersey law consonant with such a wall, subsequent court decisions on religion and education moved in quite another direction.[24]

Most Catholics probably paid little attention to liberal dismay over *Everson*. Few of them read periodicals like the *Nation*, of which Paul Blanshard was an associate editor and which had carried his best-selling book in serialized form. A good many Catholics, indeed, may have been unaware that their bishops now endorsed federal aid to education—something they had denounced for years as potentially threatening to local control of the schools. But Catholics were certainly conscious of rising property taxes in those many jurisdictions where such taxes paid for public education. With public sentiment now favoring both expansion and improvement of school systems nationally, many Catholic parents were squeezed economically as taxes rose to pay for schools they did not use and costs increased for Catholic schools as well. The dilemma ensured that Catholic leaders would continue their ultimately futile efforts to secure some form of public funding for sectarian education.

A second cause of postwar tension centered on civil liberties. Liberals complained bitterly about Catholic initiatives in the realm of censorship, especially of books and movies. Catholic opposition to birth control, which sometimes made it difficult to modify laws or policies that inhibited access to such, was another irritant. Where Catholics' numbers were large, they were usually able to prevent the provision of contraceptive services at public hospitals, although at a heavy cost with regard to public relations. The proponents of such services played skillfully on their humane intent and, given the typical client of most public hospitals, their obvious benefit to the taxpayer. Contention over a nineteenth-century Massachusetts law that prohibited the dissemination of all contraceptive devices exacted an especially heavy cost, given the attendant publicity. Modification of the law was twice the subject of statewide referenda, in 1942 and 1948. In both instances, but especially in 1948, the state's Catholic bishops played a prominent role, ordering their priests to preach against the proposed amendment, the purpose of which was the law's liberalization, and underwriting an ambitious advertising campaign. Although Catholics did not constitute a majority in the state, the amendment twice went down to defeat, partly because some voters believed that repeal would legalize abortion—a confusion that

Catholic advertising, especially in 1948, seemed designed to promote. Liberal reaction was predictably outraged.[25]

When liberals in the 1930s spoke, as they frequently did, of Catholic affinities for fascism, they often pointed to Father Charles Coughlin as a principal case in point. Catholic service in the Second World War did temporarily mute the argument. But postwar tensions over civil liberties brought it back in modified form, with Wisconsin's Senator Joseph McCarthy playing the Coughlin role. First elected as a Republican in 1946, the hitherto-obscure junior senator exploded into public view with an early 1950 speech in Wheeling, West Virginia, in which he charged the State Department with housing numerous communists. From that moment until his censure by the Senate at the end of 1954, McCarthy was the nation's most prominent anticommunist, orchestrating smear campaigns against individuals, sometimes on the grounds of their alleged homosexuality, in various government and military bureaucracies. Until he unwisely took on the Army at the end of 1953, his destructive course looked unstoppable to many liberals and moderates.

McCarthy was indeed endorsed by some prominent Catholics, most notably New York's Cardinal Spellman, whose See city, along with Boston, was the leading center of Catholic support for the senator. Most public-opinion polls, moreover, showed majority support for McCarthy on the part of the Catholic laity, at least until late in 1954. But Catholics also numbered among McCarthy's more prominent detractors, while Catholic support for the man rose and fell with public opinion generally. Outside the notoriously defensive bastions of northeastern Irish America, in the view of one authority, Catholic support for McCarthy was broad but thin—largely the product of reflexive anticommunism. "The debate over McCarthyism was thus predominantly an affair of elites, of conservative editors, politicians, educators, business leaders, and leading clergymen—all ranged against liberals drawn largely from the same ranks," according to Donald Crosby. As such, it was consistent with the elite composition of postwar anti-Catholicism.[26]

Toward a Catholic President

Tensions between Catholics and liberals of other stripes moderated after the mid-1950s. McCarthy's demise was surely a help. So was a growing emphasis by Catholic leaders on the immorality of racial segregation. Certain

Catholic institutions, it is true, retained a color bar into the early 1960s, al-though Catholic schools in the North and West were generally open by the late 1940s to Catholics of all races. But non-Catholic liberals were impressed by the several southern bishops who moved to desegregate their schools and colleges prior to the *Brown* decision in 1954—men like Washington, DC's Archbishop, later Cardinal, Patrick O'Boyle and Archbishop Joseph Ritter of St. Louis—and impressed as well by the bishops' collectively branding segregation a sin, which they did in 1958. Even the problem of contraception lost a bit of its edge, as Catholic liberals publicly admitted to doubts, not yet about church teaching on the matter but about the use of Catholic power to keep repressive laws in place. In a general sense, it can also be said that the public posture of Catholics in the later 1950s was less truculent than had previously been the case.[27]

In these more irenic circumstances, it was increasingly possible for Democratic liberals to contemplate their party's nominating a Catholic—an option that arguably made excellent political sense. With Catholics now constituting close to a quarter of the electorate and emerging as a swing vote, a Catholic on the ticket might well be key to the Democrats recaptur-ing the White House. Such was the logic of an internal party memo pro-duced in 1956 by Theodore Sorenson, a youthful aide to Massachusetts Senator John F. Kennedy, who was then being touted for his party's vice-presidential slot. Passed over for that nomination, probably to his ultimate advantage, Kennedy began a quiet campaign for his party's top slot four years hence. Acting on the advice of Bishop John Wright—a Boston auxil-iary who was moved to Worcester, Massachusetts, in 1951 and Pittsburgh in 1959—Kennedy confronted the "religion question" early on, meeting with Protestant leaders and even Paul Blanshard, while assuring the press of his firm commitment to separation of church and state. Well before 1960, Ken-nedy had announced his opposition to both the public funding of sectarian schools and the appointment of a U.S. ambassador to the Holy See.[28]

Despite such proactive maneuvering, religion persisted as an issue in the 1960 campaign. Evangelicals and other conservative Protestants invoked the specter of Kennedy's Catholicism to considerable effect in the South and the rural Midwest, where Kennedy polled fewer votes in November than did Democrats farther down the ticket. Although he had hoped that the issue would lie dormant, Kennedy was forced to address it head-on, most famously in a September speech before the Greater Houston Ministerial Association, in which he distinguished between the realm of faith and morals, where the church might properly instruct its members, and public policy, where it could not. "I do not speak for my church on public matters, and the church does not speak for me." If the distinction seems in retrospect to be more than a little problematic, the speech at the time was widely praised. But for all his telegenic charm, Kennedy defeated Nixon by one of the narrowest margins in history. Polling some 83 percent of the Catholic vote was essential to his victory.[29]

As his massive Catholic support attests, Kennedy's election had everything to do with the Catholic past. It was less about issues, even Catholic issues, than Catholic claims to full membership in the national polity. Kennedy was "one of us"—heir, no matter his privilege, to a history of exclusion and contempt. Tellingly, perhaps, the Catholics least likely to vote for Kennedy were those on the Catholic margins, who attended Mass irregularly and did not identify strongly with the church. But Kennedy's distance from the immigrant past was a source of pride as well. His wealth and elite education, his wife's cultured taste and personal elegance—these signaled Catholic arrival as powerfully as his election did. What a distance Catholics had traveled from the rough-hewn days of Al Smith, when Catholics—according to one diocesan paper—were forced to defend both themselves and their candidate from Protestant claims that, as a group, Catholics lacked "the refinement other Americans have." Upwardly mobile Catholics could see their own aspirations reflected in the Kennedy White House, along with their hopes for the Catholic future.[30]

Catholic confidence was also buoyed by the popularity of the recently elected Pope John XXIII, whose sunny persona had immense appeal to a global media audience. Rotund and engagingly jocular, the new pope afforded a striking contrast to Pius XII, his austere and aristocratic predecessor. Shortly after his election in 1958, Pope John stunned the Catholic world by announcing that he would convoke an ecumenical council—the first in almost a century. Most Catholics in the United States assumed that the council would focus on ecclesial housekeeping rather than major reform initiatives. The American church, after all, was in seemingly robust health. "We have not lost the working class," as one American bishop reminded his European confreres in the course of a council debate. American Catholics watched the council's televised opening ceremonies in October 1962 with excitement and pride, although their minds were at least partly distracted by the Cuban missile crisis, which was simultaneously threatening a

nervous world with nuclear disaster. But they did not for the most part expect that the grand Roman meeting would have much effect on their lives.[31]

In this regard, of course, American Catholics were quite wrong. The
council's reforms altered the experience of being Catholic in fundamental
ways and accelerated a process of change among Catholics that had roots in
the preconciliar years. One unhappy result was polarization. Many Catholics, like many Protestants, came increasingly to identify with conservatives
or liberals in other churches rather than members of their putative denominational family. The effects were nowhere more evident than in the realm of
politics. When a second Catholic ran for president—John Kerry, as a Democrat, in 2004—the more devout the Catholic voter, as measured by frequency of Mass attendance, the more likely that voter was to vote for the
Republican candidate. Ethnoreligious loyalties had long since given way to
the politics of the culture wars.

Part V
A World Unbound, 1963–2015

Patricia Caron Crowley

(1913–2005)

T he year is 1968. A most unusual press conference is in progress in the nation's capital, where six lay Catholics, veterans of the Pontifical Commission on Population, Births, and the Family, are delivering their verdict on *Humanae Vitae*, the papal encyclical that has just reaffirmed their church's absolute ban on all modes of "artificial" contraception. Notwithstanding the encyclical, according to spokesman John T. Noonan, Catholic married couples should decide for themselves when it came to birth control. Indeed, the group believes that the encyclical's logic is so flawed that a successor pope will eventually repudiate it. Had the bishops on the papal commission after months of deliberation not urged Pope Paul VI to modify Catholic teaching so as to permit married couples to make their own prayerful choices about family planning? Despite their service on the commission, it should be noted, none of those who convened the Washington press conference have received prior notice of the encyclical's publication. Like other Catholics, they got the news from the media, where it was the stuff of banner headlines.[1]

The lone female member in the press-conference group is Patricia Crowley, always called Patty, who with her husband, Pat, had been a lay pioneer in the Catholic family-life movement. Born in 1913, Patty might seem an implausible embodiment of the turbulent years that followed the Second Vatican Council. Her religious sensibilities having been formed in the preconciliar church, she had prior to *Humanae Vitae* never questioned papal infallibility—a doctrine that, whatever the ahistorical nature of its nineteenth-century formulation, defined the Catholicism of her generation. Nor had she and her husband ever employed a forbidden mode of contraception in a marriage that eventually produced five children before Patty's 1947 hysterectomy brought an end to Crowley fertility. (The couple subsequently adopted one of the numerous foster children they took into their home.) But despite her roots in the Tridentine church, Patty Crowley was in fact a key transitional figure—a woman whose story makes clear that change in the wake of the council had roots in the preconciliar era. Indeed, the long-lived Crowley—she died in 2005—emerged after 1968 as a prototypical Vatican II Catholic, openly critical of church authority and fiercely committed to social justice. "I long for a church that is honest about its teachings, that admits its errors and faces the effects of rigidity with openness," she wrote in 1993 with specific regard to *Humanae Vitae* and indirectly to a good deal more.[2]

Crowley, a lifelong Chicagoan, was born to a prosperous family, although her Quebecois immigrant father had not gone beyond the sixth grade. She attended none but Catholic schools, including Washington, DC's Trinity College, with a junior-year stint at the Sorbonne. Among her Trinity electives was a class taught by John A. Ryan, then in his heyday as the "Right Reverend New Dealer" but of whom young Patty had not previously heard. Ryan's was reputed to be a "gut" course—he read aloud from his various books while many of the students caught up on their correspondence—but Patty, who sat in the front row, found that questions could prompt him to talk about his life in politics. For the daughter of a staunch Republican, Ryan's musings were close to revelatory. "When Ryan and Patty happened to take the same train to Chicago at Christmastime and he bought her dinner, his influence was set." Patty was neither an outstanding student at Trinity nor a class leader, but she did return home upon graduation with broadened horizons. She had also acquired an ardent suitor: fellow Chicagoan Patrick Crowley, a Notre Dame graduate whose family was even more prosperous than hers. The couple married in 1937, upon his completion of law school.[3]

The early years of the Crowley marriage followed a conventional pattern for the Catholic upper middle class. The couple moved to suburban Wilmette in 1941, where life passed pleasantly in a child-centered round of parish and neighborhood socializing. Pat's status as the father of very young children won him repeated exemptions from the local draft board. But the sufferings of a war-torn world could not be held completely at bay. "As the headlines became more and more tragic," Pat later wrote, "the hunger to do something positive and permanent gnawed deeper inside—though perhaps it didn't show much outside." By 1943, Pat had joined a six-man discussion group that, with the help of a volunteer priest-chaplain, was exploring how Catholic laymen might "restore all things in Christ." (The phrase comes from St. Paul's Letter to the Ephesians.) After some months of talk, the group decided to devote its initial efforts to exploring ways to combat divorce. By this time several of their wives had organized a companion group with a similar focus on marital health. Patty Crowley was active in the women's group, where she displayed her hitherto-untapped abilities as a leader. But she resented the sex segregation, especially given the groups' avowed interest in supporting family life.[4]

Despite the small size of these discussion-cum-action groups, they pioneered two major pastoral initiatives in postwar Catholic Chicago: Cana Conference for the married and Pre-Cana programs for the betrothed. Both initiatives subsequently migrated to other dioceses, where they were lynchpins of Catholic family-life ministry well into the 1960s. In 1949, moreover, representatives of the now-numerous adult discussion groups concerned with family life—such groups could be found by then in at least twenty cities—came together in Chicago to establish what soon became known as the Christian Family Movement. CFM, as it was invariably called, was a couples' movement—the first in a church with a long tradition of segregating the sexes. In Chicago, as elsewhere, it was largely a movement of affluent suburbanites—itself something new in a church long dominated by the urban working class. Perhaps most important, CFM was a movement with a broad social focus. Since families could not flourish in a less-than-Christian social order, social action was integral to the CFM agenda. The group's national program was generally progressive, favoring labor unions, cooperative ventures, internationalism, and civil rights, although its membership was ideologically diverse. Minnesota's Senator Eugene McCarthy, a liberal Democrat, addressed the 1959 convention on "politics and the Christian life."[5]

CFM spread rapidly in the 1950s, due in good part to the Crowleys' vigorous leadership. Anyone who wrote to movement headquarters in Chicago received not only a personal reply from Patty but also very likely—at least in the early days—a visit from the Crowley duo and often enough their children.

Some thirty-two thousand couples nationwide were participating in CFM by 1957, by which time the movement had international affiliates. The Crowleys made the first of several global tours in the movement's service in 1956. The intense domesticity of the postwar years helps to explain the movement's appeal. It was also fueled by lay assertiveness—the perhaps-inevitable consequence of an increasingly educated Catholic population. Well before Vatican II, CFM emphasized the essential role of the laity in Christianizing the social order. "We must move into places forbidden to bishops and priests," in the words of the movement's newsletter. Every CFM group—these were composed of six couples who met every two weeks—did have a priest-chaplain. But the chaplain's role was confined to brief comments at the meeting's end. The liturgy at CFM functions was nearly always a dialogue Mass, with the congregation taking an active role, while the concluding Mass at the 1959 convention was said with the priest facing the people.[6]

Although the Crowleys served for many years as CFM's "Executive Secretary Couple," Patty was the principal activist. "Those who saw Pat and Patty live and work together say she was the energizer, the organizer, the 'motor,'" in the words of the couple's biographer. If her growing experience of leadership caused Patty to question her church's restrictive views on gender and sexuality, she never so indicated. Even in the early 1960s, with lay dissent going public around the teaching on contraception, CFM continued to celebrate the large family as an emblem of Christian discipleship. But matters changed for Patty when she and Pat were appointed late in 1964 to a Vatican commission exploring the problem, from a Catholic perspective, of "population, births, and the family." The commission, initially secret, had been established in 1962 by Pope John XXIII, largely—or so it appears—as a means of removing the nettlesome problem of birth control from the purview of the council fathers. Once its existence became public and especially after its membership was expanded to include a number of laypeople, the "papal birth-control commission"—as it was popularly known—became for Catholics a sign of incipient reform in Catholic sexual teaching. In the United States and elsewhere in the industrialized world, a good many Catholic couples began to employ still forbidden modes of contraception in anticipation of the change. At least in the United States, most opted for "the Pill," the oral contraceptive approved for American sale in 1960.[7]

As members of the papal commission, the Crowleys saw themselves as agents of the laity and especially highly committed lay Catholics like those in CFM. By the time the Crowleys arrived in Rome for their first meeting in 1965, it was clear to them that even the CFM faithful had doubts about church teaching. Invariably conscientious, the Crowleys had spoken with numerous CFM members in preparation for the meeting and solicited written comments from others. Impressed by the testimony they had marshaled, several leading members of the commission asked the couple to conduct a more systematic survey of the CFM membership. Patty coordinated the effort, in conjunction with a Notre Dame sociologist, who was also a commission member. Since few CFMers were even then ignoring the ban on contraception, the survey focused primarily on their experience with the rhythm method, which most reported as damaging to marital happiness. "Is not the sex drive instilled by God a normal one?" Patty asked, when she spoke to the assembled commission on the survey's findings. "Should not husbands and wives be encouraged to express their love without adding a series of do's and don'ts?" Patty also spoke frankly, as commission leaders had asked the group's three married females to do, about her own experience of marriage.[8]

Although voting privileges at the commission were restricted by papal fiat to its episcopal members, some of whom began their service as defenders of the status quo, a substantial majority of those members voted in June 1966 to recommend to the pope a change in Catholic teaching on contraception. While Christian marriage had by definition to be open to children, according to the commission majority, each act of marital sex did not. Couples might therefore make licit use of contraceptives in a variety of marital circumstances. Flushed with triumph, the exuberant Crowleys left for home, certain that the pope would soon implement the commission's recommendation. After an imprudently long interlude, the pope declined to do so, with devastating consequences for church authority as it was generally understood. Although younger Catholics in the wake of *Humanae Vitae* were more apt than their elders to reject the doctrine of papal infallibility, a decidedly middle-aged Patty Crowley arrived in the same territory. It was not enough for the pope to speak, she maintained, along with many others; his teaching must also be accepted by the faithful. Such had not been the case with *Humanae Vitae*.

Patty Crowley remained a committed Catholic for the rest of her long life, although she often felt marginalized. "No priest ever talked to me about *Humanae Vitae*," she explained. "No one asked how we felt. We never even got a letter of thanks from the Vatican." Pat's death in 1974 and her waning interest in CFM, much diminished in numbers after 1970 and increasingly focused on family dynamics, channeled Patty's energies in new directions. She served on the boards of numerous civic and women's organizations, as well as the Chicago Housing Authority. She supported the Women's Ordination Conference and other groups championing reform in the church. Along with several friends, she established Deborah's Place, a shelter for homeless women on Chicago's near north side, which eventually grew to include a day shelter and transitional housing. Sister Patsy Crowley, a Benedictine and the Crowleys' eldest child, was the shelter's second director; she also regularly accompanied her mother on weekly visits to Chicago's women's jail. Patty remained active too at Holy Name Cathedral, her parish church since 1969, when she and Pat had moved to a spacious apartment on the eighty-eighth floor of Chicago's John Hancock building. "I say the only important thing is Jesus' message, and the rest of the rules are for the birds," she said bluntly of the church toward the end of her life. "So give food to the hungry, give drink to the thirsty, help the sick, and visit those in prison."[9]

Patty's funeral in 2005 was so well attended that Holy Name was nearly filled—hardly a usual phenomenon when someone dies at ninety-two. Those in attendance were well aware that the Catholic Church was in trouble. Weekly Mass attendance had fallen precipitously since the late 1960s, especially among the young, many of whom knew surprisingly little about Catholic theology and tradition. Vocations to the priesthood and religious life had virtually collapsed. Venerable Catholic centers like Chicago had witnessed massive church closings—a new experience in a church whose past had been defined by growth. Catholics themselves were deeply divided over politics and ecclesial issues—a polarization sufficiently bitter that the bishop of Lincoln, Nebraska, had publicly labeled Patty Crowley "a very old degenerate who roams about promoting sexual immorality." And every mourner present had been numbed by recent revelations of covered-up clerical sex abuse in Boston and elsewhere.[10]

Many in the congregation at Holy Name were old enough to have roots in the preconciliar church. Men and women like these, in the words of Peter Steinfels, "often have a kind of bred-in-the-bones Catholicism. If they come from the younger generations, well, it's a different story." Thus in bidding farewell to Patty Crowley, the mourners were also saying good-bye to an era of Catholic flourishing. Some of their own children, in all likelihood,

were numbered among the many Catholics who have left the church in recent decades—a number sufficiently large that it was estimated in 2007 to
be equal to 10 percent of the nation's population. "Patty Crowley and her
peers never doubted that the church had something to say, but after 1968
they began to wonder whether it was interested in listening," Steinfels concluded his Crowley obituary in the *New York Times*. "For millions of their
children and grandchildren, that doubt apparently looms larger and larger."
The reforms of the Second Vatican Council were initially welcomed by
most American Catholics, whose mood was buoyant at its close in 1965.
How and why the picture changed is the complicated subject to which we
now turn."

T·H·I·R·T·E·E·N

Something Like a Revolution

The Second Vatican Council met in four sessions in Rome from October 1962 to December 1965. Attended by some twenty-two hundred bishops and heads of male religious orders, the council was by far the largest such gathering in church history and certainly the most diverse—a veritable showcase of what was now a truly global communion. The council was also attended by a number of Protestant and Orthodox "observers," a first in the long history of church councils; a much smaller number of lay Catholic "auditors" were invited to the second and subsequent sessions. Even women made a nominal appearance: a handful of women religious attended sessions three and four, while other lay female auditors were invited to the fourth and final session. After extensive formal debate and even more extensive behind-the-scenes deliberation, the council issued sixteen documents. Taken together, those documents represent a judiciously worded repudiation of the militant opposition to modernity that had characterized the papacy since the time of the French Revolution. The council fathers endorsed religious liberty and ecumenism; authorized a gradual reform of the Tridentine liturgy, including use of the vernacular; and embraced a new posture of openness to both the contemporary world and historical-mindedness. In the felicitous words of Father John O'Malley, "Liberty, equality and fraternity . . . knocked at the door and gained entrance to the feast."[1]

Not many Catholics, then or now, have actually read these documents. Catholic impressions of the council, at least in the United States, came primarily from the secular media, which provided generous coverage. The dominant media narrative cast the event as a struggle between an enlightened majority—the "progressives," in media parlance—and their reactionary opponents, housed disproportionately in the Curia, or Vatican bureaucracy. A good many Catholics seem to have found the narrative compelling, resonating as it did with their own experience as Americans. It had always been easier to blame the Curia rather than the pope for Rome's failure to grasp the genius of U.S. constitutional arrangements or the dynamism of free societies generally. Curial cardinals and their allies thus made excellent villains, especially the ubiquitous Cardinal Alfredo Ottaviani, to whom the media regularly went for colorful invective against the mildest of proposed reforms. True, it was somewhat surprising to see the council depicted in terms that were usually saved for coverage of city hall. But most Catholics knew that their bishops had differences and that they could play a political game. How else, the cynics might plausibly ask, did a man become an archbishop? Even the secular media, however, seemed to grasp that the mood of the council, and especially its language, represented something attractively new. This was a council without anathemas. Whatever struggles took place behind the scenes, the public face of the council was winsomely irenic.

Since American Catholics had long ago made their peace with political modernity, many of the council's reforms came as welcome validation. It seemed only natural that the church should embrace such obvious goods as religious freedom and respect for non-Christian religions, especially Judaism. Pope John himself had endorsed religious liberty as a fundamental human right in his 1963 encyclical *Pacem in Terris*. The positive tone of the council's principal documents was also congenial to most American Catholics, as sanguine about the world they inhabited as other postwar Americans. Highly educated Catholics were especially delighted by the council fathers' apparent respect for lay expertise and the importance of dialogue—themes implicit in the very language they chose to employ. The fathers regularly invoked terms like "cooperation," "partnership," and "the priesthood of all believers"; they spoke of the church as the "people of God." Products of a culture that celebrated innovation, most American Catholics were even able to assimilate the most startling reality affirmed by the events in Rome: that the Catholic Church, which apologists had long insisted stood above the tides of history, could and did change—that its pilgrimage through time took place in history and not apart from it. But few, in all likelihood, grasped the full implications of what was a virtual paradigm shift.[2]

The American bishops, with one or two exceptions, played a minor role at the council. Their principal contribution came in the 1965 declaration on religious liberty, largely written by the Jesuit John Courtney Murray, who had until quite recently been muzzled by the Vatican. (Murray came to the council as a theological adviser to New York's Cardinal Spellman, whose hyperdiverse See city made him something of a natural ecumenist.) Germany, Austria, France, and Belgium supplied most of the council's dominant members. But like many other national episcopates, the U.S. delegation moved away from its largely reflexive conservatism as the council proceeded. For some American bishops, indeed, the council provided an experience akin to conversion. Exposed to new theological currents and encountering the church in its splendid global variety, such men returned home as apostles of *aggiornamento*, Pope John's oft-repeated term for updating the church. To the displeasure of the Vatican bureaucracy, in short, the council assumed a life of its own, and the tide ran strongly toward reform—tempered always, it should be added, by the need for each of the council documents to command a voting majority of at least 80 percent.

The changes wrought by the council were so startling that a good many Catholics failed to note what the council neglected to do. Nearly every Catholic was of course aware that the council fathers had not addressed the problem of birth control. But since a much-expanded papal commission was deliberating the issue, many Catholics assumed that change was in the offing. Fewer noticed the council's omissions with regard to the priesthood in what is widely regarded as one of its least innovative documents. Perhaps most important, in view of subsequent developments, that document failed to address the discipline of mandatory celibacy, which, like birth control, was removed from the council's agenda by order of two successive popes. Nor did the document adequately address the meaning of priesthood in an updated church. The council fathers had acknowledged that an increasingly educated laity had of necessity to play a more prominent role in the church and as leaders in Catholic life. As for the world's bishops, their council experience was a powerful source of new morale and a spur to the organization or strengthening of national episcopal conferences. "But no fresh rationales for being a priest or a religious emerged," as

Martin Marty has cogently noted, "while the old ones were effectively undercut by the advances in understanding of bishop and lay person."[3]

The council also failed to resolve the vexing problem of tension between the center in Rome, where authority had become hyperconcentrated, and a diverse global church. Former missionary churches in Asia and Africa were asserting the need for a more "inculturated" form of Catholicism, stripped of extraneous Western influences, while even bishops from the industrialized West were chafing under Roman strictures. All bishops, moreover, had had an experience of shared decision-making at the council, and most thirsted for more of the same after the council's close. What was needed, in the view of the majority, was externally led reform of the Curia and a structure that would permit the world's bishops to share on a permanent basis in papal decision-making. Pope Paul resisted the first option—the Curia, he assured the council fathers, could and would reform itself. And while he did create a Synod of Bishops that would meet periodically in Rome to deliberate issues of importance, he did so unilaterally—itself an exercise in papal supremacy. The pope, moreover, defined the Synod as a purely advisory body "with no authority beyond what the pope conceded to it." Under Paul and his successors, the Synod has been a toothless body, while the Curia has continued in a more or less unreformed state. As for the means by which the world's bishops are chosen, which is both secretive and centered in Rome, it was not even raised by the council fathers.[4]

Imbalance between the center in Rome and what might be called the ecclesial periphery has arguably grown even more extreme in the decades since the council. This imbalance is just as arguably key to some of the most urgent problems facing today's church. Papal stands against contraception, homosexual practice, the admission to the Eucharist of any Catholic who has divorced and remarried without an annulment, a married clergy, and even the ordination of women are opposed by a great many Catholics, at least in the developed countries. Their bishops and priests have mostly responded by refusing to discuss such issues or simply endorsing the popes' positions—"prohibitions without adequate reasons," in the words of one theologian. Lay Catholics with serious doubts about some or all of the contested teachings can only conclude that no one is listening. The crisis caused by clerical sex abuse, moreover, was arguably worsened by Rome's long refusal to take the matter seriously. Attempting to have egregious offenders removed from the priesthood, American bishops were often rebuffed by

Rome, where such matters must be adjudicated. Those in the relevant Roman congregations and even the recently canonized John Paul II evidently regarded the problem as peculiarly American, fueled by the nation's supersexualized culture and exaggerated by the media.[5]

Despite the problems it failed to resolve, Vatican II unquestionably inaugurated a new era in global Catholic history. True, most of the council's initiatives reflected change already under way among Catholics, at least in Europe and North America: the activism of an educated laity, as seen in movements like CFM; the growing interest in liturgical reform; a new commitment to democracy on the part of Catholics in war-torn Europe. But the council, both as a phenomenon and in terms of its documents, helped to accelerate those changes, especially in conjunction with the cultural upheavals that defined the 1960s. Postconciliar change could be disconcerting, in both its speed and direction, for which many Catholics were unprepared. "Never before had such radical adjustments of viewpoint been so abruptly required" of Catholics, to quote John O'Malley again. Institutional crisis was the unintended but wholly predictable result. At the same time, the postcouncil church, perhaps especially in the United States, evinced new signs of vitality. Lay ministries proliferated, as did Catholic involvement in various social-action movements; new modes of spirituality flourished; while Catholic charities, which increasingly served a broader-than-Catholic population, assumed new prominence both locally and nationally.[6]

Implementing the Council's Reforms

The council fathers authorized reform of the liturgy toward the close of its second session late in 1963. The fathers were concerned above all else to encourage lay understanding of and participation in the Mass, for which reason they endorsed a limited use of vernacular languages in place of liturgical Latin. Every Mass would now be a "dialogue Mass," with the congregation responding collectively to the priest's greetings and invocations. The fathers gave new prominence to the reading of Scripture, hitherto pointedly subordinated to confection of the Eucharist, and summoned priests to center their preaching on the Word. Certain prayers and gestures, accretions of recent centuries, were eliminated: the Mass should be characterized by a "noble simplicity," as befitting its origins in the Last Supper. Preconciliar Catholics had been taught to regard the Mass as a sacrifice—a literal reenactment of Christ's suffering and death on the Cross. The fathers affirmed that understanding but also broadened it. The Mass, they reminded Catholics, encompassed the whole of the Paschal Mystery, culminating in the Resurrection—an emphasis that subtly reoriented the liturgy's emotional tenor. The fruits of the Mass should include both joy at the world's redemption and a lively solidarity with humankind. In the words of Peter Steinfels, "the liturgy ceased to be private, passive, other worldly, ahistorical; the readings, homily and prayers reminded the worshipers that they were part of a people chosen to be disciples, light and salt to the world."[7]

Shortly after the council approved the schema on the liturgy, Pope Paul created a commission to oversee the complex business of its implementation. It was this commission that encouraged a reform implied by the schema but not included in it: that the priest celebrate much of the Mass facing the congregation. (The priest had hitherto faced the altar for most of the ritual.) This particular reform was quickly implemented throughout the United States. National episcopal conferences were authorized to decide how extensively the vernacular should be employed in their churches, although for a few years after the council the Eucharistic prayers were everywhere required to be said in Latin. The American bishops, generally partisans of liturgical reform, were generous in their permissions. By the later 1960s, the Mass was being said entirely in the vernacular in the great majority of parishes; a revised order of the Mass, entirely in the vernacular and further simplified, was made mandatory for the American church in 1971. After that date, even the staunchest opponents of reform had to accept its inevitability.

Liturgical reform entailed more than language. Most parishes even in the mid-1960s were using laymen as lectors to proclaim the day's Scriptures. (Readings from the Old Testament would be included as of 1969.) Reception of communion under both species was permitted to the laity in a majority of dioceses by then on such special occasions as weddings. Since only priests had hitherto been allowed to consume the consecrated wine, the change was experienced as a kind of upgrade in the laity's status. Communion under both species would eventually be standard practice at every weekday and Sunday Mass. A minority of dioceses at mid-decade permitted the faithful to stand rather than kneel when they received—again a practice that eventually became general. Congregational singing was widely encouraged too, as per the council's instructions, although many Catholics were less than responsive. "A passerby couldn't tell us from the Methodists," my grandmother complained in 1966, at least according to family lore. But Methodists, being notably full-throated, would in fact have sounded quite different to a remotely discerning passerby.

Catholics were unevenly prepared for these momentous changes. For veterans of Catholic Action movements, the logic behind the reforms was thoroughly familiar. But for the majority of Catholics, many of whom had never experienced a preconciliar dialogue Mass, the changes might easily smack of the arbitrary. Most American bishops did try to ease the transition, holding liturgical workshops for their clergy and providing model sermon texts to explain the reforms. But they could not guarantee that every priest would do an effective job of explaining or even do the job at all. Priests themselves performed with varying competence in their new role as liturgical presiders—facing the congregation was a particular difficulty, particularly for older men—and many were initially awkward as they employed new ritual gestures and articulated vernacular texts that were themselves often awkwardly worded. But despite these considerable obstacles, the reforms were apparently popular. Two studies done in 1966 found both broad adoption of the reforms and general enthusiasm among the laity, which subsequent studies confirmed. Even when reform was clumsily implemented, most lay Catholics seemed to appreciate its evident intent of making the Mass a communal experience.[8]

Division, not to say polarization, did eventually surface with regard to the liturgy. By articulating the need for updating to make the Mass comprehensible to contemporary peoples in all their variety, the council fathers might be read as endorsing continual reform. Every diocese had its avant-garde, priests and their lay supporters who pushed the liturgical boundaries. Many liturgical innovations eventually blessed by the bishops, like receiving communion in the hand rather than on the tongue or permitting women to be lectors, began as unauthorized practice in self-styled progressive parishes. And although their numbers were usually small, every diocese had its liturgical laggards—priests and outspoken laypeople who opposed nearly all liturgical change. As Catholics were increasingly divided in the later 1960s over nonecclesial issues like race and the limits of wartime dissent, differences over the liturgy assumed an overtly political cast. Growing numbers "shopped around" for liturgies to their liking—typically those that validated the shopper's own worldview. Most Catholics, of course, remained in the ideological mainstream. But even they could intuit that the Mass had ceased to be an invariable source of Catholic unity.

Liturgical reformers typically had scant sympathy for popular devotions, despite their participative element. The Mass should stand at the center of every Catholic's prayer life. As churches were reconfigured to accommodate the new liturgy—a table-like altar facing the congregation had to be added and the communion rail modified or removed—any number of devotional statues were quietly retired. Growing numbers of parishes either cut back on their devotional offerings or eliminated them entirely. Even Eucharistic devotions declined with the postconciliar emphasis on the Eucharist as a meal. Marian devotions remained more or less sacrosanct, at least in a rhetorical sense. But they too withered in popularity. Mary was a problem for Catholic ecumenists, as well as Catholic feminists—still small in number but ardent in their new commitment. The Mary of Catholic tradition "was sometimes more plaster goddess than friend," in the not atypical words of a Sister of Mercy. Mary's role in the 1950s as a symbol of Cold War militancy and emblem of female chastity often tarnished her image for the young as the 1960s moved into high gear.[9]

Additional reforms, some legislated and some not, altered the texture of Catholic life in the wake of the council. The American bishops in 1966 ended the requirement that Catholics abstain from meat on Fridays and modified the rigorous fasting rules that governed Lent. The Eucharistic fast was eased as well. Catholics who wished to receive communion had once been required to fast from the previous midnight—a burden lightened by Pius XII, who in 1953 reduced the precommunion fast to a mere three hours. By further reducing the fast to one hour in 1964, the American bishops effectively ended a venerable Catholic tradition. The bishops did not intend to disparage either penance or spiritual discipline; their reforms were meant to encourage both frequent communion and a more interior attitude toward penitential practice. In lieu of Friday abstinence, the bishops urged Catholics to engage in a mode of devotion conducive to personal spiritual growth. Perhaps the bishops also sensed the waning power of episcopal mandates over a restive Catholic populace. They could do little about the spread of unauthorized liturgical practice, particularly when it proved popular. (The archbishop of Milwaukee in the mid-1960s embarked on a failing crusade to ban guitars and drums at Mass.) Nor could they force Catholic women to cover their heads in church—few were doing so by the early 1970s—or police consumption of popular culture. The Legion of Decency died a quiet death in dioceses around the country.[10]

Reform of the liturgy and changes like those in the rules about fasting were the principal means by which Catholics encountered the reforming logic of Vatican II. In some but not all dioceses, that logic was also apparent in a heightened concern among Catholic leaders for racial equality. Although the American bishops had condemned southern-style segregation as sinful in 1958, they had almost never addressed the manifold racial inequities evident in the North or indeed the segregative practice that even in the early 1960s could still be found in Catholic institutions. Many became more proactive, however, as the council proceeded and civil rights activism moved into the public spotlight. Catholic champions of the civil rights movement, whether bishops, priests, or laypeople, invariably invoked the council to justify their agenda. Had it not summoned Catholics to concern for the world and its manifold social ills? Northern civil rights activism, however, posed particular problems for Catholics, centering as it frequently did on segregation in housing. In a great many northern cities, the neighborhoods targeted for desegregation were heavily Catholic.

Catholics had for generations been taught to cleave to their own—to send their children to Catholic schools, support local Catholic institutions, and center their social lives on the parish. Pastors encouraged home ownership among their people to shore up the neighborhood's Catholic identity and continued parish vitality. When Catholics were mostly working class, moreover, even social Catholicism—support for unions, for example, or minimum-wage legislation—also seemed like care for one's own. But northern civil rights activism challenged Catholics to care for the mostly non-Catholic other, even at the expense of exclusively Catholic schools and communities. By the late 1960s, indeed, the parochial schools were being condemned by certain Catholic progressives as bastions of white privilege. "It is almost impossible in some [Catholic] circles to be a liberal on the subject of racial justice and poverty and be an advocate of aid to parochial schools," a Detroit woman noted in 1968, when public aid to sectarian schools was again an issue in Michigan politics. In many racially divided cities, the new social ethic was a far more serious source of intra-Catholic division than reform of the liturgy ever was.[11]

The Impact of Reform: The Laity

In the immediate aftermath of Vatican II, American Catholics were, for the most part, almost giddily optimistic. The new liturgy, still in the process of implementation, was generating excitement—at the very least, it was harder now to daydream during Mass—and the church itself appeared to be thriving. Vocations to the priesthood and religious life in much of Europe had been in decline even prior to the council, and anxieties were already rising there about a shortage of clergy. But seminary enrollments in the United States ticked upward during the council years, and at its close the number of priests and religious was greater than ever before. (Or, for that matter, ever since: priests' numbers peaked in 1965, those of women religious in 1966.) Weekly Mass attendance was holding strong, despite minor slippage since the late 1950s, and Catholics still went regularly to confession. Catholic schools enjoyed record enrollments—here too the peak was reached in the mid-1960s—while Catholic colleges, energized by the council's opening to the world, looked to update their curricula and strengthen their faculties. The vexing problem of contraception seemed close to resolution, given the continued existence of the papal birth-control commission. More than 60 percent of American Catholics, according to a 1965 Gallup poll, expected their church to change its teaching on birth control. Almost as many expected the change to occur within the next five years.[12]

The picture was strikingly different by the end of the 1960s. Weekly Mass attendance had declined significantly and by all indications would continue to do so. Only half of American Catholics in 1974 attended Mass every Sunday, according to a study directed by Andrew Greeley—a 20 percent decline since 1963. A similar drop was reported in the practice of monthly confession. Fully 30 percent of those who were polled in 1974 "seldom or never" availed themselves of the sacrament. Startling numbers of priests had asked to be laicized, which, coupled with a collapse in seminary enrollments, foretold a critical shortage of clergy. Women religious were abandoning their vocations in even larger numbers, with swift and deleterious impact on Catholic schools, many of which would soon be closing. The birth-control problem had indeed been resolved, but in the worst possible manner. After Pope Paul reaffirmed the traditional teaching in 1968, most American Catholics simply ignored him—bolstered, presumably, by the storm of protest that greeted *Humanae Vitae*. "It is likely to be a very long time before the church recaptures any kind of credibility in terms of sexual morality," Andrew Greeley opined in 1972. Most of his clerical colleagues sensed that he was right.[13]

The suddenness of this seeming collapse caused certain Catholics to blame the council. Had it not happened, they seemed to think, the American church would still be in a state of robust health. There are plentiful reasons to doubt this, however. The preconciliar church in the United States, incontestably vital, was largely a subcultural phenomenon. But for all their subcultural rhetoric, suburban Catholics in the 1950s had at least one foot in the secular world that had been so good to them. With their children attending non-Catholic colleges in unprecedented numbers, the next generation was even more likely to move with ease in the cultural mainstream, absorb its values, and acquire non-Catholic friends and spouses. Not surprisingly, the decline in Catholic observance in the postcouncil years was most pronounced among the young. Unbeknownst to themselves, American Catholics on the eve of the council were already in the throes of change, as Patty Crowley's story suggests. The council arguably accelerated the subcultural implosion that followed. But it was not the cause. Had the council never happened, the cultural ferment of the 1960s might plausibly have had the same effect, especially on the young.

Certainly it made a difference that the council's reforms were introduced just as that cultural ferment was intensifying. The pace and direction of Catholic change were inevitably affected. Consider the alterations that took place in Catholic minds and hearts with regard to matters of sin and authority. Catholics prior to the council had not always agreed with their church when it came to certain hard teachings, as their priests and bishops certainly knew. A slight majority, according to a 1952 poll, thought marital contraception was not invariably sinful; almost as many said the same about remarriage after divorce. Context and motivation mattered, or so many Catholics seemed to think. But their behavior suggests that such Catholics accepted their church's authority even when it came to hard teachings. They regularly confessed their sins, including behavior they might think justified, while Catholics who used contraceptives nearly always refrained from receiving communion. "If there is one thing our religious educations have taught us," in the words of a Catholic college professor, "it is the conviction of sin." Remarried Catholics, for their part, assumed that they were out of the church, annulments being in those days nearly impossible to secure.

Their friends and relatives did not disagree, sometimes refusing to socialize with a couple now branded as "public sinners."[14]

Attitudes changed gradually after the council, albeit more swiftly among the young. Priests increasingly told hard-pressed married penitents to consult their consciences with regard to birth control, advice that might plausibly be applied to other areas of moral decision-making. *Humanae Vitae* raised the stakes, and change accelerated thereafter. Following one's conscience postencyclical meant opting for moral autonomy, which growing numbers were ready to do. By the mid-1970s, Catholic contraceptive use was rapidly approaching the American norm. Many fewer Catholics by then were going regularly to confession; those who did, by all accounts, seldom mentioned contraception. Indeed, the subject virtually disappeared from Catholic discourse—from theological journals, popular periodicals, episcopal pronouncements, and sermons of every variety. Birth control, in effect, had been tacitly ceded to the private choices of the laity. Given the prevailing sexual climate, it is hardly surprising that young Catholics should claim the right to decide for themselves when it came to premarital sex or that the unhappily married should do so with regard to remarriage after divorce. By the early 1970s, some priests were prepared to preside at such marriages when annulment procedures in their dioceses were, in their view, being liberalized too slowly.[15]

Catholic attitudes on sex and authority had changed profoundly by the mid-1970s, as neatly illustrated by polls conducted with a similar Catholic sample in 1963 and again in 1974. While 74 percent of those polled in 1963 thought premarital sex was always wrong, 35 percent were of this opinion in 1974—a change most evident among the young but found in every age group. Only 32 percent in 1974 thought that the pope was "infallible." It had not occurred to the pollsters to ask such a question in 1963. Perhaps most startling, fully 72 percent queried in 1974 thought that abortion should be legal if the child would be born with a serious handicap—this at a time of fevered episcopal rhetoric against the recent Supreme Court decision in *Roe v Wade*. Here too was a question the earlier pollsters had not thought worth asking. The same was true when it came to asking whether missing Sunday Mass was a sin—hardly a matter of contention in 1963. But 53 percent of those responding in 1974 said that it was not. Many were probably young adults, whose Mass attendance was apt to be spotty. But change was also found among older Catholics, reflecting in part the reluctance of parents to brand as sinners their own disaffected offspring. Later polls, rephrasing this particular question, found majority support for the notion that one could be a "good Catholic" without regularly attending Mass.[16]

Accompanying these changes, and indeed undergirding them, was the evident disappearance of hell, perhaps the most striking of postcouncil developments. Although mission preachers in the 1950s sometimes reported complaints about graphic sermons on hellfire, the doctrine itself was not publicly challenged. It featured in standard catechisms and in the ubiquitous talk about mortal sin—sin that severed one's connection to God and that, if not sincerely repented, would send one to hell for eternity. In an era of frequent confession, the list of such sins grew ever longer. Murder was a mortal sin—that was self-evident. But so was birth control, even in difficult marital circumstances, and the willful consumption of meat on Friday, even in the form of a meat-based broth. In the wake of the council, however, the term "mortal sin" fell rapidly into disuse—*Humanae Vitae* does not invoke it—and Catholics, including the clergy, also ceased for the most part to talk about hell and seemingly to fear it. In the broadest sense, Catholics were belatedly moving, as most Protestants had long since done, toward what we might call a humane understanding of God—a God, in the Catholic case, who embodied the qualities hitherto associated mainly with the Virgin Mary. But purely Catholic developments played a role as well. The culture of fear that permeated preconciliar Catholicism was almost bound to elicit a backlash as Catholics rose in educational attainment and social standing.[17]

Although the church was roiled by change well into the 1970s, it was not without signs of vitality. The worst of the turmoil appeared to be over by the final years of the decade, when many fewer priests were resigning and the decline in Mass attendance ebbed and then stabilized, albeit temporarily. New religious movements had surfaced, an apparent response to what some were calling a "piety void" occasioned by the abrupt decline in traditional devotions. Most startling, from a Catholic perspective, was the Charismatic Movement, which emerged more or less simultaneously in 1967 at Notre Dame, at Duquesne University, and in Ann Arbor—home to the University of Michigan. The movement's lay leaders, all of them men, had earlier been active in the Cursillo—a lay retreat movement, imported from Spain, that made its first inroads in the United States among Spanish-speaking Catholics in the 1950s. Like its various Catholic Action predecessors, Cursillo promoted both personal holiness and an active role for the laity in the church and world. The Charismatic Movement was similarly focused on personal holiness and thoroughly lay in its ethos and leadership. But it differed from previous lay movements in some unprecedented ways. The movement's more esoteric practices included speaking in tongues—a biblical gift of the Holy Spirit encouraged in Pentecostal churches but hitherto alien to Catholicism—along with healing and prophecy. Many charismatic groups also included non-Catholic participants, some of whom may have strengthened in parts of the movement an obsession with an imminent end of the world.[18]

The success of the movement, which quickly moved beyond college venues, excited many Catholic observers, even as it unnerved others. The spiritual ardor of these mostly young Catholics stood in sharp contrast to the growing disaffection of their Catholic contemporaries. For precisely this reason, most American bishops lent the movement at least cautious support. Certain priests and religious supported it too, often having found in the movement new life for their vocations. Belgium's Cardinal Leo Suenens, a voice for reform at Vatican II, was the movement's most famous convert, saying Mass for a global gathering of Catholic charismatics in Rome in 1975, when St. Peter's Basilica rang with the unaccustomed sounds of glossolalia. But the movement's ecumenism worried most bishops, who feared that its Catholic members might eventually drift from the church. Self-styled progressive Catholics, including priests and women religious, decried the movement's insistence on male leadership and what they often saw as its authoritarian tendencies. Nor did they like its inward focus: impressively charitable to their own, charismatics generally held aloof from movements for social reform.

The Charismatic Movement was but one sign of widespread spiritual hunger in the wake of the council. For its adherents, the movement provided not only certitude—something they seemed not to find in a church in the throes of a seismic upheaval—but also the experience of community. Full commitment to the movement immersed the believer in a world even more encompassing than the Catholic subculture at its zenith. Similar hungers were also evident in a variety of widely disparate developments: Catholic traditionalism, a mostly fringe movement to restore the Latin Mass; the House of Prayer movement among women religious; and a new interest among the laity in contemplative prayer. Catholic feminism had a strong spiritual component, perhaps especially among women religious, and underwrote for its adherents a firm sense of communal solidarity and purpose. The same was true of Catholic movements for peace and social justice, including quickened Catholic activism around the issue of abortion. One might even see lay enthusiasm for participation in diocesan synods, which many bishops convened postcouncil, as rooted in part in a thirst for community.

Developments like these unleashed new energies in the church, even as they signaled a decline in Catholic cohesion. Both phenomena were poignantly evident at the massive Call to Action Conference that assembled in Detroit in 1976. The event was the culmination of a two-year process of consultation among Catholics across the country on the council's call for Christian action in a troubled world. How might the American church best fulfill this mandate? The bishops themselves had inaugurated the project, without doubt the most remarkable experiment of its kind in the history of American Catholicism. Rightly called "the first national assembly of the American Catholic community," the conference was attended by some thirteen hundred delegates, including more than one hundred bishops, a number of priests and women religious, and a lay majority— most of them chosen by local bishops or their surrogates—from a wide range of dioceses and Catholic organizations. After three days of impassioned debate, the conference approved position papers on topics as varied as "church," "family," "nationhood," and "humankind." These were forwarded to the National Conference of Catholic Bishops for subsequent action.[19]

Call to Action was decidedly progressive with regard to social policy, calling for a guaranteed income, universal health care, and, most controversially, unilateral nuclear disarmament by the United States. It also endorsed the Equal Rights Amendment and other legislation to protect women's rights. (That such rights at this juncture did not necessarily include abortion is indicated by the delegates' additional endorsement of a constitutional amendment protecting fetal life from the moment of conception.) Many bishops regarded at least some of these measures as unwise and potentially divisive, although most could recognize their roots in recent iterations of Catholic social teaching. Far more troubling for a great many bishops were conference calls for reform of the church. Among other things, the delegates endorsed a reevaluation of church teaching on mandatory clerical celibacy, homosexuality, and women's ordination. The mostly lay delegates had no right to trespass on such sensitive ecclesial turf, in the view of nearly every bishop, many of whom regarded the ban on women's ordination as rooted in doctrine rather than law.

In the wake of the Call to Action Conference, many bishops were apparently prepared to issue a testy rejoinder to its recommendations. They were dissuaded from doing so by Detroit's Cardinal John Dearden, under whose auspices Call to Action had assembled. The conclusions to which the group had come mattered less, Dearden argued, than the process of consultation and dialogue that the entire project had embodied—a process he regarded as "theologically inspired." Call to Action had been "a hope-filled experience for so many," he noted, pleading with his episcopal brethren to refrain from dashing those hopes and increasing lay alienation. Dearden won a limited victory: rather than issuing a denunciatory statement, the bishops mustered a coolly polite response—and then proceeded to distance themselves from Call to Action and the consultative mode it represented. The estrangement intensified as time went on. Dearden himself retired in 1980, after which year the American hierarchy grew gradually more conservative.[20]

Critics at the time contended that the Call to Action delegates had not been representative Catholics, which was undoubtedly true. Active in the church and their local communities, they were atypical almost by definition—but also the kinds of people no voluntary organization can do without. Nor were they wholly unrepresentative when it came to their calls for reform. A great many Catholics certainly disagreed with Call to Action's social agenda, as signaled by a conservative turn in recent Catholic voting patterns. But surprising numbers would soon be on board for ending mandatory priestly celibacy and even the ordination of women—both positions with majority lay support by the early 1990s. Many so-called ordinary Catholics also favored a more consultative mode in the exercise of church authority, especially at the parish and diocesan levels. In the aftermath of the conference, progressive Catholics and those of a conservative bent moved more than ever in separate organizational worlds, from which perspective mutual demonization was distressingly easy. Would continued intra-Catholic dialogue have lessened the resulting polarization? Given the size and heterogeneity of the Catholic population, it seems unlikely. But the situation was sufficiently painful, especially for the vast Catholic "middle," that the bishops' withdrawal from the fray looks in retrospect to have been decidedly unpastoral.

Crisis in the Clergy

The reforms of the Second Vatican Council upended the lives of even the youngest priests. A man ordained in 1963 would have spent untold seminary hours learning the rubrics of the Latin Mass and absorbing a moral theology still officially unquestioned but already under challenge by growing numbers of lay Catholics. Unless his was a highly unusual seminary, he probably came to ordination with only the most limited exposure to contemporary Scripture scholarship and minimal training in homiletics. Our 1963 ordinand was almost certainly excited by the council and the expansive role it envisioned for the church in the modern world. But in nearly all the more populous dioceses, he looked ahead to a priestly career in which his own capacity for action would be limited by more than two decades of parish assistantship—still a position, postcouncil, with almost no rights in canon law. His career, in short, would look very different from that of the many lay professionals with whom he was apt to have contact in the usual round of parish life. And although most American seminaries had undergone modest reform, he was still apt to have been socialized into a rather remote persona, allegedly useful for dealing with women but of dubious value in postcouncil circumstances.

Within three years of our young priest's ordination, he would be saying the Mass primarily in English and facing the congregation—something that placed a premium on the celebrant's ability to project sincerity and warmth. He would be expected to preach intelligent homilies on the day's Scripture readings. He could anticipate that at least some of his penitents would challenge his counsel in confession, particularly if he tried to uphold the ban on marital contraception. And he would surely have noticed that the lines for confession were growing shorter. Most priests, according to a 1964 survey, thought that hearing confessions was the aspect of priestly life for which they had been best prepared. The near collapse of the sacrament—for such was the state of affairs by the early 1970s—robbed many priests of a comforting sense of competence. Given the large size of most Catholic parishes, moreover, it was probably true, as a Jesuit claimed in 1965, that for most Catholics "confession is the only personal contact with a priest." That reality could be terribly sobering for a conscientious cleric. If confession was really "on its way out," asked a young priest from Syracuse in 1968, "How am I valuable to people? What is my role, my identity in the world?"[21]

Younger priests, not surprisingly, tended to be the most adept at negotiating change. Older men, in the words of a Chicago observer, were often
"confused and threatened by the changes in scripture, new formulations of
dogma and the new approaches to moral questions." But it was young
priests in the postcouncil years who seemed the most aggrieved, at least in
their public discourse. Their initial complaints had to do with problems of
long standing: the unnaturally long years of assistantship and resulting tensions in the rectory. The council does seem to have made a difference:
younger priests in its wake were more willing than ever before to articulate
these grievances publicly and raise them to principled status. As the various
dioceses began to establish priests' senates in the mid-1960s and after—
these were consultative bodies authorized by the council as a means of enhancing cooperation between priests and their bishops—their younger
members urged such reforms as the establishment of diocesan personnel
boards, a mandatory retirement age, enhanced financial compensation, and
greater personal freedom when it came to dress and residence. In many dioceses, genuine reform did occur. Priests by the early 1970s were generally
more equitably compensated than hitherto and often had greater control
over their assignments, while certain curmudgeonly pastors had been eased
into retirement.[22]

Even generous moves toward reform, however, failed to stanch the
flood of priestly grievance, at least among the young. By 1966 and increasingly thereafter, many younger priests were complaining that their lives
were meaningless to others and disappointing to themselves. "A growing
multitude of priests feel terribly frustrated, ineffective, and irrelevant," in
the words of a Chicago priests' group in 1969. "They see so many of their
activities and organizations as belonging to a ghetto Church which no longer exists, they see less people coming to confession, to counseling, to parish
activities." Most young priests had been raised in a world that, at least on
the surface, was a "ghetto" of sorts, where the role of the priest was clearly
defined. Insofar as the council accelerated subcultural collapse, it helps to
explain the anguish just articulated. "In some ways, I envy older priests," as
a young Dominican in 1966 articulated his sense of ominously changing
times. "I think that they are surer of themselves than those of us ordained
in the last ten or twelve years. There is more peace in them, more solidity to
them. They are less mixed up, personally and theologically." If this priest
was romanticizing the mood of his elders, who also felt battered by the pace

and direction of change, he was right to see the younger clergy as peculiarly
prey to demoralization, if only because of their sensitivity to cultural change
among their generational peers.[23]

The council also spoke in near-heroic terms when it came to Christian
life in the world, a perspective magnified on the American scene by the heroism evident in a civil rights movement that prior to the mid-1960s had obvious religious roots. The escalating war in Vietnam and the rise of a national
peace movement posed serious moral challenges too. Few priests were prepared to imitate the nationally famous Berrigan brothers—Daniel, a Jesuit,
and Philip, a Josephite—whose antiwar civil disobedience ultimately led to
long prison sentences. Nor did they flock to picket lines in the California
vineyards, where Cesar Chavez's United Farm Workers led a movement of
impoverished laborers who marched beneath the banner of the Virgin of
Guadalupe. Like most Americans, most priests watched the period's political
battles from the sidelines, sometimes for reasons of diocesan discipline but
often as well for reasons of temperament. Significant numbers were nonetheless troubled by what they saw as the decidedly unheroic nature of most
parish ministry. Given the prevailing climate, it was not hard to feel that
Christian witness at its most compelling nearly always took place outside the
sanctuary. "The meaning of priesthood is what is most at issue today," as a
Brooklyn seminary professor described his students in 1971. "Many leave because they see no meaning in it. They seek another life in an effort to do
something really helpful toward solving the needs of men."[24]

Mandatory celibacy was increasingly an issue as well. Even in the mid-
1960s, a majority of younger men believed that priests should be free to
marry. The requirement of celibacy was rooted in an unhealthy view of sex,
according to the usual argument. "The current emphasis on the sanctity of
sex makes it impossible to defend celibacy as a negation of something tainted or not quite pure," in the words of a young priest from Washington State.
It distanced the priest from the people he served and promoted ungenerous
habits. "I believe many priests would be less selfish and egotistical if they
had a family to share their immediate attention and distract them from
self," in the words of another clerical advocate. Above all else, celibacy meant
that priestly life was often intolerably lonely—a problem exacerbated by
rising rectory tensions and the era's blithe celebration of intimacy as the
highest good. By the end of the 1960s, a significant minority of young priests
were dating, despite the pope's having recently reaffirmed the celibacy re-

Priests demonstrating in support of the 1964 Civil Rights Act, then pending in
Congress, at Catholic University (Courtesy of the American Catholic History
Research Center and University Archives [ACUA], the Catholic University of
America, Washington, DC)

quirement for ordination. By that time, it is fair to say, celibacy had come
for a great many priests to stand for a more fundamental grievance—a
sense that their lives were wholly controlled by distant and often indifferent
superiors.[25]

In the circumstances, it is hardly surprising that resignations from the
priesthood began to rise in the mid-1960s, with the rate accelerating in
most dioceses at the very end of the decade. By 1975, as many as 10 percent
of all priests in the United States had left the active ministry. Most who left

were younger men, many of whom subsequently married. (It was not inordinately difficult under Pope Paul VI for such men to be dispensed from their vows of celibacy.) The departures were deeply unnerving to those who remained, although attitudes toward the men who departed often varied sharply by age. Younger priests generally regarded them as victims of the hierarchy's unhealthy obsession with celibacy; older priests were more inclined to see them as unscrupulous defectors. Assisting such men financially, as Detroit's Cardinal Dearden was wont to do, struck a group of older priests in his diocese as akin "to asking our people to subsidize married men who desert their wives and families." The departures were devastating to lay Catholics, even those who were partisans of radical reform. There had always been priests who abandoned the ministry, as most of the laity knew. But never before had the numbers been remotely as large as those in the postcouncil years, and never before had priests left so publicly or justified their departure on principled grounds.[26]

Coupled with a sudden collapse in seminary enrollments, the wave of departures led in short order to a shortage of priests in a great many dioceses. A single priest might now be in charge of a parish with as many as fifteen hundred families. Many priests by the mid-1970s were complaining of burnout, the consequence of too much work and often too little by way of results. "Priests are quite aware of declining mass attendance and of the numbers of alienated Catholics around them," a priest from the Diocese of Lansing pointed out in 1976. "This adds to the sense of powerlessness and defeat." Most priests remained committed to the priesthood—clerical departures diminished quite sharply in the latter half of the 1970s—and many found joy in their vocations. But an exhausted man might find it hard to communicate his joy to others. A substantial majority of priests, according to several surveys, had ceased by the early 1970s to promote vocations among the young. Even deeply committed priests, it seems, could regard contemporary priesthood as too heavy a burden to impose on untried youngsters, no matter how pious or gifted.[27]

As the clergy shortage grew more acute, new forms of parish ministry came into being. The Second Vatican Council had authorized restoration of the office of permanent deacon, an order known in the early church. Permanent deacons, who like priests were ordained, could preach, baptize, witness marriages, and preside at graveside prayer ceremonies. Unlike priests, deacons could be married at the time of ordination. Should a deacon's wife die, however, he was not permitted to marry again—something most council fathers thought necessary to safeguard clerical celibacy. The American bishops gave generous support to the permanent diaconate, authorizing its restoration domestically in 1968. Seven deacons were ordained in 1970; there were more than twelve thousand serving nationwide by 1998. Their numbers continue to grow: the American church has long led the world when it comes to employment of permanent deacons. Over the course of the 1970s, moreover, permanent deacons were joined in a growing number of parishes by lay parish ministers—men and women, but usually the latter, who ran catechetical programs, served as counselors and administrators, and assisted an overburdened clergy in any way they could. Their numbers grew exponentially in subsequent decades, as the clergy shortage worsened. By the turn of the twenty-first century, lay parish ministers—some 80 percent of whom were women—substantially outnumbered the priests who remained in active ministry.[28]

Older priests sometimes argued that defections from the priestly ranks were triggered by crises of faith. Radically dissatisfied priests, in other words, had simply ceased to believe. Some men who left the active ministry did eventually leave the church. But the great majority did not. Many, in fact, hoped to serve again as priests once mandatory celibacy had been abolished. Still, Catholic belief in the postcouncil years lost many of its external supports, which affected priests as well as laypeople and perhaps especially those priests who were young enough to move to a new profession. Boys in the 1950s and even the early 1960s typically entered seminary in adolescence, usually after having attended none but Catholic schools. There was ample communal support for their faith, which, sincere though that faith may have been, was apt to be corporate as well as personal. In the aftermath of the council, such communal support eroded with astonishing speed, as newly assertive lay Catholics challenged certain of their church's teachings and priests and religious openly questioned the value of their ministries. "Faith may very well be a problem for many of us," Andrew Greeley acknowledged in 1972, eighteen years after his own ordination, "not in the sense that we reject explicit doctrinal formulations but in the sense that we find it hard to shift in the middle years of life from an externally supported faith to an internally committed faith." Men who accomplished the transition could be radiant examples of Christian commitment. But the journey was apt to be lonely.[29]

Sisters: Called to Be Leaven

The council fathers called on the world's religious orders to adapt "to the changed conditions of our times" by returning to both the sources of Christian tradition and the inspiration of their founders. What this meant in practice was left of necessity to the orders themselves. Among women religious in the United States, who thanks to the work of the Sister Formation Conference were probably the world's best educated, the council's injunction led in short order to far-reaching moves toward reform. In the five years after the council's close, nearly every community of active religious debated such changes as modifying the habit, liberalizing the rules of enclosure, and broadening the order's understanding of ministry. Most orders endorsed an updated habit for those sisters who preferred it—typically a skirt of modest length, along with a jacket and shoulder-length veil. A few went further, with the Sisters of Loretto being the first to abandon the habit altogether. Rules of enclosure were relaxed, with sisters now permitted to drive, visit family— most orders had hitherto limited such visits to funerals—and travel on their own. Most consequentially, at least for Catholic education, numerous orders granted sisters new freedom when it came to deciding what work to perform. Growing numbers soon opted for ministries other than teaching, historically the principal task of American sisters. In 1966, almost 64 percent of all professed sisters were teachers or school administrators; that figure had fallen to just under 30 percent by 1980.[30]

Reform divided sisters in virtually every community. "Young sisters cried in rage after every meeting," one veteran of the wars remembered. "Older ones sank deeper and deeper into depression. The middle-aged agonized over the future." Growing numbers of sisters left, with departures ticking upward in 1965 and reaching a peak around 1970. By 1982, there were 30 percent fewer sisters than in 1966—a decline far greater than that among the clergy—and those who remained were graying. Only 17 percent of sisters were older than age sixty-five in 1966; by 1982, 38 percent qualified as senior citizens. As with priests, the greatest long-term damage was done by a radical decline in entrants to formation programs. Those who left were drawn disproportionately from the ranks of the best educated, and many were young. Some left to marry, with the intended in a good many cases being a priest who had left the active ministry. Others cited frustration with the slow pace of reform. Still others, often middle-aged, found religious life intolerable without the support of traditional structures. A well-educated sister in middle life was eminently employable in the world and could nearly always support herself comfortably.[31]

Sisters who remained embarked on a variety of new ministries, many directed toward social justice. Civil rights activism was often the spark. When a handful of sisters, still in full habit, marched in Selma, Alabama, in 1965, the televised footage electrified Catholics throughout the nation, including many women religious. Growing numbers of women religious subsequently volunteered for service projects in black neighborhoods, ranging from summer tutoring programs to friendly visiting and social work. One such experiment was Project Community, inaugurated in Detroit in 1966. That program brought sisters from several orders for a summer's residence on the city's impoverished near-east side, a once Polish neighborhood now home primarily to African Americans. Although they hoped that their training as teachers might prove useful to their needy neighbors, the sisters arrived without an agenda other than simply being present. They thereby anticipated what Benedictine Joan Chittister later described as the essence of her postcouncil vocation: "the new vision says that religious are not called to be a labor force but a leaven: a caring, calling presence that moves quickly into new needs."[32]

As was often the case with such ventures, Project Community had transformative effects on its sister-participants. The sisters used their bodies more freely as local children demanded hugs and kisses. By opening up their place of residence to those in need, including a young parolee from the local women's jail, they embraced a less restrictive common life. "She really is a good girl—and her staying with us is as good for us as it is for her," one sister wrote of their unexpected guest. "*So much of our traditional 'convent mentality' is breaking down, thank God!*" Encouraged by a sympathetic priest, the sisters embarked on their own version of liturgical reform, singing folk hymns at Mass, engaging the priest-homilist in dialogue, and holding a communal penance service. Perhaps most important, they lived for the first time in their lives surrounded by non-Catholics, whose spiritual resources they came to admire. Project Community staged a farewell gathering in August for a group of older neighborhood residents to whom many of the sisters had become attached. Toward the end of the afternoon, a guest named Louise Finch asked if she might say a few words, since she had to leave soon to preach at a local church. "She spoke of the love she has for the Sisters who have been

present these weeks and who have been so lovingly helpful to all the neighbors," one sister recorded. "And then she commented on the need for all of us
Christians to love one another in the Spirit of Christ." Resplendent in a "long,
flowing yellowed-white satin preaching robe," Finch especially impressed a
visiting sister who had recently come from a summer's study of theology:
"This woman *knows* St. Paul's doctrine on love!"[33]

The sisters from Project Community dispersed soon thereafter to
their convents and teaching assignments. Although their numbers were
small, they almost certainly wielded disproportionate influence on debates
in their orders about postcouncil renewal. The prestige that their service
had accrued to them almost guaranteed it, as did the altered view of the
world with which they returned. The most significant strand in their new
thinking was doubtless a nascent feminism. (The sisters who heard Finch
preach, after all, could not yet be lectors at Mass.) Not every sister became a
feminist, although sisters were a major presence in Catholic feminist movements as these evolved in the 1970s. Indeed, the 1975 organizational meeting
of what became the Women's Ordination Conference was attended primarily by women religious. But every order was affected by feminist convic-
tions, which emboldened at least some of their members when it came to
redefining ministry. Sisters by the late 1960s were training in fields like law,
medicine, and theology, frequently at secular institutions. They worked as
immigration attorneys and physicians in public health clinics. Some served
on the faculties of non-Catholic universities, while others worked as spiritual directors, occasionally giving retreats to priests. They pushed the
boundaries of Catholic theology by pioneering outreach to homosexuals
and enlarged the notion of Christian service to include political action.
Network, a grassroots organization devoted to lobbying for various progressive causes, was organized by women religious in 1971.

By the early 1970s, sisters were also serving in significant numbers as
lay parish ministers. Nearly all who served in this capacity expected to work
as part of a pastoral team—a concept initially resisted by many priests but
to which their diminishing numbers could hardly offer long-term resistance. Rooted in the parish, such sisters could witness firsthand the effects
of widespread parochial-school closings, for that was a principal consequence of change among women religious. The rising costs of education,
coupled with sisters' departures from the teaching ranks, made schools too
expensive for growing numbers of parishes. The number of Catholic

schools nationally decreased by 24 percent between 1965 and 1975, while enrollment fell even more dramatically—by 35 percent. Many pastors were secretly relieved to be out of the business of running a school, although a school's closing nearly always weakened a parish's social fabric, which was hardly beneficial to priestly morale. Parents, by contrast, were often distressed. Although lay Catholics had experienced a sea change when it came to their thinking about sexual morality, support for Catholic schools had not wavered in the postcouncil decade. Parents undoubtedly knew intuitively what a 1966 study had demonstrated: that Catholic schools were a major assist in raising religiously committed offspring.[34]

Many women's religious orders also ran colleges, significant numbers of which were founded after the Second World War. Not all of these schools were accredited, and most had little or nothing by way of endowment; it was the close-to-free labor of their sister-faculty that had enabled them to survive. These schools too eventually suffered from decline in the numbers of women religious, although college teaching was often more attractive to well-educated sisters than teaching in the parish schools. A more immediate blow arrived with the advent of coeducation at Catholic colleges for men. Both Notre Dame and the College of the Holy Cross admitted women in 1972, while Georgetown was fully coeducational as of 1969. The new option had almost immediate impact on enrollment at Catholic women's colleges, many of which eventually responded by admitting men. That response was not always sufficient: significant numbers of the weaker schools run by women religious had ceased to exist by the end of the century. An increasingly affluent Catholic populace did not necessarily miss them, given a dramatic increase in the 1960s and after in Catholic enrollment at elite secular universities.[35]

Those sister-run colleges that survived often retooled themselves to accommodate disadvantaged minorities, with particular attention given to women returning to college in midlife. Trinity College—now University—in Washington, DC, is a prime example. Long a favored institution for the daughters of affluent Catholic families, Trinity's enrollment suffered severely due to competition from nearby Georgetown. Looking to survive, the school reinvented itself over the course of the 1980s to serve as an engine of upward mobility for less-than-affluent Washington residents and especially the women among them. Trinity's College of Arts and Letters—essentially the Trinity of old—remains single sex, although its graduate and professional programs are open to men. Still under the sponsorship of the

Sisters of Notre Dame de Namur, the school received a lay president in 1989 and today serves a mostly non-Catholic student body. Rather than identifying as a Catholic school, Trinity now presents itself as an institution supportive of faith where students of all creeds are welcome.

Today's Trinity could be said to exemplify the transformation of women's religious life since the council. Like many sisters today, Trinity defines its purpose in terms of social justice. It does not court well-to-do Catholic students, although they would surely be welcome. Its principal goal is to serve those long excluded from affluence by institutional racism—a goal that most sisters today regard as profoundly Christian. A sister's vocation, in their view, cannot be defined by the needs of Catholics alone, especially given the affluent cast of the Euro-American Catholic population. Sisters must minister instead to the world's most needy and oppressed, even when that ministry means that a sister might have to live apart from her community. "Religious life is, like any Christian vocation, a state of search: open, listening, changing, growing, not a checklist of ministries, schedules and spiritual devotions," in the words of Joan Chittister. Once defined by a norm of rigorous obedience, women religious after the council emerged as startlingly self-directed.[36]

Many Catholics today admire sisters for their independence and social justice commitments. But hardly any have opted to join the communities that formed them. Women religious have continued to age—the median age in many orders is now north of seventy—and fewer and fewer are available for full-time work. The demographics alone could dissuade a would-be entrant. But the near collapse of support for vowed religious life, both institutional and ideological, might be even more daunting. The erosion of traditional community life in most orders—a significant minority of sisters in recent decades have lived alone or with a roommate—places a heavy burden on the individual to generate meaning and initiative as she goes about her work. Would-be entrants "want to be part of something that sustains them," according to Sister Catherine Bertrand, head of the National Religious Vocations Conference, speaking in 1993. "And that's not [provided by] independent living." Indeed, the only orders in recent years that have reliably drawn new members have been contemplative communities or the handful of those, mostly devoted to teaching, that have retained a traditional communal life.[37]

Many women's communities today face the very real prospect of dissolution in the not-too-distant future, which places a further premium on their members' possessing a high degree of psychic maturity. "When one has to live a life that may not live on in the next generation," explains Janet Ruffing, a Sister of Mercy, "the validation all has to come from inside." Given the outsized role played by sisters in the history of American Catholicism, their near disappearance is arguably the single most powerful signal that this history has passed through a period of fundamental reorientation. Not only did sisters make possible the institutional matrix that kept Catholics separate from other Americans, thereby enabling a Catholic subculture to flourish for several generations. But sisters also modeled, and thus reinforced, an ethic of eschatologically oriented self-renunciation that increasingly distinguished American Catholics from their Protestant fellow citizens. Since Vatican II, growing numbers of sisters have challenged Catholics to a new mode of selflessness—to care for the poor and dispossessed regardless of race or creed. Can this challenge survive sisters' near disappearance? If it does not, we will all be the poorer.[38]

Two Milestones

Two political developments in the postcouncil decade must be noted here, for they have shaped the contours of American Catholic history up until the present. The first was a major reform of American immigration law in 1965. The 1965 law, rightly understood as an achievement of the civil rights era, ended the national-origins quota system set in place in 1924 and had the effect of significantly raising the ceiling on legal immigration. To the surprise of its framers, who assumed that the law would stimulate new immigration from southern and eastern Europe, its principal beneficiaries were immigrants from Asia and Latin America. Their arrival in growing numbers ushered in a new chapter in the nation's immigration history and that of the Catholic Church. A significant minority of the Asian entrants were Catholic, given the influx from war-torn Vietnam. So were most of those from Central and South America and the Spanish-speaking Caribbean, along with the Mexicans who at the time of the act constituted nearly all the Hispanic population resident in the United States. Since the 1965 act also imposed, for the very first time, a numerical quota for immigrants from the Western Hemisphere, growing numbers of those Latin arrivals would be undocumented.

Quickened immigration in the 1970s and after shored up American Catholic numbers—a gift, indeed, in light of the growing rate of defections from the church and declining birthrates among the native-born. Were it not for immigration, Catholics in the twenty-first century would no longer constitute just under a quarter of the nation's population. It also brought new energy and devotional vigor to a church in danger of losing its sense of identity and connection to the past. Our Lady of Guadalupe, mother to the dispossessed, has enabled more than a few American Catholics to reappropriate a devotion to Mary from which they had become estranged. Immigration meant new challenges for a dwindling corps of clergy, thereby complicating an already serious problem. But the newcomers often revivified the vocational commitment of the priests who served them. Among the immigrant flow, moreover, were foreign-born priests and seminarians, who helped to shore up the priestly ranks in their new homeland. Roughly a quarter of Catholic seminarians in recent years have been born abroad, while foreign-born priests now make up a significant minority of the nation's Catholic clergy.

The second decisive event was *Roe v. Wade,* the Supreme Court decision that in 1973 legalized abortion in the United States. The decision capped a struggle of some years standing to liberalize the law of abortion at the state level—a struggle in which Catholic leaders orchestrated most of the opposition and in which they had recently enjoyed some success. A referendum in Michigan to reform the state's law had gone down to decisive defeat in 1972, just two months prior to *Roe,* although the state had a history of resistance to the demands of its Catholic minority. For the rest of the 1970s, opposition to *Roe* came mainly from Catholics, many of whom were distressed by what they saw as the ruling's extreme nature. (In western Europe, most nations still confine unrestricted access to abortion to the first trimester of pregnancy.) Given the logic of the ruling, most bishops saw no option but to press for a constitutional amendment establishing fetal personhood—a measure that, at least potentially, could prohibit all abortions. The effort was bound to be divisive. Catholic teaching on abortion— direct abortion is never permitted, no matter what the circumstances—may be admirably consistent. But it cannot serve as the basis of law in a society like ours. Even prior to *Roe,* after all, roughly a third of the states had already liberalized their law of abortion.[39]

The bishops' effort to overturn *Roe* by amending the Constitution never came close to succeeding. (Their lobbying was mainly carried out via the National Right to Life Committee, created in 1973 as an entity distinct from the church—something of a legal fiction.) Nor, as of this writing, have the various court challenges they have supported done substantive damage to the decision, despite a long-standing Republican majority on the nation's highest court. But the bishops' campaign did invigorate the pro-life movement among Catholics over the course of the 1970s—a movement, it should be noted, that was heavily female in its membership. Critics of *Roe* could then be found in both political parties. A number of Catholic Democrats were outspoken opponents of the decision, although their numbers dwindled as the decade wore on. The tide turned definitively in 1980, when the issue assumed an overtly partisan cast, with the Republican Party officially committed to overturning *Roe* and the Democrats committed to its protection. Allied with evangelicals, new recruits to the cause, Catholic antiabortion activists cast their fortunes with the Republican Party, even as it drifted right with regard to other social policies—a transition that was doubtless eased by growing white Catholic conservatism on a variety of domestic issues. A number of their coreligionists were deeply troubled by this development, in which they saw abandonment of Catholic social teaching and, for some, a disregard of women's fundamental rights. Already serious divisions among the nation's Catholics were in consequence exacerbated almost intolerably.[40]

F•O•U•R•T•E•E•N

Toward an Uncertain Future

No previous chapter in American Catholic history was ushered in by a papal election. But the election of John Paul II late in 1978, noteworthy as the year of three popes, did mark the beginning of something new. The newness had to do in part with changing Catholic demographics—a growing Hispanic presence and growth as well in the number of Catholics mostly or wholly formed by the postconciliar church. The man himself, however, played an indisputable role. When he was chosen to succeed John Paul I, who lived only a month after having succeeded the late Paul VI, Kraków's Cardinal Karol Wojtyła was a vigorous fifty-eight, relatively young for a pope. An ardent sportsman who skied, hiked, and kayaked, Wojtyła was also known as a poet, playwright, and actor, as well as an academic philosopher. Ebulliently masculine, he exuded magnetism. "His personality dominates," as theologian Yve Congar noted in a diary he kept during the Second Vatican Council. Since no non-Italian had served as pope in the previous 455 years, Wojtyła's election seemed to confirm the council's embrace of Catholicism's global diversity. That he had lived most of his life under totalitarian regimes strengthened his appeal as a man who had known firsthand many of the century's horrors.[1]

Perhaps most important, John Paul II was far and away the most visible pope in history. Previous popes had seldom or never traveled outside Italy; Paul VI was the first to come to the United States when he addressed the United Nations in 1965. But John Paul II made multiple extended visits

327

to each of the inhabited continents, where he was invariably greeted by massive crowds and vast popular excitement. His first "pilgrimage" to the United States—for so the pope called these extended visits—came in 1979, when he was greeted by adoring fans in Boston, New York, Philadelphia, Des Moines, Chicago, and even Washington, DC, never heavily Catholic, where the pope embraced President Jimmy Carter and said Mass on the National Mall. He made two subsequent American pilgrimages, in 1987 and 1995, in addition to three shorter visits, the most memorable of which occurred in 1993. That was the occasion of the Fourth International World Youth Day in Denver, when the pope said an outdoor Mass before an estimated five hundred thousand attendees, nearly all of them teens and young adults. Cherry Creek State Park rang with the now-familiar shouts of "JP II, we love you!" in what some in the media had taken to calling a "Catholic Woodstock."[2]

Despite living under a communist regime, then-Archbishop Wojtyła had managed to attend all four sessions of the Second Vatican Council, at each of which he spoke and presented written interventions. He regarded himself as a man of the council, not only as bishop but also as pope—a characterization supported by substantial evidence. John Paul was an ardent ecumenist who met and prayed with the leaders of various Protestant and Eastern Orthodox churches. He reached out to Jews and even Muslims and often reminded Catholics of the sins committed against Jews in twentieth-century Europe. He spoke eloquently about care for the poor, chiding the liberal West for its failures in this regard. His global travels, which placed growing burdens on a man who had nearly died from an assassin's bullet in 1981, demonstrated his awareness that the church was no longer defined by its long history in Europe. Even his linguistic prowess—the pope spoke eight languages fluently and had limited competence in several others—signaled respect for culture in all its diversity. A hero in his native Poland, he became an icon of human freedom as he championed the rights of those behind the Iron Curtain.

The pope had his critics, however, most of whom saw him as anything but a man of the council. His wholehearted support of *Humanae Vitae* was a neuralgic issue. During the first year of his papacy, John Paul initiated a four-year series of audience addresses on what he called the "theology of the body"—an abstruse but highly personalist discourse on the meaning of sexual differentiation and the physical language of love. The addresses were

Pope John Paul II at Catholic University in Washington, DC, 1979 (Courtesy of the American Catholic History Research Center and University Archives [ACUA], the Catholic University of America, Washington, DC)

philosophically demanding—too much so, surely, for their immediate audience—and what most Catholics doubtless heard was simply a reiteration of the prohibition on birth control. Given current rates of contraceptive practice among Catholics in the developed countries, this was bound to be divisive. The pope's affirmation in 1994 that Catholic doctrine forbade the ordination of women carried potential for division too. Most Catholic women did not feel called to the priesthood. But by the 1990s, feminism had made sufficient inroads in most Western nations that excluding women from a role or office simply on the basis of gender could easily seem immoral. John Paul had had to retreat, in 1980, from his effort to prohibit the use of girls as altar servers—a practice by then quite widespread in Europe and North America. The public outcry had been too strong. A reluctant Vatican gave its blessing to "altar girls" in 1994.

Other controversial papal initiatives mostly affected elites. The Vatican moved against several prominent theologians, most notably Hans Kung in 1979 and Charles Curran in 1986, stripping them of their right to teach on a Catholic theological faculty. Many academic theologians, an increasingly venturesome crew, felt threatened by the actions. Both Kung and Curran, moreover, were known to many educated Catholics, who generally appreciated their efforts to update Catholic moral theology. Curran's dismissal from Catholic University, indeed, was prompted mainly by his stance on birth control. The pope's imposition of a "personal delegate" to govern the worldwide Jesuit order in 1981 was similarly alarming to Catholic academics, given the prominent role played by Jesuits in Catholic education. For many Jesuits, the move was nearly as demoralizing as the 1773 suppression of the order by Pope Clement XIV, although the Jesuits were free, as of 1983, once again to choose their own superior general. John Paul's repeated insistence that abortion at any stage of pregnancy was among the greatest of crimes posed problems too, perhaps especially in the United States, where the issue was shrouded in rights talk. Here too, however, the impact fell most heavily on elites, in this case Catholic politicians, who had to wrestle publicly with the issue in all its complexity.

Notwithstanding his critics, John Paul was immensely popular among American Catholics, certainly in his most vigorous years but also toward the end of his life, when he was visibly impaired. Many young Catholics, not all of them regular Mass-goers, saw him as a beacon of faith and hope. Some saw in his "theology of the body" a potent response to the sexual chaos of the times, even those who ultimately discovered that they could not live by its particulars. Not a few Catholics, resigned to the realities of an imperfect world, still thrilled to his passionate defense of life at all stages. The priests ordained in the course of his papacy were frequently men in his image, committed to upholding papal authority, firm in their support of

Catholic sexual teaching, and seeing in priesthood a mode of witness enhanced by otherness in dress and liturgical conduct. (Most such priests, it
should be noted, were publicly silent in practice when it came to contraception, saving their fire for abortion and gay marriage.) The American bishops appointed by John Paul II were chosen principally for their fidelity to
Rome, particularly with regard to sexual teaching, clerical celibacy, and the
ordination of women, rather than their pastoral qualities. That bishops
were still being appointed with minimal local consultation was made easier
to swallow by the pope's popularity.[3]

The U.S. Church under John Paul II

The legacy of the pope's time in office—he died in 2005—was both increased polarization among Catholics and vibrant pockets of Catholic renewal. Generational tensions among the clergy continued unabated, with
the "JP II priests," as they liked to be called, finding fault with their elders as
insufficiently orthodox and their elders responding that these relative
youngsters were both psychologically insecure and insufficiently pastoral. A
striking number of JP II priests were ordained past the age of thirty, often
after a time of estrangement from the church. Some were even recent converts. The worsening priest shortage—too few priests were ordained during
John Paul's papacy to alleviate the problem—meant that many younger
priests became pastors within a few years of ordination. With far less firsthand experience of parish life than their elders had had prior to becoming
pastors, some JP II priests found it hard to deal with such grassroots realities as the irregular Sunday attendance of many Catholics, their frequent
indifference to confession, and dissenting views on sexual morality and
gender roles. Some found it difficult to work with women as equals, although most parishes depended heavily on female labor, either as volunteers or as poorly paid lay ministers. Unless a man possessed the charisma
of his papal model, tensions could easily result.[4]

The bishops were increasingly divided too, especially after the mid-
1980s. In the wake of Vatican II, the American bishops had slowly coalesced
into a national presence on both ecclesial and social matters, greatly aided
by the 1966 reorganization of what was now the National Conference of
Catholic Bishops / United States Catholic Conference, complete with an
expanded permanent staff. The bishops' antiabortion activism caused many

to perceive their conference as part of a right-wing resurgence nationally. But prior to the mid-1980s, the tenor of most episcopal pronouncements was decidedly progressive. Most notable were two pastoral letters: *The Challenge of Peace*, on nuclear policy and just-war theory, issued in 1983, and *Economic Justice for All*, issued in 1986. Both were the products of widespread consultation with lay and clerical experts. Both spoke to the nation as a whole, rather than to Catholics alone. And both were sharply critical of the Reagan administration, notwithstanding—in the case of the 1986 letter—Reagan's landslide reelection just two years before. Both letters challenged reigning political orthodoxies at a time of conservative dominance: that the use of nuclear weapons could be justified by the ends sought, that the market alone could produce an acceptable measure of economic security for all. No statements issued by the U.S. hierarchy had ever elicited such widespread notice and discussion.

By the close of the 1980s, however, the American bishops had backed away from such high-profile public statements, in part because of objections from Rome. They were also a less unified body than had been the case just a few years earlier, due to retirements and new appointments. JP II bishops, often theologically more conservative than their immediate predecessors, preferred to focus on their dioceses rather than broad collective initiatives. A few could be notably aggressive when it came to promoting particular papal agendas, even when these were divisive. Both New York's John O'Connor and Boston's Bernard Law—future cardinals who were appointed in 1984—criticized Geraldine Ferraro by name when she ran for vice president on the Democratic ticket in that same year as a supporter of abortion rights. As a Catholic, they insisted, Ferraro should not pretend that any diversity of opinion was possible with regard to church teaching on the issue. O'Connor went so far as to say that he did not see "how a Catholic in good conscience can vote for a candidate who explicitly supports abortion." None of his episcopal colleagues regarded abortion as anything but a grave moral wrong. The question was one of emphasis. Prior to the end of the 1980s, most bishops steered away from single-issue politics as unduly divisive.[5]

As episcopal unity eroded, however, single-issue politics seemed more and more to top the bishops' agenda. In part this was due to the media, quick to pounce when the bishops spoke to issues involving sex or gender but often less interested in their pronouncements on other areas of social policy. The behavior of certain prelates also played a role. JP II bishops tended toward a more confrontational approach to the world than had most of their immediate predecessors, which sometimes generated controversy. When a Catholic Democrat ran for president in 2004 as a supporter of abortion rights, several bishops announced that Senator John Kerry of Massachusetts was not free to receive communion in their dioceses. The contrast with 1960, when the bishops took care to seem scrupulously neutral, could hardly have been more pronounced. Peremptory gestures of this sort might even be directed at one's fellow bishops. When Chicago's Cardinal Joseph Bernardin in 1996 introduced an initiative aimed at promoting intra-Catholic dialogue and lessening Catholic polarization, it did not take certain of his confreres long to denounce the effort publicly. The Catholic Common Ground Initiative was but a few hours old when Boston's Cardinal Law dismissed it as a liberal smokescreen: "Dialogue as a way to mediate between the truth and dissent is mutual deception." He was echoed on the following day in even less charitable terms by Washington, DC's Cardinal James Hickey.[6]

Bishops invariably live at substantial remove from the people they serve. By the 1990s, however, most American bishops appeared to be more than usually isolated—one might say dangerously so. To many Catholics, their bishops seemed curiously fixated on abortion and gay marriage—both issues on which a substantial number of lay Catholics did not agree with their leaders. The bishops seemed strangely passive about the worsening shortage of clergy, which even in the 1980s was leading to churches being closed and forcing some priests to "ride circuit" among multiple parishes like their frontier forebears. Nor did they have much to say about mounting Catholic defections, evidence for which was plentiful by the turn of the twenty-first century. And as Catholics learned to their horror in 2002, some bishops had been criminally derelict with regard to priests who had sexually abused the young. The bishops' conference had, in fact, agreed on guidelines for addressing the problem back in 1993, in response to an earlier wave of reports about abusive priests. When scrupulously followed, those guidelines represented a significant first step toward protecting the young from abusers. But they were not made mandatory and were not universally adopted. Cardinal Law of Boson, where a second wave of sex-abuse scandals broke spectacularly in 2002, was reportedly one of the principal opponents of a mandatory policy.[7]

If the sex-abuse scandal in 2002 elicited from Catholics of every variety a surge of anger toward their bishops, it did not create the well of distrust in which that anger was rooted. "Conservatives and liberals might have different lists of complaints," journalist Peter Steinfels explains. "What they had in common was a festering sense that church leaders too often said one thing in public, believed another in private, and acted in ways not necessarily consistent with either." That "festering sense" was evident by the 1990s even with regard to one of the more remarkable and arguably humane reforms set in motion by the American bishops a few years after Vatican II. That reform concerned procedures in diocesan marriage tribunals, the juridical bodies that issue annulments to Catholics whose marriages have ended in divorce. Prior to and immediately after the council, annulments were exceedingly hard to procure—only 338 were granted nationwide as late as 1968—and without an annulment no Catholic could remarry in the church. A rapidly rising divorce rate, to which Catholics were not immune, brought matters to a head. By the early 1970s, the American bishops had secured permission from Rome to streamline their annulment procedures and make them more user-friendly, while the grounds for annulment were also substantially broadened.[8]

In 1991, the peak year for annulments issued to American Catholics, almost sixty-four thousand were granted—the great majority for "defects of consent," a category employed more generously in the United States than anywhere else in the world. It meant that at least one party to the marriage had been too immature at the time to enter into a sacramental union. But although well over 90 percent of all petitions for annulments in this country are granted, fewer and fewer Catholics sought them after 1991. Only thirty-five thousand were granted in 2007, although the United States, with roughly 6 percent of the world's Catholic population, still accounted for some 60 percent of the world's annulments. The decline may reflect in part an ebbing Catholic marriage rate, as well as the greater stability of marriages contracted at later ages. But it also reflected an increasingly jaundiced view of the annulment process as a whole. Was it not inherently dishonest, given the near-universal success rate and the willingness of judges to grant an annulment over the objections of one's former spouse? There were high-profile cases, after all, in which an annulment permitted the participants in an extramarital affair to marry in a Catholic ceremony. Was the process not invasive of privacy and even unintentionally cruel, especially when children were involved? Better, perhaps, to remarry in an other-than-Catholic ceremony, as growing numbers of the divorced were doing. They presumably numbered among the 67 percent of Catholics who, according to a 2005 poll, believed that one could be a "good Catholic" even if one's marriage was not approved by the church.[9]

John Paul's impact on the laity is somewhat harder to discern, despite his manifest popularity. As World Youth Day in Denver suggests, many young Catholics idolized the pope, which sometimes led to—or reinforced—a far more intense religious practice on their part than typically found among their peers. Even on secular college campuses, the Catholic chapel often attracted a core of devout participants, while certain Catholic college campuses witnessed a resurgence of Eucharistic devotion among students. Young Catholics also volunteered for service projects in impressive numbers both at the parish level and in more sustained form through organizations like the Jesuit Volunteer Corps. Devoted to the pope, ardently pro-life, and oriented to social service, such "evangelical Catholics," as theologian William Portier describes them, often confound post-council categories of liberal and conservative. Their hunger for boundaries can seem alien to Catholics for whom escape from the "Catholic ghetto" bespoke liberation. But it makes sense to Portier, who rightly points out that Catholics like the students he teaches "have to figure out how to be Catholic" without the supports of a subculture. While certain of their elders see retrogression in their love for the pope or traditional devotions, post-subculture Catholics, according to Portier, see spiritual ballast and sources of Catholic identity.[10]

Devout Catholics like these have constituted a distinct minority of the Catholic young over the past few decades. This is not surprising: the youthful devout are typically a minority in any generation. But lacking the supports of a subculture, the less-than-devout majority in recent years has been far less anchored in Catholic belief and practice than its predecessors. A 2005 study of Christian teens in the United States concluded, to the distinct surprise of the authors, that the Catholics in their sample stood out "among the U.S. Christian teenagers as consistently scoring lower on most measures of religiosity." Catholic teens, who now include numerous Hispanics, were less likely than their Protestant counterparts to attend church regularly, participate in a parish youth group, or know even basic information about the tradition to which they allegedly belong. The disengaged teens in the study had, for the most part, relatively disengaged parents, all of them raised in the postcouncil years. These Catholic parents were less likely than their evangelical or African American Protestant counterparts to say that religion was "very" or "extremely" important to them and less likely to participate in parish activities or organizations. The Catholic parents were also more likely than the Protestant parents to be married to someone belonging to a different faith tradition.[11]

The authors of the study were also impressed by the relative weakness of the Catholic Church when it came to youth ministry. Catholics simply invest less money and human capital in youth ministry than Protestants do. When large numbers of Catholic children attended parochial schools for at least a portion of their education, those schools provided a plausible substitute. But the great majority of Catholic youngsters in recent decades have had no Catholic schooling at all. Those who have, moreover, were seldom taught by any but lay teachers—only 5 percent of Catholic school faculty in 2005 were priests or religious—and not every lay teacher is well grounded in Catholic theology or even necessarily a Catholic at all. The upper-middle-class parents who are today the most likely to send their children to Catholic schools often place a premium on their academic quality and value faculty competence above all else. Most parishes do try to provide religious education to children in the congregation, although these classes vary in quality, since most are taught by lay volunteers with usually limited training. And teens are often resistant to attending such classes. Forty percent of the Catholic teens in the aforementioned study claimed never to have attended a parish religious-education program, while a 1993 study estimated that just 21 percent of Catholic high school students were receiving any formal religious training.[12]

Young adult Catholics—liberally defined as those in their twenties and thirties—have also proved a challenge. A study published in 2001, whose sample population was both better educated and more likely to have attended a Catholic school than others in their cohort, found that roughly 30 percent claimed to attend Mass weekly—a figure almost certainly inflated by the peculiarly American propensity to overestimate personal church attendance when asked about it by pollsters. Did Catholics in the immigrant slums of antebellum New York or Boston attend Mass any more regularly? Very likely not. But for those long-distant Catholics, religion and ethnicity were fused in a way that is no longer true for many young Catholics, while rampant anti-Catholicism placed a premium on loyalty to the church. That too has largely disappeared, save for liberal hostility to aspects of Catholic sexual teaching that many young Catholics also oppose. Thus even in a sample population that had received a more rigorous Catholic formation than most of their counterparts, the study found a certain fragility when it came to Catholic commitment and perhaps, by extension, Catholic identity. Although most were pleased to be Catholics and could not imagine being anything else, they regarded their Catholicism as an accident of birth. Most were hazy about recent Catholic history—roughly half had heard of the Second Vatican Council—and inclined to regard all religious traditions as "equally good" in leading believers to ultimate truth. Some who described themselves as Catholics almost never attended Mass, while a few attended churches of other denominations.[13]

The 2001 study included Hispanic young adults in its sample population, albeit a group mostly born and educated in the United States. Since Hispanics now constitute more than half the Catholic population under the age of twenty-five, their inclusion was more than appropriate. "What the Irish have been to the Church in the twentieth century," in the words of theologian Allan Figueroa Deck, "the Hispanics will be to the next." Immigration from Mexico and Central America has already shifted the center of Catholic geographic gravity from the Northeast of the country to its Southwest. The 2001 study found that despite having family backgrounds that were more than usually church connected—the sample population was drawn from parish confirmation lists, and confirmation is a sacrament received by only about a third of young Hispanic Catholics—Hispanic young adults in the study attended church no more frequently than their non-Hispanic counterparts. They were also far less informed about recent church history—27 percent had heard of the Second Vatican Council, compared with 56 percent of the non-Hispanics. And they were just as likely as non-Hispanic young adults to agree that one could be a "good Catholic" without regularly attending Mass.[14]

At the same time, young adult Hispanic Catholics tended to see their faith as inseparable from their ethnic identity. Very few in the 2001 study had left the Catholic Church, although an estimated 30 percent of Hispanics nationwide have evidently done so—many prior to emigration, others after American arrival, and most for various forms of evangelical Protestantism. Hispanics in the study also engaged in many more devotional practices than their non-Hispanic counterparts, such as saying the Rosary,

wearing a scapular or medal, and praying to particular saints. Much of this
devotional activity took place at home rather than in the parish church—a
reflection, presumably, of a long history in Mexico and elsewhere during
which priests were scarce and women, primarily mothers and grandmoth-
ers, were the principal agents of religious socialization. Home altars are
common in Hispanic households, along with statues of the Virgin and perhaps a favored saint. Relatively low levels of churchgoing, then, did not
seem to undermine Catholic identity for Hispanic young adults, who were
far more likely than non-Hispanics in the 2001 study to say that the Catholic Church was the "one true Church" and more likely as well to marry within the faith.[15]

About 40 percent of Hispanic young adults had been to confession in
the two years prior to the study, with women more likely than men to have
done so. Roughly half of the non-Hispanics who regularly attended Mass
also said they had been to confession within the past two years. The numbers are fairly consistent with those reported in two studies of the Catholic
population as a whole, one published in 1995, the other in 2003. The proportion claiming to go to confession at least once a year ranged between 43
and 46 percent; 57 percent (1995) and 53 percent (2003) said they seldom or
never went. A subsequent study, done in 2007 and presumably impacted by
the sex-abuse scandal, placed 75 percent of respondents in the "seldom or
never" category. Thus some forty years after Vatican II, confession continued for a great many Catholics to be the "optional" sacrament it had so evidently become by the early 1970s. The causes were institutional in part.
Diminishing numbers of penitents, coupled with a growing priest shortage,
led in most parishes to greatly reduced hours when the sacrament was regularly available. A postcouncil emphasis on frequent communion, which for
many Catholics came to mean receiving the Eucharist whenever they attended Mass, broke a long-standing link in the Catholic mind between the
two sacraments. Most American dioceses, in fact, had begun by the later
1960s to have youngsters receive first communion three or more years before first confession. Rome ordered an end to the experiment just a few
years later. But it had been popular with parents.[16]

The long-term decline in confession, however, had more fundamentally to do with altered Catholic views on sin and judgment. Lay disagreement with aspects of Catholic sexual teaching grew increasingly pronounced
in successive postcouncil generations. Asked in 1999 whether church leaders

or the individual or a combination of both should determine the morality of homosexual acts, remarriage without an annulment, or advocating free choice with regard to abortion, a plurality of Catholics surveyed opted for the individual. The youngest group in the sample gave majority support to the lone individual as the locus of moral decision-making. Postcouncil Catholics arguably possessed a livelier sense of social sin than most of their forebears, with many believing—at least in the abstract—that racial injustice and poverty are offenses against God. But how does one confess personal guilt for what are typically "structural sins"—for being born to a favored race or living in relative comfort? The God of the postcouncil Catholic, moreover, is preeminently a God of love and mercy—attributes that can, especially for the poorly instructed, make confession seem superfluous. "Why would I want to speak with a priest and ask for confession to a man?" asked a twenty-something Hispanic male, speaking for many in his generation. "God is here with me and he's the only person who understands."[17]

Even reform of the venerable ritual did not resuscitate confession. Although the council spoke only briefly to confession, a simplified and more Scripturally oriented rite was introduced in the mid-1970s as a council-endorsed reform. Under the new rite, penitents might choose to sit face-to-face with the confessor, with a small "reconciliation room"—oddly similar in feel to a therapist's office—taking the place of the confessional box. This, it was hoped, would make the sacrament a true occasion of spiritual direction. Priests overwhelmingly favored the face-to-face option; lay Catholics were less enthusiastic. Only 20 percent of those still going to confession in the late 1970s chose to confess in this fashion. Nor has the option become more appealing in the intervening years. Most laypeople, it seems, still think of confession as acknowledging specific instances of wrongdoing, rather than as an opportunity for reflecting on their spiritual lives. Wrongdoing sufficiently serious to merit confessing it would presumably be an occasional occurrence, with the penitent nearly always preferring to remain anonymous.[18]

A second postcouncil innovation, the communal penance service, did prove more popular. But its very popularity created difficulties that ultimately caused the option to be less and less available. When hundreds came to a communal service—"they are mass services of from 700 to 1400 people," according to a 1969 report from Detroit—how could every person present conclude the service by confessing privately to a priest? Such was the initial expectation for services of this sort. Should the priest-presider at the service

issue mass absolution to everyone present? Some in fact did. But under
pressure from Rome and often enough their own consciences, most bishops
forbade their priests to do so. (When Carroll Dozier, named first bishop
of Memphis in 1970, gave mass absolution at two penance services in 1976,
he received swift notice of Rome's displeasure.) The very ambiguity of communal penance—might attendance at such a service cause Catholics to
believe, quite erroneously, that they had satisfied their obligation to confess
privately?—caused many JP II bishops, along with growing numbers of
priests, to eschew such services altogether or offer them only occasionally.[19]

If the American church under John Paul II suffered from growing
institutional weakness, it was still a formidable institution and a major
presence in the nation's life. The pope himself was admired by many non-
Catholics. The American bishops in these years participated more visibly
than ever before in national political debates on issues ranging from abortion to immigrant rights. Catholic voters, no longer adherents of a particular political party, had emerged as a critical "swing vote" and were courted
assiduously by politicians across the political spectrum, while Catholics
were overrepresented in Congress and many state legislatures. Large numbers of recent immigrants were at least nominally Catholic, and their church
stood at the forefront of efforts to assist and assimilate the new arrivals.
Many hospitals nationwide operated under Catholic auspices, while Catholic charities were often contracted by various levels of government to aid
the poor and homeless.

The church also served as a voice of conscience when it came to foreign policy, especially during the Reagan years when the heavily Catholic
nations of Central America were wracked by civil war. When four Catholic
missionaries—two Maryknoll sisters, an Ursuline, and a laywoman—were
raped and murdered by government soldiers in El Salvador as they ministered to the victims of war in 1980, the resulting outcry helped to build resistance to U.S. military intervention there in support of the offending
government. That no such intervention occurred on Reagan's watch—
many members of his administration were pressing for it—was largely due
to Catholic pressure, including that of the bishops. Pope John Paul II, now
in visible physical decline, pleaded publicly with President George W. Bush
in 2003 to refrain from invading Iraq, citing the inevitably deadly consequences for its civilian population. He was echoed by the American bishops, hitherto courted by the president for obvious political reasons. An

invasion, they warned, "could impose terrible new burdens on an already suffering civilian population, and could lead to wider conflict and instability in the region."[20]

There were signs of health at the local level too. Nearly every parish had a core of devout, highly active members, whose example was often admired by the more tenuously connected. Some Catholic parishes were alive with activity and offered genuinely compelling liturgies. Laymen and especially laywomen continued to volunteer for poorly paid jobs as parish ministers, and the number of permanent deacons also grew apace. Although issues pertaining to gender equity continued to be a source of tension, Catholic women had made—thanks to grassroots pressure—impressive gains within their church. The altar was no longer a male preserve: parish after parish had permitted females to be lectors, Eucharistic ministers, and altar servers, innovations that the bishops eventually blessed. Women even held prominent jobs in some of the nation's chanceries. There were numerous ceremonial events as well where members of the nation's most heterogeneous church came together to celebrate what held them together. The dedication in 2002 of a strikingly contemporary new cathedral in Los Angeles is one example; the funeral of Chicago's Cardinal Joseph Bernardin in 1996 provides another. "For a week the event overshadowed everything else in the news media," Peter Steinfels recalled of the latter occasion. "Mourners lined up around the clock for three days and nights to pay their respects."[21]

The Catholic institutions that play so prominent a role in American life have, it is true, lost some of the clear-cut Catholic identity they once possessed. Catholic health care and Catholic social service agencies today often serve a predominantly non-Catholic clientele and typically receive generous infusions of public money. Relatively few priests or religious now serve on their staffs, whose lay members, even those in leadership, may not invariably be Catholics. Institutions of this sort are increasingly governed by professional norms and, in the case of health care, the dictates of a medical regime increasingly driven by technology. What, then, makes Catholic health care or Catholic social service distinctively Catholic? The most obviously "Catholic" attributes of such institutions tend to be those that generate hostility from the liberally minded and even the occasional lawsuit: the refusal of Catholic hospitals to perform abortions and, in most cases, sterilizations, or the refusal of Catholic foster-care and adoption agencies to accept gay couples as clients. Catholic institutions often find it hard to articulate a moral vision in which such prohibitions possess plausible integrity in the context of American pluralism.

The problem has been especially visible in the nation's Catholic colleges, although a significant number still serve a mostly Catholic student body. At those many institutions founded and sponsored by religious orders, diminishing numbers of priests and sisters has meant more and more laypeople on the faculty and even in leadership. College after college laicized their boards of trustees in the late 1960s and after, which severed the institutions in question from control by priests or religious or at least limited their authority. Council-era euphoria ignited a passion for campus intellectual freedom, with students and faculty at Catholic colleges demanding an end to speaker bans and compulsory classes in philosophy and theology. Catholic University students and faculty successfully reversed the firing of priest-theologian Charles Curran in 1967 by going on strike, while a meeting of Catholic college leaders in that same year issued a statement endorsing "true autonomy and academic freedom" as essential attributes of Catholic higher education. The more affluent Catholic institutions also strove for academic improvement, measured inevitably by the standards prevailing in the nation's best secular schools. Their success was often impressive: Notre Dame, Georgetown, and Boston College rose to national prominence academically, as did many smaller institutions in their regional markets. If their stellar new faculties now included many non-Catholics, the diversity was often welcomed as a happy emblem of liberation from the parochial past.[22]

For a number of years, the impact of such changes was seldom discussed in public. That changed abruptly with the 1990 publication of *Ex Corde Ecclesiae* (From the heart of the church), Pope John Paul II's Apostolic Constitution on Catholic Universities. Despite its thoughtful discussion of the nature and function of Catholic higher education, the document generated immediate controversy. A set of appended "norms" to be implemented at all Catholic colleges was the principal point of contention. According to those norms, every theologian who taught on a Catholic faculty had to receive a "mandate" from the bishop in whose diocese he or she served, which most observers assumed was equivalent to a certificate of orthodoxy. Catholics were to constitute a majority of the faculty at every Catholic institution, while non-Catholic faculty would have to respect the school's explicitly religious mission in their teaching and conduct. The guidelines made no mention of tenure or other contractual obligations that would obviously inhibit rapid change in the composition of faculties. Nor did it recognize the vastly different profiles of the various Catholic colleges in the United States, which ranged from tuition-driven institutions with a heavy vocational emphasis to highly selective research universities.

Given the country's unusually large number of Catholic colleges and universities, *Ex Corde* posed particular problems for the United States. How were the American bishops to impose such far-reaching changes on the nearly 240 Catholic colleges and universities nationwide? For much of the decade of the 1990s, the bishops' conference dickered with Rome, arguing for a gradual approach to reform in consultation with Catholic educational leaders. The bishops ultimately lost the argument, although neither of John Paul's successors has made *Ex Corde* a top priority in dealing with the American church, if only because the sex-abuse crisis has proved a major distraction. Some prominent Catholic institutions since the 1990s have placed a new emphasis on recruiting Catholic faculty. Others have continued to rely primarily on campus ministry to shore up "Catholic identity" on campus. Still others see their religious mission as service to the poor and sometimes non-Catholic minorities who constitute most of their students. But the larger problem remains: in a post-subcultural world bereft of priests and religious, Catholic institutions are bound to struggle when it comes to defining what makes them distinctive. This "is not a matter of something we have lost and must retrieve," in the words of theologian Monika K. Hellwig. "It is a matter of discovering how to do something we have never done before."[23]

Church Closings

American Catholics had long defined themselves in terms of building. Catholics claimed American space and staked their claim to American acceptance as the builders of churches, schools, rectories, convents, hospitals, and social service agencies. Some parish plants at the Catholic zenith occupied entire city blocks. The successful bishop was invariably a builder; Philadelphia's Dennis Dougherty, not otherwise a leader among his confreres, gloried in being popularly dubbed "God's bricklayer." By the 1970s, however, growing numbers of bishops were facing the need to close churches, especially in what had historically been the heart of American Catholic settlement: the Northeast and upper Midwest. The problem had three causes: white flight to the suburbs, which depopulated scores of center-city parishes; declining religious practice, especially among the young; and a rapidly worsening priest shortage. Understandably reluctant to confront the problem, most bishops temporized. There was palpable relief at the chancery when freeway construction or urban renewal forced closure of a church and muted rejoicing when the occasional parish—typically one founded by a small and now-dispersed ethnic congregation—could be discreetly dissolved. Prior to the 1980s, however, no bishop addressed the problem in all its gathering immensity. Protestant churches and Jewish synagogues typically moved from neighborhoods that their people were abandoning. Catholics had no history of doing so.

Detroit's Edmund Szoka, who assumed office in 1981, was the first to close large numbers of churches. After years of study by various committees, he announced late in 1988 that forty-three churches in his See city would be closed by the following summer. That fully one-third of the parishes in what had only recently been a heavily Catholic city would close shocked Detroiters of every variety. Suburbanites wrote angry letters. Members of the affected parishes held prayer vigils in their doomed churches and even at the archbishop's residence. Protestant clergy decried the decision, noting the importance of Catholic churches as purveyors of neighborhood social services. Even the City Council held hearings. The protests, which included threats to withhold contributions to the archbishop's annual fund-raising campaign, gained reprieves for some churches: only thirty-one were closed in the summer of 1989, with the remainder given a year to demonstrate their "viability." But since viability required both a parish membership of five hundred families and an annual income of $100,000, at least half of which had to come from the Sunday and Christmas collections, most of the remaining parishes and a good many more faced a limited future.[24]

Detroit's problems were unusually acute, given the scale and rapidity of its white flight. The chancery also handled the closings with stunning ineptness, applying a set of rigid criteria for parish viability and refusing to consider the use of nonordained personnel to maintain parishes in deeply troubled neighborhoods. No one from the chancery visited the affected parishes prior to the final decisions about closure or notified their pastors in advance of the public announcement. Bishops subsequently forced to close parishes have tried to proceed in more consultative fashion. But the sheer number of closures—almost twenty-five hundred Catholic churches were shuttered nationwide between 1990 and 2017, with particularly massive closings in Chicago, New York, and Boston—often led to Detroit-style shock and anger. Parishioners have appealed to the Vatican, albeit without success, and have on occasion occupied churches slated to be closed. Closings occurred in suburbs and towns in addition to cities, as was emphatically the case when the Archdiocese of Detroit underwent two additional waves of closures after the initial round in 1989. Growing numbers of the affected parishes were financially stable, at least in the near term, and drew respectable numbers to Mass. But given the shortage of clergy and, in some cases, financial losses due to clerical sex abuse, even seemingly viable parishes sometimes found themselves in the crosshairs.[25]

Most Catholics probably recognized that churches had to be closed. No one was prepared, however, for the scale of the closings that took place or the emotions they generated. Even hitherto-docile Catholics were stirred to anger and bitter distrust of the local chancery. Bishops in Boston and New York were accused of closing churches to profit from rising property values. (Many of the emptied buildings were subsequently offered for sale.) One could hardly hurl such charges in a declining city like Detroit, where some closed churches were eventually reduced to ruin by weather and industrious scavengers. But angry parishioners in such cities found other reasons to distrust their shepherds, even if—as was clearly the case in Detroit—demographic change locally meant that at least some closings were long overdue. "I think the Archbishop is trying to force vocations by doing this," a Detroit woman asserted in the wake of that city's initial wave of closures. She had hitherto been opposed to both married priests and the ordination of women, but the closings had changed her mind on both counts. Closures that occurred after 2002, when the sex-abuse scandal broke nationwide, were invariably seen by angry lay Catholics as occasioned by hefty settlements to the victims of clerical predators. Nothing a bishop could say would persuade them otherwise.[26]

Bishops who were forced to close churches expected to generate anger. They presumably also expected that the anger would eventually dissipate. But the closings' effects went beyond anger. They severed Catholics from their pasts, both personal and communal. Family history ran through parishes. "Although I never knew them, my great-grandparents' memory is still alive because of their church," a suburban woman told Detroit's Szoka about St. Boniface, a German parish in the city targeted for closure in 1989 and eventually demolished. The woman's childhood parish was also slated for closure, as was the church in which her father had been baptized. "It is the saddest thing I have ever seen in my 32 years of life." Large-scale closings sometimes obliterated substantial portions of an area's Catholic past, eroding collective memory. The closings also distanced Catholics from a distinctively Catholic orientation to the material world, aspects of which were imbued with the sacred. A church was never just a building but a literal locus of the holy. The closing and selling of churches, however, especially on a massive scale, could only make sense if a church was in fact nothing more than a building, a perspective arguably consonant with the logic of the council but a break nonetheless with Catholic tradition. And who could ignore the most fundamental message sent by massive church closures: that the local church now lacked the resources essential to future flourishing? This too was an orientation new to American Catholics.[27]

The Clerical Sex-Abuse Crisis

The sex-abuse crisis in the Catholic Church continues at the time of this writing. Despite massive media coverage, moreover, there is still a great deal we do not know, even with regard to recent decades and certainly about the more distant past. Complaints of priests abusing minors were apparently rare for much of the church's American history. Was such abuse correspondingly rare? It seems unlikely, but we simply do not know. Abundant evidence suggests that abuse of this sort exploded between the mid-1960s and the early 1980s, but we still do not know why or whether the extent of this abuse was truly unprecedented. And while it seems clear that reforms in most dioceses had significantly reduced the incidence of abuse by the mid-1990s, media coverage of the problem, especially in 2002 and after, created the widespread impression that it was growing worse. Many Catholics responded accordingly. The following paragraphs, then, will surely be subject to revision in the not-too-distant future. All that can be said with certainty is that the scandals, which first surfaced in the mid-1980s, have done more than anything else to weaken a church already suffering from excess levels of distrust and alienation.

The most definitive study of the problem to date, commissioned by the bishops in 2002 but carried out autonomously, charted a gradual increase in credible accusations of clerical sex abuse between 1950, the study's starting date, and the early 1960s. Probable instances of abuse subsequently skyrocketed, with the highest numbers being recorded in the 1970s, and then fell steadily between 1980 and 2002, the study's terminal date, when credible accusations were lower than those for 1950. Relatively few of the accusations were levied immediately after the alleged abuse occurred; some victims waited decades to report the crime, especially those whose abuse had been prolonged and particularly egregious. Delays in reporting, especially when lengthy, meant that some abuse went unreported. Actual cases of abuse, especially those dating from the 1950s, are doubtless more numerous than the accusations suggest. But because accusations came forward in very large numbers at times of peak publicity—approximately one-third of the accusations made public in 2002 concerned abuse that had taken place an average of thirty years earlier—delayed reporting also meant that public perceptions of the problem were apt to be badly distorted.[28]

Catholics in 2002, a year of near-saturation publicity about Catholic priests and sex abuse, were in no mood to hear that the problem had a history. Few crimes arouse more visceral emotions than the sexual abuse of children, and Catholics responded in kind. But the problem does seem to have had a history: although some victims continue to delay reporting their abuse, reporting patterns in recent years do indicate a sustained decline in abuse after the early 1990s. Not every chapter in the history is flattering to the nation's bishops. Prior to the 1980s, priests accused of abuse were almost never removed from ministry. Some bishops essentially ignored the problem, failing to investigate cases that lacked corroborative evidence, paying monetary settlements when such could not be avoided—always with the stipulation that the victim remain silent—and, having received the offending priest's pledge to sin no more, sending him to a new assignment. More enlightened bishops sent offending priests for treatment, usually to a church-sponsored facility, which might or might not be up to prevailing professional standards. But reassignment generally followed. Even when well intentioned, a great many bishops can only be said to have enabled serial abusers.[29]

Matters began to change when the case of one such abuser burst into the headlines in 1985. He was Gilbert Gauthé, then a priest in Louisiana. His multiple victims cost the Diocese of Lafayette dearly, both financially and with regard to public outrage, and bishops nationwide took note. A closed-door discussion of the problem of sex abuse took place at the bishops' annual meeting that year, although no initiatives were forthcoming. But many bishops did begin to take the problem seriously. "They engaged experts, studied the medical realities, met with victims, revised local diocesan policies, and scrutinized the quality of treatment centers," as Peter Steinfels sums things up. Most bishops, moreover, were ready for more concerted action when the arrest and trial of another multiple offender, James Porter of the Diocese of Fall River, stunned the nation in 1992. The bishops adopted stringent new guidelines in that same year for handling future abuse cases—guidelines that emphasized swift response, empathy for the victim, and compliance with relevant civil law. A number of chronic offenders were subsequently removed from ministry, and media response to the reform was overwhelmingly positive. But the guidelines were not made mandatory—certain powerful prelates opposed such a step—and actual progress varied sharply from one diocese to the next.[30]

Matters came to a head in 2002, when the *Boston Globe* published a devastating series on clerical sex abuse locally. The horrific acts described had in most cases taken place years earlier. The two most notorious abusers chronicled in the series had both been removed from the priesthood prior to 2002, and neither had functioned as a priest since 1993. But both men had histories of abuse that spanned several decades, and both had been repeatedly assigned to parishes by bishops who were well aware of their problems. The outcry in Boston was so intense that Cardinal Bernard Law was obliged to resign at the close of 2002, only to be rewarded—or so it appeared—with a plum assignment in Rome. And the story quickly went national, as reporters discovered the backlog of cases in virtually every diocese. Most of the perpetrators were now gone, either dead or no longer in ministry, but an earlier history of indifference or misplaced tolerance came back to haunt the bishops. When they met in June 2002, the nation's bishops finally took decisive action. According to the protocols adopted at their meeting in Dallas, a priest with a single credible accusation of abuse had to be removed from ministry forthwith—a mandatory policy to which Rome gave its blessing. Little was said at this juncture about offending bishops, either those who were themselves abusers or those who were flagrant enablers. That problem lay in the future.

The Dallas protocols have been remarkably effective. But as the scandal has gone global, abuse continues to make headlines, and Catholics' anger at their bishops has remained intense. If Catholics of every variety have shared in this anger, however, they have not agreed on the root cause of the scandals. Why did an estimated 4 to 7 percent of American priests—most estimates fall within this range—abuse at least one minor? Conservative Catholics generally blame a long-standing tolerance of homosexuals in the clergy, given that roughly 80 percent of known American victims since 1950 have been males, many of them postpubescent. Progressives point to mandatory celibacy and a failure to ordain women. Neither approach, however, can explain the varied incidence of abuse. Why did it achieve such shocking levels in the 1970s, when for some ordination classes the rate of credible accusations exceeded 10 percent? Presumably we must look to cultural change, in the context of which many aspects of Catholic sexual teaching came under sustained challenge, and perhaps to lax vetting of candidates at many seminaries as the applicant pool dried up. Mandatory celibacy, after all, has been required of priests for well over a millennium; it is also a principal reason that there have probably long been disproportionate numbers of homosexuals in the ranks of the Catholic clergy.

Pope Francis Comes to Washington

Both of John Paul II's immediate successors traveled abroad frequently, and both visited the United States—Benedict XVI in 2008 and Francis I in 2015. Both were greeted by large and enthusiastic crowds, and both were received at the White House. The ebullient Francis generated greater excitement than the scholarly Benedict did, in part for reasons of personality but also due to Francis's emphasis on Christian obligations to the poor and marginalized—aspects of Catholic teaching, in the view of many American Catholics, that their bishops had tended to subordinate to the politics of abortion and gay marriage. The reception accorded both men suggests that even some wounded Catholics still felt affection for their church and took pride in its global stature. As politicians across the denominational spectrum jostled to be photographed with both popes, moreover, the nation was reminded of the enduring power of the Catholic vote. George W. Bush traveled to Andrews Air Force Base to greet Pope Benedict, rather than waiting—as presidents had hitherto done with foreign dignitaries—to welcome him at the White House.

Francis was the first pope to address a joint session of Congress, both of his predecessors having declined the honor. Invited by the Catholic Speaker of the House and the Catholic House minority leader, Francis spoke to a body in which 30 percent of the members were Catholic. They were joined by several members of the majority-Catholic Supreme Court, the Catholic vice president, and the Catholic secretary of state. Invoking the lives and legacies of four Americans—Abraham Lincoln, Martin Luther King Jr., Dorothy Day, and Trappist monk Thomas Merton—Francis proposed a "dialogue" with the Congress "through the historical memory of your people." "Most of us were once foreigners," the Argentinian pope reminded the Congress, speaking not simply of Americans but all the peoples of the Western Hemisphere. Thus we know that we should not fear the foreigners in our midst today. "We must not be taken aback by their numbers," he said with regard both to Hispanic migration and the swelling population of refugees fleeing Africa and the Middle East, "but see them as persons." He spoke movingly of the urgent need to address both global warming and poverty. The pope also urged the Congress "to protect and defend human life at every stage of its development," which brought lusty cheers from the Republican side of the aisle, but pleaded in the very next sentence for "the global abolition of the death penalty."[31]

The day before Francis's address to Congress, he said Mass at the Basilica Shrine of the Immaculate Conception on the Catholic University campus, where he canonized Junípero Serra, Spanish California's most famous missionary. The basilica's iconography, it will be recalled, reminds the viewer that Catholics have played an integral role in the nation's history. Serra's canonization both underscored that message and championed the American belonging of the nation's Hispanic inhabitants. Serra's canonization drew fierce criticism, especially from advocates of Indian rights, who saw him as an agent of cultural genocide. But the pope fast-tracked it nonetheless, waiving the requisite second miracle, and chose to canonize Serra on American soil. Francis did not deny the tragic side of mission history, having previously apologized publicly for the "grave sins ... committed against the native peoples of America in the name of God." But he clearly saw in Serra a man whose life, for all its unhappy consequences, pointed toward a more generous vision of human solidarity than that implied by a static concept of culture. The missionary enterprise in the New World brought new peoples into being and enriched the spiritual storehouse of Catholic Christianity. The descendants of those new peoples, in whose veins ran the blood of their conquerors, their indigenous forebears, and often African slaves, saw in Serra's canonization an affirmation of their worth. Who belonged more fully than they to an American story defined by the mixing of peoples?[32]

The strengths of the American church were on display during the pope's five-day sojourn. His visit to a homeless-services center at Washington, DC's St. Patrick's parish reminded Americans of the church's vast charitable network. His visit to a Harlem parochial school saluted the very real achievements of the nation's Catholic schools and colleges, diminished in number, to be sure, but still by far the most numerous of the country's private educational institutions and among the most successful with poor minority students. The cheering crowds that hailed the pope were testimony to the church's continued moral authority, despite the devastating impact of the sex-abuse scandal. Catholic success in a worldly sense was on display at every stop of the pope's itinerary but perhaps most especially at the Congress. Catholic variety was evident too, presumably to the delight of a pope whose own parents had been immigrants. That so heterogeneous a church had managed to hold together was itself no small achievement. Whatever the current weaknesses of that same church, it was good for Catholics to be reminded of their still considerable strengths.

One might plausibly ask, however, whether those strengths are not mostly a legacy bequeathed by the past—the dwindling inheritance of a time when the church possessed far greater unity and spiritual élan than it does in the present. The American church can boast an astonishing complement of lay leaders, many of whom are committed to a generous vision of social justice. But those leaders are aging. Will younger lay Catholics be willing and able to take their place? Can lay leadership ever fully substitute for the labor and inspiration of the male and female religious who underwrote not just the Catholic schools but also the various Catholic movements for spiritual renewal and social reform? We laypeople, after all, have families to nurture and worldly employment to attend to. Even the most committed lay activist, moreover, cannot say Mass or hear confessions. Given the shortage of clergy, which worsens with every passing year, it is not unreasonable to fear for the sacramental orientation of a future American Catholicism. The Eucharist is still the principal source of Catholic unity and identity. Will that continue to be true if the Catholic future brings more and more priestless Sundays?

My own ambivalence about the future—the narrative turns personal here—is captured by two successive visits to Our Lady of the Angels Cathedral in Los Angeles, shortly after its opening in 2002. The building is

strikingly contemporary—among other things, it is one of the few cathedrals in existence to include an underground parking garage—and not entirely welcoming at first glance. The poured-concrete exterior, jutting at
various acute angles, can only be called fortress-like. But the interior is
breathtaking. Enormous alabaster windows flood the soaring space with
natural light, and no interior pillars interrupt the sweep of its spectacular
length. (The church was purposely designed to be one foot longer than New
York's St. Patrick's.) Especially touching are the earth-toned tapestries that
line the north and south walls of the nave. Collectively titled "The Communion of Saints," the tapestries depict 135 men, women, and children of
various races and national origins. Some are canonized saints, including a
number from North America, while others are church leaders familiar to
the locals. Still others are anonymous—ordinary Christians whose holiness
is certainly known to God and presumably also to those who love them.
Those tapestries moved me to tears.

My first visit took place on a weekday. I joined a goodly number of
other tourists surveying the sumptuous interior with evident appreciation.
As an aesthetic experience, the visit was wholly satisfying. I could not help but
notice, however, that no one was praying in the pews, although a number of
people were kneeling in an adjacent Blessed Sacrament chapel, to which the
tabernacle housing the Eucharist had been transferred. Had I felt moved to
say a prayer, I too would probably have retreated to this more intimate space.
The cathedral's magnificent sanctuary on that weekday morning seemed
conspicuously lacking in what I would call a devotional atmosphere. It was
no more conducive to prayer, at least of the unselfconscious variety, than the
atrium of an art museum. The cathedral was clearly a monument to Catholic
success—its construction had cost close to $200 million—and Catholic cul-
tural sophistication. But did it bespeak a community of living faith—a faith
that could be handed down to subsequent generations? I left the sanctuary
with nagging doubts on precisely this question.

Some ten days later, I returned to the cathedral for Sunday Mass. The
liturgy was in Spanish, which I understand imperfectly. But no translation
was needed when it came to the liturgy's mood. I have seldom experienced
so joyful a Mass or seen such wholehearted congregational participation. As
the worshipers sang and prayed, a sanctuary that had previously felt rather
cold seemed not just conducive to prayer but, in its beauty, a kind of prayer
itself. A living faith indeed! This was the Archdiocese of Los Angeles, I re-

minded myself—by far the most populous in the United States, where Mass is said every Sunday in forty-two languages. With a heavily immigrant membership, the local church does indeed face enormous obstacles, both financial and with regard to ordained personnel. But what is more central to the immigrant experience than hope? That Sunday Mass at the cathedral spoke the language of hope—hope for the nation, hope for immigrant peoples, hope for the church. And on that Sunday morning, even I was ready to accept the gift and look to the Catholic future with joyful expectation.

Notes

PROFILE Eusebio Kino, S.J.

1. On Catholic reform in Europe, see Jean Delumeau, *Catholicism between Luther and Voltaire* (London: Burns and Oates, 1977; French-language original, 1971); and R. Po-Hsia, *The World of Catholic Renewal, 1540–1770* (Cambridge: Cambridge University Press, 1998).

2. On Kino's missionary labors and conditions in the missions of the Pimería Alta, see Fay Jackson Smith, John L. Kessell, and Francis J. Fox, S.J., *Father Kino in Arizona* (Phoenix: Arizona Historical Foundation, 1966); and John L. Kessell, *Mission of Sorrows: Jesuit Guevavi and the Pimas, 1691–1767* (Tucson: University of Arizona Press, 1970).

3. Quoted in Herbert Eugene Bolton, *The Padre on Horseback* (1932; repr., Chicago: Loyola University Press, 1963), 83.

ONE Spain's North American Frontier

1. Invaluable on Spanish exploration and subsequent colonization in what is now the United States is David J. Weber, *The Spanish Frontier in North America* (New Haven, CT: Yale University Press, 1992); population figures at the time of contact are discussed on page 28.

2. Ibid., 28.

3. Kevin Starr, *Continental Ambitions: Roman Catholics in North America: The Colonial Experience* (San Francisco: Ignatius Press, 2016), 101; John H. Hann, *A History of Timucua Indians and Missions* (Gainesville: University Press of Florida, 1996), 142.

4. John E. Worth, "Catalysts of Assimilation: The Role of Franciscan Missionaries in the Colonial System of Spanish Florida," in *From La Florida to La California: Franciscan*

Evangelization in the Spanish Borderlands, ed. Timothy J. Johnson and Gert Melville (Berkeley: Academy of American Franciscan History, 2013), 140; Rose Marie Beebe and Robert M. Senkewicz, *Junípero Serra: California, Indians, and the Transformation of a Missionary* (Norman: University of Oklahoma Press, 2015), 251–52.

5. Quoted in Hann, *History of Timucua Indians and Missions,* 161.

6. Jerald T. Milanich, *Laboring in the Fields of the Lord: Spanish Missions and Southeastern Indians* (Washington, DC: Smithsonian Institution Press, 1999), 138–39, 141–42, quote on 145.

7. Population estimates ibid., 160.

8. Ibid., 131.

9. On the Áncoma massacre and its aftermath, see Starr, *Continental Ambitions,* 121–29.

10. Ramón A. Gutiérrez, *When Jesus Came, the Corn Mothers Went Away* (Stanford, CA: Stanford University Press, 1991), 92–93; Robert C. Galgano, *Feast of Souls: Indians and Spaniards in the Seventeenth-Century Missions of Florida and New Mexico* (Albuquerque: University of New Mexico Press, 2005), 57.

11. Gutiérrez, *When Jesus Came,* 93.

12. Galgano, *Feast of Souls,* 62; quoted in Gutiérrez, *When Jesus Came,* 123, which provides no context for the Freitas document, found in the National Archives in Mexico City. See also Starr, *Continental Ambitions,* 131; and Weber, *Spanish Frontier,* 332.

13. On the *encomienda,* see Weber, *Spanish Frontier,* 128.

14. For a vivid summary of scholarship on the Pueblo Revolt, see Starr, *Continental Ambitions,* 136–38.

15. Pedro Tamarón y Romeral, *Bishop Tamarón's Visitation of New Mexico, 1760,* ed. Eleanor B. Adams, Publications in History 15 (Albuquerque: Historical Society of New Mexico, 1954), 48.

16. The estimate, from Gutiérrez, *When Jesus Came,* 156, is based on research in the matrimonial archives of the Archdiocese of Santa Fe.

17. Weber, *Spanish Frontier,* 118.

18. Starr, *Continental Ambitions,* 142–46.

19. I have not included in this summary any reference to the missions that were twice planted near San Clemente, Texas, in 1632 and 1684. They were simply too evanescent, lasting only months.

20. Jay T. Harrison, "Franciscan Concepts of the Congregated Mission and the Apostolic Ministry in Eighteenth-Century Texas," in Johnson and Melville, *From La Florida,* 337; Mariah Wade, "The Missionary Predicament: Conversion Practices in Texas, New Mexico, and the Californias," ibid., 293.

21. Robert E. Wright, O.M.I., "Spanish Missions," *Handbook of Texas Online,* http://www.tshaonline.org//handbook/online/articles/its02.7-8 (accessed May 23, 2017); Starr, *Continental Ambitions,* 172.

22. Phelipe Segesser, S.J., quoted in John L. Kessell, *Mission of Sorrows: Jesuit Guevavi and the Pimas, 1691–1767* (Tucson: University of Arizona Press, 1970), 54.

23. Quoted in Fay Jackson Smith, John L. Kessell, and Francis J. Fox, S.J., *Father Kino in Arizona* (Phoenix: Arizona Historical Foundation, 1966), 64.

24. Lt. Cave J. Couts, 1848, quoted in John H. Kessell, *Friars, Soldiers, and Reformers: Hispanic Arizona and the Sonora Mission Frontier, 1767–1856* (Tucson: University of Arizona Press, 1976), 207; Phelipe Segesser, S.J., quoted in Kessell, *Mission of Sorrows,* 95.

25. Joseph Och, S.J., quoted in Albrecht Classen, *Early History of the Southwest through the Eyes of German-Speaking Jesuit Missionaries* (Lanham, MD: Lexington Books, 2013), 135.

26. Quoted in Kessell, *Friars, Soldiers, and Reformers,* 207.

27. James A. Sandos, *Converting California: Indians and Franciscans in the Missions* (New Haven, CT: Yale University Press, 2004), 15.

28. Quincy D. Newell, *Constructing Lives at Mission San Francisco: Native Californians and Hispanic Colonists, 1776–1821* (Albuquerque: University of New Mexico Press, 2009), 117.

29. Steven W. Hackel, *Children of Coyote, Missionaries of St. Francis: Indian-Spanish Relations in Colonial California, 1769–1850* (Chapel Hill: University of North Carolina Press, 2005), 142.

30. Ibid., 341, 353–56, 360.

31. Steven W. Hackel, *Junípero Serra: California's Founding Father* (New York: Hill and Wang, 2013), 122.

32. Quoted in Gregory Orfalea, *Journey to the Sun: Junípero Serra's Dream and the Founding of California* (New York: Scribner, 2014), 275; quoted in Beebe and Senkewicz, *Junípero Serra,* 197, 369; Sandos, *Converting California,* 179.

33. Sandos, *Converting California,* 85; Hackel, *Children of Coyote,* 97, 101, 103, 106–8, 110.

34. On this subject, see Benjamin Madley, *An American Genocide: The United States and the California Indian Catastrophe, 1846–1873* (New Haven, CT: Yale University Press, 2016).

35. Quoted in Hackel, *Children of Coyote,* 430; Orfalea, *Journey to the Sun,* 240; Newell, *Constructing Lives,* 163–64.

36. Sandos, *Converting California,* 45; Starr, *Continental Ambitions,* 145–46. On the evolution of the cult, see also William H. Taylor, "Mexico's Virgin of Guadalupe in the Seventeenth Century: Hagiography and Beyond," in *Colonial Saints: Discovering the Holy in the Americas, 1500–1800,* ed. Allan Greer and Jodi Bilinkoff (New York: Routledge, 2003), 277–98.

TWO France in America

1. Alan Taylor, *American Colonies: The Settling of North America* (New York: Penguin Books, 2001), 100.

2. Laura M. Chmielewski, *The Spice of Popery: Converging Christianities on an Early American Frontier* (Notre Dame, IN: University of Notre Dame Press, 2012), 111, 170, 202–3.

3. John Webster Grant, *Moon of Wintertime: Missionaries and the Indians of Canada in Encounter since 1534* (Toronto: University of Toronto Press, 1984), 38; James T. Moore, *Indian and Jesuit: A Seventeenth-Century Encounter* (Chicago: Loyola University Press, 1982), 68; quoted in René Latourelle, *Jean de Brébeuf's Writings: A Study* (St. Mary's, ON: William Lonc, 2001), 50.

4. Latourelle, *Jean de Brébeuf's Writings*, 92, quote on 158; Moore, *Indian and Jesuit*, 43; Jean de Brébeuf, "Relation of What Occurred among the Hurons in the Year 1635," in *The Jesuit Relations and Allied Documents: Travel and Explorations of the Jesuit Missionaries in North America, 1610–1791*, ed. Edna Kenton (New York: Vanguard, 1954), 111.

5. Moore, *Indian and Jesuit*, 139–42, 164, 169, 171.

6. Claude Dablon, "Of the First Voyage Made by Father Marquette toward New Mexico," undated, in Kenton, *Jesuit Relations*, 351–52; Allan Greer, *Mohawk Saint: Catherine Tekakwitha and the Jesuits* (New York: Oxford University Press, 2005), 9–10.

7. Grant, *Moon of Wintertime*, 29.

8. Quoted in Joseph P. Donnelly, S.J., *Jean de Brébeuf, 1593–1649* (Chicago: Loyola University Press, 1975), 82. For a thorough if contentious account of the martyrdoms and their context, see Emma Anderson, *The Death and Afterlife of the North American Martyrs* (Cambridge, MA: Harvard University Press, 2013), 14–46.

9. Tracy Neal Leavelle, *The Catholic Calumet: Colonial Conversions in French and Indian North America* (Philadelphia: University of Pennsylvania Press, 2012), 135, 145, quote on 1.

10. Quoted in George Paré, *The Catholic Church in Detroit, 1701–1888* (Detroit: Gabriel Richard, 1951), 229, 230.

11. Michael Pasquier, *Fathers on the Frontier: French Missionaries and the Roman Catholic Priesthood in the United States, 1789–1870* (New York: Oxford University Press, 2010), 27; quoted in Sister M. Dolorita Mast, S.S.N.D., *Always the Priest: The Life of Gabriel Richard, S.S.* (Baltimore: Helicon, 1965), 146.

12. Anderson, *Death and Afterlife*, 71–72, 103–4, 127.

13. Definitive on the life of Catherine Tekakwitha and the principal source of my account is Greer, *Mohawk Saint*. On the lengthy process of Tekakwitha's canonization, see Kathleen Sprows Cummings, *A Saint of Our Own: How the Quest for a Holy Hero Helped Catholics Become American* (Chapel Hill: University of North Carolina Press, 2019), 16–17, 20, 24–25, 62.

14. Paul Le Jeune and Jean de Brébeuf, "Relation of What Occurred in New France in the Year 1635," in Kenton, *Jesuit Relations*, 94.

15. Natalie Zemon Davis, *Women on the Margins: Three Seventeenth-Century Lives* (Cambridge, MA: Harvard University Press, 1995), 79, 95–97; see also Dominique Deslandres, "In the Shadow of the Cloister: Representation of Female Holiness in New France," in *Colonial Saints: Discovering the Holy in the Americas, 1500–1800*, ed. Allan Greer and Jodi Bilinkoff (New York: Routledge, 2003), 132, 142.

16. Emily Clark, *Masterless Mistresses: The New Orleans Ursulines and the Development of a New World Society, 1727–1834* (Chapel Hill: University of North Carolina Press, 2007), 1, 40, 58.

17. Ibid., 5, 161–62; Leavelle, *Catholic Calumet,* 154.

18. Dablon, "Of the First Voyage," 362; Claude Dablon, "Account of the Second Voyage and the Death of Father Jacques Marquette," undated, ibid., 385.

19. Quoted in Leavelle, *Catholic Calumet,* 123.

20. Dablon, "Account of the Second Voyage," 385.

21. John Demos, *The Unredeemed Captive: A Family Story from Early America* (New York: Knopf, 1994), xi–xii (emphasis in original). The English lyrics to the "Huron Carol" quoted here are by Jesse Edgar Middleton (1926) and appear in the hymnals of the Episcopal, United Methodist, and Evangelical Lutheran churches.

THREE Catholics in the British Colonies

1. The best account of Maryland's Catholic colonial history is found in Robert Emmet Curran, *Papist Devils: Catholics in British America, 1574–1783* (Washington, DC: Catholic University of America Press, 2014).

2. Robert Emmet Curran, *Shaping American Catholicism: Maryland and New York, 1805–1915* (Washington, DC: Catholic University of America Press, 2012), 32.

3. Quoted in Curran, *Papist Devils,* 179; Joseph Moseley to "dear sister," Sept. 8, 1770, and July 5, 1773, in *American Jesuit Spirituality: The Maryland Tradition, 1634–1900,* ed. Robert Emmet Curran (New York: Paulist Press, 1988), 107, 109.

4. Curran, *Papist Devils,* 180–81, Mattingly quote on 178.

5. Ibid., 183; *The Pious Guide to Prayer and Devotion,* first published 1792, excerpted in *Prayer and Practice in the American Catholic Community,* ed. Joseph P. Chinnici and Angelyn Dries (Maryknoll, NY: Orbis Books, 2000), 9.

6. Joseph P. Chinnici, O.F.M., "Organization of the Spiritual Life: American Catholic Devotional Works, 1791–1866," *Theological Studies* 40, no. 2 (1979): 236–37; Richard Challoner, *The Garden of the Soul; or, A Manual of Spiritual Exercises and Instructions for Christians, Who Living in the World Aspire to Devotion* (Dublin: Richard Cross, 1798), 297.

7. Curran, *Papist Devils,* 185–87.

8. John Carroll to Charles Plowden, Feb. 20, 1782, in *The John Carroll Papers,* vol. 1, *1755–1971,* ed. Thomas O'Brien Hanley, S.J. (Notre Dame, IN: University of Notre Dame Press, 1976), 64; James Hennesey, S.J., "An Eighteenth-Century Bishop: John Carroll of Baltimore," in *Patterns of Episcopal Leadership,* ed. Gerald P. Fogarty, S.J. (New York: Macmillan, 1989), 8; John Carroll to Daniel Carroll, Sept. 11, 1773, in Curran, *American Jesuit Spirituality,* 129.

9. Quoted in Thomas S. Kidd, *God of Liberty: A Religious History of the American Revolution* (New York: Basic Books, 2012), 73; Maura Jane Farrelly, *Papist Patriots: The Making of an American Catholic Identity* (New York: Oxford University Press, 2012); Curran, *Papist Devils,* 239.

10. Farrelly, *Papist Patriots,* 243.

11. Ibid., 244, 242, 243.

12. Kidd, *God of Liberty,* 73–74; Curran, *Papist Devils,* 273–74.

13. John Carroll to Charles Plowden, Feb. 28, 1779, in Hanley, *Carroll Papers,* vol. 1, 53; Joseph Moseley to "dear sister," Oct. 4, 1784, in Curran, *American Jesuit Spirituality,* 112.

14. John Carroll, Robert Molyneaux, and John Ashton to Pius VI, Mar. 12, 1788, in Hanley, *Carroll Papers,* vol. 1, 280.

15. Catherine O'Donnell, "John Carroll and the Origins of an American Catholic Church, 1783–1815," *William and Mary Quarterly* 68, no. 1 (2011): 120; John Carroll to Ferdinand Farmer, Dec. 1784, and Carroll to Joseph Berington, July 10, 1784, in Hanley, *Carroll Papers,* vol. 1, 148–49, 157; Curran, *Papist Devils,* 276.

16. John Carroll to Andrew Nugent, Jan. 17, 1788, in Hanley, *Carroll Papers,* vol. 1, 201.

17. Carroll to Cardinal Antonelli, Mar. 1, 1785, ibid., 179–80.

18. Carroll to Charles Plowden, June 29, 1785, ibid., 180; Carroll to Antonelli, Mar. 1, 1785, ibid., 192.

19. Carroll to Antonelli, Mar. 1, 1785, ibid., 182; Carroll to Jean Rivet, 1796, in *The John Carroll Papers,* vol. 2, *1792–1806,* ed. Thomas O'Brien Hanley, S.J. (Notre Dame, IN: University of Notre Dame Press, 1976), 164.

20. Carroll to Charles Plowden, May 8, 1789, in Hanley, *Carroll Papers,* vol. 1, 389.

21. Carroll to Charles Plowden, Dec. 5, 1808, in *The John Carroll Papers,* vol. 3, *1807–1815,* ed. Thomas O'Brien Hanley (Notre Dame, IN: University of Notre Dame Press, 1976), 72; Michael Pasquier, *Fathers on the Frontier: French Missionaries and the Roman Catholic Priesthood in the United States, 1789–1870* (New York: Oxford University Press, 2010), 26.

22. Carroll to Charles Plowden, Sept. 24, 1796, in Hanley, *Carroll Papers,* vol. 2, 189; Thomas W. Spalding, *The Premier See: A History of the Archdiocese of Baltimore, 1789–1989* (Baltimore: Johns Hopkins University Press, 1989), 37.

23. Margaret M. McGuinness, *Called to Serve: A History of Nuns in America* (New York: NYU Press, 2013), 23–25, Carroll quote on 23.

24. A biographical synopsis is found in the introduction to *Elizabeth Seton: Selected Writings,* ed. Ellin Kelly and Annabelle Melville (New York: Paulist Press, 1987), 16–19; see also Annabelle M. Melville, *Elizabeth Bayley Seton, 1774–1821* (New York: Scribner, 1960). A recent biography, which now stands as definitive, is Catherine O'Donnell, *Elizabeth Seton: American Saint* (Ithaca, NY: Cornell University Press, 2018).

25. Seton, *Selected Writings,* 69, 1804 journal quote on 133 (emphasis in original).

26. Seton to Cecilia O'Conway, Aug. 1817, ibid., 298; quoted in McGuinness, *Called to Serve,* 30.

27. Carroll to Charles Plowden, June 25–July 24, 1815, in Hanley, *John Carroll Papers,* vol. 3, 338.

PROFILE Samuel Mazzuchelli, O.P.

1. Quotes from Samuel Mazzuchelli, *The Memoirs of Samuel Mazzuchelli, O.P.* (Chicago: Priory, 1967), 58, 83.

2. Quoted in Mary Nona McGreal, "Mazzuchelli, Samuel Charles," in *The Biographical Dictionary of Iowa* (Iowa City: University of Iowa Press, 2009), http:/digital.lib. uiowa.edu/uipress/bdi/; Mazzuchelli, *Memoirs,* 285, 300.

3. Mazzuchelli, *Memoirs,* 186.

FOUR The Frontier Church

1. Thomas W. Spalding, C.F.X., "The Catholic Frontiers," *U.S. Catholic Historian* 12, no. 4 (1994): 1–15.

2. Samuel Mazzuchelli, *The Memoirs of Samuel Mazzuchelli, O.P.* (Chicago: Priory, 1967), 67; Lorena Petit, O.P., *Friar in the Wilderness: Edward Dominic Fenwick, O.P.* (Chicago: Project OPUS: History of the Order of Preachers in the United States, 1994), 35. The friend in question, Eliza Rose Powell, taught school in Canton, Ohio, which Fenwick reached the day before his death. Alarmed by his condition, Powell resolved to accompany the bishop to Cincinnati.

3. Thomas T. McAvoy, ed., "Bishop Bruté's Report to Rome in 1836," *Catholic Historical Review* 29, no. 2 (1943): 190–91.

4. On the Baltimore councils, the definitive work is still Peter Guilday, *A History of the Baltimore Councils, 1791–1884* (New York: Macmillan, 1932), quote on 115–16.

5. Leslie Woodcock Tentler, *Seasons of Grace: A History of the Catholic Archdiocese of Detroit* (Detroit: Wayne State University Press, 1990), 35; quoted in Petit, *Friar in the Wilderness*, 13–14.

6. Frederic Baraga to Frederic Rese, Mar. 7, 1833, Baraga Letters, vol. 2, unpaginated, typescript collection housed at Sacred Heart Seminary, Detroit.

7. Quoted in James M. Woods, " 'To the Suburb of Hell': Catholic Missionaries in Arkansas, 1803–1843," *Arkansas Historical Quarterly* 48, no. 3 (1989): 227–28; Ambrose Marechal to Lorenzo Cardinal Litta, Oct. 16, 1818, in *Documents of American Catholic History*, ed. John Tracy Ellis (Milwaukee: Bruce, 1956), 216.

8. Quoted in Clyde Crews, *An American Holy Land: A History of the Archdiocese of Louisville* (Wilmington, DE: Michael Glazier, 1987); quoted in Petit, *Friar in the Wilderness*, 10.

9. Account from the *Cincinnati Telegraph* quoted in J. Herman Schauinger, *Stephen T. Badin: Priest in the Wilderness* (Milwaukee: Bruce, 1956), 282.

10. Stephen Badin to "Mon Cher Ami," *Annales de l'Association de la Propagation de la Foi* 6 (Apr. 1833): 166 (author's translation from the French).

11. Quoted in Gilbert J. Garraghan, S.J., *The Jesuits of the Middle United States*, 2 vols. (Chicago: Loyola University Press, 1983), 1:102; John Mary Odin, C.M., to the procurator general of the Vincentians, 1842, in *The Frontiers and Catholic Identities*, ed. Anne M. Butler, Michael E. Engh, S.J., and Thomas W. Spalding, C.F.X. (Maryknoll, NY: Orbis, 1999), 22.

12. McAvoy, "Bishop Bruté's Report to Rome," 190; John Cappon to an unidentified correspondent, Archives of the University of Notre Dame, Rev. John C. Cappon Papers (CAP), box 1, no folder number at time of use.

13. Mazzuchelli, *Memoirs*, 308; "Contents of the inventory of the assets of Father Gabriel Richard made by Benjamin F. Larned, Charles Moral, and Peter Desnoyer on April 22, 1833 by order of Probate Judge Joseph W. Torey," undated typescript, Michigan Historical Collections (hereafter MHC), Ann Arbor, Gabriel Richard Papers, uncatalogued at time of use; quoted in Margaret M. McGuinness, *Called to Serve: A History of Nuns in America* (New York: NYU Press, 2013), 51.

14. For a fuller discussion, see Leslie Woodcock Tentler, "'How I Would Save Them All': Priests on the Michigan Frontier," *U.S. Catholic Historian* 12, no. 4 (1994): 27–29.

15. Michael Pasquier, *Fathers on the Frontier: French Missionaries and the Roman Catholic Priesthood in the United States, 1789–1870* (New York: Oxford University Press, 2010), 157–60.

16. Quoted in Garraghan, *Jesuits of the Middle United States*, 1:239.

17. Quoted ibid., 1:247, 248.

18. Quoted ibid., 1:114; John Cappon to an unidentified correspondent, Feb. 29, 1867, Cappon Papers, box 1, no folder number at time of use.

19. John De Néve to John Cappon, Mar. 12, 1863, Cappon Papers, box 1, no folder number at time of use.

20. "Bishop Flaget's Report of the Diocese of Bardstown to Pius VII, April 10, 1815," *Catholic Historical Review* 1, no. 3 (1915): 316.

21. Jay P. Dolan, *Catholic Revivalism: The American Experience, 1830–1900* (Notre Dame, IN: University of Notre Dame Press, 1978), 18–22.

22. Quoted in George Paré, *The Catholic Church in Detroit, 1701–1888* (Detroit: Gabriel Richard, 1951), 451; quoted in Garraghan, *Jesuits in the Middle United States*, 2:54.

23. Cheverus's 1798 letter appears in *Prayer and Practice in the American Catholic Community*, ed. Joseph P. Chinnici and Angelyn Dries (Maryknoll, NY: Orbis, 2000), 12–13; additional information is found in James M. O'Toole, *The Faithful: A History of Catholics in America* (Cambridge, MA: Harvard University Press, 2008), 11–13, 311.

24. Bp. J. M. Provencher to "all the families settled in the Wallamette Valley," June 8, 1835, in Butler, Engh, and Spalding, *Frontiers and Catholic Identities*, 109; Jean-Marie Odin, C.M., to Jean-Baptiste Etienne, Apr. 11, 1841, in Ellis, *Documents of American Catholic History*, 262.

25. Quoted in Garraghan, *Jesuits in the Middle United States*, 1:204.

26. Jane Birney to "Dear Father," undated but 1859, and Bridget Birney to James Birney, undated but 1859, MHC, Birney-McClear-Hankerd Papers, uncatalogued at time of use. I have retained the original spelling in all quotes from the Birney letters.

27. Bridget McClear to James Birney, Feb. 28, 1843, Birney-McClear-Hankerd Papers, uncatalogued at time of use.

28. John De Néve to Mr. Van Dorpe, Apr. 25, 1859, *Annales de l'Association de la Propagation de la Foi* 6 (Apr. 1833): 453–54 (author's translation from the French).

29. John De Néve to John Cappon, May 18, 1860, Cappon Papers, box 1, no folder number at time of use.

30. Rev. Adrian de Montauberg, "Annual Report, St. Charles, Newport," 1868, Archives of the Archdiocese of Detroit, St. Charles, Newport, Michigan, parish file, spelling as in the original; quoted in *Life and Life-Work of Mother Théodore Guérin, Foundress of the Sisters of Providence at St. Mary-of-the-Woods, Vigo County, Indiana*, by a Member of the Congregation (New York: Benziger, 1904), 231–32. The author, who published anonymously, was Mary Theodosia Mug.

31. Barbara Misner, S.C.S.C., *"Highly Respectable and Accomplished Ladies"*: *Catholic Women Religious in America, 1790–1850* (New York: Garland, 1988), 137, 140, 168, Flaget quote on 140; Crews, *American Holy Land*, 90.

32. Quoted in Mug, *Life and Life-Work of Mother Théodore Guérin*, 228.

33. Misner, *"Highly Respectable and Accomplished Ladies,"* 239–40.

34. Ibid., 218.

35. On frontier academies, see Mary J. Oates, "Catholic Female Academies on the Frontier," *U.S. Catholic Historian* 12, no. 4 (1994): 121–36, quote on 134.

36. Quoted ibid., 123.

FIVE   An Urban Stronghold

1. On the characteristics of Irish immigrants, see Lawrence J. McCaffrey, *The Irish Catholic Diaspora in America*, rev. ed. (Washington, DC: Catholic University of America Press, 1997), 63–78; on the Germans, see Jay P. Dolan, *The American Catholic Experience* (Garden City, NY: Doubleday, 1985), 130–31, 137–39, 145–47.

2. Quoted in Jenny Franchot, *Roads to Rome: The Antebellum Protestant Encounter with Catholicism* (Berkeley: University of California Press, 1994), 136.

3. Richard Shaw, *Dagger John: The Unquiet Life and Times of Archbishop John Hughes of New York* (New York: Paulist Press, 1977), 124, 169–70, 255, 267, quote on 304.

4. Joseph P. Chinnici, "Organization of the Spiritual Life: American Catholic Devotional Works, 1791–1866," *Theological Studies* 40, no. 2 (1979): 242–51, 253–54.

5. Quoted in James Hennesey, S.J., *American Catholics: A History of the Roman Catholic Community in the United States* (New York: Oxford University Press, 1981), 117.

6. Patrick W. Carey, *People, Priests, and Prelates: Ecclesiastical Democracy and the Tensions of Trusteeism* (Notre Dame, IN: University of Notre Dame Press, 1987), 11–13, quote on 13.

7. Dale B. Light, *Rome and the New Republic: Conflict and Community in Philadelphia Catholicism between the Revolution and the Civil War* (Notre Dame, IN: University of Notre Dame Press, 1996), 5, 19, 35, 111–12, 114, 130, 134, 138, 140, 149.

8. Ibid., 128–29.

9. Carey, *People, Priests, and Prelates*, 125.

10. Ibid., 60.

11. Edith Jeffrey, "Reform, Renewal, and Vindication: Irish Immigrants and the Catholic Total Abstinence Movement in Antebellum Philadelphia," *Pennsylvania Magazine of History & Biography* 112, no. 3 (1988): 407–8.

12. David Montgomery, "The Shuttle and the Cross: Weavers and Artisans in the Kensington Riots of 1844," *Journal of Social History* 4 (Spring 1972): 411–46.

13. Jay P. Dolan, *The Immigrant Church: New York's Irish and German Catholics, 1815–1865* (Baltimore: Johns Hopkins University Press, 1975), 33.

14. Emmet Larkin, "The Devotional Revolution in Ireland," *American Historical Review* 77, no. 3 (1972): 651; Dolan, *Immigrant Church*, 56–57, 83–84.

15. Light, *Rome and the New Republic*, 126.

16. Dolan, *Immigrant Church,* 154, quote on 156.

17. *Michigan Catholic,* Jan. 28, 1892, 8.

18. Excerpt from *A Pious Association of the Devout Servants of Our Lord Jesus Christ, Dying on the Cross, and the Most Blessed Virgin Mary, Commonly Called Bona Mors, in Order to Obtain a Good Death* (Baltimore: Lucas, 1846), in *Prayer and Practice in the American Catholic Community,* ed. Joseph P. Chinnici and Angelyn Dries (Maryknoll, NY: Orbis Books, 2000), 29.

19. This paragraph draws extensively on Philip Gleason, "Boundlessness, Consolidation, and Discontinuity between Generations: Catholic Seminary Studies in Antebellum America," *Church History* 73, no. 3 (2004): 583–612.

20. James W. Sanders, "Catholics and the Schools Question in Boston: The Cardinal O'Connell Years," in *Catholic Boston: Studies in Religion and Community, 1870–1970,* ed. Robert E. Sullivan and James M. O'Toole (Boston: Archdiocese of Boston, 1985), 123.

21. Shaw, *Dagger John,* 170.

22. Dolan, *Immigrant Church,* 105; Caroline Friess to unknown correspondent, Nov. 12, 1853, in *The Letters of Mother Caroline Friess,* ed. Barbara Brumleve, S.S.N.D. (St. Louis: School Sisters of Notre Dame, 1991), 53.

23. Friess to unknown correspondent, Nov. 12, 1853, 53; quoted in Barbara Misner, S.C.S.C., *"Highly Respectable and Accomplished Ladies": Catholic Women Religious in America, 1790–1850* (New York: Garland, 1988), 197.

24. Misner, *"Highly Respectable and Accomplished Ladies,"* 197; Dolan, *Immigrant Church,* 110.

25. Anne C. Rose, *Beloved Strangers: Interfaith Families in Nineteenth-Century America* (Cambridge, MA: Harvard University Press, 2001), 1–5.

26. Eliza Allen Starr, "Miss Starr Tells the Story of Her Conversion," in *The Life and Letters of Eliza Allen Starr,* ed. James J. McGovern (Chicago: Lakeside, 1905), 34–35; quoted in Shaw, *Dagger John,* 261.

27. On Hecker, see the definitive biography, which informs this and subsequent paragraphs: David J. O'Brien, *Isaac Hecker: An American Catholic* (New York: Paulist Press, 1992); Patrick Allitt, *Catholic Converts: British and American Intellectuals Turn to Rome* (Ithaca, NY: Cornell University Press, 1997), 64–65.

28. Quoted in Franchot, *Roads to Rome,* 337.

29. O'Brien, *Isaac Hecker,* 253.

30. James Parton, "Our Roman Catholic Brethren," *Atlantic Monthly,* April 21, 1868, in Chinnici and Dries, *Prayer and Practice,* 66.

31. Ibid., 65.

SIX Slavery and the Civil War

1. Robert Emmet Curran, *Shaping American Catholicism: Maryland and New York, 1805–1915* (Washington, DC: Catholic University of America Press, 2012), 48–49, quote on 49.

2. Ibid., 92–93, 101, 110.

3. William B. Kurtz, *Excommunicated from the Union: How the Civil War Created a Separate Catholic America* (New York: Fordham University Press, 2016), 42; Peter Guilday, *A History of the Councils of Baltimore* (New York: Macmillan, 1932), 220.

4. John T. McGreevy, *Catholicism and American Freedom: A History* (New York: Norton, 2003), 49, 52–54; John T. Noonan Jr., *A Church That Can and Cannot Change: The Development of Catholic Moral Teaching* (Notre Dame, IN: University of Notre Dame Press, 2005), 102.

5. Diane Batts Morrow, *Persons of Color and Religious at the Same Time: The Oblate Sisters of Providence, 1828–1860* (Chapel Hill: University of North Carolina Press, 2002), 12–14, 207–8; Emily Clark, *Masterless Mistresses: The New Orleans Ursulines and the Development of a New World Society, 1727–1834* (Chapel Hill: University of North Carolina Press, 2007), 192, 257.

6. McGreevy, *American Freedom*, 55–56; quote from Hughes's 1854 sermon in *Complete Works of the Most Rev. John Hughes, D.D.*, vol. 2, ed. Lawrence Kehoe (New York: Lawrence Kehoe, 1865), 222.

7. McGreevy, *American Freedom*, 56–65, quote on 62.

8. Kurtz, *Excommunicated from the Union*, 43–44, 46–47, 54, 57, 60.

9. James M. McPherson, *Battle Cry of Freedom: The Civil War Era* (New York: Ballantine Books for Oxford University Press, 1988), 606–8.

10. Ibid., 491–93, 609–11; Shaw, *Dagger John*, 361–65.

11. Shaw, *Dagger John*, 360; Kurtz, *Excommunicated from the Union*, 100–102; Randall M. Miller, "Catholic Religion, Irish Ethnicity, and the Civil War," in *Religion and the American Civil War*, ed. Randall M. Miller, Harry S. Stout, and Charles Reagan Wilson (New York: Oxford University Press, 1998), 282–83; Spalding quote from McGreevy, *American Freedom*, 86.

12. Peter Welsh to Margaret Welsh, ca. Feb. 1863, in *Irish Green and Union Blue: The Civil War Letters of Peter Welsh*, ed. Lawrence Frederick Kohl (New York: Fordham University Press, 1986), 62. All spellings in Welsh's letters appear as in the originals.

13. Peter Welsh to Margaret Welsh, Feb. 3, 1863, ibid., 65–66.

14. Peter Welsh to Margaret Welsh, Oct. 11, 1862, and Dec. 25, 1862, ibid., 20, 43.

15. Peter Welsh to Margaret Welsh, Dec. 4, 1862, Dec. 25, 1862, Jan. 14, 1863, and Feb. 22, 1863, ibid., 35, 41, 57, 74.

16. Peter Welsh to Margaret Welsh, Feb. 3, 1863, and Feb. 22, 1863, ibid., 65–67, 74.

17. Peter Welsh to Margaret Welsh, Feb. 3, 1863, Feb. 8, 1863, July 17, 1863, and Aug. 2, 1863, ibid., 65, 70, 110, 115.

18. Kurtz, *Excommunicated from the Union*, 43–44; James Hennesey, S.J., *American Catholics: A History of the Roman Catholic Community in the United States* (New York: Oxford University Press, 1981), 155.

19. Peter Welsh to Margaret Welsh, Dec. 25, 1862, in Kohl, *Irish Green*, 41; Peter Paul Cooney to "my dear brother," Oct. 2, 1862, in *Documents of American Catholic History*, ed. John Tracy Ellis (Milwaukee: Bruce, 1956), 386.

20. Cooney to "my dear brother," Oct. 2, 1862, 386; Sean Fabun, "Catholic Chaplains in the Civil War," *Catholic Historical Review* 99, no. 4 (2013): 681–82, 685–87; Peter Welsh to Margaret Welsh, Jan. 27, 1863, and Feb. 3, 1863 in Kohl, *Irish Green*, 60, 65.

21. Fabun, "Catholic Chaplains," 683–85; Miller, "Catholic Religion," 264–65.

22. Cooney to "my dear brother," Oct. 2, 1862, 385; Miller, "Catholic Religion," 266, 267; Rev. Frank O'Brien, "Organization and Maintenance of Parish Societies," *American Ecclesiastical Review* 14, no. 6 (1896): 492; quoted in George C. Rable, *God's Almost Chosen People: A Religious History of the American Civil War* (Chapel Hill: University of North Carolina Press, 2010), 169.

23. William Corby, C.S.C., *Memoirs of Chaplain Life: Three Years with the Irish Brigade in the Army of the Potomac* (New York: Fordham University Press, 1992), 181–84, quote on 184.

24. Ibid., 185–86; quoted in Rable, *God's Almost Chosen People*, 135–36.

25. Margaret M. McGuinness, *Called to Serve: A History of Nuns in America* (New York: NYU Press, 2013), 93, 96; Sara Trainer Smith, "Notes on Satterlee Military Hospital, West Philadelphia, Penna. from 1862 until Its Close in 1865, from the Journal Kept by a Sister of Charity," *Records of the American Catholic Historical Society of Philadelphia* 8, no. 4 (1897): 405.

26. Smith, "Notes on Satterlee Military Hospital," 408; quoted in McGuinness, *Called to Serve*, 94.

27. Kurtz, *Excommunicated from the Union*, 82.

28. Ibid., 87; quoted in Rable, *God's Almost Chosen People*, 212.

29. McGreevy, *American Freedom*, 91–96, quote on 92.

30. Ibid., 96, 98; Thomas W. Spalding, "Martin John Spalding," in *Patterns of Episcopal Leadership*, ed. Gerald P. Fogarty, S.J. (New York: Macmillan, 1989), 113.

31. Quoted in M. Edmund Hussey, "John Baptist Purcell: First Archbishop of Cincinnati," in Fogarty, *Patterns of Episcopal Leadership*, 94; Hennesey, *American Catholics*, 168–69.

32. Hennesey, *American Catholics*, 169–71; Gerald P. Fogarty, *The Vatican and the American Hierarchy from 1870 to 1965* (Stuttgart: Anton Hiersemann, 1982), 1–9; for an extended discussion, see James Hennesey, *The First Council of the Vatican: The American Experience* (New York: Herder and Herder, 1963), 230–82.

33. Stephen J. Ochs, *Desegregating the Altar: The Josephites and the Struggle for Black Priests, 1871–1960* (Baton Rouge: Louisiana State University Press, 1990), 3–6. The three mixed-race Healy brothers, ordained in 1854, 1858, and 1864, respectively, identified as Irish rather than African American and were so regarded in their lifetimes. James Augustine Healy was named the second bishop of Portland, Maine, in 1875, while Patrick Healy, a Jesuit, served as the president of Georgetown College from 1864 to 1882. Father Sherwood Healy, the only one of the three to be visibly of mixed-race origin, was a prominent priest in the Archdiocese of Boston. That he met with acceptance from his mostly Irish parishioners is indeed remarkable. See James M. O'Toole, *Passing for White: Race, Religion, and the Healy Family, 1820–1920* (Amherst: University of Massachusetts Press, 2002).

PROFILE Mother Frances Xavier Cabrini, M.S.C.

1. Mary Louise Sullivan, M.S.C., *Mother Cabrini: "Italian Immigrant of the Century"* (New York: Center for Migration Studies, 1992), 38–41, 45–48. Sullivan's is the best researched of the generally inadequate biographies of Mother Cabrini in English. Excellent on the rapid progress of Cabrini's canonization and on her significance for American Catholics is Kathleen Sprows Cummings, *A Saint of Our Own: How the Quest for a Holy Hero Helped Catholics Become American* (Chapel Hill: University of North Carolina Press, 2019), 95–122.

2. Ibid., 79; Lucille Papin Borden, *Francesca Cabrini: Without Staff or Scrip* (New York: Macmillan, 1945), 101–4.

3. Sullivan, *Mother Cabrini*, 73–74.

4. Silvano M. Tomasi, *Piety and Power: The Role of the Italian Parishes in the New York Metropolitan Area, 1880–1930* (New York: Center for Migration Studies, 1975), 81–82, quote on 91.

5. Ibid., 113, 258.

6. Ibid., 104–5.

7. Theodore Maynard, *Too Small a World: The Life of Francesca Cabrini* (Milwaukee: Bruce, 1945), 335.

8. James W. Sanders, *The Education of an Urban Minority: Catholics in Chicago, 1833–1965* (New York: Oxford University Press, 1977), 13; Leila Hardin Bugg, *The People of Our Parish* (Boston: Marlier, Callahan, 1900), 60, 75.

9. Kathleen Sprows Cummings, *New Women of the Old Faith: Gender and American Catholicism in the Progressive Era* (Chapel Hill: University of North Carolina Press, 2009), 11–13.

SEVEN Institutional Growing Pains

1. Quoted in James P. Gaffney, "Bishops on the Fringe: Patrick W. Riordan of San Francisco and Francis Clement Kelley of Oklahoma City," in *Patterns of Episcopal Leadership*, ed. Gerald P. Fogarty (New York: Macmillan, 1989), 187.

2. John Tracy Ellis, *The Life of Cardinal James Gibbons*, vol. 2 (Milwaukee: Bruce, 1952), 110–11, quote on 630.

3. *Michigan Catholic*, May 11, 1893, 3; William M. Halsey, *The Survival of American Innocence: Catholicism in an Era of Disillusionment, 1920–1940* (Notre Dame, IN: University of Notre Dame Press, 1980), 155.

4. C. Walker Gollar, "The Double Doctrine of the Caldwell Sisters," *Catholic Historical Review* 81, no. 3 (1995): 372–97; C. Joseph Nuesse, *The Catholic University of America: A Centennial History* (Washington, DC: Catholic University of America Press, 1990), 27–34.

5. Nuesse, *Catholic University of America*, 38–43, 130–33.

6. Charles Francis Aiken, seminary diary, entry for Feb. 23, 1888, American Catholic History Research Center and University Archives (hereafter ACUA), Catholic University of America, Charles Francis Aiken Papers, collection 46, box 6, folder 9.

7. David Lodge, *Souls and Bodies* (New York: Penguin Books, 1980), 12; Joseph M. White, *The Diocesan Seminary in the United States: A History from the 1780s to the Present* (Notre Dame, IN: University of Notre Dame Press, 1989), 237–51; Rev. William E. Randall to Henry F. Brownson, Mar. 31, 1904, Archives of the University of Notre Dame, Henry F. Brownson Papers (BRH), box 3, folder 3.

8. Aiken, diary, entries for May 20 and Dec. 11, 1887; White, *Diocesan Seminary,* 238–42.

9. Donna Merwick, *Boston's Priests, 1848–1910* (Cambridge, MA: Harvard University Press, 1973), 142; quoted in John Tracy Ellis, *The Formative Years of the Catholic University of America* (Washington, DC: American Catholic Historical Association, 1946), 100.

10. Thomas J. Shelley, *Dunwoodie: The History of St. Joseph's Seminary, Yonkers, New York* (Westminster, MD: Christian Classics, 1993), 39–41; John Talbot Smith, *Our Seminaries: An Essay on Clerical Training* (New York: William H. Young, 1896), 66, 67.

11. Father LeRoy E. McWilliams, *Parish Priest* (New York: McGraw-Hill, 1953), 48. McWilliams entered the seminary in 1915. Right Reverend William Stang, *Pastoral Theology* (New York: Benziger, 1897), 297.

12. W. J. Howlett, "Memoirs," undated but ca. early 1920s, 54–64, 70–72, typescript housed at ACUA.

13. Patrick J. Cullinane, "Memoirs of Rev. Patrick Jerome Cullinane," undated but probably late 1930s, 9, 17, 47–52, 97, typescript housed at the Bentley Historical Library, Michigan Historical Collections, Ann Arbor, Michigan.

14. Smith, *Our Seminaries,* 217; Cullinane, "Memoirs," 63.

15. Cullinane, "Memoirs," 77, 100, 132–36, 147–48, 159–61, 181–82, 191.

16. Rev. T. Slater, S.J., and Rev. A. Rauch, S.J., *Rules of Life for the Pastor of Souls* (New York: Benziger, 1909), 123–25.

17. Smith, *Our Seminaries,* 216; Edward Roberts Moore, *Roman Collar* (New York: Macmillan, 1950), 85. Moore was ordained in 1919.

18. Abbé Félix Klein, *In the Land of the Strenuous Life* (Chicago: A. C. McClurg, 1905), 265.

19. Hasia R. Diner, *Erin's Daughters in America* (Baltimore: Johns Hopkins University Press, 1983), 45–53.

20. Quoted in Carol K. Coburn and Martha Smith, *Spirited Lives: How Nuns Shaped Catholic Culture and American Life, 1836–1920* (Chapel Hill: University of North Carolina Press, 1999), 81.

21. Kathleen Sprows Cummings, *New Women of the Old Faith: Gender and American Catholicism in the Progressive Era* (Chapel Hill: University of North Carolina Press, 2009), 142.

22. Quoted in James W. Sanders, "Catholics and the School Question in Boston: The Cardinal O'Connell Years," in *Catholic Boston: Studies in Religion and Community, 1870–1970,* ed. Robert E. Sullivan and James M. O'Toole (Boston: Roman Catholic Archdiocese of Boston, 1985), 157.

23. Cullinane, "Memoirs," 74.

24. Definitive on the council's origins is Elizabeth McKeown, "The National Bishops' Conference: An Analysis of Its Origins," *Catholic Historical Review* 66, no. 4 (1980): 565–83.

EIGHT A People Numerous and Varied

1. Roger Daniels, *Coming to America: A History of Immigration and Ethnicity in American Life* (New York: HarperCollins, 1990), 125, 129, 146, 188, 259.

2. Ibid., 185, 189, 194, 195, 219.

3. Quoted ibid., 220

4. Quoted in Robert Anthony Orsi, *The Madonna of 115th Street: Faith and Community in Italian Harlem, 1880–1950* (New Haven, CT: Yale University Press, 1985), 51; see also pages 22–23.

5. Quoted in Silvano M. Tomasi, *Piety and Power: The Role of the Italian Parishes in the New York Metropolitan Area, 1880–1930* (New York: Center for Migration Studies, 1975), 107, 125.

6. Quoted in Orsi, *Madonna of 115th Street*, 55; quoted in Tomasi, *Piety and Power*, 81.

7. Quoted in Tomasi, *Piety and Power*, 77.

8. Quoted in Silvano M. Tomasi, "The Ethnic Church and the Integration of Italian Immigrants in the United States," in *The Italian Experience in the United States*, ed. Silvano M. Tomasi and Madeline H. Engel (New York: Center for Migration Studies, 1970), 167; Tomasi, *Piety and Power*, 77.

9. Quoted in Tomasi, *Piety and Power*, 100.

10. Humberto S. Nelli, *Italians in Chicago, 1880–1930: A Study in Ethnic Mobility* (New York: Oxford University Press, 1970), 193–94; Nicholas John Russo, "Three Generations of Italians in New York City: Their Religious Acculturation," in Tomasi and Engel, *Italian Experience*, 195–213.

11. Nathan Glazer and Daniel Patrick Moynihan, *Beyond the Melting Pot: The Negroes, Puerto Ricans, Jews, Italians, and Irish of New York City* (Cambridge, MA: MIT Press, 1963), 204–5; Herbert J. Gans, *The Urban Villagers: Group and Class in the Life of Italian-Americans* (New York: Free Press, 1962), 111–12; Orsi, *Madonna of 115th Street*, 82.

12. John J. Bukowczyk, *And My Children Did Not Know Me: A History of the Polish-Americans* (Bloomington: Indiana University Press, 1987), 40–41.

13. Ibid., 72.

14. Quoted in Thomas I. Monzell, "The Catholic Church and the Americanization of the Polish Immigrant," *Polish American Studies* 26, no. 1 (1969): 12; Anthony J. Kuzniewski, *Faith and Fatherland: The Polish Church War in Wisconsin, 1896–1918* (Notre Dame, IN: University of Notre Dame Press, 1980), 4.

15. Joseph John Parot, *Polish Catholics in Chicago, 1850–1920* (DeKalb: Northern Illinois University Press, 1981), 224.

16. Ibid., 221–22.

17. *Michigan Catholic*, Feb. 20, 1913, 8; Kuzniewski, *Faith and Fatherland*, 24–25.

18. Quoted in Kuzniewski, *Faith and Fatherland,* 59.

19. Right Reverend William Stang, *Pastoral Theology* (New York: Benziger, 1897), 177.

20. Quoted in John A. O'Brien, *Why Not Receive Daily?* (Paterson, NJ: St. Anthony's Guild, 1944), no pagination.

21. *Michigan Catholic,* Feb. 20, 1913, 8.

22. Ruth Harris, *Lourdes: Body and Spirit in the Secular Age* (New York: Viking, Penguin, 1999), 172–75; Colleen McDannell, *Material Christianity: Religion and Popular Culture in America,* 136–42.

23. McDannell, *Material Christianity,* 154–62.

24. Quoted in Paula M. Kane, *Separatism and Subculture: Boston Catholicism, 1900–1920* (Chapel Hill: University of North Carolina Press, 1994), 23.

25. Quoted in Kathleen Sprows Cummings, *New Women of the Old Faith: Gender and American Catholicism in the Progressive Era* (Chapel Hill: University of North Carolina Press, 2009), 69; Leila Hardin Bugg, *The People of Our Parish* (Boston: Marlier, Callahan, 1900), 195.

26. Cummings, *New Women,* 173–77; Kane, *Separatism and Subculture,* 221–24, 227–31.

27. Cardinal James Gibbons to "Your Eminence," Feb. 20, 1887, in *Documents of American Catholic History,* ed. John Tracy Ellis (Milwaukee: Bruce, 1956), 470.

28. Quoted in James Hennesey, S.J., *American Catholics: A History of the Roman Catholic Community in the United States* (New York: Oxford University Press, 1981), 215.

29. Quoted in Margaret M. McGuinness, "Body and Soul: Immigration and Catholic Social Settlements," *U.S. Catholic Historian* 13, no. 3 (1995): 73.

30. Glazer and Moynihan, *Beyond the Melting Pot,* 229.

31. John A. Ryan, *Social Doctrine in Action: A Personal History* (New York: Harper, 1944), 44–45.

32. John A. Ryan, "Family Limitation," *Ecclesiastical Review* 54, no. 6 (1916): 684–85.

33. Leslie Woodcock Tentler, *Catholics and Contraception: An American History* (Ithaca, NY: Cornell University Press, 2004), 23–40; Rev. Antony Koch, *A Handbook of Moral Theology,* vol. 2, *Sin and the Means of Grace* (St. Louis: Herder, 1919), 163.

34. Tentler, *Catholics and Contraception,* 27–29; Franz Xavier Weninger, *Die Heilige Mission und Praktische Winke für Missionare* (1885; repr., New York: Arno, 1978), 430. Author's translation from the German.

35. Tentler, *Catholics and Contraception,* 53–57.

36. Hennesey, *American Catholics,* 225–26, 228.

NINE "They Are Afraid of Democracy at Rome"

1. Hugh McLeod, *Piety and Poverty: Working-Class Religion in Berlin, London, and New York, 1870–1914* (New York: Holmes and Meier, 1996), 120–24.

2. Definitive on Ireland is Marvin R. O'Connell, *John Ireland and the American Catholic Church* (St. Paul: Minnesota Historical Society, 1988).

3. Quoted ibid., 188; Ireland's sermon was reprinted in full in the *Michigan Catholic,* Dec. 5, 1889, 1, 3, 5.

4. O'Connell, *John Ireland,* 332–25.

5. David J. O'Brien, *Isaac Hecker: An American Catholic* (New York: Paulist Press, 1992), 394; R. Scott Appleby, *Church and Age Unite! The Modernist Impulse in American Catholicism* (Notre Dame, IN: University of Notre Dame Press, 1992), 53–56.

6. O'Connell, *John Ireland,* 388.

7. Ibid., 3.

8. Quoted in O'Brien, *Isaac Hecker,* 336.

9. William L. Portier, *Divided Friends: Portraits of the Roman Catholic Modernist Crisis in the United States* (Washington, DC: Catholic University of America Press, 2013), 212–13, 232–29, 244–46.

10. Appleby, *Church and Age,* 13–52, quote on 35.

11. Quoted in Thomas J. Shelley, *Dunwoodie: The History of St. Joseph's Seminary, Yonkers, New York* (Westminster, MD: Christian Classics, 1993), 156.

12. Quoted ibid., 159–60.

13. *Michigan Catholic,* Dec. 5, 1889, 1.

14. Quoted in James Hennesey, S.J., *American Catholics: A History of the Roman Catholic Community in the United States* (New York: Oxford University Press, 1981), 221; William M. Halsey, *The Survival of American Innocence: Catholicism in an Era of Disillusionment, 1920–1940* (Notre Dame, IN: University of Notre Dame Press, 1980), 2–3, 6, 8.

15. Portier, *Divided Friends,* 168, 267–81; Philip Gleason, *Contending with Modernity: Catholic Higher Education in the Twentieth Century* (New York: Oxford University Press, 1995), 27.

PROFILE John C. Cort

1. John C. Cort, *Dreadful Conversions: The Making of a Catholic Socialist* (New York: Fordham University Press, 2003), 38, 72, 75.

2. Ibid., 2.

3. Ibid., 3, 17, 22.

4. Ibid., 25.

5. Ibid., 17.

6. Ibid., 203.

7. Ibid., 298, 319.

8. Will Herberg, *Protestant, Catholic, Jew: An Essay in American Religious Sociology,* rev. ed. (Garden City, NY: Anchor, 1960), 159, 234, 241.

9. John L. Thomas, "The Factor of Religion in the Selection of Marriage Mates," *American Sociological Review* 16, no. 4 (1951): 487–91.

10. Herberg, *Protestant, Catholic, Jew,* 161.

TEN This Confident Church

1. Samuel A. Stouffer, "Trends in the Fertility of Catholics and Non-Catholics," *American Journal of Sociology* 41, no. 2 (1935): 143–66; Joseph V. Nevins, S.S., "Education to Catholic Marriage, Part II: Adverse Influences," *Ecclesiastical Review* 79, no. 6 (1928): 622.

2. Gavin Jones and Dorothy Nortman, "Roman Catholic Fertility and Family Planning: A Comparative Review of the Recent Literature," *Studies in Family Planning: A Publication of the Population Research Council* 34 (Oct. 1968): 5.

3. James M. O'Toole, "The Name That Stood for Rome: William O'Connell and the Modern Episcopal Style," in *Patterns of Episcopal Leadership,* ed. Gerald P. Fogarty, S.J. (New York: Macmillan, 1989), 179; O'Toole, *Militant and Triumphant: William Henry O'Connell and the Catholic Church in Boston, 1859–1944* (Notre Dame, IN: University of Notre Dame Press, 1992), 245.

4. John T. McGreevy, *Catholicism and American Freedom: A History* (New York: Norton, 2003), 211.

5. Garry Wills, *Bare Ruined Choirs: Doubt, Prophecy, and Radical Religion* (Garden City, NY: Doubleday, 1971), 15.

6. Margaret M. McGuinness, "Let Us Go to the Altar: American Catholics and the Eucharist, 1926–1976," in *Habits of Devotion: Catholic Religious Practice in Twentieth-Century America,* ed. James M. O'Toole (Ithaca, NY: Cornell University Press, 2004), 187–89, quote on 189.

7. St. Philip Neri Mission House, Lapeer: Weekly Reports, Thomas Carey entry, week of Mar. 21, 1925, Archives of the Archdiocese of Detroit, Non-Chancery records—institutions, societies, and parishes; McGuinness, "Let Us Go to the Altar," 197–98.

8. McGuinness, "Let Us Go to the Altar," 197–98.

9. Ibid., 195–96, 209; Leslie Woodcock Tentler, *Catholics and Contraception: An American History* (Ithaca, NY: Cornell University Press, 2004), 135.

10. Msgr. Reynold Hillenbrand, notes for a sermon on confession, undated but ca. mid-1930s, Archives of the University of Notre Dame, Reynold Hillenbrand Papers, CMRH, box 4, folder 4.

11. *Michigan Catholic,* Nov. 21, 1935, 10.

12. Robert A. Orsi, *Thank You, St. Jude: Women's Devotion to the Saint of Hopeless Causes* (New Haven, CT: Yale University Press, 1995), xi, 6–9, 18–22, 24–25.

13. Flannon Gannon, C.P., "Salvation," undated typescript but probably 1940s, Passionist Provincial Archives: Holy Cross Province, Chicago, Sermons of Fr. Flannon Gannon, box 243.

14. Timothy Kelly, *The Transformation of American Catholicism: The Pittsburgh Laity and the Second Vatican Council, 1950–1972* (Notre Dame, IN: University of Notre Dame Press, 2009), 40–51; Andrew M. Greeley, "Popular Devotions: Friend or Foe?," *Worship* 33 (Oct. 1959): 569–73; James McCartin, *Prayers of the Faithful: The Shifting Spiritual Life of American Catholics* (Cambridge, MA: Harvard University Press, 2011), 106–8.

15. Keith F. Pecklars, S.J., *The Unread Vision: The Liturgical Movement in the United States of America, 1926–1955* (Collegeville, MN: Liturgical Press, 1998), 39, 52, quote on 60.

16. Ibid., 55, 63.

17. Ibid., 175, 201, 281.

18. Joseph H. Fichter, *Southern Parish,* vol. 1 (Chicago: University of Chicago Press, 1951), 203.

19. Flannery O'Connor to "A," Mar. 10, 1956, in *The Habit of Being,* ed. Sally Fitzgerald (New York: Farrar, Straus and Giroux, 1979), 145.

20. Timothy B. Neary, *Crossing Parish Boundaries: Race, Sport, and Catholic Youth in Chicago, 1914–1954* (Chicago: University of Chicago Press, 2016), 10–14.

21. William D. Dinges, "'An Army of Youth': The Sodality Movement and the Practice of Apostolic Mission," *U.S. Catholic Historian* 19, no. 3 (2001): 35–49.

22. Angelyn Dries, O.S.F., *The Missionary Movement in American Catholic History* (Maryknoll, NY: Orbis, 1998), 78, 114, 121, 127.

23. Ibid., 89, 91, 125, 136.

24. *Michigan Catholic,* Aug. 1, 1935, 3.

25. Dries, *Missionary Movement,* 148, 173, 176, 181.

26. John J. Burke, C.S.P., "Our Blessed Lady," typescript sermon for a women's retreat, undated but probably early 1930s, Archives of the Paulist Fathers, John J. Burke Papers, PPBURLKJJo33, folder FFo5.

27. Cardinal George Mundelein to Rita McGoldrick, July 18, 1932, Archives of the Archdiocese of Chicago (hereafter AAChi), Mundelein Chancery correspondence, box 13 (1932M-N), folder 11; Mundelein, notes for a sermon to his priests, undated but 1932, AAChi, Mundelein personal papers, box 8, folder 3. This and subsequent paragraphs draw from Tentler, *Catholics and Contraception.*

28. Joseph Reiner, S.J., to Wilfrid Parsons, S.J., Mar. 2, 1933, Georgetown University Library and Special Collections, Washington, DC, Wilfrid Parsons Papers, box 8, folder 12.

29. Rev. Walter J. Imbiorski, ed., *The Basic Cana Manual* (Chicago: Cana Conference of Chicago, 1957), 67.

30. Tentler, *Catholics and Contraception,* 133–34, 200.

31. Thomas A. Tweed, *America's Church: The National Shrine and Catholic Presence in the Nation's Capital* (New York: Oxford University Press, 2011), 164, 182–83; Walter J. Ong, *Frontiers in American Catholicism: Essays in Ideology and Culture* (New York: Macmillan, 1957), 8.

32. Tweed, *America's Church,* 181–82.

33. Dorothy Day, *The Long Loneliness* (New York: Harper and Row, 1952), 166.

ELEVEN Catholic Minds

1. William M. Halsey, *The Survival of American Innocence: Catholicism in an Era of Disillusionment, 1920–1940* (Notre Dame, IN: University of Notre Dame Press, 1980), 8.

2. Ibid., 2–3, 6, 50–51, 176.

3. Walter J. Ong, *Frontiers in American Catholicism: Essays in Ideology and Culture* (New York: Macmillan, 1957), 8.

4. George N. Shuster, *The Ground I Walked On: Reflections of a College President* (New York: Farrar, Straus and Cudahy, 1961), 23–24.

5. James W. Sanders, *The Education of an Urban Minority: Catholics in Chicago, 1833–1965* (New York: Oxford University Press, 1977), 185–86.

6. Ibid., 5, 193, 204.

7. Philip Gleason, *Contending with Modernity: Catholic Higher Education in the Twentieth Century* (New York: Oxford University Press, 1995), 81, 83, 95, 96.

8. Ibid., 168, 209.

9. Shane MacDonald, "The Archivist's Nook: A Flapper, a Nurse, and a Nun Apply to Catholic University," University Libraries, Catholic University of America, Mar. 15, 2018, http://www.lib.cua.edu/wordpress/newsevents/10269.

10. Ibid.

11. Halsey, *Survival of American Innocence*, 93; John Tracy Ellis, *Catholic Bishops: A Memoir* (Wilmington, DE: Michael Glazier, 1984), 103.

12. Gleason, *Contending with Modernity*, 200.

13. Ibid., 220–21, 287–95.

14. Ibid., 227; Sandra Yocum Mize, *Joining the Revolution in Theology: The College Theology Society, 1954–2004* (Lanham, MD: Rowman and Littlefield, 2007), 32–33.

15. Gleason, *Contending with Modernity*, 228; Margaret M. McGuinness, *Called to Serve: A History of Nuns in America* (New York: NYU Press, 2013), 158, 160; Patricia Byrne, "In the Parish but Not of It: Sisters," in *Transforming Parish Ministry: The Changing Roles of Catholic Clergy, Laity, and Women Religious*, by Jay P. Dolan, R. Scott Appleby, Patricia Byrne, and Debra Campbell (New York: Crossroad, 1989), 117.

16. Darra D. Mulderry, "Educating 'Sister Lucy': The Experiential Sources of the Movement to Improve Higher Education for Catholic Teaching Sisters, 1949–1964," *U.S. Catholic Historian* 33, no. 1 (2015): 56–61, quotes on 59–60, 60–61.

17. McGuinness, *Called to Serve*, 160; Lora Ann Quinonez, C.D.P., and Mary Daniel Turner, S.N.D.deN., *The Transformation of American Catholic Sisters* (Philadelphia: Temple University Press, 1992), 10.

18. Quoted in Mulderry, "Educating 'Sister Lucy,'" 64.

19. "Minutes, Advisory Committee to the Bishop in the Matter of Planning Sacred Heart Seminary," Apr. 6, 1921, Archives of the Archdiocese of Detroit (hereafter AAD), Chancery records—seminaries.

20. Joseph M. White, *The Diocesan Seminary in the United States: A History from the 1780s to the Present* (Notre Dame, IN: University of Notre Dame Press, 1989), 274, 280.

21. Ibid., 351–54; Steven M. Avella, *This Confident Church: Catholic Leadership and Life in Chicago, 1940–1965* (Notre Dame, IN: University of Notre Dame Press, 1992), 37–41; Henry Offer, "Active Catholic Action," *Gothic* 14, no. 4 (1938): 48–49.

22. Thomas J. Shelley, *Dunwoodie: The History of St. Joseph's Seminary, Yonkers, New York* (Westminster, MD: Christian Classics, 1993), 223; Jerome Fraser to Edward

Farrell, June 18, 1954, Archives of the University of Notre Dame (hereafter AUND), Jerome R. Fraser Papers (CJRF), box 1, folder: "Farrell and I, 1953–57."

23. Rev. Lyman Fenn, S.S., "Sixth Annual Report of the Rector to the Bishops of the Province of Detroit," May 11, 1955, AAD, Chancery records—seminaries.

24. Edward Farrell to Jerome Fraser, Feb. 8, 1954, AUND, Fraser Papers, box 1, folder: "Farrell and I, 1953–57."

25. Edward Farrell to Jerome Fraser, Feb. 25, 1957, and Farrell to Fraser, Feb. 10, 1954, AUND, Fraser Papers, box 1, folder: "Farrell and I, 1953–57."

26. There were 388 Catholic seminaries in the United States in 1950 and 525 a decade later. In this same period, the number of seminarians grew from approximately twenty-six thousand to almost forty thousand. David J. O'Brien, *The Renewal of American Catholicism* (New York: Paulist Press, 1972), 139; Cornelius M. Cuyler, "Perseverance Trends in the Seminary," *National Catholic Educational Association Bulletin* 63, no. 1 (1966): 151–56; Jerome Fraser to Edward Farrell, Dec. 20, 1956, AUND, Fraser Papers, box 1, folder: "Farrell and I, 1953–57."

27. Author interview with Rev. Joseph Gallagher, Feb. 3, 1999, Baltimore; Edward Farrell to Jerome Fraser, Pentecost 1955, AUND, Fraser Papers, box 1, folder: "Farrell and I, 1953–57"; Leslie Woodcock Tentler, "'To Work in the Field of the Lord': Roots of the Crisis in Priestly Identity," *U.S. Catholic Historian* 29, no. 4 (2011): 1–18.

28. Shuster, *Ground I Walked On*, 23.

29. Quoted in Gleason, *Contending with Modernity*, 129.

30. For a pithy summary of Cooper's career, see Elizabeth McKeown, "From *Pascendi* to *Primitive Man*: The Apologetics and Anthropology of John Montgomery Cooper," *U.S. Catholic Historian* 13, no. 2 (1995): 1–21; for Haas, see Thomas E. Blantz, "Francis J. Haas: Priest and Government Servant," *Catholic Historical Review* 57, no. 4 (1972): 571–92.

31. Gleason, *Contending with Modernity*, 283.

32. Thomas F. O'Dea, *American Catholic Dilemma: An Inquiry into the Intellectual Life* (New York: Sheed and Ward, 1958), 80.

33. Rodger Van Allen, "*Commonweal* and the Catholic Intellectual Life," *U.S. Catholic Historian* 13, no. 2 (1995): 71; Patrick Allitt, *Catholic Converts: British and American Intellectuals Turn to Rome* (Ithaca, NY: Cornell University Press, 1997), 192–93.

34. O'Dea, *American Catholic Dilemma*, 9.

35. Allitt, *Catholic Converts*, 317.

36. Una M. Cadegan, *All Good Books Are Catholic Books: Print Culture, Censorship, and Modernity in Twentieth-Century America* (Ithaca, NY: Cornell University Press, 2013), 2–4, 21–26; Paul R. Messbarger, "The Failed Promise of American Catholic Literature," *U.S. Catholic Historian* 4, no. 2 (1985): 155, 157; Halsey, *Survival of American Innocence*, 100–107.

37. Messbarger, "Failed Promise," 144.

38. Flannery O'Connor to "A," July 20, 1955, in *The Habit of Being*, ed. Sally Fitzgerald (New York: Farrar, Straus and Giroux, 1979), 90; Halsey, *Survival of American Innocence*, 122.

39. Quotes from J. F. Powers, *Morte D'Urban* (1962; repr., New York: Vintage Books, 1979), 104, 306.

40. Quoted in Arnold Sparr, *To Promote, Defend, and Redeem: The Catholic Literary Revival and the Cultural Transformation of American Catholicism* (New York: Greenwood, 1990), 158; Betty Wahl Powers, journal entry, Aug. 26, 1958, in *Suitable Accommodations: An Autobiographical Story of Family Life: The Letters of J. F. Powers, 1942–1963*, ed. Katherine A. Powers (New York: Farrar, Straus and Giroux, 2013), 314; J. F. Powers to Betty Wahl, Dec. 5, 1945, in Powers, *Suitable Accommodations*, 40; quoted in Paul Giles, *American Catholic Arts and Fictions: Culture, Ideology, Aesthetics* (Cambridge: Cambridge University Press, 1992), 432.

TWELVE Public Catholicism

1. Syllabus, *Pierce v Society of Sisters,* 268 U.S. 510 (1925), https://supreme.justia.com/cases/federal/us/268/510/ (accessed Nov. 12, 2018).

2. James M. O'Toole, *Militant and Triumphant: William Henry O'Connell and the Catholic Church in Boston, 1859–1944* (Notre Dame, IN: University of Notre Dame Press, 1992), 133–34.

3. Quoted in John T. McGreevy, *Catholicism and American Freedom: A History* (New York: Norton, 2003), 148.

4. Thomas J. Shelley, "'What the Hell Is an Encyclical?': Governor Alfred E. Smith, Charles C. Marshall, Esq., and Father Francis P. Duffy," *U.S. Catholic Historian* 15, no. 2 (1997): 88–91, 95–99, quotes on 91, 98, 99.

5. Quoted in William M. Halsey, *The Survival of American Innocence: Catholicism in an Era of Disillusionment, 1920–1940* (Notre Dame, IN: University of Notre Dame Press, 1980), 70.

6. Quoted in David J. O'Brien, *Public Catholicism,* 2nd ed. (Maryknoll, NY: Orbis, 1996), 167.

7. George Q. Flynn, *American Catholics and the Roosevelt Presidency, 1932–1936* (Lexington: University Press of Kentucky, 1968), 17, 50, 54, 78–79, quote on 17.

8. Ibid., 240.

9. Leslie Woodcock Tentler, *Catholics and Contraception: An American History* (Ithaca, NY: Cornell University Press, 2004), 124–25.

10. Gregory D. Black, *Hollywood Censored: Morality Codes, Catholics, and the Movies* (Cambridge: Cambridge University Press, 1994), 1–2, 86, 103, 149, 163, 173–74, 180, 186–87; Charles R. Morris, *American Catholic* (New York: Random House, 1997), 161, 165–67, 202–6.

11. *St. Vincent's News,* Sept. 3, 1939; quoted in O'Brien, *Public Catholicism,* 184.

12. Gerhard Lenski, *The Religious Factor,* rev. ed. (New York: Doubleday, 1963), 9; quoted in Matthew Pehl, *The Making of Working-Class Religion* (Urbana: University of Illinois Press, 2016), 92.

13. Charles Coughlin, *Father Coughlin's Radio Sermons Complete, Oct. 1930–April 1931* (Baltimore: Knox and Leary, 1931), 57.

14. Leslie Woodcock Tentler, *Seasons of Grace: A History of the Catholic Archdiocese of Detroit* (Detroit: Wayne State University Press, 1990), 323–24; quoted in Alan Brinkley, *Voices of Protest: Huey Long, Father Coughlin, and the Great Depression* (New York: Vintage, 1982), 108.

15. Tentler, *Seasons of Grace*, 324–25.

16. Maria Mazzenga, "Toward an American Catholic Response to the Holocaust: Catholic Americanism and Kristallnacht," in *American Religious Responses to Kristallnacht*, ed. Maria Mazzenga (New York: Palgrave Macmillan, 2009), 94–99; quoted in Charles J. Tull, *Father Coughlin and the New Deal* (Syracuse, NY: Syracuse University Press, 1965), 197–98.

17. Donald Warren, *Radio Priest: Charles Coughlin, the Father of Hate Radio* (New York: Free Press, 1996), 233–45, 303.

18. Tentler, *Seasons of Grace*, 325–28, 332–40.

19. Ibid., 340–42; Archbishop Edward Mooney to Franklin D. Roosevelt, May 9, 1942, Archives of the Archdiocese of Detroit (hereafter AAD), Edward Mooney Papers, preliminary cataloguing at time of use.

20. James Hennesey, S.J., *American Catholics: A History of the Roman Catholic Community in the United States* (New York: Oxford University Press, 1981), 280–81.

21. Rev. Boguslaus Poznanski to Archbishop Edward Mooney, Mar. 29, 1944, AAD, Boguslaus Poznanski file; Rev. Hubert Maino to Archbishop Edward Mooney, Oct. 3, 1944, AAD, Hubert Maino file.

22. John Cooney, *The American Pope: The Life and Times of Francis Cardinal Spellman* (New York: Times Books, 1984), 125.

23. McGreevy, *Catholicism and American Freedom*, 166–70, quote on 168.

24. Ibid., 182–86.

25. On the Massachusetts referenda, see Tentler, *Catholics and Contraception*, 168–72.

26. Donald F. Crosby, S.J., *God, Church, and Flag: Senator Joseph R. McCarthy and the Catholic Church, 1950–1957* (Chapel Hill: University of North Carolina Press, 1978), 343.

27. McGreevy, *Catholicism and American Freedom*, 211–12.

28. Shaun Casey, *The Making of a Catholic President: Kennedy vs. Nixon, 1960* (New York: Oxford University Press, 2009), 4, 19, 22.

29. Ibid., 100–111, 126, 145–47, 168–69, 177–78, 201.

30. J. Matthew Wilson, "The Changing Catholic Voter: Comparing Responses to John Kennedy in 1960 and John Kerry in 2004," Rooney Center for the Study of American Democracy, Jan. 2007, 10–11, https://rooneycenter.nd.edu/assets/11309/wilson.pdf; *Michigan Catholic*, Sept. 13, 1928, 5.

31. Bishop Stephen Leven, quoted in Gerald P. Fogarty, *The Vatican and the American Hierarchy from 1870 to 1965* (Stuttgart: Anton Hiersemann, 1982), 394.

PROFILE Patricia Caron Crowley

1. Robert McClory, *Turning Point* (New York: Crossroads, 1995), 137.

2. Quoted in Robert J. McClory, "Patty Crowley, Giant of Catholic Laity, Dies at 92," *National Catholic Reporter*, Dec. 9, 2005, http://www.natcath.org/NCR_Online/archives2/2005d/120905/1209050.php.

3. John N. Kotre, *Simple Gifts: The Lives of Pat and Patty Crowley* (Kansas City, MO: Andrews and McMeel, 1979), 30.

4. Quoted ibid., 35.

5. Ibid., 6–7, 20–24, 28–31, 66–67, 70.

6. Jeffrey Burns, *Disturbing the Peace: A History of the Christian Family Movement, 1949–1974* (Notre Dame, IN: University of Notre Dame Press, 1999), 8–9, Kotre, *Simple Gifts,* 64–65.

7. Kotre, *Simple Gifts,* 54.

8. McClory, *Turning Point,* 104.

9. Quoted ibid., 164; quoted in McClory, "Patty Crowley."

10. Quoted in McClory, "Patty Crowley."

11. Pew Forum on Religion and Public Life, *U.S. Religious Landscape Survey,* Feb. 2008, http://pewforum.org/docs/?DocID=279; Peter Steinfels, "The Life and Death of a Leading Lay Catholic," *New York Times,* Dec. 31, 2005, https://www.nytimes.com/2005/12/31/us/the-life-and-death-of-a-leading-lay-catholic.html.

THIRTEEN Something Like a Revolution

1. John W. O'Malley, *What Happened at Vatican II* (Cambridge, MA: Harvard University Press, 2008), 306.

2. Ibid., 121. The "language" theme informs the whole of O'Malley's excellent narrative.

3. Martin Marty, "What Went Wrong?," *Critic* 34, no. 1 (1975): 53.

4. O'Malley, *What Happened,* 252.

5. Gerard S. Sloyan, *Catholic Morality Revisited: Origins and Contemporary Challenges* (Mystic, CT: Twenty-Third, 1990), 100.

6. John O'Malley, "Developments, Reforms, and Two Great Reformations: Towards a Historical Assessment of Vatican II," *Theological Studies* 44 (1983): 398.

7. "Constitution on the Sacred Liturgy," in *The Documents of Vatican II,* ed. Walter M. Abbott, S.J. (New York: Herder and Herder, 1966), 149; Peter Steinfels, *A People Adrift: The Crisis of the Roman Catholic Church in America* (New York: Simon and Schuster, 2005), 171; see also O'Malley, *What Happened,* 140–41, 295.

8. Joseph P. Chinnici, O.F.M., "The Catholic Community at Prayer, 1926–1976," in *Habits of Devotion: Catholic Religious Practice in Twentieth-Century America,* ed. James M. O'Toole (Ithaca, NY: Cornell University Press, 2004), 26–29.

9. Quoted in Paula M. Kane, "Marian Devotion since 1940," in O'Toole, *Habits of Devotion,* 108.

10. Steven M. Avella, *Confidence and Crisis: A History of the Archdiocese of Milwaukee, 1959–1977* (Milwaukee: Marquette University Press, 2014), 73.

11. See, for example, Leslie Woodcock Tentler, "Through the Prism of Race: The Archdiocese of Detroit," in *Catholics in the Vatican II Era: Local Histories of a Global Event,* ed. Kathleen Sprows Cummings, Timothy Matovina, and Robert A. Orsi (Cambridge: Cambridge University Press, 2018), 95–102; anonymous "request to speak" form,

Archdiocese of Detroit, presynod feedback session, undated but 1968, Archives of the Archdiocese of Detroit (hereafter AAD), Synod Implementation Committee, box 2, folder 15. The definitive overview is John T. McGreevy, *Parish Boundaries: The Catholic Encounter with Race in the Twentieth-Century Urban North* (Chicago: University of Chicago Press, 1996).

12. Gallup, "Majority of Catholics Think Church Will Change Stand on Birth Control," Aug. 19, 1965. The document was a press release from the Gallup polling organization. Copy in American Catholic Research Center and University Archives, Catholic University of America, Washington, DC, National Catholic Welfare Conference (NCWC) Papers, 10/86/8.

13. Andrew M. Greeley, William C. McCready, and Kathleen McCourt, *Catholic Schools in a Declining Church* (Kansas City, MO: Sheed and Ward, 1976), 29–30; Andrew Greeley, "Is Catholic Sexual Teaching Coming Apart?," *Critic* 30, no. 4 (1972): 33.

14. Leslie Woodcock Tentler, *Catholics and Contraception: An American History* (Ithaca, NY: Cornell University Press, 2004), 200; "Professor of English at a Catholic College, New England" to the editor, *Jubilee*, dated Dec. 3, 1958, almost certainly erroneously (the correct year is 1963), typescript of the original in Georgetown University Special Collections, Washington, DC, Ed Rice Papers, box 4, folder 55.

15. Tentler, *Catholics and Contraception*, 273–75.

16. Andrew M. Greeley, *The Catholic Revolution: New Wines, Old Wineskins, and the Second Vatican Council* (Berkeley: University of California Press, 2004), 37–40.

17. Martin Marty, "Hell Disappeared. No One Noticed. A Civic Argument," *Harvard Theological Review* 78, nos. 3–4 (1985): 381–98.

18. The Charismatic Movement awaits a scholarly history. But see Joseph Fichter, *The Sociology of Good Works* (Chicago: Loyola University Press, 1993), 75–94, for a helpful discussion.

19. Alice Gallin, "Called to Action: The Historian as Participant," *U.S. Catholic Historian* 25, no. 2 (2007): 1–2; "Call to Action Conference, Introduction to the Working Papers," undated but 1976, 1, found at http://www.elephantsinthelivingroom.org/structures/Call_to_Action_Conference_1976.pdf (accessed Jan. 22, 2019).

20. Cardinal John Dearden to "Father Kelly," Mar. 29, 1977, AAD, Dearden Papers, box 2, folder: Call to Action.

21. Joseph H. Fichter, S.J., *Priest and People* (New York: Sheed and Ward, 1965), 186; Lawrence A. Castagnola, S.J., "Pastoral Reflections: Wanted: Confessors with Time," *Pastoral Life* 13, no. 12 (1965): 687; Joseph M. Champlin, "Sex and Confession," part 1, *Pastoral Life* 16, no. 5 (1968): 272.

22. Unknown correspondent but probably Rev. Walter Imbiorski to Rev. Edmund J. Fitzpatrick, July 10, 1967, Archives of the University of Notre Dame, Association of Chicago Priests Papers (ACP), box 1, folder: "Vicariate Study Days."

23. Clerical discontent is discussed in many period sources. See, for example, David P. O'Neill, *Priests and Maturity* (New York: Sheed and Ward, 1965), 51; Timothy McCarthy, O.P., "The Role of the Priest," *Pastoral Life* 14, no. 12 (1966): 657–60; Association of Chicago Priests, "Role of the Priest Committee Position Paper: A Time for Action,"

Apr. 16, 1969, Archives of the Archdiocese of Chicago (hereafter AAChi), Catholic Action Federation Papers, box 2, folder 10; Timothy McCarthy, O.P., "The Role of the Priest," *Pastoral Life* 14, no. 12 (1966): 659.

24. Quoted in "Summary, 47th Meeting" (of the Brooklyn Priests' Senate), Feb. 22, 1971, Archives of the Diocese of Brooklyn, "Senate Notes, Dec. 1966–March 1972."

25. Richard A. Schoenherr, *Goodbye Father,* ed. David Yamane (New York: Oxford University Press, 2002), 24; Rev. L. J. McCloskey, "The Case for Optional Celibacy," in *Study and Discussion Papers Prepared for the National Federation of Priests Councils,* undated but 1968, 25, AAChi, Catholic Action Federations Papers, box 2, folder 3; "Religious priest" to the editors, *Liguorian* 52, no. 4 (1964): 30.

26. Anthony J. Blasi with Joseph F. Zimmerman, *Transition from Vowed to Lay Ministry in American Catholicism,* Roman Catholic Studies 20 (Lewiston, NY: Edwin Mellen, 2004), 6–7; "Proposals to the Archdiocesan Synod by the Priests' Senate Group, 1929–1932," undated but late 1967, AAD, Synod Implementation Committee, box 2, folder 20.

27. Rev. Charles Irvin, "Expectations and Hopes," Jan. 1976, 3, AAD, Dearden Papers, box 9, folder: Michigan Federation of Priests' Councils.

28. Yamane, introduction to Schoenherr, *Goodbye Father,* xxi.

29. Andrew M. Greeley, *Priests in the United States: Reflections on a Survey* (Garden City, NY: Doubleday, 1972), 92.

30. O'Malley, *What Happened,* 301; Marie Augusta Neal, S.N.D.deN., *Catholic Sisters in Transition: From the 1960s to the 1980s* (Wilmington, DE: Michael Glazier, 1984), 24.

31. Joan D. Chittister, "No Time for Tying Cats," in *Midwives of the Future: American Sisters Tell Their Story,* ed. Ann Patrick Ward (Kansas City, MO: Leaven, 1985), 13; Neal, *Catholic Sisters,* 18–21.

32. Definitive on the subject is Amy L. Koehlinger, *The New Nuns: Racial Justice and Religious Reform in the 1960s* (Cambridge, MA: Harvard University Press, 2007); Chittister, "No Time for Tying Cats," 19.

33. Sister Maria Goretti, S.N.D.deN., "Report on Project Blecki," Aug. 3, 1966 (emphasis in original; "Blecki" was the name of the local community center), and "Summary of Project Community," undated but Aug. 1966 (emphasis in original), both in AAD, Archbishop's Commission on Human Relations, box 2, folder 28. Other documents in the same file provide additional information on the project.

34. Greeley, McCready, and McCourt, *Catholic Schools in a Declining Church,* 36–37; Andrew M. Greeley and Peter H. Rossi, *The Education of Catholic Americans* (Chicago: Aldine, 1966), 64, 73, 78, 95.

35. Thomas M. Landy, "The Colleges in Context," in *Catholic Women's Colleges in America,* ed. Tracy Schier and Cynthia Russett (Baltimore: Johns Hopkins University Press, 2002), 55, 65, 82–83, 94–95.

36. Chittister, "No Time for Tying Cats," 17.

37. Quoted in Carole Garibaldi Rogers, *Poverty, Chastity, and Change: Lives of Contemporary Nuns* (New York: Twayne, 1996), 273.

38. Quoted ibid., 130.

39. Steven P. Milles, *Good Intentions: A History of Catholic Voters' Road from* Roe *to* Trump (Collegeville, MN: Liturgical Press, 2017), 53–59.

40. Ibid., 36–39.

FOURTEEN   Toward an Uncertain Future

1. Quoted in George Weigel, *Witness to Hope: The Biography of Pope John Paul II* (New York: Cliff Street, 1999), 168.

2. Ibid., 683.

3. Thomas J. Reese, S.J., *Archbishop: Inside the Power Structure of the American Catholic Church* (San Francisco: Harper and Row, 1989), 30–35, 41–45; Dean R. Hoge and Jacqueline E. Wenger, *Evolving Visions of the Priesthood: Changes from Vatican II to the Turn of the New Century* (Collegeville, MN: Liturgical Press, 2003), 53–59, 61–69, 194–97.

4. Katarina Schuth, *Seminaries, Theologates, and the Future of Church Ministry* (Collegeville, MN: Liturgical Press, 1999), 74–79; Dean R. Hoge, *The First Five Years of the Priesthood* (Collegeville, MN: Liturgical Press, 2002), 1–4; Andrew M. Greeley, *Priests: A Calling in Crisis* (Chicago: University of Chicago Press, 2004), 75–85.

5. Steven P. Milles, *Good Intentions: A History of Catholic Voters' Road from* Roe *to* Trump (Collegeville, MN: Liturgical Press, 2018), 83; quoted in Robert D. McFadden, "Archbishop Calls Ferraro Mistaken on Abortion Rule," *New York Times*, Sept. 10, 1984, 1, B9.

6. Peter Steinfels, *A People Adrift: The Crisis of the Roman Catholic Church in America* (New York: Simon and Schuster, 2005), 17–25, quote on 25.

7. Ibid., 46–63.

8. Ibid., 66; Pierre Hegy, "Catholic Divorce, Annulments, and Deception," in *Catholic Divorce: The Deception of Annulments*, ed. Pierre Hegy and Joseph Martos (New York: Continuum, 2000), 9–11, 19–21; J. J. Ziegler, "Annulment Nation," *Catholic World Report*, Apr. 28, 2011, https://www.catholicworldreport.com/2011/04/28/annulment-nation/.

9. Ziegler, "Annulment Nation"; Russell Shaw, "Catholic Marriage Trends Mirror US Statistics," *OSV Newsweekly*, May 20, 2007, https://www.osv.com/OSVNewsweekly/ByIssue/Article/Tabld/735/ArtMID/13636/ArticleID/1781/Catholic-marriage-trends-mirror-US-statistics.aspx.

10. William L. Portier, "Here Come the Evangelical Catholics," prepublication paper, undated, in the possession of the author, 16. A revised version under the same title appears in *Communio* 31, no. 1 (2004): 35–66.

11. Christian Smith and Melinda Lundquist Denton, *Soul Searching: The Religious and Spiritual Lives of American Teenagers* (New York: Oxford University Press, 2005), 194, 209.

12. Ibid., 212; Dean R. Hoge, William D. Dinges, Mary Johnson, and Juan L. Gonzales Jr., *Young Adult Catholics: Religion in the Culture of Choice* (Notre Dame, IN: University of Notre Dame, 2001), 135–39.

13. Ibid., 40–42, 46–48, 57–63.

14. Ibid., 116, 118, 120, 124, quote on 113.

15. Ibid., 118.

16. Ibid., 76, 122; James D. Davidson, *Catholicism in Motion: The Church in American Society* (Liguori, MO: Liguori/Triumph, 2005), 154; Patrick W. Carey, *Confession: Catholics, Repentance, and Forgiveness in America* (New York: Oxford University Press, 2018), 227, 235–41.

17. William V. D'Antonio, James D. Davidson, Dean R. Hoge, and Katherine Meyer, *American Catholics: Gender, Generation, and Commitment* (Walnut Creek, CA: AltaMira, 2001), 76, 79; quoted in Hoge et al., *Young Adult Catholics,* 170.

18. James M. O'Toole, "In the Court of Conscience," in *Habits of Devotion: Catholic Religious Practice in Twentieth-Century America,* ed. James M. O'Toole (Ithaca, NY: Cornell University Press, 2004), 183.

19. "Archdiocesan Newsletter for Priests," 1970, reporting on the meeting of the Episcopal Vicars of Dec. 12, 1969, 24, Archives of the Archdiocese of Detroit (hereafter AAD), Archdiocesan Newsletter, box 1, bound volume: Newsletter, 1966–1970; O'Toole, "In the Court of Conscience," 184–85; Carey, *Confession,* 242–46.

20. U.S. Conference of Catholic Bishops, "Statement on Iraq, 2002," Nov. 13, 2002, www.usccb.org/issues-and-action/human-life-and-dignity/global-issues/middle-east/statement-on-iraq.cfm.

21. Steinfels, *People Adrift,* xiii.

22. Philip Gleason, *Contending with Modernity: Catholic Higher Education in the Twentieth Century* (New York: Oxford University Press, 1995), 305, 313–14; Steinfels, *People Adrift,* 133–37.

23. Quoted in Steinfels, *People Adrift,* 161. Very useful on this subject is Melanie M. Morey and John J. Piderit, S.J., *Catholic Higher Education: A Culture in Crisis* (New York: Oxford University Press, 2006).

24. Bishop Patrick Cooney to Cardinal Edmund Szoka and Jay Berman, memo re: "History of the Task Force, Implementation Committee, Urban Advisory Board," Sept. 19, 1988, AAD, Parish Closings collection, box 1, folder 39; Bishop Thomas Gumbleton to Cardinal Edmund Szoka, memo, Sept. 8, 1988, and Gumbleton to Szoka, memo, Oct. 6, 1988, both in AAD, Parish Closings collection, box 1, folder 38.

25. See John C. Seitz, *No Closure: Catholic Practice and Boston's Parish Shutdowns* (Cambridge, MA: Harvard University Press, 2011), for a discussion of church occupations in the Archdiocese of Boston, where they have been most numerous.

26. A.M.M. to Enzo Paparelli, Oct. 9, 1988, AAD, Church closings collection, box 1, folder 11. I have opted to protect the writer's privacy by withholding her name.

27. D.K. to Archbishop Edmund Szoka, Jan. 27, 1989, AAD, Church closings collection, box 1, folder 18. I have opted to protect the writer's privacy by withholding her name.

28. John Jay College of Criminal Justice, for the United States Conference of Catholic Bishops, *The Nature and Scope of Sexual Abuse of Minors by Catholic Priests and Deacons in the United States, 1950–2002* (Washington, DC: United States Conference of

Catholic Bishops, 2004), 5, 28; United States Conference of Catholic Bishops, *The Nature and Scope of Sexual Abuse of Minors by Catholic Priests and Deacons in the United States, 1950–2002, 2006 Supplementary Report* (Washington, DC: United States Conference of Catholic Bishops, 2006), 32.

29. Steinfels, *People Adrift,* 46.

30. Ibid., 48–50.

31. Leslie Woodcock Tentler, "Pope Francis Comes to Washington," *Religion & Politics: Fit for Polite Company* 1 (2018): 57–61; quotes from the official transcript of the speech, found at http://time.com/4048176/pope-francis-us-visit-congress-transcript/.

32. Quoted in Jamie Mason, "What Is Driving Pope Francis' Canonization of Junípero Serra?," *National Catholic Reporter,* Sept. 16, 2015, https://www.ncronline.org/blogs/grace-margins/what-driving-pope-francis-canonization-jun-pero-serra.

Index

abortion, 191; anti-abortion activism, 311,
325–26; and Catholic health care, 341;
Catholic teaching on, 325, 330, 331; in
early 1930s, 236; lay views on, 308, 311,
326, 333, 349; and politics of birth
control, 281–82; and U.S. Catholic
politicians, 330, 332, 333, 350. *See also*
Supreme Court, U.S.

Ácoma pueblo, 13, 18–19, 20

African American Catholics, 137–38; and
Catholic Youth Organization, 231; lay
Catholic congresses, 185

Ágreda, Abbess Maria de, 14

Aiken, Rev. Charles, 153, 154, 155–56, 157

Allouez, Claude, S.J., 37

Altoona, Pennsylvania, 224

American Catholic Historical Association, 204

American College at Louvain, 83, 109

American Federation of Labor, 189

Americanist controversy, 148, 149, 193, 261;
chronology of, 198–99; conflicting
ideologies in, 197–98, 199; lay response
to, 204–5; and modernism, 199–203,
204; principal players in, 195–96

American Revolution, 47, 261; Catholics

and, 53–55, 83; and legal status of
Catholics, 55–56

Ancaria, Sister, 113

annulments, Catholic, 300, 307; lay views
on, 334–35; liberalization of U.S.
procedures, 308, 334–35; number of
(1968, 1991, 2007), 334

Anti-Catholicism, 56; of abolitionists, 122;
and American Revolution, 53, 55; in
antebellum decades, 71, 81–82, 87,
92–93, 97–98, 111–12, 114; in British
colonies, 47–49; and Catholic solidarity, 221, 336–37; and Civil War, 118; and
First World War, 148, 166–67, 192, 193,
205; in later nineteenth century, 113,
134, 136, 165, 170; and nativist political
parties, 103–4, 112; post-*1945*, 280–82;
and Spanish-American War, 148; in
1920s, 267, 268–69; *1930–1945*, 213, 215,
258–59. *See also* immigration

antimodernist crusade, 156, 199–200,
201–3. *See also* Americanist controversy

Asian Catholics (in U.S.): 324–25

assimilation, 144, 145; to an American
Catholic identity, 181–82, 184, 204,
213–14, 221, 239, 240; Catholic schools

Harvard University, 187, 209, 212, 263; and anti-Catholicism, 100, 280; Catholics at, 155, 205
Haye, Helen, 211
Hayes, Carlton J. H., 262
Hayes, Cardinal Patrick, 221–22
Healy, Bishop James Augustine, 366n33
Healy, Patrick, S.J., 366n33
Healy, Rev. Sherwood, 366n33
Hecker, Isaac, C.S.P., 115–17, 124; and Americanist controversy, 195, 199
hell, 4, 23, 35, 52, 129; evident disappearance of, 309; in mission preaching, 106, 227, 229
Hellreigel, Msgr. Martin, 229
Hellwig, Monica K., 343
Hennaert, Rev. Peter, 106
Herberg, Will, 213–24, 215, 221
Hickey, Cardinal James, 333
Hilger, Sister Mary, 246
Hillenbrand, Rev. Reynold, 225, 254
Hispanic Catholics in the United States, 30, 31, 73, 86; and canonization of Junípero Serra, 30, 350–51; and Cursillo, 309–10; pastoral provisions for, 255; post-1965, 324–25, 335, 337; from Puerto Rico, 218, 255; religious practice, 337–38; from twentieth-century Mexico, 218, 255, 324
Hodur, Rev. Francis, 181
Hogan, Rev. John, 155, 156
Holy Cross Fathers, 184, 186
Holy Cross Sisters, 133, 200
homosexuality: and Catholic adoption agencies, 341; in Catholic clergy, 349; Catholic teaching on, 300, 331; lay perspectives on, 311, 321, 333, 349
Hoover, Herbert, 269, 270, 276
Houston, Sam, 22
Houston, Texas, 79; and 1960 presidential campaign, 283–84
Howlett, Rev. W. J., 158
Hughes, Archbishop John, 98–99, 105;

and Catholic education, 111; and Civil War, 126; and papal infallibility, 135; on race, 121–22
Hunter College (New York), 248

immigration: in antebellum decades, 95; and anti-Catholicism, 97, 103–4, 167, 169–70; Catholic attitudes toward, 103, 170; challenges of, to U.S. Catholic Church, 96–97, 99–100, 104–5, 145, 168, 170; in late nineteenth and early twentieth centuries, 141–42, 145, 147, 169; legislation governing, 168, 206, 217, 218, 239, 267, 324; post-1965, 240, 324–25; sources of, 169, 176, 218; in 1930s, 217. *See also various national groups*
Independent, 205
Index of Prohibited Books, 200
Indian missions, Catholic: in antebellum decades, 69–70, 72, 74; in Arizona, 22–25; in California, 25–31; catechesis and religious practice, 8, 11, 14, 15, 17, 23, 25, 26, 30–31, 34–35, 37, 44–45; chronology of founding, 9, 20, 22, 25; collapse of, 8, 11–12, 17, 21–22, 24–25, 29–30, 37, 83; in colonial Maryland, 48; in context of conquest, 5, 6, 7; disease in, 8–9, 11–12, 15, 26, 29, 35; evangelizing strategies in, 10, 11, 14, 21, 23, 25, 33–35; fugitivism, 21, 27; and intra-Indian warfare, 8, 14, 20, 21, 24, 25, 36, 48; literacy training in, 15; motives for conversion, 10, 14–15, 22, 26; in New France, 33–37, 44–45; in New Mexico, 13–19; physical punishment in, 12, 15, 27, 28–29; rebellions in, 6, 8, 9, 12, 16–17, 24, 25, 28; role of interpreters in, 10, 14, 25, 44, 70, 78; secularization of, 21, 29, 86; sexual discipline in, 6, 11, 15, 21, 26, 27, 35; in Spanish Florida, 9–13; and syncretism, 11, 17, 18–19, 24, 45; in Texas, 19–22. *See also* confession

Indians: Algonquin, 44, 45; Apache, 20, 24, 25; Apalachee, 10, 11; Arkansas, 44; enslavement of, 7, 12, 13; Guale, 9, 10, 12; Hasinai, 20; Illinois, 35, 36, 37, 44–45; Iroquois, 33, 36, 45; Kiskakon Ottawa, 37, 45; Mohawk, 35, 40; Ottawa, 70; Petun, 36; Pima, 22, 24; population decline among, 8–9, 11–12, 15, 29–30, 35; Potawatomi, 78; precontact population in North America, 7, 25: Pueblo, 14, 19; Rumsen, 10, 28; sexual practice among, 15, 26, 35; as slaveholders, 44; Tewa, 16; Timucua, 9, 10, 11, 12; Tunica, 34; Wabanaki, 33; Wendat (Hurons), 33, 34, 35–37; Winnebago, 70
International Ladies' Garment Workers' Union, 211
Ireland, Archbishop John: and Americanist controversy, 195, 196, 198, 199; and Catholic schools, 197; education and early career, 196; ideology, 196–97, 203, 269
Irish Catholics in the United States, 65, 70, 73; and American Revolution, 54; arrival in antebellum decades, 95; arrival in early twentieth century, 169, 181; in Civil War, 123, 124, 125–27; crime among, 104; ethnic consciousness of, 153–54; and First World War, 192; Gaelic-speaking, 76, 96; and New York Draft Riots, 124, 127; in politics, 189–90; poverty of, 96, 104; and racism, 121–22, 125; settlement patterns, 96; social mobility among, 103; and trusteeism, 101, 103; women's religious vocations among, 162–63
Irish Land League, 194
Italian Catholics in the United States, anti-clericalism among, 171, 173; and Catholic schools, 171, 175; and church support, 171, 172, 174; dearth of religious vocations among, 175; emigration from Italy, 141, 169; immigrant sex ratios, 170;

poverty of, 142–43; settlement patterns among, 169–70, 171; social mobility among, 177; religious practice among, 171–73, 175; remigration of, 170; tensions with U.S. clergy, 172–74

Jackson, Carol, 262
Jackson, Helen Hunt, 30
Jesuit Relations, 36, 42
Jesuits, 3, 4, 6, 44, 114; *America,* 204; and Americanist controversy, 196; in antebellum United States, 85; and antimodernist crusade, 201; colleges, 245; in colonial Maryland, 48–49, 50–52; and devotionalism, 226; expulsion from the Americas, 6, 22, 24; martyrdom among, 5, 9, 24, 36, 39–40; missionary ethos, 5, 8, 22, 33–35, 37, 44, 45–46; as mission preachers, 85, 105; in New France, 33–37, 44–45; in New Spain, 8, 22, 23–24; and Pope John Paul II, 330; as slaveholders, 43–44, 49, 119; spirituality of, 50, 51–52; suppression of, 24, 37, 53, 330; *Thought,* 249; in twentieth-century foreign missions, 233; in U.S. Indian missions, 83
Jesuit Volunteer Corps, 335
Jogues, Isaac, S.J., 36, 40, 41
John XXIII, Pope, 202, 212, 299; and birth control, 292; *Pacem in Terris,* 298; popularity of, 284
John Paul I, Pope, 327
John Paul II, Pope (Karol Wojtyła), 72, 349; on abortion, 330; and "altar girls," 330; and birth control, 328–29, 330; and dissenting theologians, 330; election of, 327; *Ex Corde Ecclesiae,* 342–43; global travels, 327–28; impact on U.S. hierarchy, 331; popularity of, 328, 330–31, 335, 340; and Second Vatican Council, 328; and sex abuse scandals, 301; on U.S. invasion of Iraq (2003), 340; U.S. visits, 328, 329; and women's ordination, 329–30

Ripley, George, 115
Ritter, Archbishop Joseph, 283
Rivera, Diego, 273
Roosevelt, Franklin Delano, 232; and
  Catholic support, 266, 270–71; and
  Father Charles Coughlin, 276, 278; and
  Myron Taylor appointment, 280
Roosevelt, Theodore, 149, 150
Rosecrans, Bishop Sylvester, 123
Rosecrans, William, 123
Ross, Eva, 262
Rouensa, Marie, 44
Ruffing, Sister Janet, 324
Ryan, Msgr. John A.: on birth control,
  190–91, 192, 231; *A Living Wage,* 190; and
  Program for Social Reconstruction, 167,
  190; in 1930s, 260, 270, 271, 290
Ryan, Archbishop Patrick, 186

Sacred Congregation for the Propagation
  of the Faith (Propaganda), 53, 56; on
  Catholic schools, 197; on frequent
  communion, 182; jurisdiction over U.S.
  Church, 57, 65, 152; on religious
  intermarriage, 81; on race, 120
Sacred Heart devotions, 51, 107, 183
saints, cult of, 11, 52, 100; Catherine
  Tekakwitha, 40–41; decline of, 227–28,
  304; gendered dimensions of, 51, 107–8,
  226–27; among Italian Catholics,
  172–73, 175; North American Martyrs,
  36, 39–40; St. Anne, 107, 183; St.
  Anthony, 183; St. Blaise, 178; St. Francis
  Xavier, 226; St. John the Baptist, 178; St.
  Joseph, 107, 178, 183; St. Jude, 226–27;
  St. Thérèse of Lisieux, 226
Saints Cyril and Methodius Seminary
  (Detroit), 179
San Antonio, Texas, 21, 86, 252
San Diego, California, 25, 28
San Francisco, 30, 153; Archdiocese and
  diocese of, 74, 149; Italians in, 171;
  Spanish mission at, 31

Sanger, Margaret, 191, 192, 235
San Jose, California, 30
Santa Fe, California, 13; Archdiocese and
  diocese of, 74, 153
San Xavier del Bac mission (Arizona), 22,
  23, 24
Satolli, Archbishop Francesco, 198
Satterlee Military Hospital, Philadelphia,
  131–32
Scalabrini, Bishop Giovanni Battista, 141
Scalabrinians (Missionaries of St.
  Charles), 141, 142
schools, Catholic: antebellum colleges,
  109; antebellum primary schools, 72,
  90, 91, 98, 110–14; Catholic critics of,
  242, 305; Catholic demands for public
  funding, 97–98; 111–12, 280–81, 305;
  decline of, post-*1966*, 321–22, 336;
  desegregation of, 283; diocesan
  governance of, 166, 219, 243, 244;
  enrollment in, 112, 164, 243, 244–45,
  306; female academies, 91, 93, 108, 165,
  243; language of instruction in, 113, 144,
  177–78; lay teachers in, 245, 251, 336;
  and minority student achievement, 351;
  non-Catholic critics of, 111, 134;
  number of, 114, 164, 241; quality of,
  112–13, 241; religious socialization in,
  183, 223, 233, 322; secondary schools,
  231, 243–44, 245; sex segregation in,
  244; as sources of religious vocations,
  244; and Third Plenary Council of
  Baltimore, 113–14, 136. *See also* women
  religious
School Sisters of Notre Dame, 112–13
Scranton, Pennsylvania, 143
Seattle, 143
Second Vatican Council, 212, 215, 235; and
  birth control, 292, 299; Declaration on
  Religious Liberty, 84, 260, 298, 299;
  documents of, 297–98, 299, 301; impact
  on lay Catholics, 214, 240, 265, 285, 289,
  290, 301, 307–9; lay attitudes toward,